The People of Paris
An Essay in Popular Culture in the 18th Century

Studies on the History of Society and Culture
Victoria E. Bonnell and Lynn Hunt, Editors

DANIEL ROCHE

The People of Paris
An Essay in Popular Culture
in the 18th Century

Translated by MARIE EVANS
in association with GWYNNE LEWIS

University of California Press
Berkeley and Los Angeles

University of California Press
Berkeley and Los Angeles

© Berg Publishers Limited 1987

Originally published as *Le peuple de Paris*.
Translated from the French by permission of the publishers,
Aubier Montaigne.
© Aubier Montaigne 1981

Library of Congress Cataloging-in-Publication Data
Roche, Daniel.
  The people of Paris.

  Translation of: Le peuple de Paris.
  1. Paris (France)—Popular culture—History—18th
century. 2. Paris (France)—Social life and customs—
18th century. I. Title.
DC715.R6413 1987   306'.094436   86–24506
ISBN 0–520–05857–7 (cloth) (alk. paper)
      0–520–06031–8 (paper)

Printed in Great Britain by Billings of Worcester

Contents

Statistical Information

Tables

Figures

To Olivier, for her patience

Foreword
to the French edition

'Peuple, le': a collective noun difficult to define, because it conveys different ideas in different places, at different times, and according to the nature of governments. . . .

L'Encyclopédie

This book is the result of a collective effort. The tendency today is for large-scale investigations to be undertaken around a particular project by researchers united by their interest and (usually) by their funding. But this is also a time of financial crises and economic cuts; French historical research now has to rely on itself and its own ingenuity. About 1974, I directed my teaching efforts to uniting for a common purpose some students who were beginning their postgraduate studies and two or three colleagues, loyal even in times of austerity. However, French historians have acquired some bad habits: quantification and a taste for serial history which demand significant statistics, and the expectation, if not in theory at least in pedagogic practice, that every project should confront a specific problem; for us, the way the popular classes of Paris felt and thought in relation to both the modes of production and social life. For this joint endeavour to succeed and for the group to fulfil its aims with no resources but its own energy, and at the same time for the effort to prove formative, the students required a great deal of patience with their supervisor and director of research studies. The numerical data gathered are modest, but undoubtedly are more important than the reader can appreciate by examining the tables which illustrate some of the results obtained. The data seek to show that there is a humane way of using figures, which depends on the questions asked.

In an exercise which took more than five years to complete, the weaknesses and errors must be attributed to the leader; the originality, approach and critical spirit to his team. I should particularly like to thank François Ardellier and Rémi Arnette, whose research in 1976–7

1

provided one of the chief sources for my thinking. I am one of those who use students' work, because I think that the relationship between student and teacher is much more than one of consumer and producer, and because I consider I have a great deal to learn from them. I do not think that standards fall as my hair grows grey and the years pass. On the contrary, I believe that, for those who were working in 1981 for masters' or doctors' degrees, having been subjected to a rigorous process of selection, they were as high as ever: simply, different generations have different qualities. If university entrants, who enjoy history and believe in research, were to be given the resources we owe them — especially grants and institutes equipped with the necessary material and staff — we could undoubtedly do still more. This is why, in spite of the major crisis affecting French universities, it is still essential that one enjoys archival research, working in libraries, exercising one's trade. It is up to us to work together and not to lose heart.

Why did I choose to work on the culture of the people, when my earlier work was concerned with the culture of the learned, the rich and the cultivated? First because academicians, aristocracy and the educated bourgeois become finally wearisome; their conviction (which can be touching) that they are working for the progress of all, their consciousness of being the 'upper crust', confident yesterday and today of their social strength and calm self-sufficiency, demands a counterpart. The disdain for the popular classes manifested by yesterday's elite and the powerful men who govern us today deserves a reply.

Secondly, because the world of the student (a mobile milieu in a constant state of transition, while their teachers stay put) has for several years experienced a nostalgia for the revolutions they could not make; often students will appeal to a past which was, if not mythical, at least one which they feel would have suited them. They are seeking prototypes for their dreams of the future. Peasants are in fashion; the old rural rebels sell books like 'mere Denis' sells washing-machines. I am a fifth-generation Parisian and, although I do not dislike the countryside, I love the town and its freedom and one can only speak well of what one loves. In this book I have attempted both to supply a need whose social implications do not escape me, and to work for my own pleasure. The book is therefore the outcome of an educational process which shows that in seeking one does not always find what one expected, and that for an historian it is important to admit this difference, as well as to appreciate the significance of time passing. This is one of the ambitions of cultural anthropology.

But at the same time, and as a final point, my enquiries have been guided by two loyalties. The first is to the sort of social history which my teacher Ernest Labrousse taught me to enjoy. The second is to the history of material culture for which Fernand Braudel provided an exemplary programme. I am not one of those who think, like Richard Cobb whom I very much admire, that there are two types of history and therefore of historian: one who displays imagination and sensibility based on personal experience, the historian of the individual, and one who accepts figures and the concerns of sociology, the historian of social economy, preoccupied with abstractions and lacking understanding.[1] I think that the history of societies is woven out of the history of individuals, and that one cannot ignore some fundamental, even theoretical, questions. So I offer apologies to the empiricists and accept my incompetence in the eyes of the theoreticians. For me, social history has not gone out of fashion; the study of popular culture enables us to perceive its importance for everyone. By this I mean not so much an investigation determined by the economy as the sum of the relations and the different types of logic at play within the popular classes. They did not live in an isolated cultural world, but formed a cluster of kinds of behaviour and practice in which one may perceive, by attempting to understand their world, a certain unity. The emphasis in this book will be on daily habits and ways of living, but without ignoring more intellectualised consumer activities — reading and writing, for example — or those which reveal a sensibility, a sociability of family and collective life. Through their manners and their nous, that is, their *savoir-vivre* and *savoir-faire*, we may glimpse the way in which the culture of the poor[2] was created between appearances and production.

I should like to thank Anne-Marie Andrade, Serge Beiss, Marc Botlan, Martine Champeau, Françoise Changeux, Elisabeth Caulier, Anne-Marie Escureix, Valérie Hanin, Corinne Jolivet, Sabine Juratic, Marie-Hélène de la Mure, Sylvie Lartigue, Isabelle Lehu, Pascale Krumnow, Francis Mabilat, Bernard Minot, Marcel Moulon, Gilles Picq, Maryse Pradines, Caroline Rimbault, Olivier Romagné, François Roger, Martine Sonnet and Catherine Ungerer. I also remember Jean Chatelus, Daniel Brun, Jean Duma, Robert Descimon and Jean Nagle, whose works and suggestions helped me and who listened to me with patience and fortitude over a period of several years.

Finally, this book would not have been what it is without the attention of Maurice Agulhon, Jean Boissière, Arlette Farge, Marie-Madeleine and Dominique Julia, Marcel Lachiver, Jacques and Mi-

1. R. Cobb, *La protestation populaire en France (1789–1820)*, Paris 1975, p. 13.
2. R. Hoggart, *La culture du pauvre*, Paris, 1970; N.Z. Davis, *Les Cultures du peuple, rituels, savoirs et résistances au XVIe siècle*, Paris, 1979.

Foreword
to the English edition

I am well aware of the significance of this translation of my work into English. It offers me a chance to renew the open dialogue with English-speaking historians and to discuss our differences of approach — for example, in the work of Richard Cobb or Georges Rudé. It seems to me that the French historian of social history reveals a different picture of everyday life from his British counterpart. By comparing the different use of sources shown in *Death in Paris* it is possible to see how the British and the French historian differ with regard to the risks they are prepared to take. With Richard Cobb, a fascinating tableau of a part of a society reconstituted in all its different aspects such as language, life-styles and continual motion, reveals a portrait that is impressionistic, intuitive, imaginative and, above all, true. With *The People of Paris* it is different. The reader is shown that what are normally described as 'the popular classes' develops as an historical entity; from degrees of fortune to life-styles, and from ways of dressing to leisure pursuits and encounters, all are seen from a different angle so that the same habits and ways of life are embedded in a larger social environment with a longer perspective. Again, if the reader were to compare Rudé's *Les foules révolutionnaires* with the present book, he would discover in the former a similar world whose cultural and social luggage is in the process of being formed. *The People of Paris* has laid emphasis on the teeming days and a militant consciousness, because the eighteenth century saw the mobilisation of minds through the transformation of customs and of the intellectual and material spheres. In short, a different but equally true image of the popular classes.

A final chance is accorded to the writer who reaches a new public through the translation of his work: that of recognising the limits of his contribution. In my case, I can now see three shortcomings which some friendly critics have already been kind enough to point out:

insufficient weight was given to popular religion; there was a discernible indifference to the twin phenomena of marginality and criminality; and not enough consideration was given to the organisation of labour. I have tried to deal more fully with these questions in my critical edition of *Journal de ma vie*, written by the Parisian glazier Jacques Louis Ménétra.[1]

It is always easier for an author to dream of a revised and up-dated edition of his work than for a publisher to provide it. I am therefore especially grateful to my translators, Marie Evans and Gwynne Lewis, and to my publisher, Marion Berghahn, who were faced with these problems and had to solve them. Such is the fate of history books! As for the critical remarks concerning the study of history that I made in 1981, I fear that there is little reason to change them. For French universities the last few years have been ones of tension and of transformation. Financial problems and the general crisis at home have hit historical research particularly hard, despite the good will of both the teachers and the researchers; in particular, the problem of how to bring in a younger generation has not yet been resolved. For the British or American reader, these last remarks may be of interest for comparative reasons and also because they underline the fact that books do not exist in a vacuum, neither do they appear of their own volition out of a clear blue sky.

Daniel Roche   *Florence, January 1986*

---

1. Paris 1982 (English transl. in preparation, Columbia UP, with a preface by R. Darnton).

PART I

Paris and her People

CHAPTER I

Space and Population

I marvelled at the way in which Paris devours its surroundings, converting nourishing gardens into sterile streets.

Rétif de la Bretonne

To write a new *Tableau de Paris* is a difficult exercise; on the one hand too many essential elements have never been studied, and on the other too many books, hastily thrown together, repeat the same hackneyed descriptions. Nevertheless the city was there, immense, slowly creeping into the surrounding belt of marshland, market gardens and fields; everywhere the country was close at hand; five minutes from the *barrière* Saint-Jacques, Parisians walked through fields of barley, filling their lungs with the scent of flowers; young people of both sexes from the faubourg Saint-Marcel jostled along the leafy lanes.[1] In early summer the lawyer Des Essarts, a man of sensibility and a lover of fresh air, chatted with homely farmers contemplating the early corn only a quarter of an hour's walk from the Ecole Militaire. Even if the French capital quickly became the very symbol of a monstrous city devouring the food supplies of an agricultural kingdom, one must never forget its proximity to a very different style of life, one, moreover, that has lasted for a very long time, whose effect was both to lessen and reinforce the contrasts with nature. For the Parisian who sought a rural retreat, the countryside was close at hand, a place for walks, leisure and adventure; on an evening's spree, one could easily get lost between the Porte Saint-Germain and Vaugirard.[2] For both the provincial and the country-dweller, the astonishment, sometimes disappointment, arising from the discovery of a strange new world was largely due to this abrupt opposition. The still world of nature contrasted with the noisy world of cobbled streets

1. Rétif de la Bretonne, *Les Nuits de Paris ou le spectateur nocturne*, London (Paris) 1788, 7 vols., 14 parts, 3,359 pages, pp. 2493–4.
2. MS 768 – BHVP – p. 28 – Mémoires de Ménétra; the critical edition of this text is in active preparation.

9

and roads, whose reverberations struck the ear of the young Rétif de la
Bretonne. People were guided by their ears along the royal road into
Paris: 'I heard a frightening noise, which seemed to me like the sound
of rolling thunder . . . .' Rétif was charmed by its grandiose air, the
magic of the buildings and parks bordering the route. He was disappointed by the jostling crowds, the summer dust and the winter mud.
At the gates the foot-traveller stopped short in astonishment:

> Leaving Villejuif, we alighted upon a great mass of houses overhung by a
> cloud of smoke. I asked my father what it was? 'It's Paris. It's a big city, you
> can't see it all from here'—'Oh! how big Paris is! Father, it's as big as
> Vermanton to Sacy, and Sacy to Joux'—'Yes, at least as big. Oh! what a lot
> of people! So many that nobody knows anyone else, not even in the same
> neighbourhood, not even in the same house . . .'[3]

What remained etched in the memory of the country lad from
Basse-Bourgogne was, above all, the sense of astonishment at the
unimaginable size of the capital, exceeding any limits he knew and
bearing no relation to the scale of ordinary geographical relationships.
Then he recalled paternal pronouncements which took on a prophetic
air — in this vast world with its jostling throngs one could feel very
lonely. The city was fascinating but one could be quite alone in it. We
must think again about this statement as it in no way differs from the
critique of urban mores to be found in the works of many other
writers.[4]

> How different was the sight of Paris from what I expected . . . I had
> imagined a town as beautiful as it was large, with a most imposing aspect
> including nothing but superb streets, palaces of marble and gold. Coming in
> through the Faubourg Saint Marceau, I saw only dirty, stinking alleys, ugly
> black houses, an air of filth and poverty, beggars, carters, mending women.
> The cries of women selling their herb tea and old hats. I was so struck by all
> this at first that all the truly magnificent things I have since seen in Paris
> could not efface this first impression, and I have been left with a secret
> distate for life in this capital city . . . [5]

For Rousseau, disappointed in his boyish dreams of a glorious,
sumptuous city, the image of Paris was based on a contrast which has
been reiterated continually by his imitators and by many historians:

3. Rétif de la Bretonne, *Monsieur Nicolas, ou le coeur humain dévoilé*, Paris, 1959,
6 vols. pp. 175–85.
4. 'La Ville au XVIIIᵉ siècle', colloque d'Aix-en-Provence, 1973, Aix-en-Provence,
1975.
5. Rousseau, J.J., *Les Confessions*, in *Oeuvres Complètes*, Paris, 1962–9, 4 vols., vol. 1,
p. 154.

the social misery of Paris, the material and moral alienation of most of its citizens, were inseparable from the luxury of the privileged and the city's seductive charm. The pact which bound the city to poverty and wealth was reinforced by all 'the indescribable weight of the charms of nature'.[6] It was impossible to comprehend the totality of Paris at a single glance; its spatial and social breadth became ever more complex as the century wore on.

Where did the city begin and end? The urban authorities could not say exactly, any more than could the travellers or bewildered young provincials disembarking from the passenger barge at the Port Saint-Paul or from dusty stage-coaches in the yards of coach companies. For more than a century the war as to where Paris stopped had been waged in silence, experiencing a decisive defeat at every engagement. Previously, under Louis XIII, the royal administrators had decided (in vain) to set limits to Paris; under Louis XIV, a further attempt was made to establish a perimeter, broad but firm and well beyond the fortifications. In the suburban fields, along the principal roads and paths, posts, wooden fences and milestones reflected the King's determination to contain the growth of Paris within reasonable limits. This war revealed the decisive change which the capital underwent in the seventeenth century in the wake of transformations affecting the state. The measures taken to control the expansion arose from a multiplicity of motives: a desire to limit the number of Parisians benefiting from fortunate tax exemptions; fear of bourgeois and popular agitation, so vividly manifested in the Frondes of the mid-century; fear of epidemics aggravated by the increase in population; the wish to provide food for the masses, and, finally, a concern to preserve the defensive value of the urban perimeter. The end of the seventeenth and the beginning of the eighteenth centuries would see a decisive war waged, for the town was advancing towards the suburban villages at a growth-rate which was difficult to define, but which always involved population density. To understand how the people lived, one must analyse in some detail these essential changes. Our analysis will be focused on two main questions: first, what were the decisive changes in the physical size of Paris and how did they affect population movements? Secondly, what upheavals occurred in urban morphology and how did they awaken a new awareness of the town?

Paris was constantly changing in shape and size.[7] To record this, the authorities kept making new plans, and at the end of the seventeenth

6. J.-C. Perrot, *Genèse d'une ville moderne, Caen au XVIII*, Paris, 1975, 2 vols., vol. 1, p. 25.
7. M. Reinhard, *Paris pendant la Révolution*, CDU, Paris, 6 parts, 1962–3, part 1, pp. 14–19.

century Sébastien Mercier could state: 'We are on the tenth plan and Paris still overflows its limits. The boundary is not yet fixed, and cannot be. The *marais* which produces vegetables retreats in order to make way for buildings . . .'.[8] A history of Parisian cartography has yet to be written, but the way in which the town was envisaged in successive plans is clearly significant. Between the end of the seventeenth century and the Revolution, the growth of the city led to the drafting of more than a hundred maps. However, it was not until 1785–90 that the first geometric plan, whose accuracy is incontestable, was drawn up by the engineer Verniquet. Until then, inexactitude was the rule and the topography of the town remained full of contradictions. The need to create a detailed geometric plan was implicit in the city's growth, and was demanded by the informed elites. The establishment of boundaries produced maps and descriptions, but failed to overcome two main difficulties: the first arose from the divisions between the various administrative bodies on which the capital depended. Parisian cartography was submitted to the watchful eye of several rival institutions whose initiatives were not always coordinated — the King, of course, along with the 'ministre de Paris' and the controller of buildings, but also the Academies of Science and of Architecture; the Treasury, which controlled the streets and highways; the *Parlement*, whose *procureur général* watched over police affairs; the *lieutenant général de police*, who was in charge of all traffic and who also authorised building and alignment plans; and lastly, the city itself, its administrators and *Prévôt des marchands*. The final achievement was to come from the city authorities, after the creation of a proper body for drafting plans and the nocturnal measuring of Verniquet. But the triumph of geometry also corresponded to a profound evolution in the way that the town was represented.

These new experiments and the traditional labours of the Parisian geographers were part of the conflict between mathematical figuration and surveying on the one hand — the first survey of the city was not made until the second half of the eighteenth century — and the representation of the 'City Portrait', which was the basis of the well-known masterpiece of the *Prévôt des marchands*, Turgot. Adherence to the values of the picturesque was implicit in a mode of cultural representation which remained faithful to the illusion of the bird's-eye view. A global view, the use of three dimensions, a perspective rendering of the high points of the city, when the map-maker was working in two dimensions, revealed an ideal of urban culture in which the concrete spectacle was more important than the abstract image, the

8. L.-S. Mercier, *Le Tableau de Paris*, Amsterdam, 12 vols., 1781–8, vol. 1, pp. 13ff.

glorious city dominated the trivial suburbs, and urban virtues proclaimed the rule of wealth and power. The perspective plan suggested a
future narrative and commanded a view of Utopia.[9] The geometric
map imposed the imperatives of measurement and planning; space was
rendered in its totality, empty, waiting to be filled, controllable; the
city thus measured was no longer the living organism adorned with all
the prestige of culture and originality, but a terrain for a policy which
rejected the relationship between wealth and space, population and
growth.[10] The first modern town planning embodied in a monumental
morphology, in a new system of public buildings, a new concept of
public space, was revealed, for example, in Boullée's speculations
aimed at redrawing the map of Paris.

The publication dates of map editions are significant; based upon
132 plans registered and divided by decades we find the following:

1700–09	10
1710–19	7
1720–29	4
1730–39	11
1740–49	8
1750–59	8
1760–69	14
1770–79	23
1780–89	28
1790–99	19

The average is one to two plans a year. The first quarter of the century
already shows an increase: whereas ten maps had been published in the
last quarter of the previous century, over twenty appeared in the
ensuing three decades. After 1770 the rush of publications reveals both
an increase in the problems which arose as well as the fact of spatial
expansion, which occurred despite the well-documented cyclical shifts
in the economy affecting leading sectors of production.[11] All this
reflects, after a pause during the years 1725–60, a renewal in
the concentration of men, wealth and power.

The maps of the beginning of the eighteenth century, and the
ordinances and decrees of 1700 and 1702, reveal the heterogeneous
nature of the Parisian terrain. Administratively a decisive stage was
reached in 1702 when, in response to the demands of policing and

9. L. Marin, *Utopiques: jeux d'espace*, Paris, 1973, pp. 257–90.
10. B. Fortier and B. Vayssière, *L'Architecture des villes. Espaces, cartes et territoires*,
in Urbi, 1980, pp. 53–63.
11. F. Braudel and C.-E. Labrousse, *Histoire économique et sociale de la France*, vol.
II, 1970, pp. 529–62.

cleaning, it was decided that the old *quartiers* should be made more equal in size, taking them from seventeen to twenty: fourteen for the right bank, one for the *îles de Paris*, five for the left bank. The faubourgs, even though they still had different functions and populations, became the growth area for these *quartiers*. The centre was freed of its former restraints but also was better controlled, since the new divisions produced a better representation of town notables in the municipal councils. The reformers had learned the lesson to be drawn from government decisions making Paris an open city, freed from its archaic and restrictive boundaries, giving free rein to the activities of the *lieutenant de police* and his agents.[12] Within this framework the expansion would occur in two stages: in the first thirty years Paris — less than 1,000 hectares with the suburbs — grew in size and in population density; after a pause about which not much is known, between 1760 and 1790 the city became a vast building-site. Verniquet's plan shows the capital enclosed within fiscal boundaries of 23 kilometres, and extending over 3,400 hectares.

The constructions cut across the ramparts which had been demolished and replaced by a broad tree-lined walk, embellished at the sites of the gateways with Roman-style triumphal arches. New buildings stretched along the main axes and the streets advanced towards the countryside. To the south of the town boulevards were developed in an empty, almost entirely rural space across gardens and cultivated land. On all sides building plots began to fill the empty spaces in the continuity of the urban network. On the right bank, on the open spaces of the Faubourg Saint-Honoré, in the marshes of Ville l'Evêque, new *quartiers* were built out of the profits of financiers and the nobility — la Grange-Batellière, where Bourret de Vezelai was a leading speculator, and the Chaussée d'Antin; mansions enhanced streets such as the rue de Richelieu and the rue Vivienne; the rue de Grammont and the rue Royale became building sites. At the end of this first phase, the construction of the Cours la Reine/Champs-Elysées complex by the duc d'Antin was a prelude, in this sector, to the rash of plans for the place Royale.

On the left bank, the interest of the builders centred on the Faubourg Saint-Germain, since the opening of the Pont-Royal made it easier to extend and develop there. The upper aristocracy bought large stretches of land to build their great houses. The quai d'Orsay made way for a concentration of buildings on the south bank of the river. Overall, an intense building fever was revealed in the countless work-

12. R. Descimon and J. Nagle, 'Escape et fonction sociale: les quartiers de Paris du Moyen Age au XVIIIe siècle', in *Annales*, ESC, 1979, pp. 966–83.

sites which, after the death of Louis XIV, were encouraged by the presence of the Court in Paris. 'Since His Majesty has settled in Paris, many government officers and seigneurs have taken up residence around the Louvre, Saint-Honoré and the Butte Saint-Roch districts, where several mansions have been built, which has forced artisans of various professions who lived in and around this district to leave and settle elsewhere . . .'; this from a document of 1720 which underlines the difficulties created by these upheavals, especially the high price of land and of rents. Moreover, the financial speculations of the Regency, business movements, drastic changes in some fortunes, bankruptcies which forced financiers or wholesale contractors to sell their houses, played an important part in the development of Paris at the time.[13] 'Since 1715', writes the author of the monumental *Traité de Police*, *commissaire* Delamarre, 'we have seen the remaining empty spaces in the town filled in and there are also a number of streets newly opened and many others extended . . . .' This fact aroused the usual terrors in the hearts of administrators when faced with the growth of the city. 'The immense size which Paris would certainly have reached then inspired fears that, if rapid expansion were given free rein, it would finally experience the fate of the great cities of Antiquity which collapsed under their own weight . . . .' A royal declaration in 1724, regulations and ordinances in 1726 and 1728, attempted once again to limit the growth of Paris. The 1674 perimeter, clearly marked on Jouvin de Rochefort's plan, had been overrun at all points. Acceptable limits were needed; what was not yet the city must not become the city; for to accept the tentacular growth and the building-lots which accompanied it would produce a population which would be impossible to feed and control. Finally, there was the risk that the centre of Paris would be abandoned in favour of the outskirts where more building land was available, both for the elegant mansions of the aristocracy, and for the hovels and cheaper rented houses of poor *faubouriens*. The royal edicts heralded an operation of great interest for the information they give about Enlightenment Paris — the *Travail des Limites* in which, for the first time, building and the demarcation of boundaries were accompanied by a survey of existing buildings in the faubourgs in order to prevent new constructions.[14] In less than five years, 294 milestones were set up, 188 street plans and 1,417 sketches of houses drafted, a prodigious effort which, however, did nothing to prevent the growth of Paris. The city continued to expand, sublimely

13. M. Poète, *Formation et évolution de Paris*, Paris, 1910, pp. 145–8.
14. J. Pronteau, 'Le Travail des limites de la ville et faubourgs de Paris', in *Annuaire de l'Escole Pratique des Hautes Etudes*, IVᵉ section, 1977–8, Paris, 1978, pp. 707–45.

indifferent to the fears of the police and the injunctions of the monarchy. The failure of the undertaking is significant, for it underlines a basic problem of urban history: how far do political and fiscal constraints influence urban development? The two are not always in harmony, but the addition of a new district to a grand urban scheme might depend on it. From this angle, the *Travail des Limites* of 1724 encouraged the process of urbanisation which it was intended to curb.[15]

The middle years of the century were not favourable to expansion, except for some limited programmes. Michel Gallet shows how, from 1740 to 1765, the burden of military expenditure during the War of the Austrian Succession and the Seven Years War slowed down royal town planning and indirectly — by increased pressure of taxes — private building.[16] After 1766 there was an obvious renewal, encouraged by the commercial upswing, financial activity and state initiatives. New regulations in the field of building legislation encouraged construction. In 1767 the duc de Croy explored the city with the architect Soufflot and noted the number of substantial buildings under construction: 'It proved that there was money in the country and showed the effects of the Peace. But perhaps Paris was ahead of the rest of the Kingdom . . .'. In the 1780s Sébastien Mercier estimated that the 'building fraternity' had rebuilt a third of the town in twenty-five years. People were speculating in land, summoning regiments of masons from Limoges, 'immense blocks of building rise from the ground as if by magic and new *quartiers* are composed of the most magnificent mansions. This fever of construction gives the town an air of grandeur and majesty . . . they are building on all sides. . . '.[17] The capital of Louis XVI was handed over to contractors; the daily life of its inhabitants was disrupted by the creation of building sites and the increased traffic of great carts laden with dressed stone and wood. Overgrown gardens disappeared, and the houses attracted inhabitants. All these movements gave Paris a new look, and took place in two directions which determined its development for a long time to come.

To the west, rich, airy, spacious districts spread out both on the right bank and south of the Seine. After 1737–40, when the great sewer which had poisoned the air was covered over, development was possible to the north-west, towards le Roule and Monceau. Financiers invested beyond the boulevards — the rues de Provence, d'Artois, Chauchat, Taitbout and Laberde. On the left bank of the Seine the

15. O. Zunz, 'Le quartier du Gros Caillou', in *Annales*, ESC, 1970, pp. 1024–65.
16. M. Gallet, *Demeures parisiennes, l'époque Louis XVI*, Paris, 1964, pp. 17–18.
17. L.-S. Mercier, *Le Tableau de Paris*, vol. 1, pp. 17–18, 222–3, 263–9.

quais, the Invalides, the École Militaire provided the focal point for expansion towards le Gros Caillou and Grenelle. The townscape of the eastern suburbs, on the other hand, became typical of working-class accommodation for a long time afterwards, and the semi-rural, occasionally aristocratic features still lingering there disappeared or diminished.

In the faubourg Saint-Marcel, on the left bank, largely attached to the old central districts of place Maubert and the rue Saint-Jacques, the streets on both sides of the rue Mouffetard were crowded with small shops and booths housed in narrow buildings. For contemporaries like Mercier this was uncharted territory, an area marked by extreme poverty and a capacity for revolt, where one ventured only out of necessity or curiosity.[18] On the right bank, from the faubourg du Temple to the faubourg Saint-Antoine, building took place primarily near the boulevards where densely built-up and heavily populated zones stood face to face with open, often rustic, patches of land along the access roads into the city. The southern part of the faubourg Saint-Antoine between the rue de Charenton and the Seine was not much built on; gardeners lived in huts and shanties in the marshy land which produced vegetables. As on the right bank, the land along the river was taken up by depots for timber floated downstream, and other materials.[19] All these zones were a familiar landscape to the people of Paris in which a whole traffic of daily and weekly travel for work and play revolved around three main components: the toll-gates, the gardens and the agglomerations of houses, building sites and taverns. Thus the irresistible thrust of the town had ignored all the royal declarations which had attempted to halt it in 1740 and in 1765. When towards the end of the 1780s the tax-farmers got permission to build the 'mur des fermiers-généraux' to control fiscal matters more effectively, the new perimeter thus defined embraced a vast zone, often undeveloped, with fields and vineyards, a temporary no man's land difficult to control, encouraging fraud and, in the eyes of the police, crime. This construction, which cordoned off the town from south to north and made it 'murmur',[20] struck a blow against the traditional patterns of consumption and imposed a limit to the development of the 'physical mass of Paris' (S. Mercier). For a time, the city enjoyed some breathing-space, for the city of Louis XIV had concentrated about

18. H. Burstin, 'Le Faubourg Saint-Marcel à l'époque révolutionnaire', Thesis 3ᵉ cycle, Paris, 1977, pp. 30–50.
19. R. Monnier, 'Les Classes laborieuses du faubourg Saint-Antoine sous la Révolution et l'Empire', Thesis 3ᵉ cycle, Paris, 1977, pp. 15–20.
20. In the French text, 'murmurer', a pun that needs explanation here: 'Le mur murant Paris rend Paris murmurant', A. Babeau, *Paris en 1789*, Paris, 1889, p. 28.

450,000 inhabitants within fewer than 1,000 hectares, but under Louis XVI there were fewer than 800,000 in more than 3,000 hectares. Nevertheless, to explore the relationship of Parisians to their space, we must reflect upon the significance of population curves.

The way in which many eighteenth-century writers deplored the exodus towards Paris has contributed to our historical understanding in ways we cannot ignore. However, this immigration could not substantially alter the traditional and stable characteristics. These newcomers were few when compared with the overall total. The place they occupied in picturesque literature or in the street, in Mercier's descriptions or police reports, should not be exaggerated. The town grew chiefly through the surplus of births over deaths. This demographic fact, which we have outlined, is all that counts and, in consequence, we should re-read and evaluate the qualitative documentation in the light of this fundamental criterion.[21] This quotation by Louis Chevalier, in an admirable book written twenty years ago, showed rather paradoxically the point at issue in a history of the population of Paris in the century of the Enlightenment. His viewpoint is entirely dominated by the demographic movements of the nineteenth century. Before the Revolution, Paris was demographically stable with a slow growth-rate due essentially to the increase in indigenous families — noble, bourgeois and artisan — which only exceptionally absorbed an immigrant population which settled in the lower-class *quartiers* and faubourgs, performing labouring tasks and preserving their social diversity. In short, there were two cities confronting each other in a way that should not surprise anyone from the late twentieth century, when migrants are playing a similar role. The Revolution disturbed this equilibrium by putting the 'barbarians' in the place of the 'civilised' and preparing the future role of the *classes dangereuses*.

The above is interesting in two ways: it clearly poses the problem of population stability — were there more Parisians in the eighteenth century who were 'real' Parisians? What was the relative place of the migrants? It also emphasises the different mores of established city-dwellers and shifting migrants. However, it needs to be examined critically for it tends to underestimate the importance of the migrant phenomenon, marginalising it and throwing into question the capacity for integration on the part of the old established social strata. Was the native–migrant frontier not as permeable as the idealised boundaries of the city? The question is not easily answered: in contrast to those for some of the larger provincial cities, the demographic sources for Paris reveal gaps and bias. There is no *état civil*; notarial documents such as

21. L. Chevalier, *Classes laborieuses et classes dangereuses*, Paris, 1958, pp. 257–8.

marriage contracts do not really enable us to study the floating population; judicial archives provide a rich variety of information but they only allow us to see things from below; hospital registers have never been studied fully and demand a rigorous approach. In short, the historian of Paris has little to go on.[22] He is better served by the Revolutionary period when censuses and especially *cartes de sureté*, issued from 1793, give more exhaustive information about the social physiognomy of the city, even if the upheavals of the period have to be taken into account. Overall, two questions must be asked: how many Parisians were there? What sort of Parisians were they?

The major population figure covering the period between the end of the seventeenth century and the beginning of the nineteenth century tend to agree, although they are not altogether convincing. Table 1.1 gives the best-known figures.

In his book on population in 1789 Brion de la Tour discusses the calculations put forward by his contemporaries: one author gives 500,000 inhabitants, eight others agree at between 550,000 and 700,000, another eight between 700,000 and 800,000, two go just over 900,000, and seven go up to a million. This diversity shows how difficult it is to get a clear, or even an approximate, picture largely because it reflects results obtained in different ways. Some calculations are fiscal, but how can one establish the real value of a *feu*, and how many people escaped the tax? Some are based on house numbers, whilst others are extrapolated from baptismal records using various coefficients. The best demographers of the eighteenth century have a weakness for this latter method, which is a somewhat debatable one for a city with a considerable number of unmarried people and a high floating population. A number of factors add to his imprecision: the question of boundaries, which were never clearly established; religious minorities, which were not always systematically registered; seasonal mobility; provincials passing through and foreigners, reckoned by abbé Expilly at 25,000 and by the 1817 census at 20,000; the inclusion in the number of births of foundlings, 10 per cent of whom came from the nearby suburbs and from the Île-de-France around 1700, 30 to 40 per cent around 1780. All in all, one hesitates to draw a conclusion; it is difficult to project the more reliable figures for the beginning of the nineteenth century to the pre-Revolutionary years, whilst the Revolutionary censuses are disputed — for the year II M. Reinhard suggests at least 560,000 inhabitants, but P. Meuriot, either less critical or more optimistic, accepts more than 627,000. In short, it is difficult to take a position; one can

22. D. Roche, 'Les migrants parisiens au XVIIIᵉ siècle', in *Cahiers d'Histoire*, 1980, pp. 5–20 (gives most of the sources).

Table 1.1. Population of Paris 1685–1789

Date	Evaluation	Source
1680–1700	500,000	Bertillon
1684	23,000 houses x 20 = 460,000 92,000 heads of family × 4.5 = 416,000	Fiscal evaluation
1695–1707	702,000	Vauban
1714	21,800 houses × 20 = 436,000	Jean de la Caille
1714	509,000	Messance (leaving out births)
1715	800,000	Joly de Fleury (mss.) (×30)
1719	509,000	Messance
1720	166,665 (hearths)	Saugrain, *Nouveau Dénombrement*
1744	800,000	Deparcieux (assessment)
1763	576,000	Messance
1766	576,630	Messance (leaving out births)
1766	658,000	Buffon (assessment) (×30)
1767	645,000 (communicants)	Denis (diocesan records)
1770	576,639	Abbé Expilly, *Dictionnaire*
1775	700,000	Buffon (assessment)
1778	640,000–680,000	Moheau (leaving out births)
1779–80	598,000	La Michodière
1780	600,000	Messance
1780	600,000	Lavoisier
1780	600,000	Le chevalier de Pommelles
1784	640,000–680,000	Necker
1796	556,000	census
1795	627,000	Meuriot
1801	546,000	census
1807	580,609–659,555 (in peacetime)	census
1817	714,000	census

reckon on a figure somewhere between 600,000 and 700,000 in 1789, even allowing at least an extra 10 per cent for a floating population. On this evaluation, one may accept a minimum growth of 30 per cent for the century, starting from 500,000 in 1700–14, a growth demonstrated by the extension in space which the tax-farmers' wall attempted to fix, and in which annual and seasonal fluctuations were very considerable. So 2 per cent of the population of the kingdom was concentrated in Paris at the time of Louis XIV and 3 per cent at the time of Louis XVI, showing an increase which is clearly less than that of the seventeenth century, when it rose from 200,000 to 500,000, and was therefore a less brutal and more controlled change. If the population was not completely stabilised, if it was not as 'Parisianised' as was sometimes thought, the qualitative changes took place fairly smoothly. Nevertheless, when related to the curve of births and deaths, the increase cannot be explained by natural growth.[23] The number of deaths of Parisian infants put out to nurse outside Paris increased the deficit every year and it is generally admitted that 30 per cent to 40 per cent died in their first year, a net deficit difficult to compensate. So the growth of Paris depended on migrants; the city could not develop out of its own resources,[24] and one cannot discount the hypothesis of an exodus which is difficult to quantify but is none the less real. The migratory balance was no doubt less on the eve of the Revolution than immediately after the Fronde, but its importance remains fundamental even if it is impossible to know the exact number of those who remained more or less permanently in the city. The question is important but insoluble. In the Revolutionary period, daily, monthly and yearly surveys of furnished rooms carried out by the police registered between 8,000 and 11,000 persons a month in Year III, totalling by the end of the year nearly 100,000 more people! Even if one cannot project back these figures, exaggerated as they are by the political, military, economic and social conditions of the Revolutionary crisis, they clearly suggest that the city attracted many more people than it retained.[25] Paris in the eighteenth century was extremely mobile, a melting-pot, an ant-hill, but it was not only that for, among the newcomers, a considerable number remained and established families. Between native Parisians (of the first or second generation?), provincials passing through and provincials who had settled, a multiplicity of relationships were created in a complex situation in which stability and instability constantly fluctuated according to a seasonal rhythm, economic difficulties, political celebrations and the initiatives of individuals and families. To a considerable extent this uncontrollable movement explains the obsessive fears of contemporaries and justifies police initiatives: 'What are the instruments of these public calamities? Always men whose names and dwellings are unknown: individuals who seem strangers in the very city which provides their subsistence; beings who live for the moment and also disappear as easily as they appeared.

23. E. Charlot and J. Dupaquier, *Mouvement annuel de la population de la ville de Paris de 1670 à 1821: Demographie historique*, 1967, pp. 511–19. All in all, births did not exceed deaths by more than 20,000 for the century, without taking into account nurselings who died outside the city.
24. M. Reinhard, *Paris pendant la Révolution*, part 1, pp. 35–41.
25. S. Lartigue, *Les populations flottantes à Paris au XVIIIe siècle*, Mémoire de maîtrise, Paris–I, 1980, pp. 124–7.

In short, men without roots.' The lawyer Des Essarts was voicing a general opinion, supported by other littérateurs like Mercier and Rétif.[26] The undisputed fact reflects the profound sense of the differences which distinguished the people of Paris.

Is it possible to assess the proportion of migrants in the population? From reliable studies made in the sections during the Revolution one can establish rates of about 60–70 per cent in the faubourg Saint-Marcel; provincials by birth represented nearly 67 per cent of the population in the faubourg Saint-Antoine; 63 per cent in the Fontaine-Grenelle section which corresponded to the west of the faubourg Saint-Germain; newcomers reached 78 per cent around the place des Vosges; in the section of the place des Fédérés the proportion of migrants was 73 per cent; in the section la Grange-Batellière research into the registers of lodging houses gives 69 per cent; near the Louvre, section de l'Oratoire, and near the place Vendôme the same source provides analogous figures. These very high percentages no doubt correspond to the provincial influx after 1792, and cannot necessarily be assumed for the century, but they do allow us to draw several conclusions.

In the first place, if one looks at the arrival dates, there is a constant influx of the order of 7,000 to 14,000 a year between 1750 and 1790. One may incline to the first estimate if one considers that the emigration of Parisians is negligible, but the second hypothesis is more probable if one accepts the possible departure of Parisians and the fact that not all the newcomers remained in the city. The question which must be answered is — how permanent or how temporary was the immigration? One must also accept the conclusions to be drawn from studies covering previous years. Around 1750, marriage contracts register only 53 per cent of migrants, a minimum figure if one remembers that nearly a quarter of the documents bear no indication of the place of origin. At the same time, research into 400 marriage contracts drawn up by notaries in the Marais suggests 50 per cent of newcomers (20 per cent of the contracts giving no indication). Immigration was a constant throughout the century and for the whole city. The data in the criminal archives confirm these results. In a good or bad year, only a third of the defendants coming before the Châtelet de Paris were born in the capital; foreigners and provincials made up three-quarters of those accused of stealing food, according to the studies of A. Farge;[27] again, they made up 64 per cent of those arrested for rebellion and judged by the Cour des Aides between 1785 and 1789. Questioned

26. Des Essarts, *Dictionnaire de la Police*, Paris, 1786–8, 7 vols., vol. VII, pp. 458–63.
27. A. Farge, *Le Vol d'aliments à Paris au XVIIe siècle*, Paris, 1974, pp. 118–119.

about their place of birth, three to four thousand, or two-thirds of the defendants, told the *procureur du Roi de l'Hôtel de Ville* that they had been born in the provinces; the phenomenon appears to have been more pronounced around 1789 than before 1750. In every case, if one accepts the predominantly popular character of the accused, if one remembers that rootlessness encouraged delinquency and criminality, one appreciates what a significant factor this mobility was for those who did not reside permanently in the capital. So far as hospitals are concerned the results are similar. From 1762 to 1776, out of 2,000 patients admitted to la Charité, more than three-quarters were migrants. Two registers of patients kept at the Hôtel-Dieu give a provincial origin for more than two-thirds of those entered in 1733, 1738 and 1744.[28] All in all, then, immigration compensated for the lack of natural growth. It created a changing and restless population in proportions which are difficult to evaluate, varying between, if one admits a certain stability, a minimum of 33 per cent and a maximum of 66 per cent if one takes into account the importance of departures, the mobility of Parisians as well as non-natives, and the probability of an unequal spread by *quartier*.[29] The discrepancy between these two estimates is a measure of our ignorance and the effort required to assemble the necessary facts for a more precise study.

The second lesson established by current studies is that the area of recruitment for the city remained stable from the beginning of the eighteenth century to the Revolution. Let us deal first with the problem of immigrants from other countries, who are not negligible, for they form an important percentage of travellers and sometimes represent a notable proportion in the studies undertaken — 6 per cent of the defendants before the Châtelet, 2 per cent of the population of the faubourg Saint-Marcel, 5 per cent of the accused at the Hôtel de Ville, 3 per cent of the inhabitants of the Marais, and 4 per cent in the faubourg Saint-Antoine. These proportions disguise the actual truth. On the one hand, an immigration of *petites gens* among whom contingents from Germanic countries and Savoy, '*Juifs de Nation*', Switzerland and the Austrian Netherlands predominated; servants, odd-job men and shoe-cleaners mingling with soldiers of fortune and petty adventurers attracted by the Parisian mirage. On the other hand there was a considerable contingent of qualified professionals. At the top, bankers, business men, *négociants* from Switzerland or Germany, from Brussels or Vienna, constituted a cosmopolitan society which

28. M.-C. Lorang, 'L'Hôtel-Dieu de Paris au XVIIIᵉ siecle', Thesis, l'Ecole des Chartres, Paris, 1975.
29. L. Henry, 'Deux analyses de l'immigration à Paris au XVIIIᵉ siecle', *Population*, 1971, pp. 1075–92.

was partly integrated, and partly renewed through the network created
by the Protestant diaspora in Europe and by family and business links
which favoured these newcomers. This type of person gained recognition in 1789 with the success of Necker. At the lower level, the same
phenomenon occurred among artisans, and foreigners were often
successfully integrated, like the 250 master cabinet-makers, of whom a
third were of foreign extraction, mostly German. This Germanic
influx, which contrasted with other closed *corporations* such as the
joiners, was not a recent phenomenon, but it increased in the years
before the Revolution. Professional and family relations, matrimonial
alliances and very high technical qualifications explain this special
character, and it would be interesting if we were in a position to assess
its importance for other trades.

As far as migrants from within France are concerned, the population
was drawn from two main areas: a first zone extending up to 300
kilometres radius provided the majority of the new Parisians; beyond
that the flow was less considerable and the provenance more varied. In
the faubourg Saint-Antoine and the faubourg Saint-Marcel, two-
thirds of the provincials came from parts of France north of the Loire.
In the majority were inhabitants of the Île-de-France, 15 per cent in
each district, followed by those from the departments of the Nord,
Aisne, Pas-de-Calais, Oise and the Somme. Contingents of comparable size from Normandy, Champagne and Burgundy (8 to 10 per
cent) completed the new population. The proportion from nearby
regions is considerably increased in the registers of furnished rooms
which have been preserved for the critical period of 1693–9: 60 per
cent of the lodgers had travelled less than 40 kilometres, essentially
from small towns encircling Paris: Dammartin-en-Goële, Crépy-
en-Valois, Nanteuil-le-Haudouin, le Mesnil-Amelot and Meaux. They
were mostly ploughmen, chandlers and seed merchants who came to
trade in the capital (50 per cent of those lodging in the Grève and the
Saint-Martin districts). The rest were drawn from all social milieux,
but especially domestic servants and professionals in the building,
furnishing and food trades. A century later, in lodgings in the Oratoire
and place Vendôme sections, there were many more provincials from
the north, west and east. Socially, the bourgeois — 300 out of 1,400 —
were a minority compared with the tradesmen, journeymen tailors —
300 — and servants. The geography of their social origins no doubt
varied considerably according to circumstances and time, but it had its
constant features — a predominance from nearby and northern zones,
from the alluvial chalk plains of the Paris basin, which were populous
and literate areas.

The rest of the immigrants came from all over France, each province offering an influx in inverse proportion to its distance, a characteristic which persisted to the end of the nineteenth century. This tendency, which lasted for two centuries, presupposes that the population of Paris was fed by the regular growth of nearby regions. For zones beyond a range of 300 kilometres, a cumulative effort was doubtless required, and migrations developed less by demographic pressure in the regions themselves than by people from the same provinces who had already settled in Paris sending for relatives and friends. Detailed studies of family networks and structures of social relations in different districts of Paris should confirm this interpretation. It has the merit of explaining the permanence of patterns which had been established and reinforced over long periods. These different influxes produced a very variegated image of the newly established population, a mixture of people from Provence, Languedoc, Brittany, Poitiers, Gascony, Limoges, the Auvergne and the Dauphiné. This geographical spread can be found in other districts and other population groups.

Among the newly-married the proportion from nearer zones is increased: young married couples from the Ile-de-France signed a quarter of the contracts, couples from Picardy, Champagne, Normandy and Burgundy nearly two-thirds, and the remainder came from all over France, with only the Massif Central standing out with substantial contingents (6–7 per cent), as well as the faubourgs (4–6 per cent). The same applies to the origins of defendants brought before the Châtelet and the Hôtel de Ville. The Paris basin provided large contingents; the east, the north, Normandy and Burgundy made a major contribution, while south of the Loire the influx thinned out, with the exception of those from the mountainous provinces of the Auvergne, Franche-Comté and Dauphiné. At la Charité hospital, one finds the same mix from different provinces with a clear majority from the dioceses of the Ile-de-France, while the bishoprics of the north, Lorraine and Champagne provided the rest. At the Hôtel-Dieu we get the same picture of a migration drawing its main strength from the north and nearby regions. All in all, in the wards of hospices and town jails, as in the houses, hotels and furnished apartments of the centre and the suburbs, there were colourful populations from the same regions, drawn by the same fascination of the city, the attraction of anonymity and freedom, the hope of steady work and of social progress which would allow them to compete in skills with an urban population.

The fact remains that one would like to know more about the relationships that existed among these new Parisians and especially what linked them or dissociated them from the indigenous population which was not multiplying. The urban dream revealed in the literary works of Marivaux, Rousseau or Rétif had to be reconciled with reality. Conflicts are recorded in the legal archives: in 1763, on the *quais*, a casual labourer from the Limousin fought with his companions who were mocking his origins; in 1772 in lodgings in the rue Saint-Denis a violent quarrel broke out between three companions, one born in the Ile-de-France, another newly arrived from Picardy and the last from the Auvergne. The coexistence of populations of different origins, with their own culture, language, ways of eating and dressing, was not without its problems, but it is a field of study which remains completely unexplored. We must examine, behind these clashes, all those factors which encouraged, or discouraged, the integration of migrants into the city.

Undoubtedly a good starting-point would be Parisian servants, an important social group numerically — 15 per cent in marriage contracts for 1749, and nearly 40,000 souls in abbé Expilly's survey based on the 1764 tax returns — as well as being a mobile group with strong provincial recruitment, a theme which we will pursue through the study of those material and cultural factors which defined the popular classes of Paris.[30]

Geographically, more than 90 per cent of Parisian servants were recruited from the provinces; only 5.4 per cent of servants arraigned before the Châtelet were Parisians, and they represented only 4 per cent of the servants who died in Paris in the reigns of Louis XIV and Louis XVI. The main area of recruitment, the breeding-ground of the town, was to be found in a radius of 50 to 60 kilometres from the capital. The main labour force was drawn from the large peasant villages in the Ile-de-France, Brie and le Vexin, supplemented by the influx from Normandy, Champagne and Picardy. An interesting indication of the mobility characteristic of this social milieu is that they were less numerous amongst those who died in Paris (6 per cent) than amongst the group of unfortunates who were brought before the courts (18 per cent), which presupposes a certain number returning home whether they had made their fortunes or not. In all, nearly half of the servants came from this emigration zone, which suggests there were permanent channels of recruitment to Paris and to the ancillary services. Few of them came from towns (15 per cent) and these were spread throughout France with one dominant zone, the urban east, which included Reims, Metz, Strasbourg, Troyes, Besançon and Dijon. The proportion of townspeople from the 300-kilometre zone around Paris is markedly lower (6 per cent); beyond that it reaches 30

30. M. Botlan, 'Domesticité et domestiques à Paris dans la crise (1770–1790)', Thesis, l'Ecole des Chartes, Paris, 1976.

per cent or more. The move towards Paris occurred after a first migration of country people towards their nearest towns. We should also note that the women came more often from the neighbouring countryside than men; less urbanised, they did not travel so far and many returned home. The immigration of servants was principally a movement from rich, cultivated regions, and in most cases those country-folk moved alone, leaving their families in the village. Their adventure might have been prompted by prosperity — this is the case with Jacob in *Paysan Parvenu*, or Edmond in *Paysan Perverti* — or by poverty or crises. There is the example of the innkeeper's daughter in *Jacques le fataliste*.

Even more than novels, archives bear witness to the power of the city in attracting a considerable percentage of the population who hoped to find their fortune there, or at least some degree of status. As a result of family or social situation, many were classless or outsiders, drifting along various seas before reaching harbour. Two factors played a decisive role in this: their age and the stages along the road to Paris. The towns where they broke their journey were the points where itineraries and roads converged, to which migrants flocked from several provinces: Troyes for people from Lorraine, Champagne and Burgundy, Versailles for those from Brittany, Normandy and Le Mans. The tramp towards the capital would be resumed from these relay towns and would finally reach its destination after a series of marches and counter-marches. More stops indicated more setbacks, since migrants did not hesitate to move on again if the servant market was over-crowded. Marie Mercier, who set out, aged 33, from Neufchâteau in Lorraine, stayed for two years at Bréviande near Troyes, then eighteen months at Saint-Pouange, which she left to work at hat-making in the Champagne metropolis. This seamstress, the daughter of a mason, arrived in Paris after six years, only to be arrested for begging. The irregularity of a typical journey such as this shows the hazards of poverty and a hesitancy arising from the unequal and problematic possibilities of employment. This story ended in failure, but for others success was not impossible and the elementary cultural and social knowledge acquired along the way was not negligible. Peasant and servant girls with no polish might turn into lively soubrettes and expert chamber-maids; inexperienced farm-hands and day-labourers might learn new methods and skills. Their ages on arrival confirm this dual training. Half the servants, men and women, reached Paris between the ages of 15 and 25; the other half arrived later, nearly a quarter of them over 30. So they went into service in Paris quite late, often after a more or less lengthy apprenticeship in various situations. This itinerary was the result of the demographic

growth of the departure zones where the young could not all be
absorbed, and the attraction of the city where ancillary employment
could be at once the last resort against misery and the means of
achieving a modest affluence. Criminal source material should not
mask the fact that a certain number of successes *could* be achieved in
the world of domestic service.

Domestic service in Paris was one of the typical areas of lower-class
immigration, and it would be interesting if one could make a precise
comparison with other social and professional strata. Let us take three
main factors which may usefully be applied to the majority of the
population of Paris: age, manner of integration and anthropological
aspects. The migrant population was young, the average age of men
arriving in the faubourg Saint-Antoine and the faubourg Saint-Marcel
in the year III was between 22 and 24, and there is no indication of
regional variables except for the remoter provinces for which age levels
were higher. So Paris saw predominantly a migration of apprentices
motivated by the search for trade qualifications, although no settled
pattern emerged before the age of 30 to 40. The youthfulness of the
newcomers made them vulnerable, at least for a time, as they were
exposed more frequently than in the country to new illnesses against
which they had no immunity. Older people, like native-born Parisians,
showed more resistance. In the two great popular faubourgs, the two
groups show up clearly; more than three-quarters had settled there
since 1755, more than two-thirds since 1770. The recent influx was
greater in comparison with the years before the Revolution, because of
the crisis which sent the provincial unemployed to Paris, and because
the authorities registered all the male population, including a floating
percentage which is difficult to determine exactly. This influx of young
men had two main consequences: it reinforced the competitive nature
of the labour market, and it helped to shore up a birth-rate which had
been seriously undermined. Both factors call into question the possibilities of integration provided by the city.

Work kept people in the capital, and the choice of work often
determined where they lived. In the main professional sectors the
levels of migration were fairly uniform and all areas of employment
and society were affected by it.

The migrants were everywhere; of course they were more numerous
in certain trades, the non-specialist professions, labouring jobs or
situations with no job security. They provided the great contingents of
servants, casual labourers, dockers and small street-traders who were
employed thus while waiting and hoping for something better. No
profession, as has often been said, was dominated entirely by one
particular provincial milieu; there were men from Normandy and the

Table 1.2. Migrant population levels (%)

	Faubourg Saint-Marcel	Saint-Antoine
Food	76	79
Building	65	66
Wood	41	61
Metal	73	66
Casual labourers	85	75
Servants	93	91
Liberal professions	56	66
Rentiers	58	69

Auvergne in all trades, and from Picardy and Champagne in all sectors. Nevertheless, a traditional geography of work seems to have existed at least for certain activities, without it really being possible to talk of a monopoly. Newcomers from nearby areas — less than 300 kilometres — were in the majority in all unqualified jobs, with people from the Paris region at the head. Some tasks devolved upon particular provincial communities, water-carriers from the Auvergne, shoe-cleaners and chimney-sweeps from Savoy, horse-dealers and coachmen from le Perche and Normandy, wood-floaters, boatmen and dockers, often from the Morvan. In qualified professions, whether free or controlled, certain provinces provided more labour for some trades than for others. Thus the building trade employed more than 1,500 workers in the faubourg Saint-Marcel, that is nearly 10 per cent of the working population; in the faubourg Saint-Antoine it employed nearly 800 people, about 7 per cent of the whole; among these professionals there was firstly a strong nucleus of real Parisians — a third — and the provincials came from all over France, with three regions predominating; the Ile-de-France (8 per cent), Limousin (18 per cent), Normandy (10 per cent). Normans and Limousins, stone-cutters, masons, paviours, plasterers had been coming regularly to Paris over a long period, but how can we know how many stayed on there, established families, and how many became masters? In textiles and clothing there was clearly a strong proportion of people from the north, from Lorraine and Champagne; metallurgy recruited from the northern and frontier provinces, the food trades from Burgundy and Normandy.

Some topographical differentiation corresponded in this relative integration through work. The population of the working-class districts in the centre and the suburbs was not segregated into streets and districts, but some local groupings according to region and village can be observed. In the faubourg Saint-Marcel the Burgundians settled in

the rue Saint-Victor, rue d'Orléans and on the *quais*, where they lived
alongside people from Lorraine and Champagne, as well as from
Normandy. Limousins preferred the rue Saint-Jacques and the place
Maubert, Auvergnats were encamped in the rue Mouffetard and rue de
Lourcine, where they cohabited with Picards, Flemings and Dauphi-
nois. In the faubourg Saint-Antoine some streets were partly colonised
by groups mixing with the original population, people from the Cantal
and the Aveyron rented rooms in the rue de Lappe, rue Saint-Antoine
in the cour Saint-Louis and the cour du Commerce. These groupings
occurred in the old central *quartiers*, in the rue Saint-Denis, rue
Saint-Martin, and in the Marais where Auvergnats colonised the rue
Jean-Beausire and the rue des Tournelles; they could also be found in
the working-class areas and back streets in the east of the faubourg
Saint-Germain, and in furnished rooms in the Oratoire, place
Vendôme and la Grange-Batellière sections. Migrant Paris was no
different from the Paris of the original inhabitants, and geographical
segregation was no more significant than social segregation, even if
some factors promoting cohesion encouraged partial grouping —
family relations, job solidarity, common speech and customs, eating
habits and daily routines. However, there is no doubt that this diversity tended to decrease with age and time, at least for those who stayed
on, but it was partly kept alive by newcomers who had to be integrated.

A return to the general study of marriage contracts should make it
possible to establish the nature, rhythms and conditions of the fusion
within Parisian society. In 1749, it is noticeable that there were fewer
provincials among brides than among their husbands; in the Marais
and in rue Saint-Denis, 40 per cent of the brides were daughters of
Parisians. It is true that marriage contracts underestimate the proportion of the very poor, but it seems clear that the choice of a wife was a
determining factor both in strengthening a partly stabilised position
and in furthering some modest social progress. It is well-known that
socio-professional inbreeding was the general rule, but one would also
like to know how this was combined with regional relationships and
local solidarities. The phenomenon affected the whole population.
Two fundamental questions are linked with it: the deculturalising role
of the town needs to be re-examined, for one can no longer rely simply
upon the affirmations of contemporaries who denounce urban malefi-
cence; and the exact nature of the migration which could by choice be
only temporary, rejecting urban acculturalisation, counting on a return
to the place of birth, which was the case with the Auvergnats who
migrated steadily towards Paris, as well as towards other horizons
such as Languedoc and Spain. Some migrants were happy to maintain a

minimal relationship with the town through a sort of temporary pact maintained over a greater or lesser period. Assimilation might mean a break with their origins and in daily life, as in literary representations, these constituted a more precious ideal than permanent establishment in Paris.[31]

For a long time differences persisted between natives and the majority of temporary migrants, seasonal workers whose importance is indisputable but difficult to establish precisely, and newcomers who had settled and become more or less integrated. Literary witnesses like Marivaux, Mercier and Rétif have familiarised us with this contrast, which was anthropological in nature. City-dwellers of long standing and newly arrived rustics were widely different in appearance and manners. The former were large and plump, pink and white, their complexion unspoilt by work in the fields, and their physical ideal was the round-bellied bulk of the self-made bourgeois, accustomed to good food and unwearied by manual labour. The *patronnes* of inns and brothels were always fresh and pale, real Parisians who neither knew nor liked the sun, which scarcely penetrated the narrow streets of the old *quartiers*. The city-dweller washed and the bourgeois sometimes went as far as experiencing the delights of personal hygiene. The newcomers were lean and tanned, burnt by the sun of the field and the highway, their bodies were deformed by hard labour, their clothes dirty and neglected. Ignorant of the niceties of cleanliness, they made do with a hasty rinse at the fountain before work, which gave a certain edge to the little glass of brandy gulped down at the nearest tavern. But it would be wrong to exaggerate this contrast. In part, of course, it was perpetuated by permanent migration, and by the fact that the city kept the novices in the lowest jobs, secreting its own poverty, but the effect of the city was not entirely deculturalising; it held on to men and transformed them, offering them new ways of eating and dressing, providing them with new opportunities to improve themselves and to dream. And for all Parisians, old and new, changes took place above all in relation to space.

The city in the eighteenth century was in a state of continual upheaval, and its inhabitants could not fail to be aware of fundamental changes. Two complementary, sometimes contradictory, town developments imposed a new morphology of social space. First, as a result of the continuous increase in the functions of Paris as a capital, the monarchy and its agents created a municipal administration of some magnificence, controlled and triumphal in style. On the other hand, there was an uncontrolled development resulting from the initiatives of

31. F. Raison, *La Colonie auvergnate de Paris au XIXe siècle*, Paris, 1976.

private citizens and speculators, which helped to destroy the character of old *quartiers* and construct new blocks of housing. Both increased urban mobility by their demand for labour, and fixed the population in Paris.

The first development is well known. It included monumental edifices, mobilised great architects, created an immense theatre in which the populace rarely performed except through their labour. The monumental gateways, the completed or newly built squares, the place Vendôme and place Louis XV, administrative buildings steadily altering the Parisians' daily view of Paris. However, the sumptuous buildings, la Monnaie, l Ecole de Médecine, the theatres, the rebuilding of the Théâtre français by Charles de Wailly, Foufflot's Ecole de droit and the Pantheon had an effect upon the social structure and the buildings of the old *quartiers* where they were implanted, especially if they were accompanied by a real reshaping of the site. This was the case with the left bank and the different alterations which took place around the Odéon, l'Ecole de médecine and the building lots of part of the Luxembourg. A unitary organisation of space, in which the relationship between public buildings, squares, streets and houses was changed, suggested a theatrical vision of the urban landscape where city-dwellers were experiencing a new social order.[32] Sometimes recent monuments and buildings helped to form a base for future developments, as with the area around the Ecole militaire and around the *bâtiments du garde-meuble* in the rue Royale.

The architectural intervention by the monarchy was accompanied by traffic plans which steadily altered the lives of everybody. The century of the Enlightenment did not change the civic ideal of the seventeenth century, it reiterated it with a stronger sense of the town as a place of exchange, trading, merchandise and men, it generalised it with a more economic and functional plan. In its supervision and intervention it used texts and rulings drawn up in the time of Louis XIV, created new ones, and attempted to apply them. Nothing escaped attention — highways, buildings and alignment — the regulation of 1783 would forbid the creation of streets less than 30 feet wide — bridges and lighting — the oil lamp replaced candle-lanterns — the numbering of streets, cleaning and water. By the end of the eighteenth century there had been decisive progress which accustomed the whole population to the use of a great range of amenities. In spite of its congestion and accidents which, over and above the rhetoric about overcrowding which had been going on since Horace, highlight the

32. D. Rabreau, in *Charles de Wailly, peintre et architecte de l'Europe des lumières*, Paris, 1979, pp. 64–9.

worst crossing-points in the centre of the town; in spite of the lack of pavements, the mud and the dust, Paris was a town where people could get about. The presence of the police ensured overall control. Paris was contained.

The initiatives of private developers present a different perspective. The continual rise in rents and speculation in individual houses and building lots promoted a fever of construction both on the outskirts and in the heart of the town. The lower classes worked on many sites, but depended on the combined initiatives of many actors. In their new mansions the nobility expressed their taste for display and sense of power, a new mode of spatial appropriation over vast airy tracts, partly wasted, creating a sense of isolation compared with their former habitat. Aristocrats remodelled the western faubourgs, creating a city which swallowed up seigneurial levies, state assistance and financial profits. Then there was the intervention of the clergy, whose enormous holdings of real estate in Paris mobilised, for buildings and gardens, land which served as the lungs and reserve building space for the town. They increased the value of their patrimony by building houses to let, and joined forces with financiers — as in the faubourg Montmartre — to make profits from housing. Lastly there were the speculators whose building enterprises in the new districts brought together not only builders such as Robert de Cotte and Brongniart, capitalists, bankers, financiers, tax-farmers, all buying, dividing and building up empty spaces, but also aristocrats led by the royal princes, Orléans, Artois, Provence, Condé and Conti, the great families, their agents, finance-dealers and business men. All these people were playing for big stakes in enterprises which not only changed old divisions of land but, by juicy small-scale operations in the centre and extensive, profitable ones on the outskirts, reorganised the entire layout of Paris.

Thus Paris spread out during the century, which meant slightly less crowding overall, but chiefly a new inequality in relationship to the available space.[33] Two cities coexisted, occupying more or less the same surface area: in the centre, the old, decrepit Paris which resulted from urban development in the sixteenth and seventeenth centuries, a dense, industrious city into which crowded the working popular classes and the bourgeoisie of commerce and crafts; and, on the frontiers of the non-urban world caught in the net of the fiscal ring, the *quartiers* thrusting towards the future, the new Paris of the idle classes and their servants as well as the jostling, jerry-built Paris of the working-class suburbs.

In the first of these cities there was a high population density: 1,000

---

33. P. Chaunu, *La Mort à Paris, 16ᵉ, 17ᵉ, 18ᵉ siècles*, Paris, 1978, pp. 197–210.

to 1,300 inhabitants per hectare, a minimum of 500 to 800 in the parishes of the old centre, Saint-Jacques-le-Majeur, Saint Germain-l'Auxerrois, Saint-Gervais, Saint-Leu, Saint-Gilles, Saint-André-des-Arts: the poor who received aid in the first years of the Revolution were concentrated there (more than 20 per cent of the inhabitants). Elsewhere the population was less crowded, at most 100 inhabitants per hectare, at the lowest 25. The faubourg Saint-Antoine, the Popincourt and Quinze-Vingt *quartiers* fell below 80, a density that recurs for the Champs-Elysées, the Invalides, and towards the Observatoire in the faubourg Saint-Marcel, but in the two big popular faubourgs the number of poor receiving help was almost as high as in the centre. In short, the social geography did not coincide with city development.[34] Contemporary accounts confirmed this fact with their strong emphasis upon oppositions and contrasts overlapping everywhere: extreme riches and extreme poverty, luxury and penury, work and unemployment, leisure and activity, security and disorder. The old Paris, where social segregation was only just beginning, presented a very different cultural ambience from the post-industrial city. The coexistence of different classes had, if not political virtues, at least lessons to teach about the civilising effect of manners and, more simply still, implications for material culture.

On the eve of the Revolution Paris was a town of subtle hierarchies and cultural brokers, and even if the changes that took place between 1770 and 1789 produced greater difficulties and therefore more antagonism, they raised the emotional level and made it easier to mobilise the popular classes politically. Thus the centre grew poorer, its building heritage — that of the old Parisian bourgeoisie — lost its value, its population density increased and migrants settled there; in addition, it stretched out in all directions through the impoverished zones which linked it to the faubourgs on both banks. Its narrow streets and too-tall houses were mostly slums. It was largely, though not entirely, the Paris of the popular classes. All around, the interventionist city of the kings with its squares, monuments and mansions stretched out, its population density greater in the wake of the town development of Louis XIV; the population changed, the aristocratic Marais district became *parlementaire, hôtels* and bourgeois houses stood side by side in the finest streets of the faubourg Saint-Germain. The popular classes passed through these fine areas but they did not often live there, though there may have been lower-class pockets and retreats among them. Still further out, we discover the city of speculative growth,

34. L. Bergeron, 'Croissance urbaine et société à Paris au XVIIIᵉ siècle' in *La Ville au XVIIIᵉ siècle*, Aix-en-Provence, 1975, pp. 127–34.

towards the Champs-Elysées, the hills of Monceau, the Opéra, places of money and conspicuous expenditure, heralding the birth of the new smart *quartiers*. These are the *quartiers* which symbolise for us the urbanised, refined, cultivated Paris of the Age of Enlightenment, but it was, as a result of their labour, the cluster of faubourgs and central zones which paid for this growth. From the top of the towers of Notre-Dame, Sébastien Mercier invited his readers to admire the city 'round as a gourd' in the meander of the river, covered with smoke from its countless chimneys, 'a sign of its breathing', open wide to the countryside through its system of broad avenues suspended in empty fields. His vision, conditioned by all the aesthetic assumptions of the day, establishes the juxtapositions and the opposites. The Paris of the popular classes was composed of these clashes.

CHAPTER 2

Who were 'le peuple'?

'Le petit peuple' are inaccessible to reason.
Fontenelle

For at least a decade studies of the popular classes,
whether of *ancien régime* France or of pre-Revolutionary Paris have
been chiefly concerned with frontiers. Labouring classes and lower
classes have been studied in their relationship to social norms: it is
their marginality, their instability and their poverty which attract
attention. Criminals, deviants, outsiders and fringe groups occupy the
front of the stage.[1] It is a legitimate perspective in so far as History
ceases to favour the leading actors and gives speaking parts to the more
obscure in society. It is also justified by the very fact that the speeches
of the ruling class and the archives of repression constitute a statement
about society itself, revealing the way in which fears and rejections
were worked into a consensus, and through laws and the application of
laws, created a state of exclusion.[2] Contemporary images of the people
then become as precious for our understanding of social relationships
as a reality reconstituted through various filters from which our own
prejudices cannot be excluded. To understand the popular classes of
Paris is to imagine both their character and behaviour, but also to
reconstitute a social identity by studying the system of representations
which attempted to exercise them in order to contain them. In other
words, it is a matter of questioning stereotypes and myths. But for this

1. On this subject, see the work on the marginal groups in history, *Cahiers Jussieu*, 5,
Université de Paris 7, Paris, 1979; also, and especially, the works and articles of A. Farge,
Le Vol d'aliment (1974); *Vivre dans la rue au XVIIIe siècle*, Paris, 1979. M.E. Benabou's
thesis, in preparation, will be of great interest.
2. The definitive sources for the study of criminality in Paris are: A. Abbiatecci,
'Crimes et criminalités en France au XVIIe et XVIIIe siècles', *Cahiers des Annales*, 33,
Paris, 1971; 'Marginalité et criminalité à l'époque moderne', Special issue of *Revue
d'Histoire Moderne et Contemporaine*, 1974 (July–September); A. Farge and A. Zysberg, 'Les Théâtres de la violence à Paris au XVIIIe siècle', in *Annales*, ESC 1979, pp.
984–1015.

purpose, historical investigation — in which considerable place is given to textual comments by literary historians — proves to be very uncertain. Working on images, speeches and literary representations is as legitimate as reflecting upon the reality, at once probable and vague, which the historian extrapolates from his analyses of archives. Getting to know the people of Paris means first of all attempting to evaluate the way they spoke, therefore capturing a system of social perceptions which, by a play of mirrors, questions the reality constructed by the historian.

At the same time, to study the people of Paris in the eighteenth century is to tackle a legendary and mythological historical subject, for the fact that the 'dangerous', labouring classes ended up as revolutionaries inevitably looms large. They dominate the Revolution 'for the good and the just in the writings of Michelet, for the inept and the bad with Taine'.[3] Excluded from power and culture, they are the 'canaille' of the émigré, seigneurs, the 'vile multitude' of M. Thiers, and they matter all the more today than they did previously, despite their numbers, because they carried with them all the potential of the future. So the important thing is to understand why the Parisian masses took an active part in the bourgeois Revolution, how they achieved at least some measure of political awareness and how they were able to follow the leaders of revolutionary *sans-culotterie*.[4] In doing this, which is essential, do we not risk rewriting history after our own fashion, that is to say from the perspective of a determinist future?[5]

In any case, by writing about the people we are choosing our own ground. Without going more deeply into polemics born of the Revolution itself and which are out of place here, we must show our cards at the outset. The debate which divides French historiography about the nature of the Revolution has tended to make people forget that, apart from any global interpretations, the Revolution had its actors and the event itself arose first of all from a series of daily acts in response to daily situations. The importance of the questions posed for French consciences today by the intervention of the people between 1789 and 1794 demands an enquiry into popular modes of existence and the fact that they were interested in theories 'which aimed lower than the government and which were targeted upon the society which served as its base', to use the language of De Tocqueville.[6] In other words, it is important to see how the labouring classes by their poverty, the

3. M. Reinhard, 'La Révolution', in *Nouvelle Histoire de Paris*, Paris, 1971, p. 73.
4. J. Kaplow, *Les Noms des Rois, les pauvres de Paris à la veille de la Révolution*, Paris, 1974.
5. F. Furet, *Penser la Révolution française*, Paris, 1978.
6. J.-P. Hirsch, 'Pensons la Révolution française', in *Annales*, ESC, 1980, pp. 320–33.

precariousness which in varying degrees placed constraints upon their way of life and by their different culture posed for the ruling classes, privileged and bourgeois, the important question of social equality which went far beyond its legal aspects. In short, it is less a matter of subscribing once again to the consolidation of a firmly established historical image — the Revolution, daughter of misery according to Michelet — than of seeking out the complexity of a social reality — the Revolution, daughter of prosperity according to Jaurès; that is, understanding the meaning of the ordinary life of the popular classes who did not live through the entire eighteenth century preparing for new dawns. This option which is determinedly partial in both senses, does not assume that one can reconcile opposites, but that it is the job of the historian to accept the ambiguous and the contradictory: material instability and signs of improvement, moral wretchedness and indications of some simple happiness, the phenomena of passivity and facts of protest which did not necessarily lead to the revolutionary explosion. In any case, even if we must cast off our obsession with origins when we see the people rising in revolt, it is still useful to wonder about their age-old inertia, the infrequency and limited extent of sedition, and perhaps beyond that, about the heterogeneous nature of their awareness and aspirations. A hundred years of calm, more or less, do not prove the extinction of pauperism, but it may justify a study of the ways in which the people diverted and partly appropriated the cultural heritage of others, and an analysis of the measures of social control which may have helped to create a climate of calm in spite of the problems posed by growth. The fleeting explosions, brief alerts and gestures of protest which flickered through the 'vast, age-old silence of the people'[7] will not form the basis of this study. This is a deliberate choice. As a result, the truth may well appear as a rather tepid affair; this is a risk we have to take. Between the hot-blooded people of a militant history and the cold protagonists of a too-cerebral history, we must try to rediscover the specific identity of a class in the making.

Michelet beckons us on: 'Oh, who will find a way of speaking to the people? . . . otherwise we will die', he said to Béranger, implying the existence of an original popular state condition which was for him the promised land which had to be rediscovered.[8] At a time when the first consequences of the Industrial Revolution were beginning to make an impression, it was the duty of the writer to bear witness and allow the

7. F. Furet, 'Pour une définition des classes inférieures à l'époque moderne', in *Annales*, ESC, 1963, pp. 459–74.
8. R. Barthes, *Aujourd'hui Michelet*, l'Arc, 52, 1973, pp. 19–27.

masses profondes to speak. In this way, the intervention by the people puts events and institutions into a proper perspective.[9] If the people of Paris rejected the monarchy which had existed for so many centuries, it was because it had been disqualified in their eyes and because henceforth the nation would plan its own destiny. Furthermore, Michelet's *'peuple'* was not just the object of an historic proof. It was also a familiar person, seen on Sundays at the *barrières*, heard in the testimony of a shrewd grandmother who remembered both the bad and the good times, consulted in the workshop, on the building site, at the tavern. Michelet, historian of the living moment, showed how one must deal with the writings of observers like Villermé, the 'estimable M. Buret', author of *La Misère*, Hippolyte Passy, Victor Gasparin, and Léon Fauchet, whose notes recalled memories, and the simple, daily perceptions, the 'I felt all that when . . .'. For an historian of the last quarter of the twentieth century, this is the whole problem. Can one project back the palpable unanimity which created the coherence of the Romantic 'people' to the the world of labour associated with Enlightenment Paris? Yes, to some extent, if one tries to tackle the observations of internal and external factors, if one admits that changes in the lower classes were much slower than higher up the social scale, if one allows the *petites gens* the right to be different which the forces of law and order always refuse them. If the search for a definition of the people is to be completely heuristic, it must not become trapped in preliminaries. On the contrary, we must consider three possible paths to reach our goal: first, to see how the moralists — a convenient category in which to include all those who watched how the people lived, meditating upon ways of improving their lives, writers, publicists, men of means — have handed down a certain truth about popular milieux; next, to compare this first image in which the presentation of the labouring classes is indissolubly linked with a concept of urban life, with others which we have acquired *en bloc* through recognised typologies of the lower classes, but set this time in the global hierarchy of Parisian society; in short, can one evaluate the people? And finally, to show that it is possible in certain spheres, like material culture, or culture full stop, to go further by using both the witnesses and the silent archives, especially those the notaries have left us.

The observers of the people can be grouped in three main strata: littérateurs, moral economists and doctors. Of course, it is impossible to conduct an exhaustive enquiry into the first, a vast and somewhat nebulous group in which one can conveniently include major texts and second-rank works; indirectly one may see what literary historians say

9. Paul Viallaneix, Preface to J. Michelet, *Le Peuple*, Paris, 1974, pp. 12–14.

of the 'images of the people', and more directly, it is permissible to look at one particular model, having brought the lower classes on to the stage — the 'fishwife' type, for example. The second stratum is well known, more accessible in a way, and exceptionally well illustrated on the eve of 1789 by two Parisian pedestrians: Sébastien Mercier and Nicolas Rétif. Finally, the third, with its medical topographies and scientific enquiries, reveals the dual rise of a 'medicalised' way of thought and a feeling common to the learned elites defining a truly clinical urban ideal. The whole, testimonies and reflexions, placed the Parisian popular classes at the centre of a general meditation upon growth, in which the principal figures were the city and the urbanised individual.

It is obvious that the people occupied a growing place in the works of a great number of authors.[10] Reason and paternalism, fear and class interest, sensibility and generosity, inspired this interest, and the mirror which the writers hold out to us reveals a way of seeing — if not a definition — as well as the aesthetic play of a social presence. Two main frontiers are outlined. The first places the people in the general hierarchy of society, the second proclaims the unanimous acceptance of a society divided in every sense, for manners and behaviour are as important in literature as the much-vaunted popular culture, if not more so. On the first count, eighteenth-century writers always distinguished the popular classes from what they were not. The chief criterion of the majority of authors was work, participation in a productive effort without controlling the means of production. In a sense the century of the Enlightenment spontaneously thought marxist. Abbé Coyer, the chevalier de Jancourt, the marquis d'Argenson and some others, Rousseau himself,[11] were never free from this tendency. The thinking of Condorcet and some patriots during the Revolution would tend to exalt this role; the times enabled them to make of the Saviour himself the first of the *sans-culottes*, and a number of priests followed the example of the preacher François-Léon Réguis in thinking that, as the son of the carpenter Joseph, Christ did not choose the most ignominious condition, but on the contrary the one in which true virtue and humility resided, among artisans and humble men.[12] The opposition of capital and work tended to replace the traditional division of orders. For writers, labour was the badge of the popular classes, but also a means of escape and mobility. In bourgeois, populist dramas, which in 'their emotional and exclamatory style' (G. Lanson)

---

10. *Images du peuple au XVIIIᵉ siècle*, Paris, 1973.
11. M. Launay, *Jean-Jacques Rousseau écrivain politique*, Grenoble–Cannes, 1972.
12. Henri Coulet, in *Images du Peuple*, pp. 7–8.

offered Parisians the sensitive dream image of a good society where virtue was a fact of civilisation, the heroes always succeeded through work, a symbol of inferiority, but also of new dignity. Dramas and comedies respected the hard-working moralism of the petty-bourgeois and popular classes who made up their audience. On the other hand, the most reactionary thinkers (who would soon become counter-revolutionaries) kept everything in its place, even if they used identical criteria to justify the distribution of tasks in the bosom of a society organised by Providence, for their social imagination was still fed by old medieval divisions. For all, work meant a healthy society, for without the ruled there would be no rulers, and without lower classes, no bourgeois. Marivaux could write about the leisured and the popular classes of Paris: 'They all live out their little lives, but some work; others pride themselves on making other people work . . .'.

The unanimity of this first premise, however, presupposes something else: to recognise the autonomous utility of the popular classes meant eliminating those who did not belong to them. The frontier of a fifth estate became a conceptual necessity. Below the people who were excluded from any sort of power but who included faithful, reasonable subjects, hard-working and useful, slumbered the populace, the world of the unemployed and the beggar, the great mass of the idle poor, failures, prostitutes, the undergrowth of the Enlightenment, always prone to riot. In many writers one senses a fascination with the abyss in which the people, dehumanised by misery, lose their nature, where the Beggars' Opera signifies the mutation of labouring classes into dangerous classes. No doubt the thinkers of the time found a remedy for these contradictions: repression awaited some of them, and a simple, sober happiness the others as a reward for their good will — it would all be arranged. The events of 1789–92 would have the virtue of offering the world a model for the future: 'Men in society will never be free, happy and good, as long as they include more of the populace than of the popular classes'.[13] The Revolution made men aware of *le peuple*. The ironic, unquiet gaze of a Marivaux, the anxiety of a Prévost, the disgusted compassion of a *curé* Meslier or the classical republicanism of the *abbé* Coyer do not tell us much about the slow germination of the citizen but they clearly show how the popular classes, although uplifted by their work, remained inferior by their culture. At a time when cultural barriers were beginning to break down, with a prodigious lead in the towns, fiction lagged behind reality.

13. *Les Révolutions de Paris*, no. 81, cited by M. Sicault and M. Bouloiseau, in *Images du Peuple*, pp. 53–4.

The popular classes, as presented in literary sources, were a majority stamped by irrefutable signs of their intellectual and moral backwardness. They represented ignorance, more often the silence of someone who could not speak; for some, and not the most unimportant, they were far too credulous — because of the priests, according to Meslier — 'they are lulled with fables', wrote the abbé Coyer; overwhelmed with work, it was impossible for them to become educated. Their universe was made up of caprice, unreason, credulity and all kinds of prejudice. Passion, irritability, violence were the common lot of the poor; the lexical constellations seen in many contemporary authors produce a vocabulary of sound and fury: the lower classes were blind, vicious, turbulent, unrestrained, dangerous. If this was so, should they be educated to escape their darkness?

The question was put to the elites of the academies in 1780 in the competition conceived in Berlin.[14] The replies presented two concepts of the people. To say yes was to accept a new policy, a different society, more equal and just; to say no was to remain true to the status quo, in which, however, social equilibrium required the selective promotion of the best. The political function of the *sapere aude*, soon to be taken up by Kant, expressed a fear of anarchy, a belief in slow, peaceful reforms, mistrust. The real conditions of urban work, the misery of the majority, the slow pace of progress, the rude brutal manners of the fourth — the working people — and fifth — the feared populace — estates, a vague collection of uncontrolled movements and collective passions which could be easily inflamed; in all this *les honnêtes gens* inevitably saw a testimony to their own excellence. So first it was necessary to offer the popular classes a beverage of pious readings to quench their thirst and calm their feverish instincts. Where — in Paris, for example — the people were less ignorant, or had at least more chance of instruction through the theatres, bookshops or *colportage*, the culture of the labouring classes had to be made more moral. Writers revealed to their public the existence of a fearful barbarism which had to be civilised. In the face of troubles which had to be contained, repression and communion, education and assistance were the remedies constantly evoked by authors and political thinkers. Moreover, a real popular mythology was being forged, with its roots in Marivaux, Rousseau in particular, and a few others. In contrast to the popular urban forces which were chaotic and violent — the 'rough sea', in Marivaux's felicitous words — the true popular classes could only be found in the countryside. The century was coming to an end, and the good peasant, as opposed to the evil city-dweller, was the

14. Ed. W. Krauss, Berlin, 1966.

incarnation of a new exorcism. The customs which were for Rousseau 'the morality of the people' — idealised rustic fêtes, songs which were included in the great repertoires — all promised a new fraternity. In pre-Revolutionary days when romance was triumphant, when Marie-Antoinette tended her sheep and Louis XVI polished away at his locks, academic poetry itself sang of the people in fleeting verse. Arcady was man's future, and the new image of a population which would be happier and better, because it was closer to nature, was gradually making headway. But could the popular classes ever be themselves, elusive, divided and torn as they were between rustic virtues and urban immorality? The teachings of exoticism are always ambiguous, and the success of the *poissard* myths during the second half of the eighteenth century shows how true this was for Paris.[15]

The interest of a genre which drew its lessons from the burlesque traditions of the previous century, and from the daily fare of the Italian comedy and fairground shows, lies in the fact that it brings the *petit peuple* on stage. Prose and verse, comedies and novellas, *scenettes* and almanacs[16] first restored a language, the speech patterns and vocabulary attributed to market women, the fishmongers, pea-shellers, laundry-women and darning women, or to cab-drivers, porters, boat-men, day labourers, water-carriers, coal-men, pedlars, recruiting-sergeants and soldiers and others who tramped the streets. Vulgar expressions, oaths, crude words, strange idioms, mispronunciation and capricious grammar did perhaps capture the true speech of the popular classes but they also expressed the convention of a skilful aesthetic. The people were observed as an object of amusement and their linguistic clumsiness became a comic device. Everyone laughed at Cataud the laundress and Mams'elle Godiche with her 'meals on trestle-tables' which brought together the friends of the comte de Caylus; they shook with delight at the *Académie des Colporteurs* or the meetings of the *Joyeux Sociétaires de Montmartre*. Voisenon, Vadé, Duclos, de Cury, Mademoiselle Quinault, the comtesse de Verrue, the comte de Tressan, an entire social world, rejoiced at the jests of *le bon peuple* who were never wretched, nor dangerous. Irony conferred a sufficient and necessary value upon its favourite registers: anger — the scolding dear to Mme Engueule, mother of Mme Angot — invective against the bourgeois, trivial gaiety and a rather foolish sentimentality. Vulgar Paris was a spectacle depending more on mocking irony and picturesque detail than on realism. Nevertheless, in seeking their

15. A.-P. Moore, *The 'genre poissard' and the French Stage of the Eighteenth Century*, New York, 1935.
16. J.-J. Vadé, *Oeuvres complètes*, London, 1785, 6 vols.

effects they could — like Vade — be faithful to the original.

This first distancing effect was increased by focusing, through the strangeness of customs and manners, on an involuntary but invaluable ethnology. The vulgar episodes placed their heroes in comical situations: amorous exchanges (see the *Lettres de la Grenouillère*), meetings displaying the sociability of the lower orders. These strange animals were fond of the tavern, the *barrières*, the open air of the streets, shop-fronts, river-banks and pleasure-gardens on the outskirts, settings in which the authors proved, not so much their pursuit of realism — they were very careful not to show the people at work — as their interest in the exotic moment. Before our eyes the popular classes still play the same noisy, confused comedy which fascinated the great seigneurs. They are restless, clamorous, facetious, immoral, given to beer and tobacco, often carried away, but not wicked at heart. Just good savages! The wits, the aristocrats in their little theatres, the drawing-room dilettantes, mistresses in their boudoirs, knew what they were doing when they laughed at 'those people', so astonishing and conforming so completely to the role appointed for them by Providence.

There remains one last dimension which is less well-known though easily recognisable, and which makes it impossible to view this literature of low life as a realistic witness to popular manners; the genre took the people as a political target in order to teach a lesson in conformism. All the authors of the genre, except Caylus, were close to the labouring classes; Fleury, known as l'Ecluse, was an actor and charlatan, Cailleau a somewhat pornographic bookseller, Taconner a carpenter turned actor, Vadé the son of a shopkeeper, darling of the taverns and secretary to the duc d'Agenais, Dorvigny an illegitimate actor. They were intermediaries taming savagery for the men of property, propagandists, servants of an order they rarely criticised. Many of their works close with a proclamation of eternal fidelity and a eulogy of good kings. The glorification of the simple man is accompanied by a message of peace and harmony. 'Let's drink, since our good King wishes it!' So it is easy to understand how, echoing the verve of vulgar lampoons and *mazarinades* which had been aimed at a public which liked to challenge authority, brochures and manifestos of the revolutionary period repeated the same procedures, spoke the same language to discuss events through the mouths of the same characters. From Cailleau's *Cris du coeur sur l'édit de 1774* to the *Lettres bougrement patriotiques du Père Duchesne* the political awareness of the people took shape, but it was expressed in old techniques diverted from their original purpose.

Sébastien Mercier, son of a Parisian gunsmith, and Nicolas Rétif, son of a Burgundian ploughman settled in Paris, in their abundant works give us a second opportunity of enquiring into the historic identity cards of the popular classes of Paris. To take their writings at face value would be to accept too hastily that their works were intended as evidence rather than as literature. In Mercier's case it is quite clear that the *Tableaux de Paris* was written after he had made a name for himself in the world of letters as well as gaining a solid reputation in the theatre. Writing impressions of Paris was a critical act, the affirmation of a reforming impulse, a call for independence from self and from others, but also a choice, a commentary in the margin of his readings of ancients and moderns, an effort to capture through words a truth about society. The title does not deceive us: Paris and its people are represented, but on a stage.[17] With Rétif there can be no doubt: each of his works is presented as a restructured whole which places a considerable distance between real experience and the account he gives of it. Neither *Monsieur Nicolas* nor *Les Nuits de Paris* is the autobiographical witness that the author maintained he wished to give.[18] The literary and the phantasmagoric, social criticism and self-taught erudition are mingled to make, as in Mercier, a homogeneous system out of incoherent reality; these two Parisians, indefatigable walkers and original observers, shared a common passion which made them irreplaceable witnesses of the Parisian popular classes, but their moral assumptions, their mixture of fiction and reality, the effort of transposition involved in giving an account of the lives of the deprived, all encourage doubts about the relationship between moral observation and history. Whatever people may say,[19] their works could not coincide with the labouring classes' view of themselves; as witnesses of the people, they spoke in place of them.

It is true there is a 'realism' in writing about the lower classes. Mercier and Rétif achieve a truth different from the *poissard* writers; divested of part of the populist livery, their writings are animated by procedures which raise the question of social tensions, and allow us to recreate a retrospective sociology of acts and styles of sociability. But it must be remembered that the inclusion of a superficial realism was a trick of the time to avoid accusations of the imaginary, and that the

---

17. L. Beclard, *Sébastien Mercier, sa vie, son oeuvre, son temps*, Paris, 1903 (extremely important but rather short); together with J. Kaplow's reflections in *Le Tableau de Paris*, Introduction and selected texts, Paris 1979; and G. Bollème, *Dictionnaire d'un polygraphe*, Paris, 1978.
18. P. Testud, *Rétif de la Bretonne ou la création littéraire*, Geneva–Paris, 1977.
19. E. Le Roy Ladurie, 'Ethnologie rurale au XVIIIe siècle, Rétif de la Bretonne', in *Ethnologie Française*, 1972, pp. 215–52; G. Benrekassa, 'Le typique et le fabuleux: Histoire et Roman dans la Vie de mon *père*', in *Revue de Sciences Humaines*, 1978, pp. 31–56.

image offered to the reader is more exotic than familiar. Two or three factors bias their observation and our reading: their moralising aim which justifies the contrasts of light and shade, a taste for the interesting and picturesque, a sense of the piquant, and especially an attitude which mingles observation and pedagogy. Manners were intended to be of general human interest. 'Of all our men of letters, I am perhaps the only one who knows the popular classes; by mingling with them, I wish to paint them, I wish to be the sentinel of good order. I have mingled with the lowest orders in order to observe all abuses', wrote Rétif in *Les Nuits*, a proposition which Mercier would not disavow.

In general, it is always a question of human nature and not of the concrete reality of life; the goal is the conversion of the popular classes. The undeniable 'naturalism' of the moral observers combines perfectly with an edifying and therefore simplifying bias. Reality became a decoration, a background for adventures, a springboard for the imagination, the basis of an education intended to transform lower-class customs which were to some extent strange and incomprehensible. This plunge into the *bas quartiers* is like travelling through the countryside or abroad or pursuing utopian adventures, it enables the writer to convince and edify by discovering a sense of alienation. This is why moral observers saw in the new ways of the popular classes proof of an imminent catastrophe — 'rien ne va plus', the poor are murmuring against the rich — and confirmation of the dangers of the corrupting urban show. The Revolution, engendering social fear, will provide the ultimate proof of an apprehension which was not limited to the 1780s. Knowledge of the people, and even some modified sympathy for them, could easily be reconciled with terror of the populace, and inevitably lead to a search for remedies. In this, Rétif and Mercier share the same destiny just as they shared a passion for Paris and a craze for writing. They stand together in the same posthumous history which commits their prolific writings to the dubious fate of picturesque snippets for anthologies. They are also united in a fundamental ambiguity in face of the 'Ville des hommes', for they steeped themselves constantly in the life of the city in search of a truth which cared little for probabilities, one in which the act of writing often blurred the frontiers of the real and the imaginary. The historian of the Parisian popular classes will find in their work not so much a confirmation of what he already knows as the pinpointing of ordinary acts which are more unexpected, revealing the relationship of men to their environment, 'therefore of immediate social practices which give rise to representations and attitudes at the same time as they are informed by them'.[20]

20. R. Chartier, in *La Nouvelle histoire*, pp. 448–52.

The contribution made by doctors should be subjected to a similar critique. The discourse upon the capital and its population developed by Hallé, Audin, Menuret de Chambaud, Lachaise and others was embodied in the growing number of rural and urban medical typographies.[21] It is therefore valuable as a particularly well-informed testimony, since it was based upon professional practices related to places and to real people. But at the same time, it grew out of a cultural code in which neo-Hippocratism often tipped over into anti-city ideology and reforming utilitarianism. The increasing number of questions posed gives us an idea of their normative obsessions and anxieties for, according to the medical world, the magistrates would learn the art of controlling the towns only from the doctors.[22] Paris and the Parisians were only one example among thousands in Enlightenment Europe of the way in which medical enquiry had tackled reality in accordance with an ancient schema, reviewed and corrected by the Société Royale de Médecine in 1776; ' . . . [you will enquire] about the temperament of the inhabitants, what they drink and eat, how they dress, their habits, manners, occupations, the structure of their houses, about the most ordinary illnesses . . . while paying more particular attention to the illnesses which affect certain workers . . . '.[23] A vast programme and a difficult questionnaire to complete! This is how Menuret de Chambaud responded in 1786: Introduction and general considerations, eleven pages; about the Sun and Fire, eight pages; of Air, nine pages; of Water, thirty pages; of Earth, fourteen pages; a physical history of the town, twenty-six pages; considerations on physical and moral man, thirty pages; effect of the seasons, about thirty; on smallpox, about forty; about inoculation, another thirty. The physical and human reality of the Parisian popular classes disappears behind the image of the urban organism glimpsed in the Hippocratic dissection, the working-class man gives way to an anonymous, 'medicalised' human being. Certainly, a cautious injection of economic and philosophical concern conferred an interesting sociological dimension on medical topographies, but it justified a conservatism which was only slightly qualified by a few suggestions for improvement and reform. Neither social inequalities, nor the tensions between social groups really stirred the Parisian medical reformers to action. 'How our sensibilities are moved in these painful circumstances [discovering the abjectly poor]; one sees the evil, but not the remedy, whilst the

21. V. Hanin, *La Ville dans le discours médical, 1760–1830*, Mémoire de maîtrise, Paris, 1978; J.-P. Goubert, *Médicins, climats, épidémies*, Paris, 1972; J.-P. Peter, 'Les Mots et les objets de la maladie', in *Revue Historique*, 1971, pp. 13–38.
22. J.-C. Perrot, *Genèse d'une ville moderne*, pp. 883–93.
23. *Histoire et mémoires de la Société Royale de Médicine*, 1896, Preface, p. xiv.

cause is permanent. Alas, one can only pity them . . . .'

However, medical topography, in all these comings and goings between the milieu and the subject of medicine, discovered that physical behaviour, habits and manners were linked. A new reality arose in which doctors shared the obsessions of writers and social observers — the depraved environment; medical ecology, escaping from the commonplaces of meteorological constitutions, shifted towards morality. It was essential to consider urban space in order to explain the appearance of disease — no longer the contagious epidemics, which Paris had been spared since the end of the seventeenth century,[24] having conquered the plague, 'these terrible scourges which devastate a whole country' (Audin Rouvière) — but veiled, permanent, tenacious phenomena, endemic disease, and illnesses arising from work and poverty. In the Paris of the medical topographies interest shifted towards the town as a pathological space producing illnesses which revealed physical and moral disorder. Thus, social divisions became important again; the people and their poverty became the target of enquiries, instructions and warnings. 'It is no doubt necessary to prevent the disorder and misfortune into which excessive poverty may drag the most numerous class in society. It is equally necessary to safeguard this immense and precious nursery of subjects destined to plough our fields, transport our produce, people our manufactories and workshops.'[25] So medical utility coincided with social utility. The people themselves could not be responsible for their own salvation, for they were a prey to ignorance and prejudices, 'too incredulous and too hardened to it all', according to medical and learned elites, the administration of bodies demanded the ordering of space and, in the end, in the interests of social morality, it led to the policing of souls. We need to emphasise here not so much the birth of the 'medical lobby', as the diversion of scientific rationality when confronted with social questions.

Littérateurs and publicists, moral observers and doctors shared a pathological view of the city of Paris. A whole current of thought once again began to criticise urban growth as the root of society's misfortunes, and thus identified the specific nature of the city-dweller defined and contrasted with the people of the countryside. 'Happy inhabitants of the Alps', cried Mercier, and how many bad verses of the time sang of the true happiness of the countryman! Using familiar and oft-quoted sources, let us look at a few examples.

24. B. Fortier, *La politique de l'espace parisien à la fin de l'Ancien Régime*, Paris, 1975.
25. *Essai sur l' établissement des hôpitaux dans les grandes villes*, Paris, 1787, p. 13.

The first debating point: man himself, private individual and social personage. According to many people, the city had a profoundly alienating effect, and its deculturising action affected especially the popular classes and the poor. 'How does it come about that Man is so easily perverted? Must he always, like the tree or the animal, inhabit the soil where he was born? I believe this is so', proclaimed Rétif. In the city, decline was almost inevitable, and the path to prison or hospital was marked out, for man had broken the pact that bound him to Nature. As Rousseau so clearly conveyed, to leave the country was to lose one's sensitivity to the seasons, to climate and to growing things, it was an 'uprooting' in the full sense of the word, revealed in a less warm and lively relationship with other beings, ending usually in solitude. One's surroundings weighed heavily upon one's personality; urbanised man was a creature of a lower order than man in Nature. So people must be encouraged to flee the cities 'instead of inciting them to crowd into towns, encourage them to spread out over the earth so that every corner could be enlivened'.[26] A similar attitude inspired doctors to seek the healthy man in the heart of the country, and to denounce urban pathogeny, with the result that man, isolated in the city, had to be safeguarded by a chain of assistance and medical care. Bodily and food hygiene, occupational illnesses, venereal disease became the target of anxious enquiries on the part of Parisian doctors, leading to the idea that individuals should be taken in charge by society. Enquiry procedures, demographic statistics, nosological counts caught the isolated and the irresponsible in their net. Medical care was inseparable from surveillance, and became one of the consequences of the urbanisation of human movement. Parisians would be counted, identified, better known, better controlled because a whole series of measures tended to make urban space more legible and clear. Piarron de Chamousset's plans to reorganise postal deliveries, the numbering of houses, the nocturnal drafting of the *Plan de Paris* by Verniquet, anxious to avoid incidents with the popular classes who saw the operation as a threat, police plans for a system of identity control with central files covering every individual, all this defines the dream of a city open to the human eye. Knowing people's movements, keeping a watch on delinquents, controlling disease were aspects of a policy aimed mainly at the popular classes.

At first glance, the *peuple de Paris* seem the complete opposite of our provincial city-dwellers; there, all is apathy, nonchalance, tranquillity, here bustling activity; people don't walk, they run, fly; they pay no attention to

26. J.-J. Rousseau, 2nd preface to *La nouvelle Héloïse*, in *Oeuvres Complètes*, vol. 2, p. 21.

each other, even when occasion requires it. They are all isolated parts that do
not make a whole. I think politics gains, but humanity surely loses in the
process . . .[27]

Rétif is indicating here how the control of the city depended on
maintaining a sort of personal alienation subordinated to the public
sphere.[28]

The second topic of discussions was the pathology of the city. The
popular classes were lost in its confusion, but its reorganisation did
little to rescue them. The fact is, every theme of decomposition and
evil was superimposed upon images of savage barbarism.

> If I were asked how one could stay in this filthy den of every vice and evil,
> where people are all crammed together in air poisoned by a thousand putrid
> vapours, amid cemeteries, hospitals, slaughter-houses, drains . . . in the
> continuous smoke of this incredible quantity of wood, in ceaseless exhala-
> tions of arsenic, sulphur, bitumen from workshops where men twist and
> shape copper and metals; if I were asked how men can live in this abyss
> where the heavy, fetid air is so thick that you can see and feel the atmosphere
> more than three leagues away in every direction, . . . in short, how man can
> crouch in these prisons when if he released the animals he has fashioned to
> his yoke, he would see them charge off, driven by sheer instinct. . . .[29]

In this magnificent text charged with all the metaphors of physical and
moral corruption, Sébastien Mercier translates perfectly the destiny of
the popular classes denatured in the city-tomb. Omnipresent morbid-
ity radiated from localised centres — prisons, such as the Châtelet,
Fort-l'Evêque, Bicêtre; hospitals like the Hôtel-Dieu, the Salpêtrière;
the popular *quartiers* where unhealthy workshops and trades were
concentrated in narrow, airless streets; cemeteries, the charnel-house
of Les Innocents, the cloister of Saint-Gervais.[30] Paris was a cesspit and
a hell, a domain of ever-present death, in the corpses exposed in the
morgue, in the undertakers' carts of the Hôtel-Dieu, in the surgeons'
dissecting rooms, in the mores of the professionals of death — execu-
tioners, grave-diggers, medical students.[31] It was a theatre of shadows
threatened by infection, where the ground streamed with muddy,
polluted waters, blood and excrement, and the black tide of sewage.
Water and air were infected; people were obsessed with the fear of

27. Rétif de la Bretonne, *Les Nuits*, p. 843.
28. J. Habermas, *L'Espace public*, French transl., Paris, 1978, pp. 30–50; J.-C. Perrot,
Genèse d'une ville moderne, vol. 2, pp. 899–919.
29. L.-S. Mercier, *Le Tableau de Paris*, vol. 1, pp. 6–7.
30. B. Fortier, 'L'architecture des villes', pp. 27ff.
31. J.-L. Vissière, 'Pollution et nuisances urbaines', relating to S. Mercier, *Le Tableau
de Paris*, in *La Ville au XVIIIe siècle*, Aix, 1975, pp. 107–12.

poison. The Paris of the popular classes was a necrophilic, coprophagous city inspiring terror and disgust. Rétif feeds the same images which he develops in the register of sexual pulsations. *Monsieur Nicolas* and *Les Nuits* present a city of evil where chaos and death reign, a vast sea of decay. Mud, filth and darkness were also symbols of vice,[32] regiments of prostitutes threatened the virtue and the very future of the race. Does the conjunction, attested on all sides, of these two themes — the alienation of the individual by the city and the pathology of urban space — lead inevitably to total despair for the fate of the popular classes in Paris? It is difficult to give an answer.

With Jeffrey Kaplow,[33] one may well suspect that all these observations had an element of truth; medical enquiries and demographic statistics aimed at measuring the effects of urbanisation offer a cruel proof. The ordinary life of the Parisian popular classes was spent in a habitat which was experiencing a crisis as a result of its expansion, attracting people like a magnet, and therefore invasions of microbes and viruses. Around 1770 average life expectancy was limited to twenty-nine years for 1,000 new births; for the two-thirds who survived to the end of their first year it was less than forty years. Infant mortality was appalling, general mortality probably in the order of 35 to 45 per cent, dirt and pollution being an important contributory factor. There was no effective remedy for endemic diseases like smallpox, typhoid and various fevers, and medical topographies reveal the existence of infections that were particularly deadly among the popular classes — scurvy, consumption, hydropsy and pleurisy, to which must be added injuries and illnesses resulting from work which was often dangerous.[34] The popular classes certainly did not help by remaining faithful to their traditional treatments, in spite of the doctors' onslaught against 'prejudices'. In these conditions, not only was natural growth of the population impossible, but the sanitary atmosphere of *Paris populaire* must have been deplorable.

However, apart from the fact that we have no better system for measuring the effects of misery than that of pleasure and pain, we must reject the catastrophe theory of contemporaries for two reasons. The first is that in itself, their method of describing the people and the city imposed a cult of misery. It was a method based upon the tactics of the defence lawyers and the difference which the quasi-definitive pathological condition of the popular classes suggested. The poor, the dangerous, the sick and the vicious were irrecuperable, forever uncul-

32. H. Krief, *Paris capitale du mal selon Rétif de la Bretonne*, in ibid., pp. 113–24.
33. J. Kaplow, *Les Noms des Rois*, pp. 99–119.
34. A. Farge, 'Les artisans malades de leur travail', in *Annales*, ESC, 1977, pp. 993–1006.

tured, drowned in their misery, uncontrollable whatever was done. A sense of menace prevailed due to the lack of a really effective urban policy. 'The "partie basse" of the population is in a state of ferment while the authorities only get agitated', thought Rétif, 'I am astonished that avengers do not emerge from its ranks to turn our world upside down. Do you remember the Peasants' War . . .?'[35] In the second place, it must be realised that to think of the popular classes in terms of the opposition of healthy and unhealthy, is also to be trapped in a particular intellectual system, to accept a message coded by all the assumptions about social practices common to supporters of the Enlightenment. Rather than succumbing to this approach, one should view it as part of the modernity of the century. But to follow contemporary observers without advance warning would be to confuse sociological description for what was a social exercise of science plus fiction, and risk missing the target. In fact, the texts tell us just as much about the conscience of the ruling elite, concerned about the popular classes because they knew that its safety and wealth depended upon their fate, as about the real condition of the labouring classes. The condition of the latter was to a large extent dehumanised, but that did not exclude a rich mental response, and a specific cultural capacity which is difficult to reconstitute because the popular classes were in a state of flux as well as distorted through the prism of witnesses. When writing about the poor, it is no longer good enough to 'épater le bourgeois' by picturesque terror, to rouse the militant steeped in historical certainty or to move the sensitive man persuaded of the permanence of misery and repression. One must allow a different language to be heard in a different way. We must try to see the ambivalence, along with the poverty and deculturation, the small signs of intelligence, cultural wealth, social progress, everything which shows that an historic object cannot at any time be reduced to a single, simple image.

The difficulty begins as soon as one seeks to give a precise definition and evaluation of the popular classes. How can we shape the definitive contours of our debate when too many items are missing from the dossier — almost nothing about work, nothing about the Parisian economy, not much about education and religious attitudes, if you except Pierre Chaunu's *Mourir à Paris* — and the fact that all our knowledge of the people comes from police archives, or relates to the Revolutionary period which is better documented.[36] Can one confi-

---

35. Rétif de la Bretonne, *Les Nuits*, p. 2908.
36. A. Mathiez, 'Notes sur l'importance du prolétariat en France à la veille de la Révolution', in *Annales historiques de la Révolution française*, 1930, pp. 497–524; J. Kaplow, *Les Noms de Rois*, pp. 59ff.; G. Rudé, *Paris and London in the Eighteenth Century*, New York, 1952, 1970.

dently use facts clearly established for the social history of Paris in 1789 for a study of the Regency period? It is very unlikely. While waiting for new avenues of research to be explored one can only proffer a few remarks.[37] Contemporaries help us by their reflections on social classification in the city. Among the accepted divisions, one appears completely useless from the start: the popular classes of Paris did not represent one order, they ranked as part of the third estate where poverty and wealth and inequality of fortune and opportunity were mingled. The labouring classes constituted a veritable cascade of conditions about which the least one can say is that it was not homogeneous, since it was an imponderable mixture of judgements about social value and dignity and economic realities. In the opinion of its most pugnacious defender, Roland Mousnier, the society of orders crumbles at this point into a multiplicity of strata in which a hierarchy operated according to men's chances of appropriating capital by controlling the work of others and by getting a foothold in the marketing of goods. Economics became the dominant factor in the changes which characterised the eighteenth century, manifested in the towns by strikes and the discontent of the workers.[38]

Tax returns do not offer us much more since, apart from the fact that most of the documents have disappeared in Paris, there are few surprises in the scrappy information revealed in the surviving capitation records or in the poor rate. By their occupations, condition and place in society, the popular classes were at the bottom of the twenty-two ranks liable to capitation tax. Those rated at 13 *sous* in the registers of the parish commissioners included most of the wage-earners whose occupation was either not defined or who were temporarily out of work, and artisans who were hardly ever qualified as masters or merchants, and rarely as *compagnons*; in other words the mass of artisans and shop assistants.[39] Almost 20,000 contributors in 1743 came into this 13 *sous* category (53 per cent of the total rated) which involved only a minority of wage-earners; those working at home, those undertaking temporary jobs, and the mass of the floating population living on irregular earnings or out of work, all tended to escape the tax collector. The better-off were in the category immediately above, rated at 1 *livre* 6 *sous*, representing almost 12,000 people,

37. They are largely inspired by two basic studies, F. Furet, 'Pour une définition des classes inférieures à l'époque moderne', in *Annales*, ESC, 1963, pp. 459–74; and J.-C. Perrot, 'Rapports sociaux et villes au XVIIIᵉ siécle', in D. Roche (ed.), *Ordres et classes*, Paris, 1973, pp. 141–66.

38. R. Mousnier, *Les Institutions de la France sous la monarchie absolue*, vol. 1, Paris, 1974, pp. 201–09.

39. F. Foret, 'Structures sociales parisiennes au milieu du XVIIIᵉ siècle, l'apport d'une série fiscale', in *Annales*, ESC, pp. 939–58.

most of whom were *maîtres de corporations* and shopkeepers. The frontier of the popular classes passed between these groups which included 86 per cent of the tax-payers and which were dominated by the artisan, by the world of work and selling. The 2 *livres* 12 *sous* threshold was virtually impassable for people of slender means. Servants, who constituted an important group amongst the urban wage-earners, do not appear in these registers. They are to be found among those liable for capitation tax, where they number over 40,000.[40] In all, if we compare capitations and the *taxe des pauvres* we find that considerably more than three-quarters of the population made up the labouring classes liable to tax, and this ignores the mass of the floating population. An analysis of marriage contracts for 1749, which underestimates the lower levels but covers more than 60 per cent of marriages in Paris, confirms this conclusion. Here the popular classes appeared in the 85 per cent of marriage portions below 15,000 *livres*, and made up the bulk of those with portions below 2,000 *livres*, that is 50 per cent of all newly-weds. Servants, journeymen, home-workers, manual workers, day-labourers, small street tradesmen and men in trades of indeterminate status constituted this lower stratum of Parisian society.[41]

The need for social understanding led observers to propose their own hierarchy. Pidansat de Mairobert is not much help; in his classification, which is concerned chiefly with the ruling classes, he makes a place for the third estate but without including the popular classes who remain curiously absent.[42] The medical topographies of Paris only preserve a distinction between the well-to-do and the poor, among whom workers and the destitute are jumbled together.[43] Sketchy, brutal nuances emphasise some major contrasts: unemployed and employed, comfortably off and indigent, honest poverty and misery, *peuple et populace*; criteria of trade, unemployment, income and physiological and mental characteristics are variously combined. This thinking, which is preoccupied with exclusion and incapable of taking an overview of society, is essentially vague and hesitant. It endeavours to amputate from the body of the people all the unhealthy, poor, mendicant, mad and diseased members. This can clearly be seen in all the plans prepared for the rebuilding of the Hôtel-Dieu. On the other hand, Sébastien Mercier and Rétif both prove more useful, because of

40. Expilly, *Dictionnaire historique, géographique et politique des Gaules et de la France*, Paris, 1762–70, 6 vols., vol. 5, pp. 400–03.
41. A. Daumard and F. Foret, *Structures sociales à Paris au XVIIIe siècle*, Paris, 1967.
42. M. Pidansat de Mairobert, *L'Espion Anglais*, Paris, 1777–8, 4 vols., vol. 1, pp. 137–83, 230–74.
43. V. Hanin, *La Ville*, pp. 162–6.

their perception. The former divides the population of Paris into nine classes, and the popular classes occupy the three last ranks — manual workers, lackeys, the *bas peuple* — and no doubt part of the fourth — the artisans — in this hierarchy based on profession, social utility and wealth rather than on the dignity of labour. This is a characteristic feature of the thinking of economists of the time, demographers like Messance or administrators like Turgot.[44] The labouring classes were viewed according to two great principles: utilitarianism, which favoured producers — the people at work — and exclusion which exiled from the city the useless — the populace, beggars, idle or criminal poor. But Mercier concludes pessimistically: 'In London they speak of the majesty of the English people: in Paris we don't know what to call *le peuple*'.[45] This leads him to superimpose on to his first classifications a third model in which men are no longer classified by their occupation or the financial reality lurking behind every level, but by their social and cultural behaviour.[46] The people occupy the three lowest ranks as in the first classification: petty-bourgeois, *le peuple*, *la populace*. A series of pictures set within the general portrait characterise these social types by the way they lived, their mental attitudes, ways of speaking, their *sociabilité*, dressing and eating. The impressionism of his approach and the breadth of the observation do not adversely affect the effectiveness of the divisions and relations presented. Overall, what counts is to capture the importance of mobility, social intermingling, the extent of the welcome and shelter offered by the city, the direction of changes during the century showing the increasing importance of money, the dissolution of old vertical solidarities, the growing confrontation of haves and have-nots. In the Paris of Mercier, in the *Tableau de Paris*, social categories, sociable or chance groupings existed side by side, close yet strangers; 'they have no material connection', 'hatred becomes venomous, the state is divided into two classes'. The city manufactured inequality on a massive scale, and equality only furtively. Many lived there poorer but freer, and found a new social equilibrium 'in the confusion of ranks'[47] which clearly heralds the citizen of the Age of Revolutions.[48]

Using different devices, Rétif de la Bretonne offers the same text leading to a similar conclusion. In his writing, simple oppositions like *peuple/populace*, haves/have-nots, rich/poor, operate freely, all the

---

44. J.-C. Perrot, 'Rapports sociaux', pp. 146–8.
45. L.-S. Mercier, *Le Tableau de Paris*, vol. 11, pp. 42–3.
46. Ibid., vol. 2, p. 210; vol. 3, pp. 95–6; vol. 5, p. 266; vol. 9, p. 9, vol. 12, pp. 61–5, 174–5.
47. Ibid., vol. 1, pp. 23–5, 38–9.
48. J.-C. Perrot, 'Rapports sociaux', p. 149.

more perhaps because his personal progress moved him away from one
side and towards the other. After 1765–70, the author and man of
letters frequented the beau monde and his observations of popular
customs were intended for them.[49] The structure and writing of *Les
Nuits* are based on this narrative and instructive intention. Indeed,
they do not contain an elaborate social taxonomy but an exploration,
very similar to Mercier's, which emphasises not so much the rigidity of
categories as the mobility of groups, the complexity of social relationships and nuances in the changes of customs and modes of behaviour.
'One thing that still immediately strikes you in Paris is the gradation
linking every rank; you see a man rise from the slime where he lies
below the animals to a state of divinity . . .'.[50]

> After the affluent artisan come the manual labourers, casual workers,
> pick-locks, and artisans rèduced to poverty: the domestic life of these people
> is no more consistent than a stormy sea; at one moment, feeling the sharp
> tooth of want, they curse and kick each other; at another, when money
> revives their flagging spirits, they feast and drink in their own way.[51]

The text reveals among other things the importance of conjugal relations, and the role of women which will be developed in *Les Contemporaines* and, more interestingly for our purpose, in *Les Parisiennes*.[52]
The engravings show first a hierarchy of clothing: ordinary costume of
provincial girls, bourgeois women in provincial towns, young ladies of
quality at Court, shopkeepers' daughters, and daughters of the populace. The oppositions Paris/provinces, court, town and populace express a simple social character study referring to nuances of the natural
or the luxurious. It is completed, somewhat vaguely, in the ensuing
series of prints which trace the outlines of the moral physiognomy of
the women of Paris. The interest lies in the reinforcement of the images
by the text in which the ethical phenomenology is largely developed in
accordance with a scale beginning with distance from the countryside
and the proximity of urban values, a range of concrete social situations,
apprenticeship at the workshop, education at the convent, family
relations in marriage, celibacy, parent–child relationships, ending with
a scale of emotions, laughter, tears, grief or joy. *Les Parisiennes* is
largely dominated by society girls, 'well-born', 'affluent', 'fortunate'
— precise traits indicating what those who are absent from the text
lack.

    49. T. Testud, *Rétif de la Bretonne*, pp. 57–8.
    50. Rétif de la Bretonne, *Le Paysan perverti*, Paris 1770, ed. Paris, 1978, pp. 338–9.
    51. Idem., *Le Ménage Parisien*, Paris, 1773, ed. Paris, 1978, pp. 169–70.
    52. Idem., *Les Parisiennes ou XL caractères généraux pris dans les moeurs actuelles* . . .,
Paris, 1787, 4 vols.

An introductory table gives a more explicit social cartography.[53] Twelve classes are required to convey all the gradations in the characters of *Les Parisiennes*, who are light and frivolous and, regardless of condition, incline to attach too much importance to the products of art and artifice. The text shows the same fairness as Mercier: the young women are coquettes not from heartlessness but because the market of the sexes imposes pitiless competition; they are less slanderous than in the provinces and thrifty because life in Paris is dear. At the top are (1) girls of the first quality, (2) girls of quality and (3) daughters of the nobility. Then come (4) daughters of the *noblesse de robe*, of (5) the financial world, (6) the bourgeoisie with whom we 'start another way of life because of another way of thinking', (7) the daughters of prosperous shopkeepers, (8) daughters of ordinary shopkeepers ('they people the shops but do not always remain there') and (9) the daughters of artists, a class peculiar to the capital, who may be spoilt and somewhat libertine. Lower down the scale come (10) the daughters of artisans — Mercier's *grisettes* — (11) working girls from shops and workshops, who are 'far from the manners of honest country-girls' and who 'have nothing about them, their exterior is repulsive and their manners and speech more so'. Finally (12) girls of the populace, greedy, corrupt, perverted, ignorant of any of the opportunities the city offers. Rétif's hierarchy repeats Mercier's principles of classification — occupation, utility and social behaviour — but it complements them with a moral scale. The female popular classes occupy the last five places at this banquet of nature and culture at which one can logically have only the vices of one's class.[54] For Rétif the change in manners can be measured by the growing irreverence and insubordination of the lower classes, and by the growing confusion of rank in society due to an increasing uniformity of manners.

Looking at the classification proposed by all the observers, two frontiers are constantly drawn — at the point where the social elite comes into contact with the artisan and shopkeeper class and, at the lower level, where it borders on the world of the social misfit. History might accept this as a starting-point, so long as we try to see what more may lie beyond it. J. Peuchet cites a police report of 1709 which proves that the same lines are drawn almost throughout the century.[55] Once again in presenting the familiar list of Parisian social groups, the author

---

53. Idem., *Les Parisiennes*, pp. 26–44.
54. He shares the social ideal of the Freemasons' Lodges and of the Academies, cf. D. Roche, *Le Siècle des lumières en province*, Paris, 1978, 2 vols., vol. 1, pp. 269–75, 341–2.
55. J. Peuchet, *Mémoires tirés des archives de la police*, Paris, 1838, 3 vols., vol. 1, pp. 204–10.

makes a break after the sixth — shopkeepers and master-craftsmen.

> Finally, there are the workers in the ports and various industries, journey-
> men, joiners, carpenters, plasterers, masons, locksmiths, leather-workers,
> binders, parchment-makers, tailors, tinsmiths; in short, all states and profes-
> sions, heavy labourers and manual workers, to whom one must add the
> Auvergnats and Savoyards, water-carriers, coalmen, butchers. There are, in
> addition, lackeys, equerries; pages, domestic servants, messenger-boys,
> confidential servants, grooms, ushers, kennel-boys, stablemen and boys,
> kitchen-boys. Surveillance of this last group must be particularly keen for,
> debauched by the example of their masters, the wretches often end up on the
> gallows, the wheel or the stake; one is relieved if it is only the galleys.

Then comes the listing of illicit groups, the *canaille*, from confidence
tricksters to thieves, from rogues to prostitutes. So the social frontiers
are not permeable, but there are many defectors from one milieu to
another, and moreover they do not function as strictly for all social
hierarchies. No doubt they are more permeable as far as mentality and
manners are concerned than for economic or status reasons: between
all categories there are imperceptible nuances. Thus the popular classes
we are studying exclude guild-masters, who are distinguished by
owning capital, by exercising power over their wage-earners and by
the hope of social mobility.[56] There is no rigorous class barrier, but
mobile fringes beyond the wage-earners strictly define who benefits
from a community of work and the daily routine and who will emerge
more clearly in the political solidarity of the Revolution. In all probability we are referring to between 300,000 and 400,000 people in the
middle of the century,[57] and 350,000 to 450,000 at the beginning of the
Revolution — allowing for fluctuations.[58]

At the lower end of this group the world of beggars and the *canaille*
will escape our net, for they are the concern of other researchers. One
should not underestimate their numbers or their links with the rest of
the labouring classes. Crowded into the *hôpital-général* at a rate of
1,000 to 2,000 a year they saw their situation worsen each year as the
harvest approached and social crises developed.[59]

The fact is that more than a tenth of the whole population was close
to penury at the beginning of the reign of Louis XV; the *comité de
mendicité* estimated in 1790 that the number of unemployed, indigents

---

56. Here we are indebted to J. Kaplow, *Les Noms des Rois*, pp. 61ff.
57. L. Cahen, 'La population de Paris au milieu du XVIIIe siécle', *La Revue de Paris*,
1919, September–October, pp. 146–70.
58. G. Rudé, *Paris and London*, pp. 25–7 and J. Kaplow, *Les Noms des Rois*, pp. 66–7.
59. P. Goubert, 'Le Monde des errants, mendiants, vagabonds à Paris et autour de
Paris au XVIIIe siècle', in *Clio parmi les hommes*, Paris, 1976, pp. 265–78.

and those receiving aid was more than 100,000.[60] In short, before the
Revolution, almost a seventh of the population was living from day to
day: a minority of outright idlers and rogues — 20 to 25 per cent — a
minority handicapped by age, illness, accident or family failure, and a
majority intermittently unemployed, who came from agriculture, the
non-specialist trades, and even the guilds. The banal theme of the
confrontation of luxury and misery is eloquently illustrated by these
figures. No doubt the capital was experiencing an unprecedented crisis
which explains the number of incidents, disturbances, and abortive
uprisings and finally the collective mobilisation of the labouring masses. But between these two periods, other changes occurred which
require more precise investigation. In the sphere of material culture of
spontaneous intellectual life, the Parisians who rose in 1789 were not
exactly the same as those who had submitted almost passively to the
crises at the end of the reign of Louis le Grand. Rather than describe
yet again the cavalcade of impoverished wretches, our aim is to
understand the ordinary life of the popular classes.

For this we need a different perspective and different sources. These
can be found piled up in the offices of the Parisian notaries where they
make up the most complete archive possible in the sphere of cultural
anthropology. With access to the notarial and judicial archives, the
historian might discover the standards and ways of living, daily habits,
and the cultural choices of the labouring classes. In the records of *post
mortem* inventories we can find the two complementary aspects of any
social analysis: the objects and material necessities which describe a
way of life, thus allowing us to identify behaviour patterns, and the
economic support which brought them together in a legacy. But in
order to evaluate from notarial sources a century-long evolutionary
process, it is important, in addition to documentary analysis, to define
clearly what were the choices, ambitions and limitations confronting *le
peuple*.

The use of inventories is open to three fundamental objections: that
one should not generalise on the basis of a specific act made at a certain
stage of one's life; that inventories reflect a particular situation; and
that the documents themselves are often deceptive and incomplete.
These three criticisms merit a reply. The taking of an inventory after
death corresponds to a period which is the reverse of that identified by
the marriage contract, the product of an exceptional moment; it is
stamped by old age and death. A calculation based on a sample of 400
documents shows that for three-quarters of them the notaries were
called in after ten years of married life; in other words, if one takes an

60. M. Reinhard, 'La Révolution', pp. 93-103, 236–7.

average age of 27 to 30 at marriage, the majority of documents were
drawn up after the age of 40 and before 50, which corresponds to the
maximum life expectancy for Parisians at that time. Consequently, it is
certain that the document will show the effects of age, either from the
standpoint of worldly success consolidated at the threshold of old age,
or from that of the difficulties encountered by those who had little but
their own strength and for whom illness and death were the cause of
increased expense — medical expenses, the cost of enforced unemployment, or the expense of having children taken into care. From this
point of view, the will emphasises contrasts and no doubt gives a false
idea of the scale of wealth, but our concern is not so much to
reconstruct a false hierarchy or to pursue meaningless realities as to
compare the *relative* stages of social reality and evaluate changes. It
does not matter if the source distorts, since we are seeking to trace an
evolution, not in relation to an elusive external reference, but in
relation to some term of the same kind, situated in the same temporal
series.[61]

The inventory is also the reflection of a particular situation. This
stems from the judicial nature of the notary's act itself, a way of
defending heirs, minors, and creditors confident of their rights. Thus
the class of document is not representative of a wide spectrum of
society as there are less than 10 per cent of inventories compared to the
number of deaths around 1730, 13 per cent in the middle of the century
and some 14 to 15 per cent on the eve of the Revolution; that is, about
3,000 documents a year. To circumvent this fault it is necessary to take
wider chronological bands, so that the samples on which the present
work is based cover 15- to 20-year periods (1695–1715 and 1775–90).
Moreover, this objection applies particularly to the *petites gens*, for an
inventory is the document of a rich or, at least, comfortably-off man.
So to find one inventory for a servant it is necessary to read twenty, for
one concerning a wage-earner some thirty to forty. All in all, to
constitute a sample — qualitatively still inadequate — of about 400
inventories, you have to look at nearly 7,000 documents. The milieu
studied risks being less homogeneous if you broaden the time-span but
this drawback may be ignored in view of the interest of an enquiry
which deals for the first time with a number of documents of such
importance.[62] Behind this danger one can detect very clearly the

61. On the problems of social history and a general analysis of sources, see D. Roche
(ed.), *L'Histoire sociale, sources et méthodes*, Paris, 1967; L. Bergeron (ed.), *Niveaux de
culture et groupes sociaux*, Paris, 1967; D. Roche (ed.), *Ordres et classes*, Paris, 1973;
B. Vogler (ed.), *Les Actes notariés, sources de l'histoire sociale XVIe–XIXe siècles*,
Strasbourg, 1979.
62. By way of comparison for similar social milieux, the reader is directed to the
figures in inventories after death used in the most recent urban and rural studies:

connection between the cost of the document and its socially selective character: around 1700, the notary charged on average 15–20 *livres*, around 1780 it was 30–40 livres — in both periods more than twenty days' work.[63] The inventory favours those who could pay, therefore those who had some possessions, and if we find few really negative inheritances, when debts are substracted from assets, this shows that they exclude a whole section of the population, those who owned nothing or almost nothing.

Then there are the gaps people always complain of in inventories drawn up after a death. They are of four kinds: judicial, economic — resulting from under-estimates — fraud, and those indicating un-doubted and significant omissions. The first gap may arise from the application of rules which, according to the Parisian custom, governed the handing on of private property which was often left out of the inventory. However, where lower-class inheritances are concerned this defect is really not very important. It chiefly concerned real estate which was rare and usually represented either by the revenue derived from it, which would pass into the community, or by fictitious assets, listed very clearly and often involving a few pieces of silver and personal jewellery. As for under-estimating, this was normal, since valuations were always carried out before the effects were sold by auction or divided among the legatees. So far as the labouring classes are concerned, this is not very important, since we are concerned mainly with a comparative study. What we must ensure is that we are comparing values affected by the same margin of under-estimation. It is true that fraud is often cited when inheritances are discussed, and one has a mental image of prowling, grasping heirs, or complaisant notaries. The reality was quite different; there was often the guarantee of the seals placed before the valuation; then there was the professional code of ethics for notaries. Generally speaking, fraud was neither conceivable nor financially rewarding — think of the notaries' charges — certainly not common, especially in judicial proceedings to which

J. Sentou, *Fortunes et groupes sociaux á Toulouse sous la Révolution*, Toulouse, 1969 (143); R. Lick, 'Les intérieurs domestiques dans la seconde moitié du XVIIIe siècle d' après les inventaires après décès à Coutance', in *Annales de Normandie*, 1970, pp. 293–402 (42); R. Mousnier, *La stratification sociale à Paris aux XVIIe et XVIIIe siècles*, Paris, 1976 (37); M. Garden, *Lyon et les Lyonnais*, Paris, 1970 (98); M. Baulant, 'Niveaux de vie paysans autour de Meaux en 1700 et 1750', in *Annales*, ESC, 1975, pp. 505–18 (70); H. Burstin, *Le Faubourg Saint-Marcel*, 1977 (59).

63. AN, Minutier central, Etude XVIII, 1. 885, 23 August 1783ff. An important document could cost 100 *livres* or more. For example: fee for an official valuer, 16 *livres*; draft, 3 *livres*; registration costs, 14 *livres*; insinuation, 7 *livres*; paper, 15 *livres*; seals, 1 *livre*; fee for the *substitut du procureur du Roi*, 16 *livres*; costs of valuation, 12 *livres*; costs relating to a will, 12 *livres*; costs for recovering a *rente*, 3 *livres*; total 99 *livres*.

the poorer classes were economically and culturally unaccustomed. In popular milieux the notaries were perhaps less inclined to trust relatives and witnesses — they exercised powers which demanded minute verification — than at higher social levels where the professional man was often a friend, sometimes a confidant. In other words, the trustworthiness of the notaries' descriptions may be reckoned in inverse proportion to the level of the fortune. Finally, it should not be forgotten that the claimants and the creditors kept a careful watch on each other which guaranteed at least a comparative objectivity, if not the absolute truth of the document.

The indisputable omissions concern three kinds of object. Firstly, food reserves which, unlike in rural areas, were rare in Paris, with the exception of wine, the presence of which would indicate a level of affluence. Secondly, clothes; the wardrobe of children under age was never described, and the wardrobe of the dead was rarely kept for more than a few weeks and was sometimes sold to cover the extra expenses incurred during illness; sometimes even the clothes of the survivors, if few or of little value, were not included in the inventory. Finally, a host of small inexpensive household objects seems to have gone unchecked. Combs, pocket-knives, brooms, knick-knacks and the many pamphlets did not interest the notaries or heirs or creditors, for they made little difference to the amount of the inheritance. They constitute a sub-stratum we can only guess at, which is regrettable in so far as these pieces of evidence which have no economic importance are an interesting indication of cultural behaviour.

Having said this, it is possible to state precisely the objectives to be pursued. A study of the culture of the popular classes in Paris assumes two procedures: one must first draw up sufficiently representative samples of the labouring classes (we will indicate later the spread and principles involved); one must reconcile economic and social analysis — starting with the economic — with analysis of cultural behaviour which defines ordinary life. First, one must compare inheritances to discover, as the century progresses, a hierarchy of categories and the general trends which transformed them. Starting with the content of legacies, one must try to discover coherent models or attitudes. Next, an exhaustive résumé of *everything* the inventory describes will enable us to approach, at least from outside, the world of things owned by *le peuple de Paris*. The logic of the valuers' descriptions will help us to reflect upon the social meaning of things belonging to a familiar world and the psychological behaviour which went with them. We glimpse the character of the popular classes only through the mediation of a notary who had these particular sociological and psychological insights and a text which has its own coherence. Both depend on a system of values and level of culture which are not those of the manual worker nor of precarious life-styles. But this distortion is no different from that encountered in other sources: literary observations, reports of police commissioners, documents of judicial proceedings. By taking them into account we are outlining the possibilities of creating a methodology with a social anthropological approach.

It is essential to break with a narrative history of daily life in order to rediscover the 'prose of the world' (Henri Lefebvre), which exists outside the world of buying and selling. In the culture of the poor possession is nine-tenths of the law and reveals multiple layers of significance; objects define a life-style. But it is difficult to pass from a functional reading based on common practice to the lesson of a symbolic analysis which requires other materials and other sources, and it is almost impossible to reconstruct the essential elements, that is to say the specific acquisitive strategies in societies characterised by scarcity and stability. We must resign ourselves to measuring the inheritance with little hope of knowing how the part of being and having was resolved in it, which in all human communities constitutes the essence of the possession of things; how the pressures of desire might beset obscure people faced with objects that were less ephemeral than in the mass consumer societies of today.

In eighteenth-century Paris a strange phenomenon was taking place. The exceptional quality of one of the great capitals of the modern world was founded upon an extraordinary accumulation of intelligence and goods. For the leisured society, freed from productive labour, traditional stable values were becoming blurred just when, in the material sphere, they were passing from an age when there was no artificial obsolescence of basic needs to a time of cheap exchange and rapid transformations. Fashions confer a swifter moral ageing process on things; Paris was experiencing an extraordinary acceleration of time. To what extent did the popular classes participate in this movement which has accelerated to the present day? In what way and to what extent were they associated with 'unchanging procedures handed down from time immemorial' and the innovations which helped to change, if not to liberate them?

CHAPTER 3

Popular Fortunes and Misfortunes

In this world fortune and misfortune abound. (*Proverb*)

The poverty of eighteenth-century France was appalling; it was part of the daily scene in which the contrast, often remarked upon by contemporaries, existed between the poor committed to a precarious existence and the lucky ones who had found their place, a job and a home. Ordinary life was made up of this confrontation. 'The multitude of poor and wretched in every part of the city is such that, in a carriage, on foot, or in a shop, you can do nothing because of the persistent hordes of beggars. It is lamentable to hear the recital of their miseries; and if you give to one of them, the whole swarm at once descends upon you . . . .' For the worthy Doctor John Lister, it was proof of the flaws of Papism which was too indulgent towards idle poverty, of the will 'of God's Providence which orders all things in this world', as well as of the incontestable superiority of the beef-eating English over the 'Lenten-fasting French'.[1] This sort of observation, made in 1697, continued until 1789 and proved the attachment of the cultural elites to the idea of an irremediable social destiny:

> The poor in a State are rather like shadows in a painting, they provide a necessary contrast about which humanity sometimes groans, but which honours the decree of Providence. . . . It is therefore necessary that there should be poor people, but there should not be wretches; the latter are nothing but a shame to humanity; the former, on the contrary, are part of a particular order and a political economy: they create the wealth of the towns . . . the Arts which flourish. Do not these many advantages which we receive from the poor demand that we furnish them at least with what is needful to bear patiently with their hard condition. . . .[2]

1. J. Lister, *Voyage à Paris, en 1697*, Paris, 1873, pp. 34–5.
2. P. Hecquet, *La Médecine, la chirurgie et la pharmacie des pauvres*, Paris 1740, 3 vols., vol. 1, pp. 1ff.

The good Doctor Hecquet offers us, with candid cynicism, a clear example of the basic split in Enlightenment thought: by his work the poor man was indispensable to society which must eradicate misery, always a threat to social order. Through charity, they might become God's poor; through philanthropy, they might attract the attention of charitable ladies.[3] In any case, prompting this thinking was an awareness of the economy, of work, therefore of wages. The popular classes who narrowly escaped misery were those who were lucky enough to have a 'daily job' (Necker); those who 'include all men without property or revenue, without *rentes* and without security; who live on their *salaires* when these are sufficient; who suffer when they are too low; who die of hunger when they receive none' (Linquet); '*travail* is their only partimony' (Cliquot de Blervache).[4] In Paris these are the people who appear in the inventories, and whom we must now follow in their fortune and misfortune.

Two social categories provide the evidence: servants and lower-class workers. In the notarial archives it is easy to pick out the servants, even if they are an unstable group, appearing and disappearing every year, even every season. They present a particular model of urban wage-earners in the pre-industrial age. Other wage-earners present different problems. If we opt for the expression 'lower classes', rather than other more precise terms such as 'wage-earners', 'popular strata', 'labouring classes', *'petites gens'* or 'proto-proletariat', it is because each of these terms takes a definite criterion to define the identity of the group: its place in the production machine, status, economic dependence, living and cultural standards. Thus they cover only one part of reality, half-captured within imprecise limits, constantly being reshaped. Towards the bottom end of the scale, they are at the level of indigence; at the top, of micro-bourgeois consolidation in a world of artisans and shop-keepers. Within this social space, the true physionomy of the lower classes in Paris was variable and multiform.

Servants were part of the landscape. On the stage and in novels they were a familiar jostling throng; Molière and Marivaux used them to question the role of the servant oscillating between representatives of unseemly behaviour and pedagogues regulating the action. In literary confrontations, male and female servants achieved exceptional dignity which confirmed in the ruling class their view of their own superiority

---

3. A. Farge, 'Les maladies', pp. 999–1000.
4. J. Necker, *Sur la législation et le commerce des grains*, Paris, 1775, 2 vols., vol. 1, ch. XXV; S.H.N. Linguet, *Annales politiques, civiles et littéraires du XVIIIe siècle*, Paris, 1777–92, 19 vols., vol. IX, pp. 326ff.; S. Cliquot de Blervache, *Essai sur les moyens d'améliorer en France la condition des laboureurs, des journaliers, des hommes de peine vivant dans les compagnes, et celle de leurs femmes et de leurs enfants par un Savoyard*, Chambéry, 1789, vol. 1, p. 102.

to the mass of the people, whilst simultaneously revealing their fear of another culture.[5] On a different note, the myth of the successful servant who became a tax-farmer by his wits retained its hold, despite a contradictory and far more complex reality.[6] In both cases, this field of symbolic representation is called into question by the role of mediator, go-between, even trouble-maker which the servant played in the real world. Socially suspect to the middle-class deputies of the Constituent Assembly and the Jacobins — 'The notables wanted to give even servants the vote, but Necker would not consent' (Michelet) — and to the nobility and the ruling classes generally, servants were obviously social and cultural cross-breeds. For the first group, they were dubious characters in so far as they accepted a situation of voluntary slavery at the time of the affirmation of egalitarian claims for the individual; moreover, they shared the aristocrats' vices and taste for luxury.[7] For the others, they embodied the spirit of sedition, base sentiment and, all in all, constituted a danger which was certainly disturbing but more to Christian ethics than to the established order.[8] This durability as a literary theme and the costant denunciation on social and moral grounds underline the importance of an overall study of the group and its function compared with the characteristics of the wage-earning lower classes. The place of servants in Parisian society was sufficiently important to offer scope for an exploration of the phenomena of cultural circulation and the role of frontier groups in transmitting acculturising values and introducing innovative modes of behaviour into their milieu of origin. Through servants, the objects and actions of the upper classes were filtered through to the lower social categories. Conversely, servants were able to keep alive popular, rural manners and traditions in the world of their masters: from sturdy common sense to old wives' tales, from ancestral links with nature and the animal world to sensual and sentimental awakenings; how can we imagine his master without Jacques? However, the right terms of reference must be found if this notion is to prove sound methodologically. We must examine external attitudes, for who is more caught up in a web of appearances than a servant? We must relate the notion to an

5. J. Emelina, `Valets et servantes dans le théâtre comique en France de 1610 à 1700, Grenoble, 1975.

6. Y. Durand, *Les fermiers généraux au XVIII*[e] *siècle*, Paris, 1971, pp. 231–88.

7. A study of the criticism of servants in Enlightenment thought has yet to be carried out; of course, it would involve the town–country and Paris–provinces contrasts. The following might offer some leads: abbé Desfontaines, *Le Nouveau Gulliver*, 1730; A. Désiré, *L'Origine et source de tous les maux*, 1571; Chevalier Des Forges, *Du véritable intérêt de la Patrie*, 1764; C. Soret, *Oeuvres*, 1784; abbé Soulavue, *Des moeurs*, 1784; Piarron de Chamousset, *Oeuvres*, 1787; abbé Grégoire, *De la domesticité chez les peuples anciens*, 1814.

8. J. Emelina, *Valets et servantes*, pp. 287–322.

anthropology of acts of possession and culture, leaving to some future work the examination of sexual or criminal behaviour,[9] and in a general way everything that concerns the subservient relationship.[10] Between *Les Liaisons Dangereuses* and *Le Mariage de Figaro* there are various social permutations of the corrupting role of servants and of masters, but that is another story which has yet to be written. We will keep to a socio-cultural analysis of a condition which was often temporary. Some fled from it to return to their home ground, to retire as small leisured *rentiers*, or to settle in a different social world once they had gathered their small nest-egg — which depended very much on age, the position they had filled and masters they had encountered. In short, this is the ideal group with which to test both mobility and imitation.

In the middle of the eighteenth century the abbé Expilly estimated the servant population at nearly 40,000, nearly 5 per cent of the total population, more if one counts families — difficult to calculate exactly in a milieu where the unmarried state was common. It should be noted that this is the rate in other big cities studied: Lyons 4 per cent, Aix, Marseilles, Toulouse, between 5 and 7 per cent, and that it comes nowhere near the rate in fiction for low-life comedy characters, some 30 per cent. This rich imaginary society underlines the basic features of real society and the fundamental fact that an important percentage of the city population was involved in close bonds of dependence. But what matters here is undoubtedly the nature of the servant world as well as of that of the employers: like master, like valet, as the proverb says.[11]

On this point, two models present themselves, not as intangible and omnipresent realities, but as poles in the social organisation: on the one hand an aristocratic style typical of the *beaux quartiers*, but not uniquely so; on the other hand, an omnipresent bourgeois style. The former was characterised by the large number of servants to each employer and the predominance of male servants. It was mostly found in the new Paris of the west, the Faubourg Saint-Germain, the Saint-Honoré district, the Palais Royal, and the traditional Marais of the lawyers. In their great mansions and vast apartments the masters were surrounded by a swarming mass, heterogeneous in their occupations, hierarchised in their functions, varied in their geographical origins: butlers, household stewards (in the revolutionary vocabulary *hommes de confiance*), coachmen (often from Normandy), lackeys

9. M. Botlan, 'Domesticité', pp. 289–310.
10. E. Walter, *Jacques le fataliste de Diderot*, Paris, 1975, pp. 68–75.
11. D. Roche, 'Les domestiques comme intermédiaires culturels', in *Les Intermédiaires culturels. Actes du colloque, Aix, June 1978*, Aix, 1981.

(sometimes from Picardy), valets, chair porters (from Brie, Burgundy or Le Mans), chambermaids and personal maids of all sorts, coming as we have seen from nearby provinces. This was the seditious *canaille* of the contemporary scene: 'A moi la livrée', and riots would break out. . . .[12]

In the middle-class world of shopkeepers and artisans, on the other hand, each family had only one servant, almost always a woman. This was the dominant model in the central districts and the popular faubourgs of eastern Paris. In the Faubourg Saint-Marcel, the police registers number nearly 200, all men (Expilly counted more than 1,000 in 656 families), that is, one male servant to two families and one female-servant per family on average; in the Faubourg Saint-Antoine he estimated the number of servants to be 429, one to three or four homes, and even during the Revolution there were more than 200 male servants there. Altogether, there were *quartiers* that were real breeding-grounds for servants, and others where they were lost among the artisan and labouring population. This contrast is repeated in the map of unemployment and domestic criminality,[13] where the important fact is the large number of servants in the interstitial zones where the abbé Expilly did not list them. The topography of servant unemployment, as well as of delinquency, is the world of furnished rooms, of the popular *quartier*, those areas which provided non-specialist labour; in short, a heterogeneous world of multiple population shifts, obeying laws of supply and demand in a labour market which was saturated on the eve of the Revolution. The main point here is to emphasise the importance of servants as a mediating force. This occurs on two planes: first the great migrations; then the uprooting within the town accentuated by the inner mobility of the great city.

Servants were provincials, a state which gave them, like all migrants, a special linking role between country and town, province and capital. Strangers in the city, often ignorant of its ways and customs, it is understandable that they lapsed easily into criminality and that they should have been the favourite target of authors eager to denounce the impertinent folly of the popular classes. It remains to be discovered if these sons and daughters of peasants and *les petites gens* perceived their links with their place of origin. Inventories enable us to calculate the presence of families: at the beginning of the century less than a quarter of the individuals had no relations mentioned, on the eve of the

12. AN.Z1 H 652 — extract from the capitation roll for the Saint-Germain district, 1762. The house of M. le Prince d'Henrichemont: 1 steward, 1 butler, 2 valets, 2 chambermaids, 1 cook, 1 laundryman, 5 lackeys, 2 coachmen, 1 groom, 1 postillion, 1 hall-porter.
13. M. Botlan, 'Domesticité', pp. 346–8.

Revolution it was 20 per cent. Servants in Paris were not always isolated and some — more than half of the cases studied — had close relatives with them. In other words, the important point was the possibility of integration into the city — often by marriage — and the existence of a servant class taking root and playing a mediating role between the metropolis and the village, if only on the occasion of an inheritance or a family celebration. The fact remains that domestic service was not the best possible channel for urbanisation, that it did not constitute a permanent state, attracting the little man fascinated and often blinded by the lights of the city.

Within the city their mobility is still more obvious.[14] Frequent moves meant that the average stay for more than nine out of ten servants in furnished rooms in Paris was for under a month; the rapid rhythm of the period of service; the fact that nearly two-thirds of servants had been in trouble with the judges of the Châtelet (out of 300 cases studied by M. Botlan); a change of master at least once a year; all this indicates the unstable nature of domestic service though it is less striking for men who were less dependent. The special nature of the servant in society is accentuated by this extreme instability so far as employment and living quarters are concerned. This fact reflects the comparatively hard and often dramatic conditions of their existence, but it also stresses the importance, as catalysts of experience, of all those who managed to become familiar with urban life, and for whom all this uprooting was accompanied by a hope, partially realised, of integration. From this point of view, the comparison of aristocratic and bourgeois service should be reconsidered, for the possibilities of success were not the same in each; four-fifths of the richest servants who appear among the inventories of the Paris notaries were in service with the nobility, the poorest had employers of lower standing and smaller means. [15] Unequal participation in the benefits of aristocratic life was what marked out winners and losers, separated those who could assimilate the values and behaviour of the urban elites and those who would never be in a position to do so.

The working-class world poses other problems.[16] It was incoherent and heterogeneous because it exploded in a multiplicity of relationships characteristic of a hybrid economy dominated by light industry in which the small workshop and the single room dominated; that is, proto-industrial enterprise where, however, certain aspects of the

---

14. Ibid., pp. 200–25.
15. F. Ardellier, *Essai d'anthropologie urbaine au XVIIIe siècle, les domestiques parisiens d'après l'inventaire après décès*, Mémoire de maîtrise, Paris, 1977.
16. S. Kaplan, 'Réflexions sur la police du monde du travail, 1700–1815', in *Revue Historique*, 1979, pp. 17–77; J. Kaplow, *Les Noms des Rois*, pp. 71–90.

manufacturing town already existed, and where the economy was complicated by a vast commercial sector which devoured unskilled labour and services which, without demanding qualifications or training, were none the less fundamental; for example, the *savoyard* water-carriers. At the beginning of the Revolution, the average business employed no more than about fifteen workers, and factories like the Gobelins or Réveillon looked like manufacturing monsters. In the Faubourg Saint-Marcel, the weavers in the *manufacture royale* constituted a highly specialised class — identity cards often described them as *artistes* — three-quarters of them were natives of Paris and 90 per cent of them could read and write. They lived in the factory itself, and had their own disciplines and social life. Even if, on the eve of 1789 they were suffering a crisis (royal debts were eating into everything), they were none the less privileged in the world of labour, and this gave them a potential manifested in their expression of general dissatisfaction, an 'independent spirit' feared by the authorities.[17] The 500 workers at the glass manufactory in the faubourg Saint-Antoine, the thousand or so workers gravitating around the wallpaper factories, the porcelain-workers and potters of a few big enterprises, constituted another aspect of this concentrated labour force, exploited by wage restraint, but who were not always the first victims of a crisis or the last to protest violently.[18]

Any hierarchy in the world of work can only be arbitrary, as socio-economic realities in Paris are not sufficiently well-known and do not lend themselves to categorisation, mobility and confusion of status being a general, if not inevitable, rule. One may, like Steve Kaplan, accept that there is a clear social map. At the top, contemporary consensus placed the guild worker, the journeyman in a workshop or the shop assistant who stood out from other workers by his specialisation, and sometimes by his manners. What particularly differentiated this type of worker was that he was integrated into the guild system and able to aspire to the rank of master, even if the barriers erected by the guild communities grew higher as time went on. At the end of his apprenticeship the *compagnon* was finally distinguished from the rest, often after sharing the life of his master and shaping his behaviour in the ambience of the atelier or the family shop. Not all journeymen could aspire to a mastership, for two reasons. First, the number of places was limited and such as there were went first to the sons and sons-in-law of masters. Secondly, the cost of places was relatively high; in 1789, 200 days' work for a glass-worker,

17. H. Burstin, 'Le Faubourg Saint-Marcel', pp. 279–90.
18. R. Monnier, 'Le Faubourg Saint-Antoine', pp. 44–105.

800 for a wine merchant, 1,400 for a mason or carpenter and at least 2,500 days for a draper, who was at the top of the corporate hierarchy together with haberdashers, grocers, hatters, goldsmiths and furriers, in the trades which were inaccessible to the common worker. There were between 30,000 and 40,000 masterships; there were probably two or three times as many journeymen, whose solidarity was also expressed by the clandestine nature of *compagnonnages*, which often attracted the attention of the police. It is certain that the proliferation of trades, the existence of exceptional situations (the privileged artisans of the faubourg Saint-Antoine, or the shopkeepers of the Temple precincts) encouraged a dispersal of wage-earners whose study should be undertaken by economic sectors. In general, however, 'the domestic authority' of the guilds, firmly re-established after Turgot's confused attempt to remedy the abuses of the old guild system by liberalising it, distinguished journeymen and assistants from *alloués*, who were destined to work all their lives by the day without any hope of corporative status, or forced to work secretly at home, in spite of the rules.

The wage-earners who did not belong to the *corps d'arts et métiers* made up the mass of the labour-force serving masters of all kinds. Two categories predominated among the *ouvriers* not affiliated to masterships: those who received their wages, sometimes their lodgings, directly from the entrepreneurs and were always supervised by them, and those who were paid by customers; the terminology hardly distinguishes between manual labourers, day-labourers, workers in businesses and casual labourers, unloaders, porters and labourers at the ports and markets who performed countless odd jobs. They might be paid for the job or by the day, they might join gangs recruited by the host of minor officials of the town ports or markets for temporary jobs as porters — unloading a boat, emptying a warehouse — they might be linked by ties of origin, village or family in some sort of working practice. Most were poor devils, recent immigrants with no qualifications, and the great number of them in the suburbs indicated the changes in the organisation of urban work, due less to the limited increase in capitalist and manufacturing enterprise than to the development of town functions requiring an unskilled labour-force for a multitude of occasional tasks. Implicit hierarchies, solidarities and networks functioned within this lowly world. In 1786 the reorganisation of the parcel delivery service under the control of a transport authority unleashed protests and attacks on delivery men in the middle of the winter. Casual labourers from the Auvergne and Savoy, with the 'support of the dregs of the people', clashed with the watch and held up unloading at the ports. A demand for the right to work was expressed in these demonstrations which, though unsuccessful, proved the strength of combined action even in the unorganised sectors.[19] Every day countless members of small trades, socially very close to the workers' world, were engaged in a multiplicity of tasks — jobbing, building, small-scale manufacture and selling new and second-hand goods. These street salesmen, fixed or itinerant, were controlled and registered during the last quarter of the century. There were more women — mending, selling hardware, old clothes and other second-hand goods — than men — hucksters, pedlars, vendors of lottery tickets and tinkers.[20] The 'cris de Paris', a genre which had flourished among print-sellers and engravers since the sixteenth century, popularised these street people. The prints offer a double testimony: first, they are tangible proof of the growth of small trades and services linked with the increase and diversification of the population of Paris and, secondly, they are a sign of the interest in the picturesque strangeness of the lower classes felt by the ruling classes who created the principal demand for these engravings which were, however, quickly banished to the lumber-room of the popular imagery.[21] It was one of the ways in which cultivated opinion invested the world of work with a normative coherence and a homogeneity of role and function. It demonstrated clearly the social frontier of labour, and the artist's eye fixed gestures and objects from the wide range of the precarious and needy.[22] There is a distinct evolution between the images of the end of the seventeenth century and the fine series published in the eighteenth century by Boucher and Bouchardon. The print-makers in the reign of Louis XIV depicted grave, severe faces, dry bodies, supplicant gestures, men and women marked by work and the poverty of the times. A century later the misery, though still apparent, acquires a new clarity. Bouchardon presents fresh, sprightly milkmaids and charming little sweeps. The ambiguity of the lower classes and the poor as perceived by the rich is apparent everywhere in this strolling bazaar, reducing a gigantic, disparate world to an exotic and innocent condition which is barely punctuated by a few disturbing signs. The small street-traders in Paris played an essential part in the ordinary life of the lower classes, they contributed to the notorious acceleration of consumption, and they offered an important second income to many households. Neither wage-earners nor entirely self-employed, these street-criers fulfilled basic needs which were perhaps becoming more and more pressing. The popular classes were composed of such diverse elements.

The notarial archives offer a guide to this multifarious mass. Two

19. H. Burstin, 'Le Faubourg Saint-Marcel', pp. 325–32.
20. J. Massin, *Les Cris de ville*, Paris, 1979.
21. A. Farge, *Le Bazar de la rue*, Urbi, I, 1979, pp. xcvii–xcviii.
22. S. Kaplan, Réflections', pp. 20–2.

Table 3.1. Social composition, based on notarial archives 1695–1715 and 1775–90

1695–1715
Lower classes

Guild-workers	44
Unqualified wage-earners (including 22 casual labourers)	31
Tradespeople with no status	25

Servants

Upper servants	29
Personal servants	20
Subordinate and indeterminate functions	51

1775–90
Lower classes

Guild-workers	55
Unqualified wage-earners	28
Tradespeople with no status	17

Servants

Upper servants	15
Personal servants	20
Subordinate functions	65

samples of 200 inventories taken at each end of the century of the Enlightenment cast some light on the general development.[23] Table 3.1 shows the composition of the samples.

The social range of the popular milieux seems adequately differentiated; the enquiries exclude both office-workers and clerks, both of whom belonged to an employment economy, one which was specifically modern. Geographically, they cover wage-earners and servants from all districts of the city.

From the point of view of employment sectors, the different functions of servants are represented with a slight tendency to over-estimate the number of upper servants, and to under-estimate the inferior personnel of the kitchen, stables and servants' quarters; the representation of personal servants is fair. Table 3.3 shows the chief trades that are represented in each period.

Nevertheless, so far as an exact definition of this microcosm is concerned, the fact remains that it is not easy to differentiate concrete activities merely by a professional vocabulary. The multiplicity of

23. As well as F. Ardellier, 'Essai d'anthropologie urbaine', see R. Arnette, *Les classes inférieures parisiennes d'après les inventaires après décès au XVIIIe siècle*, Mémoire de maîtrise, Paris, 1977.

Table 3.2. Social range of popular milieux

	1695–1715		1775–90	
	Wage-earners	Servants	Wage-earners	Servants
Right-bank parishes, including the Faubourg Saint-Antoine	68	66	73	60
La Cité	1	2	3	1
Left-bank parishes	28	29	15	33
Others	3	8	9	6

Table 3.3. Chief trades in the popular milieux

	1695–1715	1775–90
Building	26	22
Transport	31	13
Clothing and various crafts	43	65

terms conceals real situations and positions, such as precedence among servants and the hierarchy among trades, which could provoke conflicts. It is easier to arrive at a terminology in the artisan and shop-keeping sphere, where tools and materials preserved serve as evidence. The value of words may always mask varying realities, for it is part of a strategy of social positions which may be built on usurpation or even dissembling. But the value of the general analysis is none the less real even in this relative sense.

Finally, it remains difficult to attempt to differentiate between the sexes and to allow for people holding more than one job or for family work: 10 per cent of the verified cases relating to servants, less than 15 per cent in wage-earner inventories. It is impossible to analyse the exact role of working women. Let us now try to tackle the question of lower-class fortunes and their evolution. By looking at groups of legacies and their dispersion, by comparing the results with jobs, by analysing the make-up of personal possessions, one begins to trace economic and mental behaviour patterns; one begins to see certain changes.

The first question to be answered depends on the definition of 'average fortunes'. To reconstitute them requires some audacity on the part of the researcher, owing to the difficulties arising from the notarial sources themselves, the complexity of comparative studies which

Table 3.4. Basis for a calculation of fortunes

	Wage-earners		Servants	
	1695–1715	1775–90	1695–1715	1775–90
Average fortune (*in livres*)	776	1,776	4,209	8,251
Average price of wheat per *setier* (in *livres*)	18L6	23L6		
Reduced to *setiers* of wheat	47.7	75.5	226	350
Increase (%)		81		54
Reduced to terms of a manual worker's wages (*sols*)	17 5	25		
	886 days	1,420 days	4,810 days	6,600 days
Increase (%)		59		37

involves different financial milieux and, especially, because reasoning about nominal averages for a study of inheritances poses problems. For lack of a guide to the cost of living, one may translate the values obtained into prices of products which had a decisive social value for the milieu in question, such as the price of a *setier* of wheat sold at La Halle, or of a day's work. These transpositions may be open to criticism, but they offer an effective basis for comparison. Among wage-earners at the beginning of the eighteenth century the average fortune was 776 livres, by the end it exceeded 1,700 *livres*. Translated into terms of the price of wheat this meant an increase of 80 per cent and, calculated against the average wage of a manual labourer, a leap from 886 days' work to 1,415, that is 60 per cent. The gain is undeniable, but may not apply to all wage-earners. There is a considerable difference in the evolution of servant's misfortunes. In the reign of Louis XIV the average was higher, 4,000 *livres*, and on the eve of the Revolution it was over 8,000 *livres*. This increase is slower and in its range of 37 to 54 per cent it means that in real value the world of domestic service has progressed less than in the labouring classes overall; but does the progression affect them all equally (Table 3.4)?

If we group legacies around the principal modes, in the two sectors, several types of development may be seen (Table 3.5). For the whole century the hierarchy of fortunes is strictly inverse for the two groups. Among wage-earners, the most usual fortune at the beginning of the century is between 200 and 300 *livres*, two-thirds of wage-earners die with less than 500 *livres*, as did more than half on the eve of the Revolution. On the other hand, by the reign of Louis XIV more than half the servants died with more than 1,000 *livres*, and more than

Table 3.5. Model distribution of fortunes (%)

Fortune, in *livres*	1695–1715		1775–1790	
	Wage-earner	Servants	Wage-earners	Servants
Below 500	60	30	50	16
500–999	23	15	13	8
1,000–2,999	12	19	14	21
Over 3,000	5	36	23	55
10,000	—	[12]	[6]	[26]

three-quarters did so in time of Louis XVI. In short, enrichment generally depended on a very unequal distribution of chances, which were always more favourable to the servant classes.

Among wage-earners, the improvement is due to the progress of the higher categories — the 'rich' poor — who were three times as numerous towards the end of the century as at the beginning, the average value of their succession having multiplied by five.[24] The gap has widened between the poorer and the richer, the increase calculated in wheat or average wage is 7 to 20 per cent for the latter, while the former suffer a loss of 30 to 40 per cent, a sure indication of pauperisation of crisis proportions.[25]

Among servants, the poorer category is less numerous (Table 3.6) but in real value the legacies drop by 20 to 30 per cent. The mass of servants lived on the edge of extreme poverty, their dependence was increasing and more than a quarter died empty-handed at the end of a lifetime's labour. A few affluent members, more numerous than among wage-earners, prove that it was possible to prosper, but in general Parisian servants in the pre-Revolutionary period form a group unequally divided between winners and losers. Marc Botlan has already noted this pauperisation from two pertinent indicators: 10 per cent of the servant inventories, after the placing of seals by the commissioners of the Châtelet, indicate an utterly wretched standard of living; more than three quarters of servants were obliged to stay in service in spite of age and illness.[26] Nevertheless, a close analysis of the inventories does modify this conclusion and proves that one must not overestimate the tendency of notaries to scale-up the higher fortunes.

24. Even after 1775 six legacies exceed 10,000 *livres*, an indication of real success for this milieu and period.
25. See Table 3.6 for a calculation of increases.
26. M. Botlan, 'Domesticité', pp. 259–69, exaggerates pauperisation when referring to poverty for fortunes of more than 10,000 *livres*.

Table 3.6. Evolution by categories, average fortune in *livres*

	Less than 1,000 *livres*				Over 3,000 *livres*			
	Size of sample	Average fortune	Wheat (*setiers*)	Work (days)	Size of sample	Average fortune	Wheat (*setiers*)	Work (days)
Wage-earners								
1695–1715	73	351	18.8	401	5	5,385	289	6,154
1775–90	69	308	13.1	245	17	8,182	349	6,519
Servants								
1695–1715	45	377	20.2	425	36	10,617	570	12,133
1775–90	24	354	15.0	283	55	14,280	605	11,424

The link with jobs provides a possible line of exploration.[27] The importance of what precise role a Parisian servant played is obvious. Performing a superior function which placed him near his master made him a winner. As coachman, groom or unqualified lackey, he was a loser, for they made up two-thirds of those who left legacies below 500 *livres*. However, things changed in the time of Louis XVI, the hierarchy of fortunes and functions no longer coincide so clearly, two-thirds of the servants performing responsible tasks died with more than 3,000 *livres*, and there were men from the stables and kitchen alongside them. It was in great houses especially that servants died rich, those of the Orléans, Conti, Choiseul and Condé families, whatever their level of skill. So while success and stabilisation might be explained partly by cultural capacity, it depended even more on the size of the master's fortune.

Among wage-earners the situation is more complex, for one must take into account socio-professional variables as well as the types of activity. Men not belonging to corporations are grouped in the category of legacies below 500 *livres*, with a few exceptions such as factory-workers, one of whom, E. Poiret, working in the *manufacture de glace*, died in 1709 with assets of 8,500 *livres*. At the end of the century, guild-workers were still advantaged and their group was generally more homogeneous, whilst for manual and casual labourers a few successes did nothing to hide the general mediocrity of their achievements. These were the marginals of the urban economy. This

27. It is difficult to establish a precise analysis in this area for too many elements are missing: a study of wage categories; real resources, which includes the total resources for the household especially women's wages; a comparison of income and expenses, which would require a knowledge of demographic family data. In short, a study of fortunes must not be confused with a study of living standards for one cannot deduce from inventories the basic items in a budget. See M. Baulant, 'Niveau de vie', p. 506.

first split cuts across another: highly-qualified workers under guild-masters were the top scorers, wage-earners in the building industry occupied the middle positions, while casual labourers, porters, carters and unloaders lived in the greatest poverty. But few of these men who lacked a stable trade or qualification ever came to the attention of the notaries: 30 per cent in 1715, 13 per cent in 1790. So the really poor workers simply disappear from our field of vision, for they cannot have decreased as the working population of Paris grew, and there was no technical revolution to replace men in manual tasks.[28] Outside the *jurandes*, the gap separating failure and success widened, whilst in the guild communities the advance of average fortune reduced it a little. Overall, the eighteenth century closed on a scene of sharp contrasts, substantial fortunes were more numerous but the massive impoverishment of the majority was undeniable among servants and the lower classes. The snapshot view at the end of the century, compared with the more overall picture for the beginning, is biased towards the top for two reasons: the increase in the cost of inventories, and the drop in the real value of fortunes below 500 *livres* — what was the use of having a valuation if the legacy was almost worthless and if the notary's fee swallowed a quarter of it! ... As far as servants were concerned, the chances of getting rich had increased but more than a quarter of the group remained constantly on the poverty line. Compared with the manual workers and journeymen, servants were distinguished by a more significant number of modest fortunes and more important real successes; those who lived in the shadow of the ruling classes were less liable than others to become marginals. This lesson is confirmed by an enquiry into the inventories of wage-earners in the Marais area in the middle of the century. While some servants had 20,000 *livres*, three-quarters of the wage earners had less than 500 *livres*.[29] Similarly, a study of marriage contracts for 1749 reveals an analogous social topography: 20 per cent of servants married with a portion over 5,000 *livres*, 55 per cent between 1,000 and 5,000 *livres*, less than a third had scarcely 500 *livres*; marriage reinforced and accelerated the possibility of saving and helped to integrate the servant wage-earners. On the other hand, 60 per cent of tradespeople were married with portions of 500 to 1,000 *livres*, while at the lowest levels day-labourers and other casual workers predominated at the lowest levels, with no hope whatsoever of upward social mobility. The gap was more marked between them and wage-earners belonging to cor-

28. J.-C. Perrot, *Genèse d'une ville moderne*, vol. 1, pp. 265–6.
29. D. Roche, *Recherches sur les structures sociales du quartier du Marais au milieu du XVIIIᵉ siècle*, DES, Paris, 1959, pp. 177–200.

porations than between journeymen and master-craftsmen.[30] In short, marginalisation constantly threatened unskilled wage-earners and the army of labourers committed to countless unrewarding tasks. In productive sectors where the socialisation of work was more advanced, chances of success existed throughout the century.[31] The composition of fortunes enables us to be more precise about divisions and general trends.

Legacies can be divided into two groups according to the nature of the categories of property listed: on the one hand everyday objects, furniture, utensils, clothes, tangible objects of practical value; on the other, financial reserves, investments, money, jewellery, debts, *rentes* and circulating assets. It is true that silver and real estate can be reckoned in either group, but it is more convenient to consider them with reserves or investments.[32]

In relation to theses two categories of bequests, two patterns emerge for the beginning of the century. Among wage-earners, practical possessions were more important and for a good third they were the main part of the legacy, reduced to a few pieces of furniture, a handful of kitchen utensils, a few clothes and some linen. Among servants, on the other hand, this type of possession made up of only one-tenth of legacies and, except for very small inheritances, circulating assets, jewellery, silver, *rentes*, even bonds were the general rule. Undoubtedly the most important factor is the close connection between the nature of the possessions and the level of fortune in the two classes; below 500 *livres*, and still more below 300, tangible possessions predominated, life was reduced to basic necessities; above 3,000 *livres* they made up less than 5 per cent of the legacies. Fortune rather than jobs conditioned behaviour patterns, misfortune cut down the range of choices (Table 3.7).

A century later the picture had changed a little. Among wage-earners, basic necessities tended to play a reduced part while remaining much the same for servants, but one must remember that among the latter the proportion of very small legacies had diminished while remaining constant for the lower levels of wage-earners: for these there was no change, and 80 per cent of the assets were in everyday goods.

---

30. A. Daumard and F. Furet, *Structures sociales*, pp. 25–34.
31. H. Burstin, 'Faubourg Saint-Marcel', pp. 334–5.
32. The make-up of fortunes has been classified according to the system established by Madame M. Baulant, 'Niveau de vie' (1975), that is to say, twelve categories in all: household utensils, furniture, linen, clothes, tools and professional equipment, silver and jewellery, cash, interest, *rentes*, bonds, unpaid trade debts, real estate. Two of them are under-valued (clothes and real estate), but these slight gaps do not invalidate the comparison; cf. R. Arnette, *Les classes inférieures*, pp. 30–5, and F. Ardellier, 'Essai d'anthropologie urbaine', pp. 20–32.

Table 3.7. The composition of fortunes (%)

	1695–1715		1775–1790	
	Wage-earners	Servants	Wage-earners	Servants
Furniture, linen & clothes	31.5	8.9	18.2	7.3
Silver	4.2	2.9	2.8	2.2
Cash	3.9	1.6	4.5	3.6
Rentes	19.2	49.8	45.2	61.1
Promissory notes, bonds, *offices*	22.2	28.7	20.5	21.3
Unpaid or book debts	4.1	5.2	4.2	3.0
Real estate	14.9	3.1	4.6	1.0

Above 3,000 *livres* in both groups the proportion was comparable. The contrasts between rich and poor appeared more clearly in the composition of fortunes than in their hierarchy; it is more striking on the eve of the Revolution than at the time of Louis XIV (Table 3.8). The stability of servants in this respect confirms their former advantage and the proximity of their behaviour patterns to those of the ruling classes. Where there was a change, especially for the pauperised categories, it was due to the drop, or at least shift, in established values, household utensils, tools, clothes. Household utensils depreciated and were responsible for the general fall in the value of articles of everyday use. They constituted 15 per cent of fortunes below 500 *livres* at the beginning of the century, but only 7 per cent at the end. This is due to the massive renunciation of a certain number of objects and especially to the substitution of cheap pottery and china for costly materials such as copper and pewter. Furniture and bedding maintained their position, and became more important in large legacies. This first shift had an opposite effect on both rich and poor for whom familiar objects lost value and no doubt became less durable. Tools and professional equipment diminished still more sharply, in frequency and in relative value (3 per cent to 0.7 per cent), but chiefly in the case of heavy tools and even the equipment of a small workshop; no doubt this fact indicates a loss of independence. Linen and clothes rose at all levels; above 3,000 *livres* they moved from 0.6 per cent of the assets to 1.6 per cent, below 500 *livres* they jumped from 7 per cent to 16 per cent. This indicates a new relationship to clothing consumption. Generally speaking, everyday articles had evolved in three ways: in the servant world they experienced a relative decline in importance through a transformation of every kind of job; for the more affluent wage-earners, they rose, with the exception of household utensils; finally,

Table 3.8. Composition of legacies and levels of fortune (%)

	Assets 500 *livres*		Assets 3,000 *livres*	
	1695–1715	1775–90	1695–1715	1775–90
Wage-earners				
Furniture, clothes, linen	78.0	79.0	5.0	8.0
Silver	7.0	7.0	1.0	1.5
Cash	2.0	5.0	1.0	4.5
Rentes	—	2.0	28.0	64.0
Promissory notes, bonds	3.0	3.5	33.0	16.0
Debts	3.0	3.5	4.0	4.0
Real estate	7.0	—	30.0	2.0
Servants				
Furniture, clothes, linen	51.0	40.0	10.0	7.0
Silver	2.0	13.0	3.0	2.0
Cash	2.0	5.0	2.0	3.0
Rentes	5.0	10.0	50.0	70.0
Promissory notes, bonds	15.0	20.0	24.0	16.0
Offices	—	—	4.0	—
Book debts	25.0	10.0	5.0	1.0
Real estate	—	2.0	2.0	1.0

for the majority of workers, they followed a confused path, due to the loss of some furnishings and tools, and the increased importance of clothing. So the daily horizon had changed considerably for all.

The difference between servants and wage-earners, and between rich and poor, lay in the possession of circulating assets. They made up 90 per cent of the legacies of servants around 1700, scarcely three-quarters among wage-earners, and, more importantly, they appeared in only 30 inheritances out of 100. Two worlds were contrasted here: on the one hand, clever butlers and cooks, lucky valets and maidservants, rich wage-earners who perhaps started off with a legacy and were fortunate in their activities; on the other, the poor who never entered the world of savings and paper money — the vanquished of the city. In legacies of over 3,000 *livres*, circulating assets made up 90 per cent of the whole, below 500 *livres* they did not reach 20 per cent except among servants. By 1789, the outlook hardly changed: savings, *rentes*, cash remained at the same level among the rich, rose in the middling fortunes of between 500 and 3,000 *livres*, and dropped from 21 per cent to 20 per cent among the poorest. This stability conceals varied attitudes with regard to abstract values, where the issue is not only economic but cultural.

In fact, the difference in access, according to levels of fortune and activities, to these possessions of the rich and propertied classes, indicates familiarity with writing and with the elementary mechanisms of monetary circulation and ways of managing capital. In this respect the composition of fortunes shows whether the owners were capable of following the path of social modernity.

Let us first consider coin, silver and jewels.[33] They increased everywhere from 1700 to 1790, except among those very rich servants who were already well provided; 'everywhere' is true, but distributed unequally according to the objects. The proportion of jewellery increased because more and more urban wage-earners had watches. The proportion of silver dropped; appearing at first in all the inventories, it had disappeared from the smallest legacies at the end of the century. For the rest, it must have represented a reserve which could be realised in an emergency, as well as being useful, for there is no reason to think that silver cutlery and goblets were not in daily use. For the lower classes it was a dream to be attained, a demand for social imitation. There may be several explanations of its decline: perhaps a reserve of precious metal on which one might borrow became less necessary during the reign of Louis XVI than during the repeated dramatic disturbances at the end of the reign of Louis XIV; perhaps silver no longer had the same appeal, its mimetic social significance having shifted towards other signifiers such as jewels, watches or clothes. As for coin, unusual between 1695 and 1715, it became more important at all levels. Avaricious accumulation of money was not common among the lower classes, but metal coins became more customary. The monetary stability of the century, the increase in the circulation of coins, the passing of a time when the depreciated currency was distrusted and specie in short supply, all explain this general process. The choice of the poorer people in this respect may indicate several things: ready money was a much more accessible reserve than pieces of silverware; wages in coin became more important; an age which encouraged thrift and a move towards the financial protection of the families of the provident poor; all were possible factors.

Rentes feature everywhere, with one exception — wage-earners who died around 1700, leaving less than 500 *livres*: on the eve of the Revolution such income still represented a scarce 2 per cent of their assets. With between 500 and 3,000 *livres*, journeymen, assistants, casual and manual workers, valets, lackeys and servants all had government bonds, and this appears in both surveys. Above 3,000 *livres*, assets in the form of investment vary from two-thirds to three-

33. D. Roche, 'Recherches sur la noblesse parisienne au milieu du XVIIIe siècle, la Noblesse du Marais', in *Actes du 86e Congrès National des Sociétés Savantes*, Montpellier, 1961, Paris, 1962, pp. 541–76, esp. Table 2, p. 571.

quarters. In short, the Parisian servant became a *rentier* very early, and the wage-earner who had made his fortune quickly followed suit. For the former the *rente* might have been in lieu of wages, a reward from the master for loyal service, but also a bid for security. The servant wanted to become a bourgeois, and partly succeeded. It was also the wage-earner's dream, but he succeeded only occasionally, for he had to achieve an estate of more than 3,000 *livres* to see investments outweigh the rest: of the total, 5 per cent of cases succeeded in 1700, 17 per cent in 1790. This is an important consideration, increasingly so in the century of the Enlightenment, when it conditioned the behaviour of many micro-*rentiers* who put their trust in the state (interest on customs dues and *gabelles*), the Hôtel de Ville and the church. Curiously absent from the subscribers in 1690 recently studied by Claude Michaud, the lower classes placed their modest savings in investments which could be acquired indirectly,[34] at lower cost or in part. The rise in annuities is a clear indication of such a hope of temporary security. Annuities did not feature at all in working-class fortunes and very little for servants at the beginning of the century. At the end of this period they made up a quarter of the contracts for the latter, and two-thirds for the former. For all of them, the vogue for annuities which could not be transmitted to heirs indicated a preference for rapid gains, a wager against the chance of a short life, to the detriment of family continuity and transmitted inheritances for which perpetual investments would have been more advantageous. The purchase of annuities points to an acceleration of the rhythms of economic behaviour, a distant echo of the financial growth and practices of the state, for the more affluent, perhaps, a prolonging of the average duration of life which made the initial investment more fruitful. This links up with other indications, such as the greater position accorded to clothes, jewellery and money. We are witnessing the beginning of a major new development.

With regard to debts, promissory notes and bonds, the apparent homogeneity of the people may be broken down. Financial documents, traces of an awareness of commercial capitalism, signs of financial dealings are rare except at the highest levels of fortune and among servants. Only trade debts occupied a significant place, together with tickets for the royal lottery, a way of gambling with one's gains. So far as servants are concerned, it proves that wages were lent at interest and that masters got into debt to their servants.[35] In both groups, investments with small returns were not significant and

---

34. C. Michaud, 'Notariat et sociologie de la rente à Paris au XVIIe siècle, l'emprunt du clergé de 1690', in *Annales*, ESC, 1977, pp. 1154–87.
35. M. Botlan, 'Domesticité', p. 276.

diminished in importance from 1700 to 1790, dropping by half among rich wage-earners, and by 10 per cent among servants. They played a more important part for all whose estates exceeded 3,000 *livres*. One had to be a person of means to make a profit in this area, which is why personal valets, butlers and stewards, all of whom controlled financial outlay in their own fields, invested on average twice as much as ordinary servants.[36] In the same way, a few very specialised *compagnons* (printers, cartwrights, coach-makers) were able to produce a profit from their work and from very careful saving. For all the rest, the promissory note met the requirements of urban monetary circulation, representing the customary means of payment in a world which was becoming more sophisticated.

Debts were an important part of lower-class life, becoming more widespread rather than heavier: around 1700, 65 per cent of wage-earners' estates and 60 per cent for servants; in 1790, 83 and 80 per cent respectively, with the level remaining more or less the same, 260 to 265 days' work on average, a heavy burden if one remembers that it was the small legacies which were the most heavily indebted. The nature of the debts is revealing: rent topped the list and remained stable, and the landlord or chief tenant was often present at the inventory ready to reclaim quarterly rents that had fallen due; professional debts decreased, while debts for the charges of doctors, apothecaries and burial increased (3 per cent to 8 per cent among wage-earners); debts for food doubled, the grocer, fruiterer and chocolate-seller appearing beside the ubiquitous baker and the occasional butcher. In other words, poor servants and journeymen got into debt not only to cope with the difficulties of sickness and old age, but also to enjoy a better standard of living. For this purpose they played upon close loyalties: two-thirds of the loans were contracted within the family, the professional group or the neighbourhood. Money-lenders were rare even at the beginning of the century, but everyone knew he would lend only to the almost-rich. Working-class debts constituted a closed system in which each might play the role of creditor and debtor in turn for tiny sums which rarely exceeded 100 *livres*. At the end of the *Ancien Régime*, two changes may be seen: debts owed to the heads of workshops and stores, and those owed to property-owners, suggest increasing dependence; pawn-brokers' tokens, established in 1778, appear as proof of the popularity of an institution founded to combat usury. All in all, traditional borrowing practices were changing; the burden of paying for new needs was being spread over a greater number of creditors, it was moving beyond the boundaries of the group, family and neigh-

36. Ibid., p. 267.

bours to reach the anonymity of the public credit system; it was at once a response to changing patterns of consumption and a defence against impoverishment. In 1789, the pawnbrokers' shops contained about three million objects deposited as pledges for small loans — utensils, clothes, blankets, sheets and small pieces of furniture rather than jewellery.[37] Receipts in inventories rise from 10 to 40 *livres* and mention in particular pieces of silver and clothes. They cost the unfortunate borrowers 2 *sous* per *livre* per month.[38] Sickness and death were a heavy encumbrance on the balance-sheet of a lifetime's work, accentuating the contrast between poor and rich, between the more independent servants and the dispossessed of the lower classes.

One last element in the legacies must be mentioned although it occurs only rarely — real estate. There were few property-owners among the lower classes: 18 servants out of 100 in the first study, 11 in the second, 6 among wage-earners in the reign of Louis XIV, 7 in the reign of Louis XVI. The sources here are incomplete but again clearly indicate the hierarchy of fortunes. Some of these properties — pieces of land, some acres of vineyard, parts of houses — had been inherited and were rented out for a few *livres*, a not inconsiderable addition to budgets; they symbolised links with the country, keeping alive for some the hope of a return to their roots. However, workers and servants rarely became *coqs de village*; drawn into the town, they would lose faith in the land and turned instead to *rente*. A small number managed to invest in Paris or in the suburbs, buying a house, a garden, a few plots of land, perhaps both a viable small investment and a refuge outside the city. For the great majority, it was an inaccessible dream, more so at the end than at the beginning of the century. The value of real estate in wage-earning legacies dropped by more than half, among servants by two-thirds; it was, moreover, concentrated at the top of the pyramid of modest fortunes. The better-off lost interest, preferring to be *rentiers*. All in all, it was a luxury few could dream of affording. This fact is confirmed by a comparative analysis of valuers' reports around 1710–20 and 1780–92; there were no servants or workmen in the list of property-owners, builders or house-repairers.[39] Building and property were beyond the scope of the popular classes.

37. M. Reinhard 'La Rèvolution', p. 105.
38. R. Ardellier, 'Essai d'anthropologie urbaine', pp. 118–19, just one case of expenditure at the time of death: apothecaries, 63 *livres*; surgeons, 313 *livres*; doctors 20 *livres*; twenty-five days' sick-nursing, 50 *livres*; funeral cortège, 60 *livres*; burial, 7 *livres*; insinuation of will, 30 *livres*; debts to butcher, 13 *livres*; loan during illness, 150 *livres*; cf. AN, MC, 1 583, 3 November 1780.
39. F. Changeux, '*La Maison Parisienne au XVIIIe siècle*', Mémoire de maîtrise, Paris 7, 1978. These tables are based on Series Z 1 J, 140 and 183 owners having recourse to the *juridiction parisienne des bâtiments*.

People's means, viewed according to their place in the hierarchy and their constituent parts, shed an important light on the mentality and social objectives of the popular classes. One can, at least, reach hypothetical conclusions, if only on the strength of the representative nature of the statistics in the surveys. This is why one must try to compare them with the economic and social data of the time; in other words, to talk of budgets, or more precisely of wages and resources, for it is almost impossible to arrive at the truth about incomes and daily expenses.[40] One must distinguish between servants and lower classes because the way they were paid differed considerably. Emoluments paid to servants were typical of the old wages, paid both in kind and in specie; journeymen's wages, even if they incorporated elements of the traditional model which is very difficult to evaluate, were moving steadily closer to modern forms.

It is known that a worker's wages, calculated for the whole of France and verified against regional and urban curves, remained unaffected by the general price-rise typical of the economic movement of the century; from 1726–41 until 1789 the cost of living rose by 62 per cent, average wages by 25 per cent. The worker lost out during the Enlightenment, but one cannot rest content with this bold conclusion, for we are almost entirely ignorant of the Parisian scene for the period preceding the start of this evolution, and it is difficult to make a comparison of the reigns of Louis XIV and Louis XVI. Moreover, the known data for Paris — the price of wheat at La Halle,[41] rent curves,[42] the wages of masons from 1726 to 1789[43] — do not shed much light on the overall results obtained for the whole of France by C.-E. Labrousse and his students. It must be noted that the price of wheat and its variations are representative of the cost of living, but although this may be true for the lower classes, it tends to over-simplify matters. It is also true that wages in the building industry throw some light on wages in other sectors. Around 1789, they were half-way between those of a workman in the *ateliers de Charité*, at 20 *sous* a day, and those of qualified *compagnons* at 1 *livre* 5 *sous*; during the whole

40. M. Morineau, 'Budgets populaires en France au XVIIIe s.', in *Revue d'Histoire Economique et Sociale*, 1972, pp. 204–37 and pp. 449–81, shows what can be learnt from theoretical writings, Vauban, Veran, Lavoisier, but also the difficulties involved in moving from illustrative texts to reality; R. Arnette, *Les classes inférieures*, pp. 72–82.

41. M. Baulant, 'Le Prix de grains à Paris de 1431 à 1788', in *Annales*, ESC, 1968, pp. 520–30.

42. P. Couperie and E. Le Roy Ladurie, 'Le mouvement des loyers parisiens du Moyen Age au XVIIIe siècle', in *Annales*, ESC, 1979, pp. 1010–25.

43. Y. Durand, 'Recherches sur les salaires des maçons à Paris au XVIIIe siècle', *Revue d'Histoire Economique et Sociale*, 1966, pp. 468–82; M. Baulant, 'Le salaire des ouvriers du bâtiment parisien de 1400–1726', in *Annales*, ESC, 1971, pp. 463–83.

period they rose by 40 per cent.[45] It is certain that for qualified workmen and for simple manual workers wages trailed behind the cost of living and far behind rents, which soared during the century with an average increase of 146 per cent (568 *livres* to 1,402 *livres*); the rents mentioned in inventories show an analogous increase of the order of 130 per cent. In general, then, comparing the increase in legacies with the increase in the price of wheat and rises in wages, one appreciates how difficult it was for the urban working classes to escape from their extreme poverty; nominally the increase in legacies is lower than that of rents, and translated in terms of wheat or average wages is lower still: 80 per cent or 60 per cent against 126 per cent. If one takes crises into account, the erosion of lower-class fortunes is indisputable.

In the years preceding the Revolution, economic problems and the drop in agricultural prices did not improve the situation. If wheat fell, the same was not true of wood, meat, textiles and (especially) rents, which certainly did not fall. A manual worker in Paris earned about 230 *livres* for 250 working days at the beginning of the century and 320 *livres* at the end; in the same period the proportion of his resources devoted to housing had passed from 13 per cent to 22 per cent (30 and 70 *livres* a year). The increase in housing costs partly counterbalanced the advantage of the drop in cereal prices. And finally, there remains an important unknown quantity — the level of employment. One must agree with J.-C. Perrot[45] that an increase in wages accompanied by a decrease in work is not likely to improve the situation. So if there *was* a partial respite for the Parisian *peuple* so far as wheat and wages are concerned, the progress was limited to those who had a job, and the brutal price explosion in 1788–9 served to cancel it all. The collapse of production and the resulting unemployment provoked the first outbursts of popular protest and they struck at a group with no safe reserves. The levels reached by the legacies of wage-earners on the eve of the Revolution[46] are partly explained by this decline. One would need to know the real state of the labour market in Paris to push this explanation further and to affirm that chronic under-employment followed the drop in wages, just when cyclical high costs and unemployment coincided, provoking the impoverishment of wage-earners.

However, to understand the real value of personal fortunes, one has to re-examine the significance of the legacy from the standpoint of

---

44. C.-E. Labrousse and F. Braudel, *Histoire économique et sociale*, vol. II, pp. 487–97, 665–78.

45. J.-C. Perrot, *Genèse d'une ville moderne*, vol. 2, pp. 782–97; R. Arnette, *Les classes inférieures*, pp. 79–80.

46. Ibid., pp. 82–5.

consumption. Two elements stand out: a daily level (food, lodging, fuel, upkeep), and a level of capital assets (furniture, jewellery, silver, *rentes* and so on). The inventories are informative about the second, but not about the first, except for rare clues such as debts. The composition of an estate depended on the way the relationship between these two elements developed, and it might change to some extent independent of living standards if this was dictated by conscious or unconscious social choices.[47] The composition of legacies may be interpreted in this way if one bears in mind the rise in borrowing for better food and better health, the increase in available cash and in the use of life annuities at the expense of having money tied up in more costly and unrewarding capital assets, which is indicated by the drop in the value of goods and chattels in the poorer legacies. From this point of view, the greater importance of clothing means the appearance of new consumer habits brought about, if not by fashion, then at least by the necessity of wearing something new which the ambience of Parisian life encouraged. So the inventory will provide source material for a history of consumption, a history which should be followed by a study of the feeding and medical treatment of the lower classes. Perhaps, through the relative collapse of wage-earners' legacies and the structural change they experienced, this is the only way to discover the twin aspects of a single evolution.[48]

The extremes of fortune spotlight the capacity of a few individuals to adapt and succeed. Some workmen belonging to organised guilds amassed savings which brought them close to master-craftsmen and shop-keepers, for example, Alexandre Hanotel, a journeyman shoemaker who died in 1776 with a fortune of 16,000 *livres*, or Jacques Chaudron, a mason's mate, who had more than 8,000 *livres* in 1783. But with a few exceptions the difference between fortunes did not stem from differences in profession. One must take into account the secondary activities which created a better standard of living in Parisian households. There were three main possibilities: laundering, which did not require much in the way of investment — a few wash-tubs, baskets and soap-pots; keeping a small inn or tavern, which did not need much equipment — one or two tables and benches, wine measures, a few barrels; and, finally, letting furnished rooms, which could be done with very little space or expense. To these secondary incomes might be added those of working women: 12 per cent of cases around 1700, 16 per cent around 1789, when statistics fix the women's contribution at

47. J. Baudrillard, *Pour une critique de l'économie politique du signe*, Paris, 1976, pp. 59–94.
48. As with previous cases we have relied principally upon our chief source here, which is R. Arnette, *Les classes inférieures*, pp. 83–4.

10 per cent of the men's — no doubt an under-estimate. There were two main types of activity: clothing, from making to maintenance, and small retail businesses and street trades. Nevertheless, the levels of affluence achieved by household with two incomes were still below the general average (Table 3.9).

Table 3.9. Comparative levels of affluence (*in livres*)

	1695–1715	1775–90
General average	776	1,776
Average for households with two incomes	415	1,146

Modest wages and the charges on commercial activities partly explain this fact. Additional work and supplementary activities seem to have been mostly a means of survival and not of enrichment. In the end, the family situation was the deciding factor.

During the reigns of Louis XIV and Louis XVI, single people were at an advantage, they all came into the group with over 3,000 *livres*. Widows, on the other hand, were generally extremely poor, for they were left with children to bring up. Children were a burden, but apparently less so at the beginning of the century when affluent families had more children, than at the end (Table 3.10)

Table 3.10. Size of family in relation to income

Number of children	1695–1715	1775–90
In the whole group	1.7	1.3
In families with over 1,000 *livres*	2.2	1.1
In families with under 1,000 *livres*	1.6	1.4

Families with four children and more saw a deterioration in their situation; they had on average 1,128 *livres* under Louis XIV, and 1,161 *livres* under Louis XVI, which certainly corresponds to an impoverishment when the price-rise is taken into account. This confirms the hypothesis that only bachelors and couples with small families could manage.

Examining the twenty or so estates of over 3,000 *livres*, one sees two possibilities of enrichment: savings and inheritance. Antoine Dunhan, a journeyman-printer who died in 1710 with assets worth 6,000 *livres*, was an example of the first type. Coming from Aix-en-Provence where his sister was living, he never married and must have saved *sou* by *sou*

Table 3.11. Family situation

	Wage-earners				Servants				
	1695–1715	1775–90			1695–1715		1775–90		
Couples	94	83			64		58		56[1]
Widowers/widows	3	4			15		17		30[1]
Single persons	3	100	13	100	21	100	25	100	121[1]
Average number of children	1.7	1.3			2.2		2.3		
Fortunes>1,000 *livres*	2.2	1.1	> 3,000 *livres*		2.5		1.8		
<1,000 *livres*	1.6	1.4	< 3,000 *livres*		2.0		2.4		

[1] Figures calculated by Marc Botlan, which underline the real preponderance of unmarried servants.

the Treasury bonds, the investments and the *écus* he left at his death. Etienne Poiret, a worker at the *manufacture des glaces* who left his wife and two children 8,500 *livres* in 1710 was an example of the second type: in twenty years he inherited the whole of his fortune, a house in the Faubourg Saint-Antoine and some investments from his father, his first wife (cutting out his brother-in-law), the parents of his second wife, and half the estate of his brother who died childless. It was always the family situation which made it possible or impossible to save and reach some small degree of affluence. In Paris or in Caen, 'marriage and especially the family' could, in a survival economy, compromise and destroy the delicate balance between resources and needs[49] (see Table 3.11).

The experience of the lower classes applies also to servants. The correlation between celibacy, or few children, and a higher level of affluence is clear. As with wage-earners, there has been a change of direction; at the beginning of the century it was the rich servants who had most children, at the end it was the poorest. As the rise in the cost of living hit large families more severely, the richer servants were able very quickly to adopt the contraceptive practices which were well-known to the aristocracy from the beginning of the eighteenth century. Moreover, service tended increasingly to exclude the presence of children under the master's roof: 58 per cent of servants living in had no children, but only 30 per cent of those who were living out. In short, affluence came to servants for reasons which applied to the labouring classes generally — family situation, inheritance and savings. On the last point, the possibilities of enrichment are obvious. First, servants were less likely to become marginals than the rest of the popular classes, especially upper servants and those working for the aristocracy. Secondly, their wages followed the price rises: calculated

49. J.-C. Perrot, *Genèse d'une ville moderne*, p. 791.

on about a hundred cases, the average wage for men rose by 97 per cent, for women by 33 per cent.[50] Upper and lower servants were not equally affected by the increase, which depended much more on the employers than on a hierarchy of qualifications which was essentially fluctuating. Marc Botlan, although pessimistic about the improvement in the lot of servants, confirms this fact: differences in salary depending on the employers could vary from 20 to 40 per cent. The observation was general, and it applied more to women than men; a cook might be worth his weight in gold, but a whole host of servants jostling on the ancillary labour market continued to be wretchedly paid throughout the century.[51] The most catastrophic situation was that of married women servants with children, who were obliged to live out. For others, the inherently complex nature of servants' wages determined, along with the type of job and family situation, whether or not they achieved a position of some affluence or were forced to accept mediocrity. In any case, many of the servants in the inventories were able to economise on rents, food and, no doubt, clothes. The measures taken repeatedly through the century against supplementary remuneration — tips, sale of wine or of effects and furniture — seem to prove the failure rather than the success of the attempts to combat these abuses against property.[52] Moreover, the kindness of masters, arbitrary gratuities during life and legacies after death, fostered an inequality of opportunity which cannot be measured, as it depended on personal relations which might be advanced by proximity — the chambermaid was more favoured than an ordinary woman servant, the personal valet rather than the lackey — and special functions — the butler earned more than the hall porter, the first chamber-maid more than the second lady's maid, and they had more opportunities of making additional profits. In short, favour made fortunes, and luck made favour.

Circumstances favoured servants more than the lower classes. There is no denying that being in service in Enlightenment Paris was for most poor devils a condition close to poverty, but it is clear that a minority had some chance to rise and then to become integrated into the population. Everything depended upon employment and upon consumption.[53] The effective annual income of servants in general,

50. F. Ardellier, '*Essai d'anthropologie urbaine*', pp. 17–20; translated into *setiers* of wheat, this comes to 57 per cent for men, and less than 10 per cent for women.
51. M. Botlan, 'Domesticité' pp. 60–96.
52. Ibid., pp. 66–7.
53. F. Ardellier, '*Essai d'anthropologie urbaine*', pp. 31–2; marriages and dowries should be taken into account, especially as it is possible that servants married later than the rest of the population. A contribution to the marriage of 2,500 *livres*, noted in more than a third of the contracts, puts the servant in the upper category at the time of the inventory.

taking into account advantages in kind, was no doubt higher than that of ordinary workers but, like the latter, they might in times of recession be victims of chronic under-employment, and in a crisis period face unemployment. At such time reserves would quickly be exhausted. The servant labour market would harden, and dependence on masters would increase. Adam Smith, in *The Wealth of Nations*, had clearly foreseen the problem:

> In years of scarcity, the difficulty and uncertainty of subsistence make all such people eager to return to service. But the high price of provisions, by diminishing the funds destined for the maintenance of servants, disposes masters rather to diminish than to increase the number of those they have . . . . More people want employment than can easily get it; many are willing to take it upon lower terms than ordinary, and the wages of both servants and journeymen frequently sink in dear years. Master of all sorts, therefore . . . find them more humble and dependent . . . .[54]

Finally, there is another sort of dependence and docility which makes servants' legacies a special case, and at the same time indicates the narrow passage between a subsistence and a consumer economy. Servants' emoluments and workers' wages are not exactly comparable because for the first, especially in Paris, we have to take into account needs occasioned by the service itself. The higher one rose in the hierarchy of functions, or the hierarchy of great houses, the more fundamental was the phenomenon of conspicuous over-consumption. As long as the service lasted, basic keep was provided and earnings could be invested in other things: clothes, little luxuries, personal show, jewellery, gold or silver watches, expensive embroidery, fine lace, ornate canes.[55] Needs thus created might continue to be felt in spite of crises. Pauperisation might be delayed, they might sell what was superfluous, but it could not easily be avoided by many whose wages were not enough to put something away against the threat of unemployment.[56] The only ones to escape the relentless mechanism were those with a secure job, sufficient savings, family inheritances which came in time, and few children. For the others, access to a society of mimetic needs was only a passing interlude, giving rise to the chief misunderstanding between servants and a society which dreamed

54. A. Smith, *An Enquiry into the Nature and Causes of the Wealth of Nations*, Paris, 1843, 2 vols., vol. 1, pp. 114–16, quoted by M. Botlan, 'Domesticité', p. 90.
55. M. Botlan, 'Domesticité' p. 89.
56. Ibid., pp. 226–43, makes very clear the importance of unemployment as seen in a study of servants tried at the Châtelet in Paris between 1771 and 1789: 75 per cent, with two peaks in 1771 and 1789, linked with the curve in wheat prices. He also shows that unemployment was of short duration: 42 per cent less than a month, the rest from one month to a year, with a significant threshold at six months.

of a thrifty, docile servant class and found a small nation of turbulent servants indifferent to the impossible notion of saving. The servant might sometimes be privileged among the popular classes, but not always. The moralist and observer, Piarron de Chamousset, noted these differences clearly in one of his reform projects aimed at ending the misfortunes of the city:

> There must be servants, but the great number of them is a real evil since it takes small farmers and workers away from our provinces. The absurd magnificence of liveries and the soft, idle life had by most of them attract hosts of provincials, causing them to abandon useful occupations; then licentious ways, drunkenness and debauchery in the end stifle all feeling in time; they rely on work-houses in sickness and old age. . . . I do not mean here the wise servants who, after meriting their masters' trust for many years, choose to end their days with the savings their good conduct has built up, . . . the number of such men should be increased. . . . [57]

Let us now sum up the essential facts. A study of the fortunes of the popular classes has pointed to a fundamental contrast throughout the century between small and substantial legacies, to be found in the type of things people kept. Between the two, the group of medium legacies, according to the circumstances and objects under consideration, inclines to one or the other model. The people are divided into those below 500 *livres* those and above 3,000. On the one side is the world of utilitarian values, basic necessities which are scarcely adequate, chronic debts, near-misery; a quasi-proletariat of workers and lower servants is created, the poor who cannot be happy in Paris.

> It is he who of all men works hardest, is worst fed and appears most wretched. . . . Bowed beneath the eternal weight of fatigue and labour, raising, building, forging, plunging into quarries, perched upon roofs, transporting enormous burdens, cast upon the mercy of all powerful men, and crushed like an insect as soon as he tries to raise his voice, the poor Parisian earns only by hard labour and the sweat of his brow a scant subsistence which merely prolongs his days without ensuring him a peaceful old age . . . [58]

Here Sébastien Mercier finds the right tone to depict the fate of the majority.

On the other side, capital investments, promissory notes, debts, bonds and ready cash bear witness to the creation of a modest afflu-

---

57. C.H. Piarron de Chamousset, *Oeuvres Complètes*, ed. Abbé J.B. Cotton des Houssayes, Paris, 1783, 2 vols., vol. 1, pp. 355–6.
58. L.-S. Mercier, *Le Tableau de Paris*, vol. 3, pp. 206–10.

ence. Here servants cut an exceptional figure, achieving unimaginable riches without the structure of their assets being modified. The ideal suggested is of the secure bourgeois *rentier*. Nevertheless, at the end of the century the types of inheritance underwent profound changes. For the poorest, circulating assets remained as rare as ever and the few real estate properties noted in the time of Louis XIV have disappeared. The change derives from the fall in time-honoured values — furniture, household goods, silver, tools which have either been abandoned, as with kitchen equipment and metal objects, or exchanged for others, as with pottery; but on the other hand clothes and coin grew in real and relative value. Among top fortunes, everything was maintained or enhanced; at the bottom, the disappearance of everyday objects indicates an adaptation to cyclical difficulties and at the same time a probable exchange of durable investments for consumer objects. The change in the system of borrowing no doubt worked in the same way towards a higher standard of living. All members of the Parisian popular classes were affected by a transformation which developed fully where enrichment, inheritance and personal situations made it possible, but only partially where resources were inadequate. Two-thirds of wage-earners were affected by some degree of impoverishment — and success was limited to a few sectors: misfortune did not exclude change. Servants, who participated more closely in the life of the ruling classes, but among whom women were always less fortunate than men, formed a screen between classes and diffused values and behaviour patterns from the sphere of the elite to the city of the poor. This appropriation must now be examined in order to understand a wider change in awareness and manners, a first consumer revolution which we must follow in the ordinary lives of the people.

PART II

Housing and Consumption

CHAPTER 4

Housing and Accommodation

The more disagreeable the districts and badly built the houses, the cheaper they are and the more the poorer classes are attracted to them and crowd into them. . . .

Menuret de Chambaud

The houses of the popular classes in Paris had a bad reputation: they were the home of misery. Sébastien Mercier, who depicted the Faubourg Saint-Marcel as a lair and a refuge at the limits of the known world, was amazed to discover their habitat there:

A whole family occupies a single room, with four bare walls, wretched beds without curtains, and kitchen utensils rolling around with the chamber-pots. All the furniture together is not worth twenty *écus*; and every three months the inhabitants change their hole, because they are chased out for failing to pay the rent. So they wander, dragging their miserable furniture from one shelter to another. You never see shoes in these houses; you just hear the clatter of clogs on the stairs. The children are naked and sleep tumbled together . . .[1]

In this hasty chiaroscuro sketch the fascinated observer conveys an instinctive recoil of horror. Bestiality and barbarity appear before his very eyes in the heart of a city as prestigious as Rome and Athens! The intimate life of the people is encamped in a décor devoid of culture. Yet there are accurate touches: the limited space, bare walls — cold and damp — the clutter of household objects, family promiscuity; rent too high for working-class means. Living meant finding a temporary shelter where they were unable to take root and to which they could attribute none of the familiar protective qualities which were part of the symbolic potential of bourgeois dwellings. There was no warmth in these homes of misery. They had nothing to do with the 'humble

1. L.-S. Mercier, *Le Tableau de Paris*, vol. 1, pp. 255–7.

hearth' which everyone imagined his first shelter to be: they were driven from them, thrown out into the street to search for warmth elsewhere. They had nothing in common with those Chardin homes which have too often been taken as the model of working-class dwellings, in which familiar objects construct a sense of space and by their friendly presence evoke everyday acts, a simple (but already refined) climate, conveying a certain quality of culture. The lodging depicted by the painter is as far removed from the popular habitat as it may be from aristocratic dwellings.[2]

This discovery by Sébastien Mercier is not an isolated case. In fact, the end of the eighteenth century saw the beginnings of speculation in urban housing, which indirectly raised the question of the architecture of lower-class dwellings.[3] This question was not immediately seen in its totality, in relation to the environment — as it would be in the nineteenth century — but from a biased and, as it were, negative point of view. It was simply a problem of limiting the height of houses, preventing them from expanding into the street, freezing their development on the outskirts, mainly in the faubourgs. Architects, doctors, men of science, administrators discovered the city first, and the house after; only rather furtively did they venture into the social economics of building. In pre-industrial Paris architectural forms were strictly subjected to the parcelling out of units of land. The building was defined by the unit, which considerably limited the application of architectural or sanitary norms, with the exception of aristocratic mansions whose plan required a preliminary regrouping of units.[4] Administrative decisions were directed chiefly at the whole architectural envelope, as it were, and had since the seventeenth century kept a watchful eye on alignment and the establishment of aesthetic standards for the streets.[5] All the rest was botched.

There was more rebuilding then building, in the central districts at least, and, as we have seen, it was only at the end of the century the movement accelerated, especially on the outskirts of the town. This was to change considerably the view of the Parisian house and especially the relationship of building to the environment. The dossiers of experts in the *Chambre des Bâtiments* empowered to pass judgment on plans and disputes show very clearly how the use of development land

2. G. Wildenstein, 'Le décor de la vie de Chardin d'après ses tableaux', in *Gazette des Beaux Arts*, February 1959, pp. 97–106.

3. F. Beguin, 'Savoirs de la ville et de la maison au début du XIXᵉ siècle', in *Politiques de l'habitat*, Paris, 1977, pp. 211–24.

4. F. Boudon, 'Tissu urbain et architecture: l'analyse parcellaire comme base de l'histoire architecturale', in *Annales*, ESC, 1975.

5. F. Beguin, 'Savoirs de la ville', pp. 27–2.

Table 4.1. Evolution of land development

Buildings planned	47	122
carried out	44	104
Total or partial rebuildings planned	53	42
carried out	25	8
Internal alterations	47	69
Repairs to be done	493	298
carried out	102	116

evolved.[6] Reckoned over five-year periods, operations carried out between the beginning and the end of the century look as in Table 4.1

At any time, actual building was much less important than more limited operations or the sort of work necessary to shore up a decrepit inheritance. Furthermore, the clerks of works always registered more plans than completions: what is then interesting to note is the number of work-sites started and their location. From the beginning of Louis XV's reign, building activity had left the centre of the city, and all the sites were concentrated in the new districts, on the right bank, and on the left bank towards the west; in the reign of Louis XVI the contrast was still more marked. There was hardly any building in the old parishes of the city or in the faubourgs north and south of the River Seine. Neither was there much rebuilding *in situ*, most of such operations occurring in the zones, bordering on the old city. On the other hand, repairs were going on everywhere in this part of Paris — masonry, framework, roofing, painting, woodwork, windows, flooring — but less at the end of the century than at the beginning. For the houses of the popular classes this meant two things; on the one hand the poor remained badly housed; on the other, the concept of internal space was beginning to change, and this could be seen in the nature of the repairs. Owners in the centre were profiting from the crowding together of an increased population, and speculators were investing in profitable operations on the outskirts. If old inherited property was less well maintained, it was because repairs cost more, the investment brought in a lower return, and it was possible to continue to draw a profitable rent with less outlay by dividing the original space. This is shown by the records of different types of repair (Table 4.2).

Major structural work clearly gave way to interior alterations. The basic idea was to pack people in. The new houses where apartments were bigger absorbed fewer people; in old houses repairs and alterations made it possible to crowd in more people, especially on the

6. F. Changeux, *La Maison Parisienne*, Mémoire de Maîtrise, 1978, pp. 20–30.

Table 4.2. Types of repair (%)

	1718–22	1788–92
Masonry	44.4	22.8
Framework	13.5	7.3
Roofs	12.1	8.7
Locks and ironwork	11.4	19.7
Woodwork	12.8	23.9
Plumbing	2.8	2.6
Painting	2.5	14.7

upper floors; the lower storeys were reserved for owners, middle-class master-craftsmen, shopkeepers or the principal tenants. In Paris inequality began in relation to space. About 1760 abbé Expilly reckoned the number of houses at nearly 2,400, each of which accommodated a minimum of 23 people; in 1789 there were reckoned to be more than 2,500, with a minimum of 25 to 30 people per house. As most of the houses were both very narrow, often with only two windows on the front, and shallow, and were also four or five storeys high, and as one must bear in mind that there were fewer occupants in the new apartments and in aristocratic mansions, this meant considerable overcrowding and, in less favoured districts, real slums.[7]

Doctors and authors of medical topography were clearly aware of this, since they noted the coincidence of unhealthy parishes and the poverty of their inhabitants:[8] 'The more disagreeable the districts and badly built the houses, the cheaper they are and the more the poorer classes are attracted to them and crowd into them'. Moreover, the poor wretches were exploited by owners 'who mask the defects of the houses as cheaply as possible', and relegate workers to 'neglected buildings'. In the Ile de la Cité, Audin Rouvière reckoned the density per house at more than 10 families (40–50 people).[9] Housing became one of the mainsprings of social antagonism within the city; at the beginning of the eighteenth century Doctor Lachaise admitted it freely:[10] in the upper-class *quartiers* wide, healthy, spacious streets, elegant, salubrious houses, mansions with gardens, airy, clean, dry dwellings; in the poorer districts, narrow, dirty, dark streets, humidity, open drains, gutters, mud, irregular and badly-built houses,

7. M. Reinhard, 'La Révolution', part 1, pp. 32–3.
8. V. Hanin, *Le Ville dans le discours médicale*, Mémoire de Maîtrise, 1978, pp. 143–4.
9. Audin Rouvière, *Essai sur la topographie physique et médicale*, Paris, 1792, pp. 15–16.
10. C. Lachaise, *Topographie médicale de Paris*, Paris, 1822, pp. 146–50.

damp and close-packed, dingy, tall and very crowded. This description, full of organic metaphors, marks an arrival point, for at the beginning of the eighteenth century segregation had scarcely begun; and it implies other divisions: vertical — between storeys — and horizontal — in the streets and neighbouring alleys.[11] The phenomenology of the neo-Hippocrates emphasises many basic contrasts involving the relationship between building, street, city and society. The street decided the nature of the dwelling, not vice versa, narrow streets and unhealthiness were inseparable in their thinking, which put the circulation of air at the top of the hierarchy of medical values.[12] The most fearful climatic condition was cold damp, considered to be responsible for many illnesses; warm damp inevitably suggested moisture and putrefaction. A healthy habitat therefore required healthy streets, in which the air could circulate freely, 'a vital movement of vital life'.[13] So the homes of the poor were dens of corruption, for everything opposed the free passage of air — narrowness, height, lack of openings, bad building, inadequate drains and high population density. They presented a threat to the city. Medical thinking, preoccupied with the question of the cubic capacity of air needed by patients in hospitals, prisoners in jails, sailors in ships — places notorious for crowding and a high death rate — scarcely touched on the question of the houses of the poor.[14] It skirted it, preferring to discuss the destruction of obstacles to the purifying winds in the street; the question of public amenities such as drains and fountains; a general cleaning-up of the city, cleared of its slaughter-houses, tanneries, hospitals and noxious cemeteries. It edged around the house; more effective in public space, it hesitated on the threshold of private lives; more at ease in praise of the dwellings of the rich, it picked its way cautiously into the unhealthy houses of the poor. But Lachaise did go so far as to regret the 'architecture seems always to have sacrificed everything else to appearances . . .'.[15]

As hygienists, however, these medical topographers were interested in building materials; solid, square-cut stone was infinitely preferable to the old wooden walls in ancient houses and especially to reused materials: old stone, reheated lime, old frames, decrepit laths saved from demolition. Plaster, on the other hand, won loud acclaim, for it combined three qualities: it was a means of combating humidity, if

11. Audin Rouvière, *Essai*, pp. 23–4.
12. R. Etlin, 'L'Air dans l'urbanisme des Lumières', in idem, *XVIIIᵉ siècle: Le Sain et le malsain*, 1977, pp. 123–34.
13. De Horne (D.M.), *Mémoires sur quelques objets qui intéressent plus particulièrement la salubrité de la ville de Paris*, Paris, 1788.
14. V. Hanin, *La Ville*, pp. 74–6.
15. C. Lachaise, *Topographie médicale*, pp. 128–30.

people waited long enough for it to dry out properly before moving in;
it was a protection against fire (in spite of a few alarms Paris had never
known a disaster such as the Great Fire of London); and it lent colour
and charm to the city. So plaster was rated highly according to the
symbolic values of old-style medicine: it dried and whitened, an agent
for good against the evils of damp and darkness. Parisian doctors were
moderates in their assessment of town building: houses must be
neither too high for this created an obstacle to the circulation of air,
nor too low, for this encouraged putrefying damp. Like Sébastien
Mercier, they deplored the existence of modern blocks more than five
or six storeys high which kept out the sun, forced people to live in the
dark, threatened to collapse and encouraged crowding. High rooms
and frequent apertures should prevent the accumulation of thick,
unhealthy air. Woe to the inhabitants of dark ground floors deprived
of air or sun, victims of a combination of harmful effects! The specific
pathology of districts housing the popular classes and a definition of
domestic hygiene were set in a topography of congestion. There was
already a glimmer of an idea which the nineteenth century would
develop more fully, that wretchedness arose not from poverty but
from culture, that is to say, from immorality, neglect and an inability
to shape a different environment.[16] The fundamental attitudes of the
popular classes to their habitat became one of the causes of bad health
in towns. Mercier insisted on the bestiality of suburban accommodation, like a lair or den, and this was echoed in medical topographies
that generated topoi and norms which were not applicable to the
popular classes.

For their conditions varied enormously. For one thing, the population remained very heterogeneous, with long-established Parisians
rubbing shoulders everywhere with newly-arrived migrants, different
social classes mingling in the same building, which might house solid
artisans as well as rich bourgeois, shopkeepers as well as the workers
on the upper floors. It is true that the principle 'the higher the floor,
the lower the class' applied in nearly all districts,[17] but it is important
to look more closely at how it applied, and this can be done by
examining inventories. An analysis of fortunes has revealed several
patterns of the behaviour of the popular classes which evolved differently but were in some ways comparable. These attitudes depended
largely on economic factors, but at the same time the milieu, choice of
objects and organisation of space had a wider significance, both social
and affective. All these signifiers involved a way of acting, thinking and

16. J.-M. Alliaume, 'Anatomie des discours de réforme', in *Politiques de l'habitat*, pp.
145–209.
17. J. Kaplow, *Les Noms des Rois*, pp. 120–1.

living as a family. This is why we must investigate the way people lived: first examining the function of accommodation in relation to its situation and its layout; next in the ways of using space to fulfil basic biological needs: sleep, warmth and food; finally, to rediscover every-day acts within the context of furnishing. A notary's inventory cannot always answer every one of these questions; in particular it does not throw much light on the daily relationship between space and its inhabitants in urban dwellings. It says nothing about the relation of accommodation to environment, about the distances people travelled daily; it says little about the geometry of rooms, their size, windows, age; it does not question the extension of family life outside the house; it tells us nothing about stairs, courtyard or street. In short, the finest inventory can only give what it contains, but as far as the accommo-dation of the popular classes is concerned, this is a great deal. To discover the housing conditions of the labouring classes, two sorts of evidence are particularly valuable: papers such as rent agreements, rent receipts or quarterly bills teach us the status and cost of the dwelling; and the descriptions by peripatetic notaries and assessors make it possible to build up piece by piece a concrete picture of apartments.

So far as the study of lodgings is concerned, the geography of the information is important in order to know which Paris we are talking about. For domestic service around 1700, the homes recorded belong to about fifteen parishes on the right bank, and eight on the left bank; they are generally fairly scattered, owing to the low coverage of this category in the notarial archives. However, three areas stand out: the aristocratic Marais, accounting for a third of the cases, parishes in the centre of the city, and the parish of Saint-Sulpice. In 1789, these three principal localities recur, but the faubourg Saint-Germain has gone to the top, ahead of the rich aristocratic parishes of the west, the right bank and the Marais, which has lost a little of its prestige during the century.[18] This topography of the servant class underlines the link between the position of the master's home and the servants', but there is not absolute contiguity. There were servants all over Paris, but fewer in the east and the working-class suburbs, and a great concentration in the centre and near the great houses, not only for reasons of hiring but because being near employers remained a great asset until late in life. Moreover, it must be remembered that 'the number of male servants undoubtedly proves an excellent criterion by which to evaluate the global wealth of any given district. The number of female servants is not significant'.[19]

18. D. Roche, *Recherches*, (DES, 1959), pp. 195–200.
19. M. Botlan, 'Domesticité', pp. 193–4.

The distribution of wage-earners was clearly different. At the beginning of the century the group was evenly spread between the parishes
of the Marais, the centre where the rue Saint-Denis–rue Saint-Martin
axis was well represented, the suburbs in the north and east and,
finally, the left bank, especially the eastern part of the faubourgs
Saint-Germain and Saint-Sulpice and the parish of Saint-Etienne du
Mont. On the eve of the Revolution, the number of servants in the
suburbs had increased: fifteen inventories in the parish of Saint-
Laurent and twenty-three for Sainte-Marguerite, which served the
faubourg Saint-Antoine. Overall, mention is made of every district in
Paris containing the *classes populaires* but, in spite of the uncertainties
inherent in the drafting of such surveys, the notaries' documents
indicate the beginnings of segregation and they confirm observations
of a shift of the working classes from the centre towards the outskirts,
and of the impoverishment of the *quartiers faubouriens*, especially
Saint-Marcel, about which information remains very limited. The
contrast with the map of the servant classes in Paris is striking: they
were concentrated in the rich areas, and followed the shift of the
affluent westward; the lower classes, though present in all areas, fled
from the rich western parishes and gathered in the centre and the east.
Social segregation worked in opposite directions for the two groups,
and only a map of pre-Revolutionary unemployment — if we could
draw one — might erase this opposition. In any case, a correlation
exists between the habitat of wage-earners and the geography of
poverty, as indicated by the investigations of the Assemblée Nationale
at the beginning of the Revolution in Paris.[20]

The same contrast between servants and lower classes appears when
we consider the status of accommodation. There are six possibilities:
boarding houses, free accommodation with the employer for worker
or servants, ownership, principal renting (that is, of the whole house),
renting and sub-renting — some inventories do not make a clear
distinction between the last two. Table 4.3 shows proportions for the
century.

Ninety per cent of wage-earners were tenants; servants benefited
from free accommodation provided by the master, but a considerable
number lived outside their place of work, and a small group rented a
room or apartment in addition to those allowed them by their employer. Neither group saw any change in their situation from the
beginning of the century to the end, wage-earners stayed in their
rented accommodation, servants continued to be divided between
those who lived and died in their employer's house, and those who

20. M. Reinhard, 'La Révolution', pp. 93–102.

Table 4.3. Categories of accommodation (in %)

	Wage-earners		Servants	
	1695–1715	1775–90	1695–1715	1775–90
Renting	55	47	26	24
Sub-renting	27	40	16	18
Principal renting	1	2	8	4
Ownership	4	2	1	1
Free lodging	2	7	49	53
(Double accommodation)	—	—	(12)	(16)
Boarding house	1	2	—	—

rented outside something more suited to their family life or the requirements of age, often of retirement. This is the case with Nicolas Compère, chef to a *procureur du Roi* at the Châtelet, who lived near his master's house in a room in rue de la Tournelle, continuing the service he began seventeen years before but having recently left his master's house.[21] Notarial sources give more coverage to the affluent and independent, but the picture we get from criminal archives is not necessarily more accurate, for they, conversely, are more concerned with poverty and dependence: more than 85 per cent of servants brought to trial were living in their master's house, a small minority lived outside with the help of some discreet assistance or in a situation of semi-retirement. The fact remains that the general rule for the servant population in Paris was accommodation under their employer's roof and that this might be combined with the renting of an outside apartment. There were two consequences of this particular situation: subordination had its advantages, the net wages of the servants included their accommodation; family life for married servants (although there was a high rate of celibacy among servants, marriages were not uncommon especially for men in service) meant a double life. In fact, it was quite unusual for servants to be housed under their master's roof with their wife and children. Subject to chance solutions, demographic and family behaviour may have been strongly affected. Jean-Baptiste Cary, butler, and his wife Marie, cook to the comte de Malide in the rue Saint-Roch, occupied a small room in the comte's house, but they rented another room in the same street where they joined their children after working hours.[22] So a second

21. M. Botlan, 'Domesticité', pp. 123–4, calculated on 113 cases, 86 men and 27 women for the period 1770–89.
22. AN, Min Cen, I, 590, 11 June 1782; same situation with Marie-Madeleine Amiot, a cook in rue des Tournelles, and her husband, a coachman in the rue Saint-Paul, who

lodging was often a way of creating a home for servants, but their family life must necessarily have been a divided one.

Furthermore, the term 'tenant' could cover two different situations. For the majority it meant direct renting: the rent was paid to the owner of the building. However, at the beginning and the end of the century there was a significant proportion of sub-tenants who paid their rents to a principal tenant who had taken the whole house on a lease.[23] Principal tenants were mostly shop-keepers and master-craftsmen, and the situation arose from a long-standing economic necessity, for the renting of the shop or workshop on the ground floor often entailed the renting of the whole building. The vital part played in daily life by the principal tenant — collecting rents, seeing that the house had a good name, supervising its upkeep and to some extent its social character — makes it surprising to find only wage-earners, and, to a lesser extent, servants, in houses rented as a unit by petty-bourgeois shop-keepers and artisans, and where callers and neighbours almost always belonged to the lower classes. The generally accepted principle of 'the heterogeneous character of the occupants within one house' does not always apply, whether because of local influences, or because some measure of segregation is beginning in housing, we cannot say exactly.[24]

As far as other types of accommodation are concerned, it is clear that they confirm the contrast between servants and wage-earners. There were very few owners among the wage-earners and not many more among servants, but the latter were more often principal tenants (12 against 3). The expedient of sub-letting as a means of improving a precarious existence was an impossible dream for the wage-earner; if he were poor, he lacked the ready money; if he had the money, he preferred the security of less complicated *rentes* to collecting rents. The servant, on the other hand, had a certain mobility, worldly wisdom and possibly some experience of elementary book-keeping picked up in service, which made the role of principal tenant conceivable and put him in touch with micro-speculations which could sometimes lead to resounding failure. In 1786, Jean-Marie Levasseur, butler, died a ruined man with debts of 2,400 *louis*, arising chiefly from rents he had failed to collect since 1783, the date at which he used money advanced by his second wife to take on a lease which proved too onerous. This example shows the limits within which servants

---

rented a room in the rue des Minimes in order to bring up their son, I, 608, 6 September 1786; examples taken from the beginning of the century may be found in CV, 1143, 1 July 1706.
23. R. Arnette, *Les Classes inférieures*, p. 86.
24. J. Kaplow, *Les Noms des Rois*, p. 124.

could operate in this sphere. These are mostly atypical situations in relation to the majority of tenants and lodgers. So the question of rents and their evolution is of major importance: on the one hand, they represented an increasing and burdensome part of the family budget, on the other, one of the possible paths to modest wealth on the part of servants who could always economise on accommodation expenses.[25]

Records in inventories of rents due — fifty-nine and seventy-six examples for wage-earners and twenty-four and thirty-five for servants — give an idea of average costs: 41 *livres* at the beginning of the century, 95 *livres* at the end. In fact, it cost more than 60 *livres*, paid in four quarters, at Easter, Saint-Jean, Saint-Rémy and Christmas, for two rooms in the period around 1700, and 35 *livres* for a single room. By about 1780, two rooms cost over 160 *livres* and a single at least 80. Rent increases in Paris in the eighteenth century are a well-known fact: 140 per cent reckoned on several thousand leases,[26] 130 per cent according to figures in inventories. The gap between the two calculations is less important than the increasing burden on wages, although it is not without significance, for it may correspond to the greater proportion of wage-earners to be found in the 1775–90 inventories who lived in the suburbs where rents may have been lower than in the centre; or perhaps to a decline in the quality of the accommodation.[27] Impoverished wage-earners may have moved to the older streets and houses with lower rents rather than to the new buildings and *quartiers*, or to renovated buildings, thus limiting to some small extent the effects of the rise in rents, although at the cost of poorer-quality housing. Two observations by Sébastien Mercier confirm the extent of the phenomenon: 'In the last thirty years ten thousand new houses have been built and there are more than eight thousand empty apartments. There is far more competition for small places than for the others. A hundred people will apply for a room at 50 crowns; the poor man pays proportionately more for his apartment than the rich man . . .'; and in another passage: 'In the suburbs there are three or four thousand families who do not pay their quarterly dues, and every three months they drag from one garret to another furniture which is not worth twenty-four francs in all. They move out piecemeal without paying, just leaving one of their bits of furniture in lieu . . .'.[28]

25. Two sorts of free lodging existed for wage-earners: either corresponding with the old guild custom of lodging with the master, 'à pain, pot, lit et maison'; or boarded out with a member of the family. They were not common in Paris, unlike the rest of France.
26. P. Couperie and E. Le Roy Ladurie, 'Le Mouvement des loyers parisiens de la fin du Moyen Age au XVIIIe siècle', in *Annales*, 1970, pp. 1002–23.
27. R. Arnette, *Les Classes inférieures*, pp. 88–9; M. Garden, *Lyon et les Lyonnais au XVIIIe siècle*, Paris, 1970, pp. 25–35.
28. L.-S. Mercier, *Le Tableau de Paris*, vol. 10, pp. 353–8.

Figure 4.1 Income and cost of living

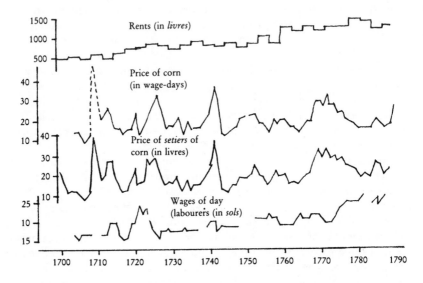

The important fact to note is that the burden of housing costs had doubled in a century and that for an increasing number of workers it became unbearable, condemning them to such expedients as moonlight flits, debts or the sacrifice of their scanty household possessions. In 1700, rent was the equivalent of 30 *setiers* of wheat, around 1780 it was more than 60 *setiers*; in the reign of Louis XIV, it represented 46 days' work, or 18 per cent of the annual wages of a labourer reckoned on 250 working days; under Louis XVI it was more than 75 days, that is 26 per cent of the same income. In short, in real or nominal values, the lower classes were paying higher prices for smaller, and no doubt poorer, places. The considerable deterioration in their living conditions,[29] was accompanied by increasing inequality (see Fig. 4.1, Income and cost of living).

The increase in the range of rents, for servants in lodgings and for the lower classes, is significant: the gap between the lowest and highest had grown (see Fig. 4.2, Breakdown of rents). At the beginning of the century 90 per cent of rents were between 20 and 60 *livres*; there were no more than 17 per cent in this range on the eve of the Revolution, and nearly 50 per cent between 60 and 100 *livres*. The increase in

29. R. Arnette, *Les Classes inférieures*, pp. 89–90; F. Ardellier, 'Essai d'anthropologie urbaine', pp. 38–40.

Figure 4.2 Breakdown of rents, (1695–1715 and 1774–91

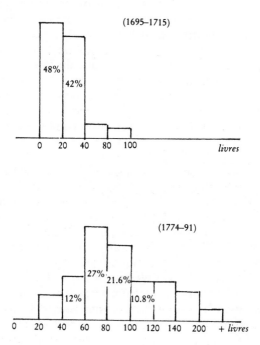

housing costs was therefore very unequally spread, whether this indicates the widening gap already noted in people's fortunes, or a change in the behaviour patterns of some people seeking comfort or privacy for their family. At his death, Jacques Louis Gay, a casual labourer, left an estate of 400 *livres* crippled with debts, but his rent for two rooms and an attic in the rue du Faubourg Saint-Denis was over 200 *livres*: he left several children. At the other extreme, Jean Chauderon, who left nearly 9,000 *livres*, was content with a modest room on Notre-Dame-des Champs costing him 36 *livres* a year: he was a bachelor.[30] The range of rents reflects an economic development more than a hierarchy of living standards, but also a change in ways of thinking and the attraction of new values. Thus servants living outside their employer's house tended to pay a higher rent than journeymen or labourers with the same means would accept. This shows that servants broke into the consumer market more rapidly, and confirms their role as intermediaries in the circulation of norms. The tendency was

30. AN. Min. Cent, XXII, 17 April 1790 and I, 28 August 1783.

perhaps limited to some extent by the excessive burden of rents in Paris compared with other cities: a silk-worker in Lyon paid less than 40 *livres* a year for accommodation; in Caen 80 per cent of *citoyens passifs* on the 1790 census paid less than 30 *livres*.[31] For the lower classes in Paris on the eve of the Revolution housing costs varied between a quarter and a tenth of wages, and the burden seems to have grown during the century, apparently without any significant change in quality, except for a minority. In the full range of rent costs in Paris — known for the Revolutionary period because of the imposition of the *contribution mobilière*[32] — wage-earners and servants were at the bottom of the scale: 85 per cent of them were laying out 40 to 50 *livres* a year on housing; only 50 per cent of all Parisians bore a comparable burden. There was not much housing available below 40 *livres* — equal to one *écu d'or*; with a few exceptions, the popular classes could not afford more than 150 *livres*. This represented a social boundary above which one can begin to talk of affluence; once the threshold of 500 *livres* rent a year was crossed, you were into the world of the rich and the ruling classes. This shows clearly the advantages enjoyed by servants living in their masters' houses. In a lifetime, the savings and micro-speculations made possible by this way of life, and the quest for other sources of income apart from wages, made up for a loss of independence which was perhaps giving rise to increasing resentment.[33] In any case, even if the question of rent is only one aspect of housing, it is a good indication of the widening differences between servants and wage-earners, between the comfortably off and the impoverished. The organisation of space will highlight other differences (see Table 4.4).

First, let us consider the vertical distribution, which began at the end of the seventeenth century and would change little with time. The popular classes lived on the upper floors, starting from the second, without any obvious increase of vertical stratification during the century. If there were slightly more servants on the *piano nobile* this was because they were sharing it with their masters, and the presence

31. M. Garden, *Lyon*, pp. 135–9; J.-C. Perrot, *Genèse d'une ville moderne*, pp. 615–16.
32. M. Reinhard, 'La Révolution', pp. 42–43. Rents ranging from:

	40–100 *livres*	10–150 *livres*
Parisian tenants (%)	33	50
Wage-earners and servants (%)	64	87

33. M. Botlan, 'Domesticité', pp. 120–3.

Table 4.4. The organisation of space

	1695–1715		1775–90	
	Wage-earners	Servants	Wage-earners	Servants
Vertical distribution (%)				
Ground-floor/mezzanine	11	12	2	20
1st floor	17	10	24	13
2nd floor	26	20	28	28
3rd floor	23	20	21	21
4th floor and above	13	17	17	9
Composite lodgings including	9	8	6	9
ground-fl./1st fl.	(8)	(5)	(6)	(4)
Outlook (%)				
On the street	56	31	40	36
On the yard (among which	33	54	52	44
those indicating garden)		(6)		(5)
Mixed	11	15	8	20
Number of rooms (%)				
1 room	57	41	63	38
2 rooms	34	26	19	40
3 rooms	6	13	8	9
More	2	1	5	5
Not stated	1	19	5	8
Distribution of rooms				
Bedrooms/rooms	106	110	119	120
Kitchens	8	12	5	11
Sitting-rooms	—	12	1	3
Annexes	4	2	5	2
Closets	3	1	—	6
Cupboards and nooks	6	3	—	2
Cabinets	4	9	12	21
Anterooms and passages	2	12	5	6
Dressing-rooms	—	—	1	2
	133	161	148	173
Cellars	5	11	3	12
Attics	5	4	6	4

of a greater number of them on the ground floor was due to a stronger representation of door-men and porters in the pre-Revolutionary census. The fact that fewer wage-earners were living at street level at that time indicates a decline in the number of workshops and shops since the time of Louis XIV. Around 1700, seven cases out of ten confirmed this arrangement, which answered an economic need: a back room behind the shop, or simply a space curtained off, served as a bedroom, and the shop was the working- and living-room. Composite vertical accommodation was very rare, but was much like this first type except that the bedroom was upstairs and bigger. The two types could sometimes be combined: Jean Martin had a corn-chandler's shop run by his wife on the ground floor, a small room at the back used as a kitchen, and a bedroom upstairs.[34]

Generally speaking, for servants and wage-earners, the archaic arrangement of accommodation on different levels, which involved a great deal of inconvenience, disappeared quite early, if only because their lodgings were so small; reduced to one or two rooms. In any case, from the beginning of the eighteenth century it was more often found among shopkeepers, artisans and middle-class proprietors, and this vertical organisation of space was finally left to them.[35] It is difficult to make sense of the other changes, but we must remember the two enquiries were taken in different areas (see Tables 4.5 and 4.6).[36] The first was based more on the centre than the faubourgs, and the opposite was true for the second. But the buildings in the faubourg Saint-Laurent and Saint-Antoine were low, and there was evidence of

34. R. Arnette, *Les Classes inférieures*; pp. 94–5, AN. Min. Cent VI, 63, 25 XI 1705.
35. P. Couperie and M. Jurgens, 'Le logement a Paris aux XVIe et XVIIe siècles, une source: les inventaires après décès', in *Annales*, ESC, 1962, pp. 488–94; J.-C Perrot, *Genèse d'une ville moderne*, pp. 787–8.
36. R. Arnette, *Les Classes inférieures*, calculates thus (in %):

	1695–1715	1775–90
For parishes in the faubourgs:		
ground and 1st floor	45	46
2nd floor	30	27
3rd floor	7	15
4th floor and upwards	15	9
For parishes in the centre:		
ground and 1st floor	29	20
2nd floor	23	29
3rd floor	29	27
4th floor	16	25

Table 4.5. Hotels and furnished rooms by *quartier*

	1757 No.	%	1765 No.	%
La Cité	12	4.0	18	3.0
St-Jacques-la-Boucherie	3	1.0	3	0.5
Ste-Opportune	3	1.0	6	1.0
Le Louvre	21	7.1	57	9.6
Palais Royal	20	6.7	57	9.6
Montmartre	6	2.0	34	5.7
St-Eustache	43	14.5	48	8.1
Les Halles	No figures available			
St-Denis	14	4.7	13	2.2
St-Martin	17	5.7	40	6.7
La Grève	4	1.3	21	3.5
St-Paul	10	3.3	26	4.4
Ste-Avoye	1	0.3	7	1.1
Le Marais	5	1.6	9	1.5
St-Antoine	1	0.3	14	2.3
Place Maubert	4	1.3	10	1.6
St-Benoist	19	6.4	31	5.2
St-André-des-Arts	59	20.0	105	17.8
Le Luxembourg	20	6.7	26	4.4
St-Germain-des-Prés	33	11.1	64	10.8
Total	295	100.0	589	100.0
Average	15		(30)	

Source: Compiled from Jèze, *Le Tableau de Paris*, 1757–65

vertical stratification in the town parishes where the higher you went, the more wage-earners you found. Vertical segregation occurred sooner there, no doubt because it answered a need to reduce the costs of rents and the higher up you lived the less rent you paid. In 1780 one first-floor room on the rue Saint-Paul cost 80 *livres*; in a nearby street an attic room could be rented for 60. While there was little change in working-class lodgings in the faubourgs through the century, in the older *quartiers* the popular classes were climbing onto the roofs! This reflects the general practice of raising the height and reorganising the storeys of houses in the central parishes.[37] Sébastien Mercier noted the phenomenon:

They have had to curb the height of houses in Paris, for several private

37. A. Chastel, 'L.'Îlot de la rue du Roule et ses abords, Paris et l'Ile-de-France', in *Bulletin et Mémoire de la Fédération des Sociétés Historiques et Archéologiques de Paris et de l'Ile-de-France*, 1965, 1966, pp. 7–110.

Table 4.6. Average rents, in *livres* per month

	1757	1765	Variation %
La Cité	18.7	11.0	−41.1
St-Jacques-la-Boucherie	20.2	8.0	−60.3
Ste-Opportune	16.8	12.0	−28.5
Le Louvre	32.3	13.0	−59.7
Palais Royal	74.7	35.0	−53.1
Montmartre	74.0	30.0	−59.4
St-Eustache	85.3	45.0	−47.2
Les Halles	No figures available		
St-Denis	25.3	26.0	+ 2.7
St-Martin	27.5	20.0	−27.2
La Grève	15.3	9.8	−35.9
St-Paul	16.0	16.5	+ 3.0
Ste-Avoye	17.2	19.5	+13.3
Le Marais	13.9	15.7	+12.9
St-Antoine	11.0	20.6	+87.2
Place Maubert	17.0	17.0	0.0
St-Benoist	15.0	15.7	+ 4.6
St-André-des-Arts	40.1	58.2	+45.1
Le Luxembourg	111.9	82.6	−26.2
St-Germain-des-Prés	143.9	106.0	−26.3

citizens had virtually built one house on top of another. The height is restricted to seventy feet, not including the roof. The poor who live up there to save money have to pay more to have wood and water brought up; the others [the bourgeois still living on the ground floor] have to light a candle at midday to eat their dinner . . . .[38]

The ascent of the popular classes living in the centre must have meant a change in their budgets, complicated the deliveries of wood and water, and to some extent changed their relationship with street, courtyards and transitional spaces such as stairs and ground-floor alleys. This movement certainly began earlier in the city than in the provinces: already by 1700, 90 per cent of accommodation in Paris was above the ground floor, compared with 25 per cent in the central parishes of Caen.[39] The way in which wage-earners and servants in Paris were living showed the cumulative effects of centuries of building which remain largely unexplored, and the picture we can only sketch here represents an average situation mid-way between real and contrasting

38. L.-S. Mercier, *Le Tableau de Paris*, vol. 10, pp. 4–5.
39. J.-C. Perrot, *Genèse d'une ville moderne*, p. 685

states which did not coincide topographically. It serves to demonstrate the limitations of accepted ideas, for vertical stratification of lower-class accommodation did exist and no doubt had done for a long time in the old *quartiers* in the centre of Paris, but it did not cross the boulevards, beyond which housing in the faubourgs was differently structured.[40]

The same applies to servants. The generally accepted view is that the eighteenth century saw the end of an ancestral way of life dominated by cohabitation with masters. But as we have seen, servants shared partly their employers' habitat, and partly that of the labouring classes. The fact is that the reality of servant life was very different from the images handed down by nostalgic observers or gleaned from architectural treatises.[41] Charles-Antoine Jombert[42] or Jean-Charles Krafft, echoing Ledoux and others, discussed servant accommodation within the content of a hierarchical concept of houses and habitat: there were as many ways of housing servants as there were types of nobles and bourgeois. At the same time, architects' notions about making new buildings more rational and practical did not benefit servants in the same way as masters. Comfort and convenience primarily concerned the latter and only indirectly the former, although there were frontier zones, like the antechamber and offices. Servants were meant above all to contribute to the well-being of their masters, and for this the *hôtel* where all these notions were possible was a better solution than a house which was less easily adapted. We can see how this reading gave a biased view of reality, since there were fewer aristocratic mansions in Paris than the bourgeois houses in which cohabitation necessarily involved either a different type of relationship, or the relegation of servants to the top floor recommended by fashionable builders: in these houses separation was inevitable. In his plans Jombert reconciled the traditional preference for servant accommodation on the spot, near their masters, with the building of quite separate accommodation in wings or attics. In Krafft's plans at the end of the century the distance was increased, menials were banished from sight and their activities relegated to shadowy zones — basements for preparing food, courtyards and annexes for coaches, attics for footmen and servants.[43] This reorganisation of space involved a complete transformation of passages, and concealed corridors and service stairs made their appearance.

40. R. Arnette, *Les Classes inférieures*, p. 96.
41. M. Botlan, 'Domesticité', pp. 97–125.
42. Ch.A. Jombert, *Architecture moderne ou l'art de bâtir pour toutes sortes de personnes*, Paris, 1764, 2 vols.
43. J.-C. Krafft, *Plans et coupes élévation des plus belles maisons et hôtels construits à Paris et dans les environs*, Paris, 1909.

Theoretically this marked the end of centuries of cohabitation. It was also the end of solidarity within the servant body, for the fragmentation of space led to an increase in specialisation and the growth of a hierarchy of ancillary functions. In the new buildings upper servants found their place near their masters and lower servants were exiled to the periphery. In princely houses veritable dormitories absorbed bachelor servants under the roofs or above the stables with the animal fodder. This cellular organisation was recognised by Mercier:[44] 'In the past all the servants were warmed at a common hearth: today the chambermaid has her fire, the tutor his, the butler his . . .'. This shows both regret for the ending of collective sociability and an acknowledgement of the individualised benefits of aristocratic affluence, therefore of the diffusion of new expectations in the lower classes. Mercier was recording an increase in anonymity and distance which made for harsher relationships, but which was seen against some golden age of master–servant relations which is not altogether proven. No doubt Laclos was nearer the truth in showing a host of servants who were indispensable to the detailed functioning of life by day or night, but who were deprived of identity or voice. Collectively they were simply *les gens*.[45]

In reality, the daily life of the bourgeoisie and the popular classes was quite different.[46] Only rich employers and their many servants lived with this sort of concrete separation. It was sought after by a certain number of servants — the more comfortably-off who had acquired greater independence *vis-à-vis* their employers or who were approaching retirement. For the majority cohabitation was still the rule, organised according to their sex and matrimonial situation. The majority of married servants enjoyed the advantage of separate accommodation, but not always the unmarried. As to female servants, for equal work they could expect inferior conditions to men. They remained in the main apartments, while the men lived upstairs or in separate quarters. Women servants and chambermaids were sometimes allowed a nook in a garret or corner, but very often they shared their mistress's room or slept in the kitchen. The valet could be sure of a small room or corner of a dressing-room, and very often his own room upstairs. Strict segregation of the sexes was fundamental. It was dictated by the division of roles — chambermaids, waiting-maids and cooks were at their mistress's beck and call at any moment of the day

44. L.-S. Mercier, *Le Tableau de Paris*, vol. 1, p. 40.
45. J. Proust, 'Les Maîtres sont les maîtres', in *Romanistische Zeitschrift für Literaturgeschichte*, Heidelberg, 1977, pp. 145–65.
46. M. Botlan, 'Domesticité', pp. 119–23; F. Ardellier, '*Essai d'anthropologie urbaine*', pp. 35–6.

— but also by lack of space, as most employers who had only one woman servant would perforce share their accommodation with her; it is significant that male servants were never housed like this in similar circumstances. In addition to this, relations within the living-space between masters and mistresses and their male and female servants were not the same, and a greater familiarity between mistress and maid combined very well with the principle of moral surveillance by the mistress of the house and the problems inevitably attached. Far from the ideal of increased segregation and special designation of private space propounded by architectural treatises, in reality there were, on the one hand, those who remained strictly dependent, more or less well housed, but certainly in their master's shadow, and on the other those who had their own apartment, with men always treated better than women, and highly specialised upper ranks treated better than unqualified lower servants. Here again, both masters and servants were distinguished by levels of affluence, and by comparison with the popular milieu in general the servant wage-earner was advantaged: he did not always have to pay rent, and if he did he was better housed, for he aspired to a higher standard of living derived from his contact with the affluent.

This contrast is apparent if we ask what was the outlook from the lodgings studied and what number and type of rooms they had. The first survey is not very conclusive (25 per cent of the cases made no mention of the outlook), but it is revealing (Table 4.4). Some lodgings with several rooms overlooked the street as well as the courtyard and gardens; these were more common among servants than wage-earners. In this case, the bedroom was in front and the kitchen at the back, leading to a polarisation of daily life — utilitarian by day and social by night, for visitors were received in the bedroom. This alternation of living-space was exceptional, and a sign of affluence. At the beginning of the century it was more common to look out on to the street; witness the number of houses with one or two bays at the front, therefore one or two windows on each floor: 67 per cent of buildings examined by official inspectors around 1720.[47] The habitat of the *classes populaires* was wide open to the street, both visually and practically,[48] allowing for ordinary curiosity and a general awareness of the lively passing show. At the end of the century the scene had been reversed and more workers' lodgings overlooked the yard, while, conversely, 36 per cent of servants now looked out onto the street.

47. P. Changeux, '*La Maison parisienne*', pp. 156–7.
48. A. Farge, *Le Bazar*, pp. 21–41.

These changes, which coincided with an increasing number of houses overlooking the outside world (51 per cent of official reports around 1780 concerned buildings with three bays or more), show a growing inequality of housing conditions. Such changes must be related to the tendency of the lower classes to live higher up, and they reveal a decline in standards and a change in attitudes and relations to the urban environment. Servants were a little better off than before and shared in the projection of private space on to public space. The number of windows, as well as balconies, went up with the price of the house. The invitation to sit at the window was now open to fewer Parisians, whose general situation was deteriorating.

In this respect, the number and type of rooms seems more significant. The total number of rooms does not change much in the two counts: in the first, 133 involved wage-earners and 161 servants, to 148 and 173 in the second. If we discount recesses and small annexes divided by wooden partitions — without forgetting their importance in the daily organisation of life — the figures drop to 144 and 134 for the first, and 124 and 134 for the second. Although servants were slightly better off, for all of them this meant scarcely more than one room per lodging. Working-class dwellings really meant living in a single room: around 1700, the number of one-room lodgings was 57 and 41 per cent; around 1780, 63 and 38 per cent. The same cross-current of development can be seen, with wage-earners occupying less and less space, and servants a little more. If we remember their double lodgings, they are seen to be still better off for space, although this was restricted to the servant elite: in the reign of Louis XIV, 60 per cent of upper servants had several rooms, in the reign of Louis XVI 55 per cent; at the beginning of the century 90 per cent of those with an estate of over 3,000 *livres* were occupying more than one room, and 77 per cent at the end. But the servant habitat also depended on the employer's means, which could have a favourable effect: 62 per cent of servants living in their master's house were allowed two rooms or more.

The degree of crowding in these lodgings is difficult to estimate, for we do not always know the exact number of servants. At the lowest calculation, among wage-earners around 1700 the average coefficient was 2.3, and it dropped to 1.9 between 1775 and 1790. If we exclude annexes from the calculation, conditions were even less imposing: 2.3 occupants per room at the beginning, 2.7 at the end. The advantage enjoyed by servants is confirmed beyond doubt by occupation rates of the order of 0.5 and 0.6. Overall, there was some improvement for a fringe of the labouring class, such as families with fewer children, bachelors, and, always, the better-off. It was not a question of an increase in the number of rooms available to all; crowding was the general rule for most of the popular classes. We must not be deceived by the terminology used in our analysis: the frequent occurrence of the word '*chambre*' simply means that for most people all the daily activities, cooking, eating, sleeping, and sometimes working, took place in a single room. It was a world of promiscuity where space was organised spontaneously, making maximum use of every nook and cranny; a noisy world with no possibility of privacy, for not only were the occupants crammed together, but the partitions were thin and failed to keep out the bustle and noise; a private world which necess-arily overflowed on to the outer, shared space of passages, landings, stairs and streets. Not only did the general verticality lead to a lack of privacy, but the relationship of living-place to environment became contingent: 'It is like a great machine, and private life is completely banished'.[49]

Any specialisation of room was, like the number of annexes, a luxury. Not more than one Parisian in ten knew what it was to have a real bedroom. Kitchens devoted solely to the preparation of food were as few at the end of the century as at the beginning, and were found only where there were legacies of over 3,000 *livres*. For everyone, domestic family life was rooted in a single living-space around one hearth. This makes the number and development of small annexes all the more interesting. They increased everywhere and at the same time changed their purpose. At the beginning of the century they were mostly dens, cubby-holes, garrets, recesses, passages used to store a hotch-potch of old junk, worn-out tools and wood, but were some-times also used as an office for stewards. In pre-Revolutionary times the terminology had changed: *cabinets, antichambres, garde-robes*; and there were twice as many in the world of domestic service as elsewhere. Often they represented another living-space, with beds and furniture. At first, annexes were not really part of the lodging; they constituted an intermediate state between interior and exterior, rather like the stairs. In the end, they had become an integral part of the living-space of the poor, in a more flexible and differentiated mode of organisation which ascribed a specific use to places, and, in an attempt to preserve some individual privacy, adjusted to the sub-division of the single room into small, juxtaposed, partitioned units. In short, the people were learning to organise their immediate environment. Rétif bears witness to it in *Ingénue Saxancourt*: 'My father brought home a young girl who seemed to me very beautiful. She called my mother sister, and I was told to call her aunt. *A bed was put up for her in the*

49. G. Bachelard, *La politique de l'espace*, Paris, 1972, pp. 42–3.

room, and I was moved into a little annexe in the attic. Next day the
bed would be tidied away and brought out again in the evening . . . .'[50]
The flexibility of the useful space available, adaptability of behaviour
to situations, a rhythm of life marked by part-removals, family solidarity towards newcomers — all this is briefly recorded in this sketch
which, however, suggests the relative affluence of a minority, who
sometimes had the use of cellars and attics to keep their lumber or their
wine. This and other indications show that we cannot reduce the
behaviour of the popular classes to a routinised existence; it was
gradually enhanced by aspirations to new values. Polyvalent space was
an archaism imposed upon them and its disappearance depended on
economic conditions and the burden of marterial constraints. The fact
remains that these new developments were more evident among servants than wage-earners, with clearer indications among the affluent
than the less well-off.

At the end of the *Ancien Régime* three main features were typical of
the accommodation used by the popular classes. First, it was expensive
and the formidable rise in rents was accompanied by stagnation, even a
decline in the quality of lodgings. Next, there was a preponderance of
single-room dwellings which increased during the century: 57 per cent
around 1700, 63 percent around 1780. As in Lyon, it was a sign of the
poor cutting back in order to economise on rent and heating.[51] More
sophisticated lodgings were less common, pertaining only to a minority. Finally, a few things nuance this confirmation of mediocre living
conditions, such as a new awareness in the organisation of family
space. For a privileged few, physical congestion, lack of privacy and
spatial polyvalence gave way to improved standards in a better organisation of space, to the hint of comfort, like a distant echo among the
Parisian popular classes of the progress known to be taking place in the
upper-class world.

However, for newcomers and for a host of temporary Parisians who
would vanish as quickly as they arrived, lodgings could be more
precarious. The social reality of *garnis*, or furnished rooms, is available
to us particularly in the police archives, since landlords were obliged to
keep a record of arrivals and departures.[52] A small number of these
documents have survived and they give us a better insight into the

50. Rétif de la Bretonne, *Ingénue Sexancourt*, Paris, Ed. 10–18, 1979, p. 41.
51. M. Garden, *Lyon*, pp. 174–5.
52. They have been preserved in part for 1693–9 (Quartier de la Grève, Commissaire
Dorival Y, 12499); 1769–73 (Quartier Saint-Eustache, Commissaire Fontaine, Y 12163);
other registers for the Revolutionary period exist in the Archives of the Prefecture of
Police; AA 174, section de la Grange Batelière. We are indebted to Madame Lanhers,
conservateur at the Archives Nationales for her invaluable suggestions; for a first essay,
cf. S. Lartigue, 'Les Populations'.

usual way of life of the floating proletariat, a way of life which was not exclusive to them, however, for other social categories used these temporary lodgings and the borderline between lodgings, inn and hotel is not always easy to trace. Moreover, this wretched temporary accommodation had a thoroughly bad name, but it was a familiar and accepted part of life, and offered a possible solution to the problems of a shifting Parisian population who were poor and rootless. For Sébastien Mercier there was no doubt: furnished rooms were repulsive, dirty, let at exorbitant prices; attics or basements, they were open to all weathers and were infected by filth and pests.[53] They were 'lairs', dens with that aura of bestiality which for the moral observer always characterised the obvious primitiveness of the *habitat populaire*. But at the same time, it was a familiar world where cheap lodgings could be found, with sprightly *soubrettes* to welcome the lonely traveller who had just arrived from his native province. In Rétif's *Les Contemporaines*, young de Billy, from Auxerre, arrives one morning by the water-coach; he asks a landlady for 'something small and cheap':

> The latter said to her niece, take the gentleman upstairs and show him our empty rooms; Julie took a light and led de Billy up a narrow, rough staircase to the sixth floor where she showed him some rooms. He chose one overlooking the street, and for six *livres* a month (the others at the back cost only four), he was sure of a lodging, bed and furniture, that is to say a table and two chairs, a mirror, water-jug, towel, basin and chamber-pot for thirty-one days. They asked him to pay a half-month in advance and to write his name in the register.[54]

This tells it all: the check on new arrivals, the necessity for new arrivals to find accommodation (as well as Parisians of longer standing, servants or workers leaving their boss or master). You could not risk being picked up by the watch for sleeping in the street; the rent for a room was not to high — 48 to 72 *livres* a year according to the view; you were provided with furniture and linen, and you were free to leave at the end of a fortnight.[55] So the world of furnished rooms had its advantages. Three questions must be asked: where were these landlords to be found? This should help to improve our knowledge of the Paris inhabited by the *classes populaires*. Who made use of them? This should give an insight into social segregation. What were these temporary lodgings like? This should give more precise information about life-styles amongst the popular classes.

53. L.-S. Mercier, *Le Tableau de Paris*, vol. 1, pp. 86–7.
54. Rétif de la Bretonne, *Les Contemporaines*, éd. Paris reprint, n.d., vol. III, *La Fille du Savetier du coin*, pp. 47–8.
55. A. Farge, *Le vol d'aliment*, pp. 162–3.

We do not know exactly the number of lodging-house keepers, or of hotel- and inn-keepers. According to the police, at the outbreak of the Revolution there were about a thousand; according to M. de Malesherbes, 90,000 people lived in furnished rooms around 1775 which, when compared with the 10,000 monthly arrivals during the Revolution, would mean a higher figure for landlords, for their accommodation was limited: nine to ten persons per landlord in 1789.[56] In fact, anyone could rent rooms and from the reign of Louis XIV to the reign of Louis XVI, the police were no doubt dealing with only a small part of the problem.[57] Nooks, attics, garrets; anything could be let without declaring it. We should note that in the registers of non-corporate professions kept by the officers of the Châtelet between 1767 and 1768, there are no more than 230 landlords and landladies;[58] and in his useful *Etats de Paris* Jèze reckons less than 600,[59] including hotels for travellers. These lodgings were all over the place, but the list drawn up by Jèze allows us to sketch a rough map of their density and cost. In both respects, two kinds of Parisian hotel can clearly be distinguished; in the west, one already stamped by tourism, where the many expensive inns were concentrated; in the east and the old central districts, the world of *garnis* and cheap working-class lodgings. In the faubourg Saint-Germain, around the Palais Royal, you find the rich travellers, English, German, Italian, or provincial gentry at the Hôtel d'York in the rue Jacob for 300 to 400 *livres* a month; at the Hôtel Impérial in the rue Dauphine, at the Hôtel de Bretagne in the rue Croix-des-Petits Champs and at the Hôtel de Chartres in the rue de Richelieu. This was the world of the Grand Tour, of business and luxury which went on until the Revolution.[60] On the other hand, in the faubourgs Saint-Laurent, Saint-Martin, Saint-Antoine, Saint-Marcel, in the old central districts, around the Grève, Les Halles, on the quais, along the ports, members of the popular class who rented furnished rooms at 4, 6, or 8 *livres* a month were concentrated. They were particularly numerous on certain main routes — the rue de la Vannerie in the Grève district (fourteen lodging houses in 1694), rue de la Mortellerse (thirteen in 1765), rue des Vieux-Augustins in Montmartre (twelve), rue du Faubourg Saint-Martin (twenty-five in 1793), rue du Faubourg-Saint-Denis (twenty-four), rue Saint-Laurent (thirteen). The Paris of cheap lodging-houses was the Paris of the popular classes, on the main axes,

56. M. Reinhard, 'La Révolution', *passim*.
57. K. Kaplow, *Les Noms des Rois*, pp. 88–9.
58. S. Lartigue, '*Les Populations*' pp. 30–48.
59. Ibid., pp. 27–46
60. M. Sacquin, 'Voyageurs anglais en France et voyageurs français en Angleterre', Thesis, École des Chartes, Paris, 1978, 3 vols., vol. 1, pp. 60–114.

Table 4.7. Social analysis: tenants of furnished rooms (%)

	Saint-Martin 1693	Saint-Eustache 1773	Grande-Batelière 1791
Artisan-shops (masters and journeymen, workers, day labourers)	21	17	57
Servants	7	22	6
Nobles (soldiers and officers)	9	36	18
Wholesalers, bourgeois *rentiers*, officers, commoners	18	11	6
Common soldiers	3	11	2
Various (including *laboureurs* only in 1693)	42	3	11
Total % (number)	100 (412)	100 (378)	100 (196)

but also in tiny back-streets and sordid alleys — the rue Pélican near Saint-Eustache — a world of trafficking, work, activity, where you could, for a few *sous*, find somewhere to sleep not too far from your work. In the more mixed districts, like Saint-Eustache in 1773, the better-built, airy streets like the rue de Grenelle and the rue de Bouloy, where private mansions stood next to blocks bringing in good rents, were the preserve of travellers and gentry, and while the popular classes could be found on arterial roads like the rue Montmartre, cul-de-sacs and alleys, streets with cook-shops and taverns took in servants and workers.[61] Geographical segregation of the popular classes living in furnished rooms functioned not only according to the *quartier* but to the street and the building (Table 4.7).

So all social levels and all professions could be found in the registers of landlords; but it was more a case of existing side by side than of mixing. Generally speaking they were provincials, 75 to 90 per cent of those registered between 1693 and 1791. The majority, 78 to 95 per cent, were men, 90 to 95 per cent of these bachelors with no family; the average age was around 30 (70 per cent under 40 of the 789 cases studied). In short, this was the mixed population of migrants looking for work or status. A close look at the activities declared by the group of workers — the sources do not enable us to distinguish master-

61. M. Botlan, 'Domesticitè' pp. 202–10.

Table 4.8. Port workers 1730–89 — 1,618 cases (as a %)

No profession stated	12
Casual labourers	26
Carters	14
Porters	5
Bargees	9
Workmen	17
Servants	1
Soldiers	3
Shopkeepers, *jurés*, artisans	11
Miscellaneous	2

craftsmen from wage-earners — reveals three dominant sectors: jobs organised within the framework of *maîtrises et jurandes* — always more than a quarter of declarations with a substantial proportion in textiles and building; small trades and day-labourers, constantly more than a third; and servants.[62] The list of all the trades constitutes a complete picture of the Parisian labour-force, from the journeyman who had just completed his tour of France, to the wretched peripatetic workers of uncertain means. It is not surprising to find many of them in police files: 54 per cent of those caught stealing food lived in rooms hired by the night or in innkeepers' rooms[63] — the interrogations reveal that the defendants were anxious to escape the suspicion of being homeless vagrants — and almost all of them were on the poverty line, although they all claimed to have work (12 per cent admit being unemployed). They peopled the cheapest, most insalubrious hovels: François Ponsart, day labourer, was paying 2 *sous* a night to his landlord in the Cour des Miracles; young Lofinot, aged $13\frac{1}{2}$, lived with his beggar father in Dame Lavallée's house, grande rue des Porcherons, for 4 *sous* a day: 37 to 40 *livres* per person per year represented the borderline of misery in housing around 1750; no doubt it was higher thirty years later. However, this is a sample strongly biased towards poverty and misfortune. Let us consider those workers thronging the ports who got into trouble with the town justices between 1730 and 1789 (Table 4.8).[64] In this crowd of petty delinquents, caught for pilfering, fights or minor fraud offences, few admitted to being unemployed, always below 20 per cent; there were many casual labourers, carters, workmen, a few watermen, and shop-

62. G. Picq, M. Pradines, C. Ungerer, *La Criminalité aux bords de l'eau*, Mémoire de Maîtrise, Paris 7, 1978, 2 vols., vol. 2, pp. 66–82; more than 3,000 cases tried in 50 years.
64. Ibid., pp. 82–3, 184–5.

Table 4.9 Distribution of port workers by accommodation, 1730–89 (as a %)

Rented accomodation	46
With an employer	18
With a relative	17
Furnished rooms	13
Homeless	6

keepers or artisans drawn to the ports by business (5 to 7 per cent), soldiers and servants on the spree. The great majority had little in the way of professional qualifications, there was a substantial element of new arrivals, there were always more than 50 per cent provincials — 70 per cent in 1789 — and they were generally young — three quarters of the delinquents were under 35 — mostly male and single. With few exceptions, this sample of the popular classes had to live somewhere, only 6 per cent of them being unable to give an address (Table 4.9). Most of them lived with a relative, an employer, a principal tenant or an owner. Less than 15 per cent were living in furnished rooms. In short, the bulk of the labour-force of Parisian trade, this host of seasonal or permanent workers on the ports and markets who carried, heaved, and trundled about the thousands of tons of foodstuffs, thousands of hectolitres of wine, thousands of cubic metres of wood essential to the daily life of the capital, were not committed to the precarious life of furnished rooms, they had some semblance of a home. Many of them shared it with members of their family: father and mother, but also brothers, sisters, parents-in-law, uncles, aunts or distant cousins. Some were taken charge of according to old guild custom, by their masters, who were mostly sellers of wood, wine, grain or fodder, or carters hiring out equipment. They were crowded in the parishes near the river, Saint-Paul, Saint-Jean-en-Grève, Saint-Germain-l'Auxerrois, the back streets of Saint Sulpice or Saint-Nicolas du Chardonnet, but many came from further afield, from the faubourg Saint-Laurent, from the parish of Saint-Médard in the faubourg Saint-Marcel, or from Sainte-Marguerite in the faubourg Saint-Antoine. This presents a familiar topography in which two components are associated: work, depending on the proximity of the river, and accommodation in the densely populated centre and further off in the cheaper housing in the faubourgs. This is the permanent geography of the popular classes traced by Richard Cobb for the closing years of the century.[65]

65. R. Cobb, *Death in Paris*, London, 1978, pp. 85–6.

To sum up the character of furnished rooms, one might simply recall the features suggested for most of the accommodation of the popular classes: they were dear for anyone who was not always sure of work; they were cramped — for most workers in such lodgings one room was already a luxury; they were congested, and people were crowded in furnished rooms as they were forced to be in the small single rooms where the labouring classes lived; it was a precarious world, and it was quite common for poor people to do a midnight flit, to the detriment of their landlord. Lack of work, inconvenience or a quarrel with the owner or the neighbours might prompt these furtive departures.[66]

But to leave it at that would be to ignore part of the reality which directly involved the way the popular classes lived. It is not at all sure that we can judge and understand their particular life-style. A feeling for the home is not a luxury reserved for those who command unlimited space and means. It may exist in a minimum of space and with very few worldly goods. There is perhaps no room so small in which people cannot shape a particular order of daily life with its own laughter and dreams. It is not at all certain that the *les gens du Peuple* wished to leave familiar places, and their customary cramped horizon of narrow, airless, sunless streets, denounced by doctors and hygienists of the soul, to abandon all the practices and strategies developed over a long period for *quartiers* where they did not feel 'at home'. In short, for the popular classes of eighteenth-century Paris, there was a relationship to space which was not ours, which modified their daily acts, influenced family life, drove the poorer people to the street, workshop or tavern; but at the same time, forced them to use their imagination in a way indispensable for the preservation of a minimal personal identity and privacy. The habitat of the popular classes in Paris speaks less of the way the die was ultimately cast for them, than of the ways in which they manipulated the rules. At the end of the *Ancien Régime* the problem of housing had become extremely pressing; it was obviously expensive, mediocre and inadequate.[67] Nevertheless, new sensibilities were appearing in *les peuples de Paris*. Dull custom and archaism, novelty and modernity were combined in their ways of organising domestic interiors, and their general life-style.

---

66. A. Farge, *Vivre dans la rue*, pp. 30–31.

67. G. Rudé, 'La Population ouvrière parisienne de 1789 à 1791', in *Annales Historiques de la Révolution française*, 1967, pp. 18–42. The author thinks that one workman out of five or six lived in furnished rooms; it is possible that the proportion was higher among small street traders and seasonal occupations. There are not enough registers of furnished rooms to allow an analysis of this point.

CHAPTER 5

Learning to be Consumers

What regulates the way men live. . . ? Health and diet? One doubts
it. . . .

La Bruyère

Through the eyes of young de Billy in *Les Contemporaines* we have seen the minimum of space and possessions available to
most of the popular classes: a small room at the top of a tall, dark
house, a bed, table, two chairs, mirror, water-jug and chamber-pot, a
towel and bedding. This was all the world of furnished lodgings
offered and one can vary the significance of this brief description by
adding a few adjectives: a lop-sided table, rickety chairs, a broken-
down bed, dubious-looking blankets, or easy chairs, a clean, comfortable bed, an elegant side-table. Any study of a domestic background is
first of all an inventory, but the final image depends on the way the
observer adjusts his distance and forces. Let an elegant blurring mask
the poverty and you have the charming, tinsel eighteenth-century,
rococo décor, and the popular classes affected by the grace of refined
living, pretty and grave in their submissive poverty; step up the
contrasts, and you have the eighteenth century of widespread poverty,
le peuple as a jostling throng of tattered wretches beginning to raise
their heads above the parapet. We must adopt a more disciplined
approach and return to the documents.

Our objective must be to draw up a repertoire of objects from the
notarial inventories and check them for significant repetitions or
flagrant gaps, in order to build up models.[1] This approach, which uses
ordinary acts and daily life seen through everyday objects, is undoubtedly the only way to escape from the tradition of picturesque descriptions which still persists. But the countless familiar things in Parisian
inventories recreate only a vast museum of words, lifeless objects
abandoned by their owners and exposed for a few moments to the
curious gaze of the valuers and people like us, of little use in recaptur-

1. S. Tardieu, *La vie domestique dans le Mâconnais rural pré-industriel*, Paris, 1964.

ing times past. So we must go further and attempt at least an approximation of the meaning of daily actions and the way objects were used. On the one hand, the groupings and combinations of objects reveal ways of living and acting through the organisation of domestic space which the popular classes both shaped and accepted.[2] Family, social and cultural behaviour patterns can be traced in the association of structures and practices. On the other hand, these constellations of objects allow us to uncover a system of distribution which determined their lives, divisions which separated the majority of those with little in reserve from those who were well off, contrasts which differentiated the open, artful group of domestic servants from the more disadvantaged, traditional and less mobile group of Parisian wage-earners. Certainly it must not be forgotten that, for all of them, the departure point one or two generations earlier was the France of the plain and the plough, fields and meadows, that flat rustic land on which everything depended, and from where the city lights could be seen flickering, remote but fascinating. And lastly, in this historicity of habits we must trace an evolution, changes whose qualitative importance may far exceed their quantitative manifestations. Minor adaptations, slow shifts and silent substitutions might gradually have shattered the weight of tradition and lead to decisive break-throughs. A basic question recurs in a different light: how could the dynamic forces of the century of the Enlightenment affect daily life?

The question may be answered in three ways: first, by the objects themselves which tell us about the popular diffusion of forms and the development of materials; secondly, by the relationship between men and objects, which may be modified by social phenomena fostered by the city where fashion and the consumer market always accelerate the forces of obsolescence; thirdly, by the structures of domestic space in which man invests in a way of life which evolves in response to the joint pressures of material changes and the diffusion of new values. By comparing the answers to these questions we will reveal a state of mind, which may be grasped first in an investigation of the primary functions of sleep, heating and eating, and then in an analysis of décor and appearances provided by a study of furniture and objects bought to provide comfort. The first procedure reveals the social style of *l'habité populaire*, in which the numbering and grouping of things show the coexistence of traditional and accepted items coming from old rural and ancestral assets, and the increasing importance of new objects which gradually altered the rationale of inherited possessions. On the other hand, when we study the elements contributing towards higher

2. R. Arnette, *Les Classes inférieures*, pp. 105–06.

standards of living we immediately adopt a perspective based upon
laws of imitation and strategies of appearance. We also accept the
possibility of the rapid diffusion of objects which the upper classes
perfected.[3] Mobility did exist for men and things in the Parisian world;
social appearances were a means of affirmation and transformation
only too obvious to contemporary observers. 'Here, one may be
oneself; a modest fortune is not subjected to malicious comment not to
the disdain of the opulent, because most people have only slender
means. . .'.[4] Mercier noted several times the levelling of manners by the
city which masked one's origins and social rank, creating the 'mélange
des individus', and a continual stimulus of contact with active minds.
Charles Peyssonnel, an academician from Marseilles turned Parisian,
observed life in the capital with a provincial eye, commenting that 'it is
fortunate that *les petits* should appropriate the luxuries that *les grands*
have renounced. Industry loses nothing thereby — it simply changes
purchaser: I even venture to believe that it gains, for *les petits* are
infinitely more numerous than *les grands*. . .'.[5] We may ignore the
remark about the renunciation by the rich, as it is well known that
antique or rustic simplicity can cost a fortune, but we may retain the
observation concerning this entry into a new world in which consumption, the driving force of economies, determines the stakes for the
success and the scale of imitations.

It has always been a well-known fact that the popular classes had to
sleep in order to keep up their strength for work, but to acknowledge
at the same time the psychological value of a night's rest is permanent
proof of the powerful *raison d'être* of the home as a refuge, a place for
sleep, an enclave of security and peace. The bed, a vital article of
furniture, becomes the symbol of the conjugal home, the last retreat of
intimacy; the only place, given the proximity and promiscuity of
family life, where one can speak of a private life. Among those
members of the popular classes who were tenants, everyone had his
bed, and they were always real beds: makeshift beds, palliasses,
trestle-beds were used only as extras in large families or for a special
occasion, to put up a visiting relative or friend. Their double beds
nearly always had a wooden frame and base. People did not sleep just
anywhere, and certainly not on the floor.[6] Between 1695 and 1715, 162
beds are recorded for servants, plus 21 provided by employers, and 176
for wage-earners: the average is 2.3 and 1.9 persons to a bed; around

3. J. Meyer, *La Vie quotidienne en France au temps de la Régence*, Paris, 1979, pp.
128–9.
4. L.-S. Mercier, *Le Tableau de Paris*, vol. 12, pp. 1–5.
5. C. Peyssonnel, *Les Numéros*, Amsterdam–Paris, 1782, 4 parts, no. 2, pp. 32–3.
6. R. Arnette, *Les Classes inférieures*, pp. 120–4.

1780, there were 110 beds for servants, plus 31, and 154 for wage-earners, which is still 1.8 and 1.9. Servants obviously had an advantage, because they could sleep in someone else's bed and sometimes have a bed with their job as well as one of their own, but the averages generally must be close to the truth: two to a bed in most cases, and at the worst two beds for three or for six. There were rare exceptions, homes where each member of the family had a bed, and not only single people. Louis Marchand, a worker at the faubourg Saint-Antoine manufactory, with a wife and two children, had two beds 4.5 feet wide, another one 3 feet (0.95 metres) wide, and an old couch;[7] he lived in two rooms and his estate did not exceed 700 *livres*. Sometimes there was incredible congestion — seven to a bed in a single room in the rue de la Mortellerie where a casual labourer, Louis Bequet, his wife and five children slept crowded into one bed.[8] That is a marginal case: there were only eleven such cases around 1700, and seven before 1789.[9] Crowding was a fact of life for some, and parents and children shared the same bed. It is rare to come across cradles or children's beds (eighteen cases, 9.5 per cent). The majority enjoyed that minimum of well-being, still associated with the basic practices of ancient civilisations in which warmth was created by bodily contact. Comfort was a matter of bodies. The bed symbolised the home and evoked for seventeenth-century authors domestic joy and harmony which won it a central place, head to the wall, facing the window, an arrangement justified by the exigencies of health, but more obviously answering a need to organise the only room around the fundamental polarities of rest and warmth. Opposite the bed was the fireplace.

The bed was important for its value as well as its function and meaning. In the estates of the poor, it represented a considerable part of the legacy: 15 per cent, which meant on average 25 per cent of the value of furniture and furnishings for the lower classes, and 39 per cent for servants. According to the levels of fortune, average values show these trends (Table 5.1).

In the reign of Louis XIV, there was a clear contrast between servants and lower classes — among the latter, poor and affluent were similarly equipped with bed and bedding. At the end of the century, the lead enjoyed by servants has not increased, which shows they had reached a point which satisfied their needs, or that their efforts were directed elsewhere. On the other hand, the gap between rich and poor

---

7. AN Min. Cent, LXXXIX 807, 23 August 1785.
8. AN Min. Cent, XXVIII, 473, 8 February 1779.
9. In 1700, four to a bed, seven cases; in 1789, three to a bed, two cases and seven to a bed, two cases; five to a bed, four cases.

Table 5.1. Value of the bed as part of a legacy (in *livres*)

		1695–1715	1775–90
Fortunes over 3,000 *livres*:	servants	179	145
	wage-earners	40	73
Fortunes below 500 *livres*:	servants	75	80
	wage-earners	33	48

wage-earners has widened: for the rich, the average price has almost doubled (+ 85 per cent), for the others it has not increased much (+ 45 per cent). In short, nocturnal comfort had been acquired by Parisian servants by the end of the seventeenth century, as long as they had secure positions, otherwise they made do with a less downy sleep in makeshift beds and couches, at the foot of their lady's bed, or in some recess. Crepuscular well-being percolated to the fortunate fringes of the popular classes, but not to the world of the wretched, some of whom were obliged to sleep as best they could on benches in the poorest of furnished rooms. This, and the practice of sleeping in dormitories, helps to explain the stupor of the wretched and the animality so often attributed to them. But within this sharply differentiated progress, the fundamental difference concerned bedding.

The appearance of beds changed in the eighteenth century. Two-thirds of the beds recorded around 1700 were couches with low or high posts, the rest were trestle beds, bedsteads or simpler couches. In the reign of Louis XVI, the latter were more numerous, together with couches with leather thonging, a certain number of beds with castors — especially among servants — and bench beds. In general, beds had become smaller, and they may have moved from a central position towards the corner of the room. This new relationship to space suggests a dual development: as regards furnishing, smaller beds helped to balance escalating costs — wood increased in price and wages rose as time went on — as regards heating, there was a change which must be examined later.

In appearance and function, the traditional bed was much more complex than a present-day one, largely because it had to protect people against cold winter nights. If servant innovators imitated the ways of the rich, it was in displaying a pronounced taste for luxury. It has been seen that the average value of the bed was 25 per cent of all the furnishings in the wage-earning group; it reached almost 40 per cent among servants. Equipment and bedding allowed for a certain well-being and taste for display, and only a few rich journeymen could fulfill this dream. Take Simon Dumont, *compagnon de rivière*:

> ... couch with low walnut posts, with base, palliasse, two mattresses, one of wool and one of *bourlanisse*, bolster and pillows of ticking filled with feathers, a white woollen blanket, counterpane of printed linen which was also linen-lined, two curtains, two covers garnishing the head and foot, and the back, canopy and surround of the said bed of green serge with a little border of green silk...

worth 150 *livres* in 1715.[10] While the poor day-labourer was spending 20 to 30 *livres* on his bed, servants and rich wage-earners would set aside more than 100 *livres* for it. For the poorest of the poor crude palliasses stuffed with straw, cheap ticking bolsters, thin, patched woollen blankets, and for the others good woollen mattresses, thick wool blankets, warm counterpanes, feather pillows. Affluence and success were manifested by imitating the ways of the rich; that is by accumulating goods and shutting themselves in. Piling on mattresses, the guarantee of cosy, sexual intimacy offered by covers and curtains; all this was already achieved by the beginning of the eighteenth century by servants, who thus enjoyed the comfort of better sleep and proclaimed that the bourgeois and aristocratic way of sleeping was the good way. In other words, the attention paid by the very rich to the second bodily cycle filtered down the social hierarchy, and in this slow migration servants were both spectators and actors, serving as models to the affluent lower classes. The ideal for all was exuberance, lavish expenditure on accessories, and a retreat to the conjugal or individual sanctum. The enclosed space of the bed shut off by its covers, where the individual was barricaded behind curtains, was available to almost all with more or less ostentatious display — two-thirds of the inventories around 1700, three-fifths around 1780. On the other hand, the protection and privacy of alcoves were rare — scarcely one-tenth — and confined to those who had rather more space. If we look at the way the popular classes chose the colours of the curtains and canopy of their beds, there can be no doubt that the patterns of sleep corresponded with a general cultural system in which necessity — the problem of warmth and crowding — was combined with symbolic values. The symbolism is old, recorded for the houses of the rich in the sixteenth and seventeenth centuries by Blaise de Vigenère and Corrozet: green predominated (60 per cent of cases), less frequently red was used (28 per cent). So people slept under the symbol of youth, gaiety and fecundity — a salute to Nature which was generally

10. AN Min. Cent, XIX, 612, 17 September 1715.

banished from the city — as well as under the sign of courage, riches and solar values. The accepted social values of colours, which had vanished from bourgeois and noble circles, persisted among the poor, no doubt as an unconscious legacy from an earlier life-style. So it is significant that Parisian servants abandoned these old symbols and rejected green serge and red blankets in favour of flowered and sprigged linens, gaudy damasks and striped silk-muslin. Later than their masters, but in advance of the provincial bourgeoisie evoked by Balzac, servants were innovators for the popular classes on the status symbols they chose from the modern range of textiles. For the rest, the old ways went on, and in the case of the very poorest they indicate the full extent of the importance accorded to sleep in the preservation of health and good digestion. The body must benefit from sleep and it was no good sleeping just anyhow; like Doctor Savot (1624), old nurses and lovable grandmothers, everyone knew that those who slept on their backs might give birth to incubuses or even risk death. It was better to sleep on the right side, at the worst the left, or on the stomach, which was better for the digestion, and perhaps too for the dreams of those who went to bed on an empty stomach.[11]

The achievement of a particular physical life-style is seen to follow a precise social trajectory. Even if sleep may be difficult in a soft bed — proverbial wisdom is not deceived by material things — none the less the quality of sleep and dreams is part of a whole range of social representations in which an investment of individual psychology is explicity revealed. But a psychoanalysis of the bed and a history of people's sleep cannot ignore the necessary priorities: at the lower levels of affluence, servants did not always aim to own a bed, they were content with those that were offered to them, but half of those who did not see fit to buy a bed owned their own bedding and fittings. Ostentation was a personal matter. Among the labouring classes, when means were lacking, there always remained, as a last resort, the primitive comfort of bodies clustered together in makeshift beds in a rough-and-ready community of family and friends.

In real and symbolic terms, the hearth stood opposite the bed. Its importance for the popular classes was equal to that of the bed, for it described the third bodily circle of common life, the sphere of warmth, the narrow zone where in the warmth of the hearth was enacted the drama of health, the contentment of eating and resting and the fight against the harsh cold. In the domestic interior the fireplace performed multiple functions — cooking, heating and lighting — and also incited

11. I am indebted to Jean Nagle for information on ways of sleeping in the Classical Age.

people to dream. The values embodied in hearth and fire made them the centre of the home. Unfortunately it is not often described in inventories for it was part of the building and we are aware of its presence and role only by the accessories attached to it. The lack of them does not prove that the deceased and his family did not keep warm, but that they did not own these things: they may have been lent by the employer. In all accommodation belonging to the popular classes in Paris there was at least one fireplace, but the relationship to the hearth is much harder to define in the case of those servants who enjoyed the extraordinary advantage of heating that was guaranteed by their master. It may be recalled that Mercier considered this a major feature in the evolution of the servant class.

What is certain is the presence of fire-irons among the popular classes; only 2.5 per cent of wage-earner inventories make no mention of them, but a good third of inventories for the servant group. More important, perhaps, is the fact that all the rooms were provided with them: 100 per cent of kitchens, which is not surprising, 98 per cent of single rooms and bedrooms, which proves how necessary they were, but only 40 per cent of secondary rooms which were less often heated; as for small annexes, they had no means of heating. For all, the fireplace was a necessity, not a luxury.

Traditional hearth equipment continued throughout the century: fire-dogs, shovels and pincers to hold back logs, poke the fire and remove cinders and ashes were general, fireguards and bellows less common;[12] other things were frankly exceptional — screens, hearth-brushes, fire-grills. All these utensils together were not worth much, 3 to 5 *livres* at least, 8 to 10 at the most; and they did not increase much in number or proportion, for the change occurred elsewhere, not as far as the accessories were concerned, but in the more general sphere.[13] The art of the humble fire calls into question the various means. What did they burn in these modest hearths?

For lack of room and money, the popular classes in Paris did not keep great stores of fuel; moreover, servants and some journeymen could draw on their employer's supplies, and more than half the inventories were drawn up in the summer when people did not care to clutter up the place in advance. When, in 10 per cent of the cases, there were stores, they were always wood; coal makes only a fleeting appearance and one cannot tell if it was charcoal (specified once) or the mineral coal sometimes used by bourgeois and aristocratic families.[14]

---

12. 30 per cent around 1700 in wage-earners' inventories, 40 per cent around 1780, 35 per cent and 45 per cent in servants' legacies.
13. R. Arnette, *Les Classes inférieures*, p. 108.
14. Coal mentioned six times in wage-earners' legacies, eight times among servants;

Compared with wood, which was to be found in all households and in every form — large faggots with four or five billets, bundles, new wood and wood floated down on the Seine, sticks or big logs — coal was still a subsidiary fuel. There were several reasons for this — problems of supply, the inconvenience, where there was no grate, of using coal in the hearth, smoke, the acrid smell, and above all the weight of stubborn prejudice against a little-known or appreciated fuel whose smoke was deemed to be harmful. In the middle of the century of Enlightenment the *Encyclopédie* still glorified wood and charcoal, proving the extent and permanence of old prejudices which thus retarded the science of combustion.[15] Wood heating, on the other hand, offered many material and symbolic advantages. It would light and burn easily, gave off no disagreeable smell or sulphorous, black smoke; you could cook on it without a grill or spit — undoubtedly a great asset for most of the popular classes. Wood was also more convenient because chimneys in Paris were technically primitive, and blew the smoke back into the rooms which were without proper ventilation; even so, it was not as dangerous as braziers, which were feared by artisans and were not to be found in their homes.[16] A smoking chimney, a leaky roof or a scolding woman, according to a seventeenth-century proverb, drive a man from his home. An entire life-style had to be adapted to cope with a technical situation; in the winter everyone had to put up with the effects of chimneys that did not draw properly. There were also disadvantages to wood as a fuel: it did not heat very well, for the poorest coal gives out twice as many calories as wood, and the old-style chimney with its straight flue was expensive and created a permanent heat loss. From the end of the seventeenth century one can see how this expense burdened the budgets of the *classes populaires*. In 1700, a cubic metre of floated wood to make their meagre fires cost eleven days' work; around 1780, the same quantity cost fifteen working days. This increase in the cost of firewood was one of the fundamental difficulties of ordinary life,[17] and one of the major preoccupations of municipal administrators. People were heating their houses more, if not better, stated M. de Gallon, *officier des*

L. Trénard (ed.), 'Le Charbon avant l'ère industrielle', *Actes du Colloque de Lille*, Paris–La Haye, 1966, pp. 53–101.

15. G. Bachelard, *Le Formation de l'esprit scientifique, contribution à une psycha-nalyse de la connaissance objective*, Paris, n.d.

16. C. Morazé, *Nouvel essai sur le feu*, Mélanges L. Fèbvre, Paris, 1953, pp. 83–95.

17. Basic source is M.H. Bourquin, *L'approvisionnement en bois de Paris, de la Régence à la Révolution*, Paris, thesis (law), 1969, pp. 146–51. Between 1726 and 1789, the national increase in the cost of wood, calculated by C.E. Labrousse, was 91 per cent; in Paris where the market was protected, new wood rose by 47 per cent, 'floated' wood of lower quality by 42 per cent.

eaux et fôrets, and supplies threatened to run short. 'What has greatly increased the consumption of wood — in 1725 — is the great number of fires today in modest homes; whereas in the past even people of distinction made only one, and received callers and worked in the communal room, now they have a number of fireplaces . . .'.[18] The lower classes were becoming sybaritic in everything, 'heating their houses more than our fathers did in the past, who, if they made fires, at least did not trouble what sort of wood it was, . . . whereas nowadays even the least little bourgeois burns only new wood, that is to say wood cut from the living tree, because the fire is brighter and gives off more heat . . .'. Wood and fire were inseparably linked in the notion of the basic elements of Mother Nature, fire was life, and a country without wood would be uninhabitable, wrote Duhamel du Monceau, with no thought of finding substitute energy for the one which soothed people's spirits and warmed the winter nights. The domestic suns of the poor depended on the physics of the elemental forest. But should wood become more costly or in short supply then the city was in an uproar. One could always advise the poor to burn the coal that the pampered rich refused.[19] One could make them try peat and especially charcoal, but the masses dug in their heels and went on consuming whole forests. The trade in wood continued to grow, flotillas jammed the ports, tottering piles of logs rose ever higher on the work-sites, timber merchants built up substantial fortunes. Around 1730, more than 400,000 loads went up in smoke in this way; around 1789 more than 800,000 (a load of wood was 2 cubic metres), in addition to charcoal — 250,000 loads according to the city administration in 1725; 765,000 loads in 1789. The rise in consumption greatly exceeded the growth of the population who were more demanding and also benefited from the solicitude of the administrators. Wood in Paris was a protected market, and its collapse was dreaded as much as a shortage of wheat. Without wood, no bread and no work; a whole civilisation was built on its forests, a whole population, poor and rich, lived with the haunting dread of a shortage of wood fuel. Stealing wood was a regular practice among the poor, as rumours arose from a fear of going without when the river was frozen or the spring thaw hampered supplies; the rumours would start in the ports and then spread through the city. During the winter of 1788/9 the people of Paris launched an onslaught upon the King's woods at Vincennes and Neuilly and pillaged them. Faced with the gangs of women and

18. M. de Gallon, *Conférences de l'ordonnance de Louis XVI sur le fait des eaux et forêts*, Paris, 1725, 2 vols., vol. 2, pp. 40–4.
19. J.-F. Morand, *Mémoire sur la nature, les effets, les propriétés et les avantages du charbon de terre*, Paris, 1770.

children laden with faggots and branches — the men were at work — the keepers preferred to decamp.[20] Like other basic necessities, fuels were a cause of riot, but these were an indication of improved consumption and a change in habits. It was a question of resisting price increases and shortages to maintain a vital minimum of warmth.

In the campaign for warmth, the people's genius for making ends meet was deployed to combat winter cold by every possible means — hot-water bottles, warming-pans, foot-warmers, small stoves, all brought in to temper the chill of a bed or slightly improve the temperature of spare rooms.[21] Above all, the people kept off draughts with tapestry hangings,[22] which covered the damp walls of 84 per cent of domestic interiors; carpets and door- or window-hangings were less common. These were signs of luxury, even among servants who were always a bit more alert and were beginning to think about interior decoration. For the popular classes, so-called Bergamo tapestry,[23] second-hand of course, took the place of the panelling of the bourgeois. It often concealed the poor quality of the walls, and there were not many journeymen or servants who did not make it a point of honour to hang a few yards of cloth upon their walls. All in all, anything might serve in the struggle to keep up the temperature, even wall-hangings.

The end of the century witnessed a distinct change in most respects. Some things remained the same: the same utensils and use of wood; fireplaces for the majority. But the Parisian fireplace became more sophisticated: instead of the vast hearth, high mantelshelf, sloping hood and wide, straight flue, the stove-makers of the Regency period began to substitute low mantels, a narrower hearth, straight hood and curving flues; 'around 1750 the fireplace was small, and people sat around instead of inside it. It consumed less fuel and, above all, gave out more heat'.[24] Inventories which listed mirrors and pier-glasses now placed on the straight mantelshelf show how general was this improvement in chimneys, no longer the preserve of the rich. Around 1700, pier-glasses appeared in 7 per cent of servant inventories, among the better-off at least, for they were expensive at 40 to 70 *livres*; there were none in wage-earners' inventories; between 1775 and 1790 notaries counted about forty in servant lodgings and about thirty among

20. D. Romagné, *Etude des délits jugés par la maîtrise des eaux et forêts de Paris a la fin de l'Ancien Régime*, Mémoire de maîtrise, Paris 7, 1975.

21. 33 per cent of wage-earner's inventories, 55 per cent of servant's inventories, 70 per cent above 3,000 *livres*.

22. Thirteen cases of carpets and nineteen of door hangings.

23. For Bergamot, read: 'Bergamot type', for most of these hangings in Paris came from textile centres in the west and from Beauvais, Picardy and Flanders.

24. J. Baudrillart, *Le Système des objets*, Paris, 1968, pp. 60–1.

journeymen. The widespread diffusion of material progress began among the Parisian popular classes long before it reached the rural world, where the old model of the high mantel would continue for a long time.

The appearance of the stove had a different importance, for it introduced new styles of behaviour and a different psychological approach to the fire. Henceforth hidden, virtually abstract, controlled and functional, it no longer played the same role in the ambience of domestic life. Stoves were unknown around 1700 among wage-earners and only four were listed for affluent servants; in 1780 there were more than thirty for both groups. Made of faience, glazed earthenware, cast-iron, more frequently tin and sheet-iron, sometimes combined with a 'cooker', with or without an oven, the stove was beginning to rival the old fireplace. Its price was modest in inventories, on average 10 to 20 *livres*. It ensured better heating, as it gave out more warmth and provided more calories for less fuel, and it could be put almost anywhere. In general, for nearly half the households of wage-earners and three-quarters of servants households, an improvement in heating had been achieved by 1789, as attested either by the presence of pier-glasses above the chimney or of a stove. It is interesting to note that this trend did not relate to levels of wealth among both groups in the same way: among ordinary workers, it was represented at all levels and legacies worth more than 3,000 *livres* do not afford more examples of this modernisation than others (48 per cent); in the house of servants, on the other hand, the improvement in comfort was limited to the rich and concentrated in four-fifths of the legacies above 3,000 *livres*. In this case affluence was linked with imitation of the upper classes; but for the majority affluence already meant a certain independence. This was the start of a new epoch for individual heating, terminating the long period when a man poking his fire 'continued his Promethean act', for he could see the moment when he had to help the wood to burn and put on extra logs at the right time.[25]

Parisian attitudes, long shaped by these daily actions repeated a thousand times over, took two centuries to change. At the end of the sixteenth century Montaigne was already singing the praises of German and Swiss stoves, and a few decades later the hymn was taken up, to the glory of philosophic meditation, by Descartes, accustomed to Dutch heating. France stubbornly continued to freeze. In 1619 the painter François Keslar launched a campaign for 'German heating', by bringing out on the French market his 'Wood-Saver', designed to give out more heat and save fuel, thanks to 'an ingenious stove which will

25. G. Bachelard, *La Flamme d'une chandelle*, Paris, 1964, pp. 54–5.

bring relief to the poor . . .'.[26] The text speaks clearly of ancient elemental values; fire had to be contained for it was essentially a subtle and evasive element; it had to be captured and controlled, seduced like a living being, fed with various materials, wood, charcoal, coal. Keslar carefully sharpened his advertising arguments on the physics of symbolic values. He proposed models suited to every purse and every use: with two levels, a grid, a boiler, an oven; of wrought iron, brick, faience; to be used in a small or a large room; with architrave and frieze, or a simple border with bourgeois decoration.[27] He attacked the fireplace: 'When I come home cold in the winter, I much prefer to warm myself at my stove than in front of an open hearth, where you are roasted in front and freezing behind'.[28] So buy German, the best of stoves, capable of providing a 'pleasant, shining heat'. This last image, deliberately deceptive for the fire was invisible, shows what the German utensil lacked: the 'Licht macht Feuer' of Novalis. France, according to the Palatine in 1701, was cold, Paris was freezing, wine turned to ice in the glasses on the King's table, but the flames shone and leapt in the chimneys. In the first quarter of the eighteenth century, when the great King had gone, a new warmth was created when the cohorts of stove-makers in Paris and Versailles experimented with the small fireplace for small apartments. The bourgeoisie and servants of the great were the first to benefit from the new mode of comfort.

After 1750, when the stove made its début, the administrators took note and installed them in their offices and guard-houses;[29] architects included them in their plans and they began to be influenced by fashion.[30] In the 1780s James Sharp offered the French his 'American stoves',[31] or grilles with a ventilator effect, based on the principles of the physicist Gaugerdans in his *Mécanique du feu* of 1709, and the basic elements of Benjamin Franklin's chimneys which circulated air from outside. Odourless and coal-burning, it 'suited the most delicate lungs'. There was a two-thirds saving of fuel, so warmth was within

26. F. Keslar, *The Wood-Saver, that is to say a new model and therefore not commonly known, an invention of certain divers artificial stoves, by the use of which one can save annually a vast amount of wood and other combustibles and nevertheless maintain the stoves at a comfortable and more salubrious heat . . .* , Oppenheim, 1619.
27. F. Keslar, *The Wood-Saver*, pp. 1, 2.
28. Ibid., pp. 8, 57–8.
29. AN.Z'H 652, an agreement passed on behalf of the office of the Hôtel de Ville for the provision and repair of cast-iron stoves to serve the Hôtel de Ville and the guard-houses, a total of 13 iron and 7 earthenware stoves in the Hôtel de Ville, and 23 in the guard-houses on the ramparts and the *quais*. 24 November 1774, installed in October by Jean-Louis Barbier, hardware merchant.
30. J.-C Perrot, *Genèse d'une ville moderne, passim.*
31. J. Sharp, *Exposé des principes et des effets des grilles à feu ventilateur*, London, n.d. (*ca* 1780).

the reach of all. 'One can rise naked from the warmest bed on the coldest morning without the slightest danger.' The old values were replaced by others — metal, friend of the human body, air-conditioning as in a hot-house — but a compromise had to be achieved, for the great advantage of the 'American Stove', soon imitated by the French manufacturers, was 'that one could see the fire, a very pleasant thing in itself which also means that the heat can emerge freely and spread around the rooms'. This combined the effect of French open fires with the freedom of movement afforded by the American, German and Dutch stoves: you no longer needed to sit close to the fireplace to be warm. All progress has its detractors, perhaps because they, compared with immediate converts, are better able to assess what is involved in the changed relationship to the elements and to things. A discontented Mercier foresaw a joyless future without flames in a city less well armed against the cold, where smoke rose feebly from the chimneys and the people grew soft. 'The sight of a stove kills my imagination and makes me sad and melancholy; I prefer the sharpest cold to this tepid, dull, invisible heat . . . .'[32] So the skills of stove-makers offered a revolution in comfort which represented symbolic change for all, a transformation in an intimate sense. Lacking the poet's prejudices, the popular classes greeted the new utensils and new ways with enthusiasm, perhaps because they had less opportunity to dream by the flames of the hearth, but especially because they could economise on their heating costs, and did not have to light the fire so often to prepare food and heat the room. But in the evenings they often went to each others' houses to spread the cost, and they poked the logs cautiously when they were cooking. In the sky above Paris, one could distinguish *les foyers populaires* by the wispy, frugal smoke[33] which rose up from the fires of the rich, tended night and day by the poor, with their thick, oily fumes.

Linked with the hearth, the preparation of meals and the meals themselves can be traced through the precise group of objects whose function is indicated in the old saying: to live by pot and fire. These objects were missing from inventories — only 6 per cent of wage-earners, mostly bachelors or journeymen, ate at their master's table, and 30 per cent of servants, who dined and supped in the kitchen and butler's room. So far as household goods are concerned, kitchen utensils, of little value if taken separately, made up an important part, but one which declined as the century went on. What was the significance of this fall in value? Two things: either an old life-style was

32. L.-S. Mercier, *Le Tableau de Paris*, vol. 10, pp. 303–11.

Table 5.2. Value of cooking utensils as part of a legacy

1695–1715			1775–90	
Wage-earners	Servants		Wage-earners	Servants
481 *livres*	2,000 *livres*	average	271 *livres*	1,015 *livres*
20	5	% of legacy	7	2

losing its hold, or changes relating to form and the materials used were being introduced. In the first case we should see a perceptible diminution in the number of these objects, in the second the appearance of new materials and products.

The drop in the average value of cooking utensils is spectacular (Table 5.2). Servants living in their own homes accumulated five times as many kitchen utensils as wage-earners, but the average investment fell at all levels, among both the affluent and the poor. So the size of the change suggests the disappearance of many items, but it is not easy to assess this, as notaries rarely detailed pottery or metal utensils, which were valued in lots. Let us, therefore, look at the most important copper or iron items which were expensive enough to be valued, and sufficiently varied to discourage the practice of weighing them all together as they did with pewter ('in pots, dishes and places, 40 lbs of sound pewter') (Table 5.3).

Servants always owned fewer items, a fact explicable by their profession, but in absolute value they could devote more money to more expensive objects. The fall in value was general, which meant people were economising on certain objects which could only be made of metal, such as sieves and skimmers; as far as other items were concerned, new materials may have appeared on the market. At the beginnning of the century an average of ten metal utensils were inventoried per household, at the end only six. In the reign of Louis XIV, table and kitchen utensils were divided between iron, copper and pewter: iron for trivets, chimney-hooks, grills, frying-pans, copper for saucepans and cauldrons, pewter for tableware;[34] in value, copper and pewter objects represented nine-tenths of the whole in wage-earning homes, two thirds among servants. In the reign of Louis XVI, iron and cast-iron maintained their lead at 95 per cent; copper dropped from 98 to 63 per cent; pewter from 98 to 61 per cent. Pottery objects appeared

33. Ibid., vol. 10, p. 311; C. Peyssonnel, *Les Numéros*, part II, pp. 35–6 (our corner stoves and Franklin chimneys).
34. A frequency approaching 98 per cent for the three metals.

Table 5.3. Availability of kitchen utensils (% owned)

	1695–1715		1775–90	
	Wage-earners	Servants	Wage-earners	Servants
Frying pan	69	60	59	30
Saucepan	73	50	32	25
Stewpans and cauldrons	86	50	54	60
Skimmer	69	55	47	37
Sieve	40	20	20	15
Chimney-hooks	79	60	60	2
Trivet	20	15	62	40
Average no. of metal objects	10		6	
Cast-iron*	98	98	98	98
Pewter	98	97	61	60
Copper	99	96	63	55

* expressed in terms of the number of times items were mentioned.

in almost 100 per cent of cases. Stoneware, glass faience and earthenware replaced pewter for ordinary dishes. In other words, the drop in value corresponded less to an overall fall in the number of items than the appearance of new products such as trivets, portable earthenware ovens — 40 per cent of domestic interiors possessed one of these new cooking devices — and especially to the appearance of cheap products, particularly pottery.[35]

In this respect too, servants had established a lead which dated from the beginning of the century and which they were able to maintain. They had more earthenware dishes, which gradually developed into real dinner services with soup tureen, plates, dishes, salad bowls, fruit bowls, sauce boats, water jugs, butter dishes, salt cellars and mustard pots. Around 1775–90 these were to be found in more than half the estates, faience and porcelain making up more than half the legacy in value. This indicates a new approach to eating. Among the popular classes no doubt these signs were part of an economic adaptation. Copper and pewter objects were worth more before the Revolution, for the price of common metals had been rising steadily. Around 1700 common pewter was worth 9 to 12 *sous* per lb., and superior pewter, mixed with lead, between 12 and 15 *sous*: around 1780 its value had risen by 75 to 80 per cent. Except for cutlery and small items, the lower

35. F. Ardellier, 'Essai d'anthropologie urbaine', pp. 51–4; R. Arnette, *Les Classes inférieures*, pp. 113–15.

classes no longer owned pewter vessels. These had been replaced by stoneware, glazed earthenware, faience and pottery, that is, by all the products of the ceramics industry which were cheaper in comparison. So the inventories clearly registered the outcome of a chain of effects which involved production and consumption, the attempts of manufacturers and merchants to develop cheaper, mass-produced ranges of goods, the researches of chemists and technicians to lower costs and improve quality, and the support of consumers for new products which had a more rapid turnover because they were more fragile.[36] In short, more things were broken in homes at the end of the eighteenth century. The loyalty shown to things handed down from generation to generation would disappear, a new obsolescence of the objects of daily life would involve another change of sensibility.

The omnipresent common ceramics — glazed earthenware for the poor, brown and white faience for the well-to-do, promoted by servants who from the time of Louis XIV had acquired a taste for the finer and more decorative pieces — appeared in toiletry items, kitchen utensils, water jars, foot-warmers, pipes, ink-wells and flower-pots. In 1789 they represented nearly 10 per cent of the total production of the skilled trades in Paris, employing a labour-force of 40,000 people, and more than 200 important business concerns. The interest of the Parisian market did not escape the entrepreneurs of Beauvais and Rouen, and encouraged the initiatives of the well-established corporation of potters who exploited the few quarries in the town and suburbs from Gentilly to Vaugirard.[37] Business flourished for faience merchants who held the rights for the sale of faience and glass-ware and who shared the monopoly on exotic, imported porcelain with mercers.[38] Hawkers and pedlars supplied the lower-class clientele at fairs and markets, and the potters from Beauvais opened up in the capital to improve their takings. Fireproof brown ware, sold by the piece and by the dozen, found working-class outlets: 7 *livres* per thousand compared with 80 *livres* for white ware. It even partly supplanted glazed ware, which hygienists considered dangerous and which was more expensive and often heavier. Fashions moved down the social scale, and in the homes of the popular classes there was occasionally a fleeting touch of anglophilia, a 'little Wedgwood pot', or an 'English-style tea service'. The change would accelerate after the Revolution.[39] In the range of cooking utensils, metal also gave way to earthenware. This accelera-

---

36. F. Espagnet, 'La céramique commune en France de la fin du XVIIIe siècle', Thesis, 3rd cycle, Paris–I, 1978, pp. 15–16, 52–5, 169.
37. Ibid., pp. 24–5, 53–4.
38. Ibid., pp. 177–80, 188–90.
39. Ibid., pp. 213–38, 258–60.

tion in consumption coincided with the breakdown of the traditional way of organising space for cooking and meals.

Domestic interiors at the end of the seventeenth century were still dominated by tradition, perhaps rural in origin but certainly familiar to the sons of peasants who made up the population of Paris. Several functions — heating, cooking, lighting — and several categories of object — kitchen utensils, crockery, cutlery — were concentrated around the hearth. Cooking was done over the fire, with the help of a chimney-hook, or less frequently a trivet. The housewife was accustomed to bend and crouch as she carried out a thousand daily tasks. The main thing was that everything should be concentrated near the fire, on the ground, on the mantelpiece, or hanging from, and placed on, shelves.[40] This arrangement, with its symbolic value, was fundamental to the system of domestic organisation; the flickering firelight, warm colour of copper, shining polish of wooden utensils, dull sheen of pewter, all bespoke a concrete scheme of values.[41] But around 1780 everything was reorganised. Chimney-hooks became less common, and almost disappeared from servant homes, always in the van of change; secondary sources of heat; small stoves, fireproof brick ovens, and new cooking devices such as grills, spits, dripping-pans and boilers became more common. Tinned-iron ovens and cookers were the preserve of the well-to-do; seventeen instances among servants, and less than a dozen among wage-earners. Utensils and ovens were still near the hearth, but crockery was kept in sideboards and dressers. When the lodging included a kitchen, the separation was still more radical.[42] The old multi-functional hearth with its symbolic complexity had begun its progressive retreat and people were beginning to cook standing up.

For cooking utensils and crockery generally, permanency outweighed novelty, except for the invasion of pottery items. But the important thing to note was the appearance of more and more objects with a specific purpose, first saucepans, then basins, sugar-bowls and egg-cups. Servants accumulated more of these items. Moreover, there is evidence of the use of *boissons excitantes* in many homes. The more

---

40. Typical example from the beginning of the century: 'One chimney-hook, one grill, one dripping-pan, two small iron frying-pans, one strainer, one skimmer, 4 medium cauldrons and 2 small saucepans of yellow copper, 2 saucepans and one apple roaster of red copper, and in a small cupboard 40 *livres* of quality pewter and 10 *livres* of common pewter', AN. Min. Cent., 466, 17 December 1710.

41. R. Arnette, *Les Classes inférieures*, p. 116; J. Baudrillart, *Le Système*, p. 61.

42. In the house of P.J. Forthomme, journeyman-shoemaker, 'In a *kitchen* overlooking the yard, one chimney hook, one tripod, one grill, diverse kitchen utensils, frying pans, saucepans, 20 pieces of glassware and pottery in different household utensils; in the *bedroom*, 6 dishes, two dozen plates, and 15 pieces of pottery in an old pine dresser . . .', AN. Min. Cent. 466, 9 December 1777.

affluent of the popular classes made their coffee at home, some servants took tea, all were setting the tone. But these advances were matched by a decline in silverware and in utensils for grilling meat. The first no doubt indicates a change — which needs to be verified — in eating habits: fries and fricassees, bouillon and boiled beef tended to replace roasts. Perhaps it suggests a change from infrequent to more frequent meat-eating, as 80 per cent of the inventories testify, but of lower-quality meats. Silver — cups, goblets, dishes, for personal use or for special occasions — became less common, but continued to make an appearance among the more affluent.[43] A shift towards different objects, and the pointlessness of collecting valuables, may explain this decline.

From all these changes three conclusions may be drawn. Non-essentials were appearing among the more well-to-do, especially servants; where basic necessities and ordinary equipment were concerned, the economic hierarchy was only a secondary factor. In the material sphere there was a slide from good-looking, solid, expensive things to ordinary, cheap, breakable materials: the loss of real value coincided with a change in attitudes. Finally, objects were being organised differently, old structures were gradually breaking down, places and things took on a specific, instead of a multi-functional, use. The popular classes had taken a first step towards a more ephemeral consumerism where needs changed more rapidly. The table-manners of the rich — changing plates after the soup, using bowls for soup, a table-knife instead of a pocket-knife, a fork instead of fingers — had moved a long way socially since the seventeenth century.[44] A glance at other domestic objects will enable us to appreciate other variations (Table 5.4).

Furniture contributed in its way to the unification of domestic space. It was to be found in every home, cluttering up the space in some, but nevertheless falling far short in amount and value of the furniture accumulated by the upper classes. The impression of over-crowding was due to the little space really available, perhaps also to choices which caused people to cling to worn-out, even dilapidated objects from a primitive attachment to the family heritage or affective hoarding. Unfortunately, an inventory can provide only a 'snapshot' of acquisition in a state of equilibrium, without telling us their story. Moreover, the lexicon of the furniture follows the logic of the notary, not of the user or of the real plan of the home; with a few exceptions,

---

43. 27 per cent between 1695 and 1715 among servants, 36 per cent at the end, average value 90 *livres* and 80 *livres*, 17 and 21 per cent among wage-earners.
44. N. Elias, *La Civilisation des Moeurs*, Paris, 1973.

Table 5.4. Availability of furniture (%)

	1691–1715		1775–1790	
	Wage-earners	Servants	Wage-earners	Servants
Storage				
Wardrobes	75	85	67	78
Chests	62	75	18	73
Sideboards	5	12	37	11
Sideboard-cupboards	—	4	16	24
Dresser	9	5	17	6
Chest of drawers	—	7	57	53
Bin	26	19	1	3
Group furnishings				
Tables	91	80	77	75
Chairs	96	80	89	75
Benches	5	5	1	2
Forms	1	5	1	2
Armchairs	59	25	57	33
Furnishings for show				
Chest of drawers	—	7	57	53
Secretaries and bureaux	1	14	6	11
Bookshelves	—	1	4	13
Cabinet	—	14	—	23
Bergère	—	1	—	11
Writing table	—	—	14	23
Chiffonnier	—	1	—	11
Console table	—	—	—	4
Coat stand	—	—	—	10
Card table	—	3	4	10
Coffee table	—	—	—	10
Sofa	—	—	—	2

we do not know where the furniture was placed or how it was arranged. So it is the function which suggests the grouping, and not the reverse. More clearly even than bedding and kitchen goods, furniture also betrays the desire to imitate and is an affirmation of success. A fine piece of cabinet-work in an otherwise undistinguished collection marks a certain choice which could dictate the harmony and relationship between the functions of furniture — arrangement, sociability and display.

No wage-earner's estate was entirely without items of furniture, but 15 per cent and 22 per cent of servant legacies were; these percentages being related both to the two kinds of servant lodgings and to rank in the servant world. The menials who slept in dormitories and corners had few belongings to store away and very little furniture to put them in. Three trends show up quite clearly. The key piece of furniture was the wardrobe, which was found in all homes at the beginning of the century, but less frequently at the end because other possibilities were available. With or without a cornice, they were massive and, in the restricted space available to the popular classes, had a monumental, imposing appearance which symbolised success for the affluent and, for all, a profusion of linen and clothes hidden away. Oak and walnut for those with estates over 3,000 *livres*, whitewood and modest pine for the poor. It was an expensive piece of furniture — around 1780 a fine walnut wardrobe cost between 15 and 30 *livres* — whose propriety could suggest a particular sense of luxury or secrecy. Inside it you might find a host of little storage devices — tiny chests, lilliputian boxes, secret cases in which papers were stored away or perhaps '*la croix de ma mère*', caskets with complicated locks which would be opened before the watchful eye of the family and witnesses or, more prosaically, frails, bags, baskets and little kegs. By its majestic size, the family wardrobe stressed possession and fecundity and at the same time it hid countless tiny possessions from the eye. As soon as you cross the 3,000 *livres* threshold, you find several wardrobes, often corresponding with the separation of conjugal goods. Each had his or her own wardrobe.

The second tendency was to find wardrobe and chest together, a survival from an old system of storage which continued well into the nineteenth century among the peasantry. Its presence in Paris testifies to the links maintained with the country: leather-bound, with a solid lock, it was the quintessential mobile piece of furniture. With a chest one could just throw things in without bothering about neat arrangement. It was not exactly an archaism; it bore witness to a different geometry of storage. Associated with mobility, it was the furniture of affluent wanderers, of servants who supplemented it with trunks and cases, of bachelors, widowers, lonely old servants or elderly journeymen lodging with their masters. Its use was not dictated by lack of means but by a particular situation. It could sum up the whole social experience of a poor wretch, deposited with neighbours or friends, it was, after his death, the only possession which recalled his life. Instability and movement favoured the chest, stability and permanence represented the virtues of the wardrobe. The Parisian popular classes hesitated between the two approaches, and finally the wardrobe carried the day, except with servants.

One last point: this chopping and changing was accompanied by a parallel decline in the system of storage once used by the peasantry —

the bins and containers which were no longer associated with food in the urban world. People no longer ground their flour or stored grain or bread. A Parisian rarely bought bread for the week, but rather for a few days, and mostly just for the day: the appearance of the 'baguette pas trop cuite' can be dated quite precisely from the years 1775–80.[45] For these meagre food supplies people in lodgings used sideboards; for household utensils, shelves and dressers; but those were already beginning to suggest affluence. If we take bins and chests together, they represented three-quarters of the storage space used at the beginning of the century; around 1780, just over one-twentieth. Storage space had been functionalised in the sense of a more orderly classification of the things accumulated. And it was by now accumulation which made the man in Paris.

Furniture required for social intercourse among family and friends did not change much. Old accessories like benches and forms gave way to the combination of table and chairs, which were only missing among servants who had lodgings with their masters, and who sometimes replaced them with collapsible arrangements like planks and trestles which were found in recesses. Ways of sitting or receiving guests among the popular classes evolved by changes in shapes and an increase in comfort. Simple tables predominated at the time of the Sun King for two purposes: first, for meals — the family gathered round them on benches and chairs; secondly, for storage. This can clearly be seen in a Lebrun drawing engraved by Duflot:[46] the father is sitting on a stool with his back to the high chimney whose mantelshelf holds vases and pots. One child sits in meditation, another little one stands praying, but with his eye fixed on the soup-tureen, while the mother stands spoon-feeding her last-born. The accent is religious and old-fashioned; the family eat from the same dish, each with his own spoon, by the light of the fire and an oil-lamp hanging in their midst. The popular-class Parisian family, grave, a touch austere, thanks God for providing their daily bread; table and seats serve as a family reunion for the sanctified meal. At the same time, another use was possible: tables with drawers could accommodate many items such as cutlery, odd pieces of paper, small items of linen. In the pre-Revolutionary years these rather massive tables, generally made of good wood, became less common, numbering only four instead of thirty among wage-earners, and nine instead of twenty-seven among servants. They were replaced by light tables, quite often round, with a specific

45. S. Kaplan, *Bread, Politics, and Political Economy in the Reign of Louis XV*, The Hague, 1976, 2 vols., vol. 1, pp. 347–89.
46. *Le Bénédicité.*

purpose: bedside tables, tables for cards, writing, coffee, eating. The total number of tables had not really changed, but its role in gathering the family together seemed to have diminished, rivalled by other lighter pieces of furniture which were more functional in designation if not in use. A different structure of family space is suggested here, but its development was strictly limited among the popular classes by the size of the home and the cost of rent. A one-room lodging would allow the functional furnishings already apparent in the homes of the ruling classes only in a modified form. The same basic trend seems to have disposed of the chairs, at first always gathered round the table except for an armchair and a few stools scattered in the other rooms or placed in corners: the ration was three chairs to one armchair. This was the furniture prepared for use at a meal or for spending an evening by the fire or perhaps just with elbows on the table. In the reign of Louis XVI the number of chairs fell and they were of poorer quality: the white-wood chair with a cane seat appeared three times as often as the walnut chair with a modest tapestry cover. This suggests a drop in the living standards of some people, the furniture echoing what has already been noted in costs and restricted space. Less welcoming homes may have helped to fragment family life for a certain number of people, and to encourage an explosion of activity in the public sphere.[47] On the other hand, for the more affluent everything was improving and progressing, starting with rich servants, who enjoyed *bergère* chairs and armchairs covered with Utrecht velvet and Bruges satin. This development of a wider range of furniture designed for comfort and display showed the importance of imitation, as well as access to models preferred by artisans, who were masters of their art and skills, but which were made inaccessible to the working majority by an economic barrier.

This barrier was crossed with the acquisition of display furniture by a successful minority: one-twentieth of examples around 1700, less than one-quarter around 1780. Some pieces of rich man's furniture would sometimes move upstairs to popular-class lodgings: a chest of drawers, cabinet, console table, chiffonnier, secretaire and bureau or a few articles worthy of a more imposing drawing-room. Very few of these advantages reached the lower classes, while servants stuck more closely to aristocratic ways: only those who made their fortune bene-fited from an advance which even today symbolises for many the refinement of the age and the triumph of the minor arts. A pale reflection of aristocratic show touched the popular classes by a slow, secret process of circulation which accelerated only for certain goods which were particularly useful or prestigious. The chest of drawers

47. A. Farge, *Vivre dans la rue*, pp. 40–1.

was one example, an ambiguous item, expensive (it cost 20, 30, 40 *livres*, sometimes more); it combined the stacked-up storage of chests in its rows of drawers with the organisation possible in a wardrobe with shelves, and offered increased storage capacity, a considerable advantage in a population short of space. It was not necessarily a rich man's whim for it could appear anywhere. Beside national woods like oak and walnut used in three-quarters of the models, one would find exotic woods like rosewood and palissandre, or Brazilian rosewood, and elaborate workmanship in which veneering was making a breakthrough. In short, by virtue of its cost, ornaments, different woods and bronze fittings, it was a prestige piece for a few affluent people, but its lighter style and its capacity to store a lot in a small space made it also a consumer item and a fashionable piece of furniture. Generally speaking, the furniture of the popular classes demonstrates the reorganisation of domestic space, the triumph of orderly storage in wardrobes and chests of drawers over stacking and hanging on hooks, and the shift of products that were dreamed up for the upper classes towards the homes of *le peuple*. Of course, their décor had none of the Regency charm, Louis XV refinement or the theatricalism of the neo-classical age, but it was influenced in its turn by an organising tendency under the sign of a consumer market concerned with show.

The valuers did not allow a broken old mirror or worn, moth-eaten tapestry to escape their notice, and this indicates the social and utilitarian investment involved. Their value was insignificant,[48] even among servants, and even then we are talking about the better-off. Concern for the appearance of the house was a luxury confined to a few lucky journeymen and servants. The only remote illusion of elite display to which they might be said to aspire involved two areas: the various types of wall decoration, and items connected with basic hygiene, whose real importance is obvious if we remember the confined space of their lodgings. The peripheral items in the room — tapestries, door and window hangings, wallpaper and mirrors determined the colour scheme and define the ambience of homes (Table 5.5).

Among servants a taste for comfort appeared very early, and with it more and more decorative novelties: fixed hangings and wallpapers replaced the old tapestries. In their own lodgings they copied the practices of their masters: tapestries ranked among a man's own

---

48. Among wage-earners: 12 *livres* around 1700, 25 *livres* around 1780, that is, one-tenth of the household goods; among servants there is a drop from 600 *livres* to 400 *livres*, which underlines the decorative role played by display furniture. Almost all the inventories in question are for estates of from 1,000 to 2,000 *livres*, except for a few items found very generally; see Table 5.5.

Table 5.5. Home décor — frequency of ownership (%)

	1695–1715		1775–90	
	Wage-earners	Servants	Wage-earners	Servants
Tapestry	100	98*	73	42
Printed cloth	—	1	4	12
Wallpapers	—	1	17	25
Silk muslins	—	—	4	7
Printed tulle	—	—	2	10
Door hangings	34	75	53	70
Window hangings				
Mirrors	65	71	61	66
Pier-glasses		7	29	33
Small mirrors				
less than 10 inches	42		15	
10 to 20 inches	52		58	
more than 20 inches	6		27	

* Of which Bergamot tapestries made up 78%

furnishings, but paper was part of the house. So the success of the new materials may also have been a way of economising — it was the proprietors who paid for decorating — and they were less expensive. Tattered Bergamot tapestries were no longer so important in lodgings that were better heated. Servant interiors partially reflected these fluctuations in architectural and decorative fashion while those of Parisian wage-earners did not change much and, perhaps indicating a general deterioration, fewer people were affected by them. In wage-earning homes, tapestries continued to be found throughout the century and new materials only appeared gradually. Servant homes were nearly fifty years behind the aristocracy, and the affluent labouring class almost a century. The lead over the rural world and provincial towns was very clear,[49] and this was another area which accentuated the role of servants as intermediaries. For them, wall-hangings could be one way of hoarding: some English and Hungarian point tapestries were worth 40 *livres* an ell, a Flemish tapestry more than 400 *livres* for 20 ells, an Aubusson 200 *livres* for 15 ells.[50] Their presence is indicative of an attempt at imitation, but this passed with time and changing tastes. Verdure was old-fashioned and less useful. At the beginning of the century you could buy cheap Bergamot at 4 to 5 *livres* an ell, and it

49. M. Baulant, *Niveaux de vie*, pp. 520–30; R. Lick, *Les Intérieurs*, pp. 293–300.
50. F. Ardellier, 'Essai d'anthropologie urbaine', pp. 87–9. The *aune de Paris* was equivalent to 1.18m. Four to six *aunes* would make an area 5 metres square, 12 *aunes* 15 metres square.

played a vital part in maintaining the delicate balance of heating. Popular-class living space tended to be completely sealed off, so as to control the meagre heat given out by the fireplaces; curtains, door-hangings and other draperies were the old way of helping to achieve this effect. In the first half of the seventeenth century all bourgeois and popular-class houses in Paris had tapestries. In the eighteenth century, Savary states that there were few artisans or humble folk who did not make it a point of honour to have a Bergamot tapestry in their bedroom as a success symbol, a sign of aesthetic conformism and an essential element of preserving warmth. The enclosing of the conjugal bed mirrored the enclosing of the family home. Door-hangings and carpets in particular were the preserve of the elite of the popular classes. Generally speaking, the décor of the majority was dominated by the green of the Bergamots or a natural grey serge, with a very little red; for a minority, narrative fantasies, bright colours, motifs, stripes, flowers and leaves introduced a more varied tonality in imitation of the privileged classes. For most people it was simply a question of combating damp walls, insidious winds and draughts; for a few, of playing upon feeble aesthetic resonances. These changes with regard to wall décor and heating were one of several indications concerning the reorganisation of space. It was about volumes rather than surfaces, for it showed the move from the confined space of the classical age to the open, airy space of pre-Revolutionary times. Wallpapers and tulle or muslin curtains suggested a much more open ambience. But all this was essentially the preserve of the well-to-do. For most of the popular classes it was inevitably limited by the constraint of a single room; problems of circulation, movement and ventilation which occupied architects and publicists were very much reduced in scale.[51] Daily movements took place over tiny distances, actions were calculated for essential routine functions, volumes were organised within a confined space, the values of warmth and comfort were proclaimed and the popular classes adopted only 'what fitted their ethos, deliberately ignoring the rest'.[52] The single room of *le peuple de Paris* was intrinsic to their way of life. Its crowding, modest decoration and real poverty did not diminish its protective function emphasised by many details. For those who had achieved some degree of stability and integration as a result of a slightly less precarious situation, it was the theatre for life's sweetness and violence, security and fragility. It was the mirror which confirmed the shift towards another life-style.

---

51. J.-C. Perrot, *Genése d'une ville moderne*, vol. II, pp. 681–2; L.-S. Mercier, *Le Tableau de Paris*, vol. I, p. 277, vol. II, p. 185.
52. R. Hoggart, *La Culture du pauvre*, Paris, 1957, pp. 62–3.

It appeared very widely and very early (Table 5.5). From the end of the seventeenth century, to own a mirror was a sign that you belonged to the town and to Paris. It was hardly a luxury, but an object of everyday use, and more affluent homes had more than one on their walls. A variety of styles developed: to the simple mirror with a frame of painted or gilded wood were added, by the end of the century, 'dauphine' and oval mirrors, and especially pier-glasses. Their growth was linked with the changing shape of chimneys, which made it Integrated in the general scheme, there were at least two mirrors in more than half the 400 inventories. They were very useful for picking up, refracting and amplifying light. Progress in this direction is shown possible now to hang mirrors on the chimney-breast. The mirror played its part in working-class décor and humble Parisian pier-glasses echoed the recommendations of Robert de Cotte and the Blondels.[53] by increasing size: around 1780, two thirds of the popular classes had more mirrors, and larger ones. This decorative fashion was made possible because increased production and improved technical conditions brought about a fall in price: around 1680 the sale of mirrors was below 200,000 *livres*; in 1788 it exceeded 2,000,700 *livres*. This reflected the triumph of Saint-Gobain and his royal manufactory,[54] a triumph which did not depend only on the increased use of mirrors by the rich, but also on a massive urban consumer market. Sales quadrupled during the century. *Le miroir du peuple* marked the success of the industry protected by the King and the efforts of the Parisian masters of the guilds mirror-makers supplying mercers, haberdashers and pedlars. During the reign of Louis XVI, progress in Paris was indicated by the multiplication of models and especially the increase in size: around 1700 a 20-inch mirror was extremely rare, but about 1780 they accounted for more than a quarter of the mirrors recorded in inventories. But the implications of these developments, copies of conspicuous expenditure, were not just economic.

The Parisian mirror symbolised the pursuit of superfluity, of a doubling of appearances for people and things. Among affluent servants its frequent and even general appearance indicated a desire to multiply objects and possessions; its superfluity meant it belonged not to a list of essentials, but to consumer goods regulated by appearances. Like clothes, the mirror made the man; it was an instrument of outward appearances, in which you not only contemplated your image, but corrected it and improved your posture. In it a man might

53. P. Verlet, *La Maison au XVIIIe siècle*, Paris, 1966, pp. 96–7.
54. C. Pris, *La Manufacture de Saint Gobain XVIIe – XIXe siècles*, Paris, 1975, 3 vols., vol. 1, pp. 730–837. The technical revolution meant that mirrors of blown glass gave way to those obtained by pouring and polishing.

seek his own truth: 'qui odit veritatem odit lucem', or, as Montaigne says, his 'right bias, his "true visage"'. The mirror was, therefore, a means of progress for the individual conscience. It afforded everyone a way of discovering, seeing and duplicating himself; so, like writing, signatures and personalised objects, its logic lay in conferring a social status, in providing an individual's importance. Mirrors helped to mimic other gestures, they were instruments of integration into the socialised world of superior practices; they helped to attain independence. Unlike the discipline of catechisms and manners, it provided a different education by which one could acquire a supple physical identity through the duplication of appearances. It is easy to understand the moral conflict which grew up around the mirror: an auxiliary of the toilet, weapon of coquetry, symbol of lust, instrument of perversion. Christian moralists since Saint Jerome had continued to thunder against this despicable object which they tried to tame and conquer by the use of the 'speculum mentis'. A war against the fascination with self was waged in its reflections. The popular wisdom of fairy tales condemns those who are lost by spending too much time in front of their mirrors. The proliferation of display mirrors does not strike me as an affirmation of bourgeois awareness.[55] The phenomenon is more complex, and reveals the wide diffusion of an aristocratic practice, the power exerted by this model of festive opulence, and of the play of Enlightenment brilliance in the mirrors of châteaux and mansions, of the prestige of psychological power confirmed and duplicated in a contemplation of reflections.[56] The endless reproduction of this conquest in the meanest popular-class interior extended to the people's consciousness a confused sense of liberation by day and night. It was a sign that they were participating in some small share of life's beauties, that they were thus more fully themselves, and at the same time it was confirmation of a fragile awareness, easily shattered. The beliefs attached to mirrors, their traditional magic which continues today in rural areas, were obviously reinforced by their scarcity.[57] Did the superabundance of mirrors in the town dispel their ancient charms? Popular magic is little understood in modern towns, but there is no reason to suppose that either Christian moralists or those skilled in optics have succeeded in expelling or exorcising ancient, hidden practices. The people's mirror, that they are afraid of breaking, remains perhaps a window opening upon invisible worlds, and one of the ways in which being comes to terms with having.

55. J. Baudrillart, *Le système*, pp. 27–8.
56. H. Polge, *Les Miroirs et les ombres*, Archistra, 1972, no. 14–15, pp. 47–63.
57. G. Lascault, *Figurées, défigurées, petit vocabulaire de la féminité représentée*, Paris, 1977, pp. 110–11.

In this order of things, domestic hygiene deserves a moment's attention. We will keep to a few hints of a change of behaviour which should not be interpreted in the light of more backward hygiene or pre-medical practices. The customs of cleanliness and uncleanliness associated by all observers with the life of the *classes populaires* are a sign of something else, a different cult of the body, different practices of civility. A count of objects connected with personal hygiene reveals a barrier between the traditional ethos arising from an order of necessity and new habits in which progress was leading to superfluity. From the start, the basic problem is the infrequent recording of these objects: does this mean that the corresponding practices did not exist, or that the low cost of the objects concerned caused them to be overlooked by the not over-zealous valuers, who evaluated them occasionaly when they were sorted in groups or when there were more than one of them? There is no doubt about certain things like brooms, brushes and feather dusters, always valued at a few farthings; an object of no value was overlooked, and toiletries were always valued if they were above a cetain price, never below, like silver-backed brushes, tortoiseshell combs and silver powder-boxes. Thus, their absence might mean the opposite of what is usually supposed, and for inexpensive utensils indicate the routine familiarity, even abundance suggested by the broom-seller, or vendor of knives, scissors and combs captured in Bouchardon's *Cris de Paris*. So the list of objects is short and the changes they indicate gain significance from this fact (Table 5.6).

First razors, scarce because they were expensive, found among servants and the better-off, and making slow headway. Valets shaved their masters and quickly adopted the habit themselves. As for the rest, they went to the barber's shop or the hairdresser's stall. Taconet evokes the daily procedure in a *poissarde* heroic ('By shaving yourself, you make a sure penny'). A change leading to the daily ritual of shaving has begun; masters themselves renounced the services of a living-in barber in favour of a valet, or even of shaving themselves. On the other hand, it marked the decline of a sociable ritual, the hasty visit to a practitioner whose shop was for many a place to meet, discuss, pause. People could warm themselves by the stove there in winter and tear Calonne and Necker to pieces. A public, male ritual retreated to the home. Other indications are difficult to interpret, and it seems that for men and women the emphasis was on appearances, a sort of bodily care based on decorum. Some syringes evoke digestive therapies in Molière, or seem already to have been an instrument of feminine hygiene in emancipated households, as Rétif noted referring to high-flown courtesans: 'Her chamber-maid, called Lépine, came in carrying a bowl, sponge and small syringe, and they went into the cabinet . . . .'.

Table 5.6. Availability of toileteries and washing utensils

| | 1695–1715 | | 1775–90 | |
	Wage-earners	Servants	Wage-earners	Servants
Razors	1	15	3	25
Shaving-dishes	—	2	8	5
Syringes	15	10	24	20
Toilet mirrors	31	36	45	46
Toilet cases	—	2	2	6
Water-cisterns	52	35	24	15
Buckets, tubs, jars	7	8	19	12
Water-jugs	1	14	5	16
Bowls	1	2	1	4
Chamber-pots	1	3	5	4
Chaises percées	—	4	—	6

Attentions to the female body were an attribute of the upper classes and prostitutes; there was no brothel without its bath, and bidets were becoming quite common there. Concern for genital health may have reached the people via servants — men and women were keen observers — and through the habit of visiting prostitutes and whores who were obliged by their rapid encounters to observe some sexual hygiene. Only occasionally could the lower classes deodorise themselves.[58] Their daily cleanliness could only be superficial and peripheral, as dictated by the text-books of manners *ad usum populi*.[59]

The body (in the puerile codes of manners published again and again from the sixteenth to the nineteenth century, of which seventy-five texts were traced before 1828),[60] was an absentee, to be hidden under clothes, kept silent and disciplined. Discourse upon cleanliness was primarily about decency; for two centuries it went in unchanging circles round the same 'proper' parts — teeth, hair, face, eyes and hands. When cleanliness became more precise, it included the feet, subject to particular care, authorised repeated ablutions and audaciously prescribed a monthly bath. For the people, to be clean was to respect appearances, and moral observers adhered to the clerical convention according to which bodily cleanliness was a reflection of spiritual cleanliness. 'This extreme cleanliness is to be found even

58. Rétif de la Bretonne, *Monsieur Nicolas*, vol. 3, p. 110, 'Agnes made the bed then washed . . . '; pp. 227–8, the story of Sephir's mother, 'They come to my place, I have 5 or 6 large bath-tubs, I wash, rub down, cut corns, deodorise, perfume, blanche . . . '.
59. R. Chartier, M.-M. Compère, D. Julia, *L'Éducation en France du XVIᵉ au XVIIIᵉ siècle*, 1976, pp. 138–44.
60. C. Rimbault, *Le Corps à travers les manuels de civilité du XVIᵉ au XIXᵉ siècle*, Mémoire de maîtrise, Paris 7, pp. 67–88.

among grisettes because it stems from the character', wrote Rétif, less religious but just as convinced that physical graces began with clean clothes.[61] The ideal woman, the real sylph of the aristocracy, represented an unattainable model: 'In the warm season frequent baths preserve her health, even in the winter she spends a few minutes, three times a week, in warm water . . .'. The Parisienne of the popular classes must be content with less thorough and less frequent ablutions. She could not claim to be the 'pearl' whose element was water, or the 'Musulmane' that Rétif liked to imagine.

Water was scarce and something of a luxury. The popular classes had only a limited number of utensils for storing it, and it cost money to fill them. Copper cisterns worth 10 and 20 livres, were not uncommon around 1700, but they became so towards 1780, being replaced by stoneware or hard faience models which were cheaper — jars, tubs and buckets. Here again one sees an indication of the decline which affected all groups, but to which servants were less vulnerable, since the better equipment of noble and bourgeois houses was available to them. Handling water was a problem for all, and many practices were almost inconceivable at that time: laundering, which was entrusted to countless washerwomen[62] who made the river ring with their noise, or which was done in the yard near the communal well; the bath, which could be taken only in the river — a male custom — or in establishments which became more common at the end of the century. The slow increase in the number of jugs and bowls, the occasional presence of chamber-pots or 'chaises percées' show that these utensils were a luxury. For the others, there was the fireplace where it was customary to piss on the ashes, and collective water-closets suggesting communal manners far removed from our deodorised sensibilities. Throwing a pot of excrement out of the window surprised nobody, even if it infuriated the receiver.[63] Pissing in the street and alleys offended only the great and the English, like Arthur Young who noted the fact as characteristic of the strange manners of the French. Elsewhere abbé Perraut commended cleanliness to the popular classes in towns, a sign that a change was taking place: 'They should wash frequently at all times. It is as important to health as to cleanliness . . .'.[64] This was an

61. Rétif de la Bretonne, *Les Parisiennes*, pp. 45–8.

62. Washing equipment was very scarce, most people had neither wash-tub nor washing cauldron, very little equipment for ironing; on the other hand, around 1780 a quarter of the servant's legacies and a third of those of wage-earners mention laundry debts.

63. A. Farge, *Vivre dans la rue*, pp. 35–6; dossiers of the *commissaires* are full of such incidents.

64. J.-A. Perreau, *Instruction du Peuple*, Paris 1786, pp. 179–80, 187–91. The dirtiness of the popular classes contributes to urban decomposition.

Table 5.7 Availability of water

	1695–1715		1775–90	
	Wage-earners	Servants	Wage-earners	Servants
1 bucket/15 litres	10 (17)	10 (26)	1 (7)	12 (54)
2 buckets/30 litres	15 (25)	9 (24)	3 (21)	7 (32)
3 buckets/58 litres	23 (39)	10 (26)	8 (58)	3 (14)
4 or more buckets/ 87 litres	11 (19)	9 (24)	2 (14)	—
2,900 litres	59 (100)	38 (100)	14 (100)	22 (100)
Averages per house 49 litres				

*shown in frequency and (%)
A 'load' of water in Paris was just under 30 litres, the usual bucket was a half-load; the capacity of a cistern has been calculated on this.

audacious suggestion which was difficult to satisfy (Table 5.7).

Elementary hygiene and privacy for the most intimate practices were luxuries, reserved only for the privileged, recent amateurs of English privies.[65] The usual horizon of the popular classes encompassed only latrines and limited supplies of water from stinking wells or the Seine. Moreover, water was precious and costly: one delivery upstairs averaged 2 to 3 *sous* around 1780, which put 1 cubic metre at more than 3 to 4 *livres*, or two days' work! It had to be used sparingly for dishes, laundry, housework, and personal ablutions. All these factors remained constant throughout the century, except for rare cases, and sometimes they got worse. They suggest a specific ambience of daily life which could not fail to offend doctors and observers, and which could not change until *le maîtrise de l'eau*[66] was achieved.

Countless projects were set up to tackle the problem in the new *quartiers*, including the fire-station established at Chaillot. But the ingenuity of the popular classes and the medical offensive of scientists could do nothing to palliate such grave deficiencies. The initiatives were not directed towards mass water consumption, they were not accompanied by an education programme to teach new rituals of hygiene. In short, the sensual and olfactory world of the popular classes was not ours. 'Not one bath in a thousand years' was Michelet's rather hasty simplification, but his astonishment revealed the curiosity

65. J.-C. Perrot, *Genèse d'une ville moderne*, vol. II, p. 915.
66. B. Fortier, *La Maîtrise de l'eau, XVIIIᵉ siècle*, 1977, pp. 193–201.

of an anthropology concerned about extreme differences.

The ordinary life of *le peuple* was a matter of crowding, promiscuity of ages and sexes; privacy was primarily a refuge for sex and not for relieving oneself, the curtained bed allowed some degree of privacy, but not the commode or chamber-pot in single rooms, or the open latrines at the tops of stairs.

So it was certainly a strange world in which micro-improvements, in heating and décor, changed the quality of life, in which minor rationalisations such as storage and the division of space were introduced furtively, and in which some acceleration was manifested by more rapid consumption. But these changes were obvious only among the more affluent, whose vision of domestic space reflected that of the upper classes. For the rest, deterioration and progress struck a balance, the restrictions of the home and the weight of habit remained immovable. The ethos of the Parisian popular classes provided a primitive sort of comfort. The historian's dream is to gain access to the demography of things.

CHAPTER 6

Popular Dress

The garment was bought: I had made my choice; it was noble and
modest . . . .

Marivaux

Clothing is a good indication of the material culture of a
society, for it introduces us immediately to consumer patterns, and
enables us to consider the social hierarchy of appearances. In
eighteenth-century Paris one was, indeed had to be, dressed according
to one's state: 'It is a poor proverb which says that the robe does not
make the monk! Of course it does! It makes him morally and physi-
cally, simply and figuratively. Let a man take the robe of an attorney,
lawyer, clerk of court, magistrate, and at once he takes on the *esprit de
corps* . . . a cowl makes a monk of the man who puts it on, whether in
jest or for a masked ball . . .'.[1] For Rétif there is no doubt, a garment is
a costume, and you must have the one that belongs to your condition,
a cobbler may be well-dressed for such a state, but he is none the less
recognisable as a cobbler; a poor Auvergnat, a day labourer, a mason
are immediately identified by their clothes: beautiful shop girls, pretty
girls from the pork butcher's, are dressed according to their occupation, which is not the same as a girl in a butcher's shop.[2] Clothing
conferred a social identity on every one, but at the same time it
revealed the character and personality of the wearer, it showed each
man's individuality and originality more clearly than his walk or
actions, his features or deformities might have done; it was an immediate means of identification.[3] In Paris everyone knew the clothes

1. Rétif de la Bretonne, *Les Nuits*, pp. 2521–2.
2. Idem, *Les Contemporaines*, pp. 73–4. ('Les Trois Belles Charcutières'). A concern
for appearance can also be found in *Les Parisiennes*, with some acuteness of observation
as an element in the social hierarchy, for example, in the engravings.
3. R. Cobb, *Death in Paris*, pp. 22–3, 70–86. The admiration owed to the intuitive
genius of the author, who was guided by his unsurpassed knowledge of Enlightenment
Paris, does not rule out the possibility of reopening the dossier in order, perhaps, to give
fuller support to certain statements. Unlike R. Cobb, we believe in a social history in
which statistics need not be dehumanising, but like him we wish to remain faithful to *le
peuple*.

appropriate to each condition, but at the same time costume made possible a game whose rules varied with the individual and the occasion. If it was primarily a question of conforming to a scale of conventions, it was also possible to escape from the burden of appearances. Functional needs affected appearances, refusal to conform would confuse the clothing codes, and the daily practices of the popular classes could change the original meaning of upper-class principles of dress. An inventory of the clothes of the *classes populaires* points us towards the history of social circulation and mimesis. We go beyond the superficial familiarity to the bodies that wore them and were masked by them. Through a study of linen and clothing a link is revealed between men and women and their bodies; man's private and public character are sufficiently combined for gestures to recover their symbolic meaning, and for us to rediscover an attachment to tradition as well as the reflected spark of fashion. Our research route is clearly set out: from the tangible fact of inheritance to the reality of the passing urban show, from inherited accumulation to daily practices in dress — a spontaneous adaptation to circumstances and to the evolution of conventions which, in town, and everywhere else, affected everyone. Like a fragile seismograph, proletarian clothing registered great changes and tiny adaptations, revealing the combined effects of necessity and of circulation between groups and classes ripe for change.

Opening cupboards and chests releases such a profusion that we find it difficult to organise things in comprehensible terms. In the first place, there are gaps which make it difficult to interpret certain points, and may cause us to underestimate the number and value of the garments owned. Why should notaries' inventories and rulings on inheritances ignore children's linen or garments? The clothing of minors is never listed — certainly not that of small babies, although this is understandable. Occasionally the garments of the surviving partner are missing from such inventories, whether because they were considered to be private property having no part in the legal sharing of goods, or because they were worth too little to merit valuation. Frequently even the wardrobe of the deceased was not assessed; it may have been sold to pay off debts during the illness; it may have been passed straight to the children in a way which confers on clothing a considerable symbolic and material value; or, more simply, because the deceased was buried in the few clothes he owned. Notarial documents are not loquacious; they say more about servants — 60 per cent of inventories from c.1700 gave adequate information, 75 per cent from c.1780 — than about wage-earners, where 45 per cent and 70 per cent offer useful information. We must bear in mind these omissions which, especially for small legacies, mean that the total value was considerably underestimated, although this became less common as time went on, proving the greater importance attached to clothing. It must be reiterated that the inventories do not reveal the ways in which things were acquired, and therefore do not enable us to appreciate the importance attached to clothing in people's budgets, which were dominated by relatively fixed food costs, rent and heating. Nor do they tell us how often wardrobes were renewed, the choices made between essentials and luxuries, the importance of inherited as opposed to purchased goods — the former of some significance to servants — and the way people dressed according to the season. The inventory offers a fleeting snapshot, it does not register movement, which, in matters of dress was clearly fundamental for the individual and the group. But Paris, and towns in general, certainly favoured movement rather than stability, for the lives of all were activated by a certain fall-out from the consumption of the rich. The corrupting luxury of towns denounced by moralists had its effects on clothing; thanks to a vast system of redistribution of aristocratic excess involving second-hand dealers and the people themselves who became salesmen in case of need, the clothes of the rich ended up on the backs of poor people who could bedeck themselves in sumptuous rags which had been worn and repaired over and over again. Essentially, bits of clothing passed from body to body on a journey at every stage of which they underwent the spontaneous changes and adaptations which composed the motley spectacle of dress.

At all levels of income clothing and linen represented a small part of the patrimony but it was undoubtedly more significant at the lower end, both among servants and wage-earners (Table 6.1). The pre-Revolutionary years saw spectacular progress in their real value and quantity, which occurred in no other area of household goods. In short, in the eighteenth century the popular classes accumulated clothing for the first time: a growth rate of the order of 200 per cent, that is, a tripling; it was clearly the beginning of a consumer market in this sector.[4] Of course the growth varied according to means and to the different categories: it was faster for the poorest, and generally more pronounced among wage-earners than servants, who started off with a considerable advantage, and it also varied according to sex. Under Louis XIV most wage-earners had a mediocre wardrobe, valued at less than 17 *livres* for men and women; in the budgets studied by Vauban

---

4. It must be remembered that the increase in fortunes was of the order of 128 per cent for ancillary wage-earners, and 90 per cent for the lower classes.

Table 6.1. Availability of clothing and linen in popular-class fortunes

	1695–1715		1775–90	
	Wage-earners	Servants	Wage-earners	Servants
Total value of general clothing categories (in *livres*)	2,704	5,472	8,534	17,505
Average out of 100 (in *livres*)	27	55	85	175
Average out of wardrobes reconstituted (in *livres*): men	17	34	36	88
women	15	61	92	151
Clothing in total fortune (%)	3.0	1.2	4.4	2.1
Goods and chattels in total fortune (%)	5.0	10.0	10.0	
Fortunes < 500 *livres* (%)	7.3	14.0	16.1	
> 3,000 livres (%)	0.6	0.4	1.6	1.3
Average value of linen (in *livres*)	15	59	48	118

the labourer devoted almost all his earnings to food and had little left at the end of a life of work. But servants' wardrobes were already twice as costly, and the clothes of serving women and chamber maids were worth twice as much as those of the men who worked alongside them. This is clearly characteristic of the behaviour of the group, and its obsession with appearances copied from the rich. And the gaps widened again under Louis XVI. A chamber-maid's wardrobe was still worth twice as much as a valet's, but wage-earners, men and women, had followed suit. The wife of a casual labourer had seen a six-fold increase in the value of her clothes, while his had only doubled. In short, all women seem to have been infected by the frivolity of the upper classes, female servants already at the beginning of the century, women from the wage-earning classes only on the eve of the Revolution. According to Rétif and Mercier it was in the 1770s and 1780s that the *femmes du peuple* began to dress more tastefully, to pay more attention to their adornment, and coquettes began to wear 'dresses trimmed with fancy-work'.[5] Reading inventories can sometimes reveal extreme cases: Jean Bertos, a cook-shop boy, died on 4 November 1784 leaving clothes worth 38 *livres*, while his wife's wardrobe was worth 346 *livres*. Such disproportion suggests a passion[6] This di-

5. Rétif de la Bretonne, *Les Contemporaines*, 'La Petite Laitière', p. 105; *Monsieur Nicolas*, vol. III, pp. 293–4.
6. AN. Min. Cent., CXI. 36 L 4XI.1784.

morphism, however, tended to decrease with an increase in wealth, especially among servants: in fortunes above 3,000 *livres*, the average was 225 *livres* for men, 230 *livres* for women. The clothes of butlers and *hommes de confiance* were elaborate and varied; they approached, relatively speaking, the refinement of their masters. This is not the case with more menial servants; the garments of porters, coachmen, lackeys and grooms had none of the elegance of their wives' or their superiors'. The value of wardrobes is a good test of the impact of economic success on the class codes of clothing among the popular classes, perhaps of the part played for both sexes by social traditions, and, in the case of the women of Paris, by dowries. Underclothing, which was only half as important as outer garments, showed the same characteristics: the same importance among the rich at the beginning of the century; the same increase in all classes, but more striking among the poor than the well-to-do; the same sexual dimorphism overtaken to some extent by the men during the reign of Louis XVI. Beneath these surface movements concerning the prices and interests of the popular market, we must seek out such hidden information as the possible increase in the number of garments and items of linen owned and the possibility of important changes in the materials used.

As far as the number of garments is concerned, analogous conclusions may be drawn, but the growth seems more evenly divided between the sexes. The usual masculine wardrobe around 1700 consisted of four or five main garments — breeches, jacket, coat, jerkin, waistcoat; by about 1780 it included nine or ten items; cloaks and frock coats, though often well-worn, were now quite common. On the other hand, there might be six or seven main garments in a woman's wardrobe in the reign of Louis XIV, and twice as many under Louis XVI. The popular classes in Paris seemed better and more warmly dressed, since they could easily supply their needs from the resale cycle; clothes and linen would circulate from one milieu to another, come and go within families, and might sometimes constitute one's sole possessions. Drowned men fished out of the Seine were sometimes wearing several trousers and jackets on top of each other in the middle of summer, so it was not a matter of keeping warm, but of keeping their meagre riches on them. [7] It was for many the beginning of new consumer habits. Moreover, in male and female wardrobes, the changes were essentially in accessories and extras; secondary items like linen, kerchiefs and ornaments were five times more common for women, four times for the men, and they became more varied. Thus the increased value of people's clothing was the result of greater

7. R. Cobb, *Death in Paris*, pp. 21–2.

variety, and, therefore, of a growing interest in new fashions, for which Paris had tended to be a prodigious laboratory; at the same time, there was a profound qualitative change which brought with it a primitive sense of luxury, and evoked in the people a fundamental response to the challenge of necessity. At the end of the seventeenth century it was still the preserve of a few, at the end of the eighteenth it was within the reach of all. But can we trace the lower limit of these changes? Notaries' inventories ignore the non-integrated population, newly arrived migrants and the poor whose estate was not contested, all those regarded by the police as routine game, pursued for the thousand misdemeanours then considered real crimes.[8] We will leave aside out-and-out rogues and persistent criminals; they loved fine clothes just as they imitated fine manners and Mandrin's red coat was long a folk legend. For the rest, clothing was reduced to essentials. Precarious lodgings and a constant shifting made this inevitable; for anyone who lived in a furnished room, a dormitory, under the bridges or in boats stationed along the river, it was impossible to store things, and the fear of being robbed meant they could not leave their baggage and bits of clothing unattended. The poor wore their whole wardrobe. Legal witnesses attested this 'very ragged' appearance of the poor, just as they could identify by their clothes workers integrated into society who wore the costume belonging to their occupations — carters, carpenters or watermen.[9] The clothes of the *malvestus*, the 'ragtag and bobtail' bore witness to their poverty, to the need to get maximum wear out of a minimal wardrobe, and the filth due to the lack of bodily hygiene. But the witnesses were like the notaries; faced with rags and tatters, they lacked detachment and revealed their haunting fears. Beggars or poorly dressed, it was all one to them: 'mean', 'worn out', 'wretched', 'threadbare', 'worn thin', 'shabby', 'torn' served to describe both their poverty and their conduct.[10] It was no use asking a clerk of court or an official valuer to understand what the rags and shabby clothing could also mean — the way in which this processing of cast-offs could contaminate habit.

Basically, changes in clothing can be measured against the evolution of three main parameters: the frequent mention of certain types of clothing revealed by the vocabulary of dress; the variety of fabrics which reflected the people's sensibilities through changes in affluence and comfort; and a spectrum of colours which evoke the street scene and a change in visual perception.

8. A. Farge, *Le Vol d'aliment*, pp. 142–70; G. Aubry, *La Jurisprudence criminelle du Châtelet de Paris sous le règne de Louis XVI*, Paris, 1971.
9. G. Picq, M. Pradines, C. Ungerer, 'La Criminalité', pp. 145–7.
10. R. Cobb, *Death in Paris*, pp. 70–3.

Let us, first of all, look at the *femme du peuple*. Around 1700–15 her wardrobe consisted of five main garments: the skirt, which appears in 89 per cent of inventories; petticoat, 53 per cent; mantle, 87 per cent; apron, 88 per cent; bodice and corset, 41 per cent. Female garb remained faithful to trends already established in the sixteenth century. The skirt was the basic garment; pleated, sometimes slashed, always attached to the hips by strings, it was worn over one, sometimes several petticoats. The apron was indispensable, pinned to the chemise, or more exceptionally to a blouse. Bodice and corset were not so common, which indicates a suppleness very different from the obvious rigidity of the costume of the rich. Shirts were ubiquitous, but no undergarment, since female drawers were only for predators and women of ill fame. Mention of a woollen mantle shows that a certain seasonal adaptability had evolved. Accessories, about a dozen, were mostly for the head: bonnets, fichus, head-dresses, caps (78 per cent); then the legs: the majority owned cotton and muslin stockings; neckerchiefs (16 per cent), kerchiefs and scarves were less common; shoes and gloves were rare — the former appear in 20 per cent of inventories, which indicates how expensive they were and that they were passed from foot to foot. Perhaps people were buried in their only pair?

A serving woman's wardrobe was the same, but included more items more carefully combined, an outfit of skirt, apron and wrap; her clothes were more varied, a brassière was added to the corset, the neckerchief was trimmed with point-lace and collars with ordinary lace, shoes — which appear in a quarter of the inventories — could be of good quality: silk, damask, Morocco or Cordoba leather. But the real difference was the quantity; where the working woman had two to three petticoats, the servant had four to five, the chamber-maid six to seven; serving women were not short of fine linen which may have come from their mistresses, in 88 per cent of valuations chemises were counted in dozens and the more fortunate also had camisoles, an expensive garment usually owned by women of the world and costing 3–5 *livres*. Cotton stockings were piled in dozens in chests, silk stockings were not unusual, and handkerchiefs were quite common. A lady's maid had fine and varied linen, whilst the working woman's remained simple and rustic. Everyone slept naked, but the first nightclothes appear in a tenth of servant wardrobes, though drawers for daytime wear remained almost unknown (only one is mentioned).

In the reign of Louis XIV, women's clothing was made from substantial materials: wool predominated (48 per cent), cotton was rare, and silk still more so; underclothes and aprons were cut from coarse cloths, linen and hemp. Camlets, *bourracans*, winceys and druggets, sometimes mixtures, dimity, thick flannel and plush dominated the range of textiles. Among female servants woollen fabrics, ratteen and poplins were found as often as in wage-earners' wardrobes; muslins and Spanish ratteens were a bit lighter and cheaper. Easy movement and light materials were available only to the comfortably-off minority. Colours were dark and uniform: 45 per cent wore black, grey or brown and not many wore warm or light colours (red cloths, 21 per cent; white, 16 per cent). Figured cloths (15 per cent) were mostly striped or flowered. Servants did not experiment with different shades, two-thirds of them chose cold, dark colours, but they did add some violet, musk colour, tan, pink, yellow and green. Checks mingled with stripes. All in all, with the exception of a few frivolous soubrettes, quick to copy their mistress, the *femme du peuple* and the servant had a severe, imposing appearance, a uniform and sombre presence, closer to the peasants of Le Nain than the women celebrated by Watteau. More touches of grace and fantasy were to be found in the upper ranks of workers and servants.

As we have seen, men had four main garments: jacket, 65 per cent; breeches, 80 per cent; jerkin, 95 per cent. A complete suit made up of these three items was rare: a quarter among wage-earners and a half of servants. Not many cloaks are mentioned (27 per cent), the better-off had great-coats for the winter. A hat completed the outfit, especially black three-cornered hats and grey felts. Shoes were twice as expensive as women's, yet more common: 37 per cent of the inventories. There were not many elegant touches; collars, cuffs, cravats (40 per cent), lent variety to a few more expensive wardrobes, especially among upper servants who liked furbelows and lace. Livery is not mentioned, as it belonged to the master, an affirmation of patriarchal possession and a sign of belonging to a house, an asset restricted to rich lords and *bourgeois gentilshommes. Hoi polloi* were content to trim their ordinary clothes, and a serving man's outfit differed from that of the poor more by its variety than its uniformity. Most servants and a few rich journeymen were distinguished by the abundance of their clothes and therefore by the possibility of changing them according to circumstances and the seasons; they had three or four pairs of breeches, four or five jackets, a beaver, a felt hat, a muff, a pair of gloves, all of which enable them to cut a dash. Their cupboards contained about ten shirts and a few *précieux* even had underpants for day and night: the poor man had only rough shirts and wore no underclothes. Cotton and muslin stockings were the usual wear (as they were for women). Archaism and simplicity conferred a peasant solidity upon the clothing of the popular classes. This can be seen in the materials used: 80 per cent woollen cloth; the rustic material of shirts — hemp and linen, 80 per cent; lighter cotton, silk, muslin and velvet were the prerogative of dandies and the well-to-do. The uniformity of the whole was accentuated by the predominance in the clothing palette of even darker shades than for the weaker sex: for three-quarters of them, blacks, greys and browns were background colours, red enlivened a tenth, whites, blues, yellows, greens sparkled here and there. Watteau's *La Marmotte* in the Hermitage, or the *homme du peuple* who is watching the boxes of paintings being opened in *L'enseigne de Gersaint* illustrate both the dominant style of clothing among the labouring classes and their sober tonality. Body and gestures were as stiff as their garb, suppleness, like colour, was reserved for the rich. In the popular crowd the servant stood out by the quality of the materials he wore — satins were not uncommon, a few calicoes added a forward-looking note — and by way of ornament, gold and silver braid, velvet borders, coloured-silk embroidery, lace and sparkling buttons. His appearance, no less than his bold gait, was a badge of service, conferring a limited but ostentatious brilliance which deceived no one.

So this was the costume of the Parisian popular classes in the closing days of Louis XIV's long reign; for men and women it was simple and solid, made to last, to stand hard work and bad weather and to help to combat winter cold. It was sombre and this absence of colour and gaiety in the streets blended with the grey cobbles and black mud. Its roughness retained a rustic quality, though people were wearing shoes rather than clogs, a significant difference. The severe uniformity of the sartorial range of the crowd appears in the fine series of *Cris de Paris* published around 1700 by François Guérard, in which we find hints of a few chosen traits, fluted bonnet, round hat pushed back, bands, and the steinkirk set at a rakish angle.[11] The popular classes in pictures, like the old knife-grinder and the men walking, drawn by Watteau in red chalk and black pencil,[12] have a grave and stately presence; days of crisis and poverty did not lend themselves to rejoicing, even of a sartorial nature, but the fear of passing for a bare-foot or a ragged wretch conferred real dignity on them all. Elegance and style were for the rich and for the intermediaries who, on the fringes of the popular classes, took on the tastes and manners of the ruling classes. If clothing and fashion were a language in the time of Louis XIV, the *peuple de Paris* were still somewhat illiterate.

Around 1775–90 it all changed (cf. Table 6.2), beginning with men's clothing. Complete suits are found in 84 per cent of the inventories,

11. Massin, *Les Cris de la ville*, Paris, 1978, pp. 52–7.
12. M. Pitsch, *Essai de catalogue sur l'iconographie de la vie populaire à Paris au XVIIIe siècle*, Paris, 1952, pp. 97–110, 197–201; see no. 648, *cabinet du dessin* in the Louvre, also 690, *cabinet du dessin*, Louvre.

Table 6.2. Fabrics and colours of garments (%)

| | 1695–1715 | | | | 1775–90 | | | |
| | Wage-earners | | Servants | | Wage-earners | | Servants | |
	M.	F.	M.	F.	M.	F.	M.	F.
Wool	76	42	62	55	60.0	6	42	10
Wool and mixture	1	6	4	5	—	—	12	1
Cotton	1	11	8	10	20.0	57	21	59
Linen	13	18	17	12	1.5	16	10	7
Silk	3	16	4	15	4.5	20	12	19
Miscellaneous	7	7	5	5	15.0	1	3	4
Brown	25	10	32	14	7.0	5	5	3
Black	40	25	25	33	21.0	7	15	8
Grey	10	10	18	22	30.0	12	25	11
Red	11	21	15	10	6.0	20	4	22
White	9	16	6	5	12.0	23	11	24
Yellow–blue–green	5	3	2	6	17.0	26	22	28
Miscellaneous	—	—	2	10	3.0	4	13	4

matching jackets and breeches are common, but the wide-skirted jerkin, so characteristic of the *Cris de Paris* of Boucher and Bouchardon, has disappeared, to be replaced by the waistcoat. In this respect paintings had not caught up with the reality revealed in the inventories, for a definitive change does not occur in the Saint-Aubins or in the Orléans images of the 1780s.[13] From now on capes and great-coats were rivalled by the frock coat, which was widely adopted by dandies at the end of Louis XIV's reign. Henceforth, where the notary had listed two items in 1700, now he found three or four. Among the more comfortably off, especially elegant servants, the dress-coat made its appearance, hats were worn by all, and 'the Swiss-style three-cornered hat had won the day, routing all the round hats, because it gave its wearer a much more frank, proud, resolute air . . . .'.[14] But trousers pose a problem to the historian of material culture; one expects to find them, for the Revolution established them as the symbolic garment of the *sans-culotte*, but they never appear in the inventories of those who were to participate in the *journées*. They are known to have been worn at work by sailors and rivermen, and they were worn by a few small street tradesmen; in 1775, in the series of *Cris parisiens* by Jean-Baptiste Leblond, the chandler, the machinist Turpin and Scaramouche are wearing trousers; which makes three as against twenty-

13. Massin, *Les Cris*, pp. 63–5, 67–9, 84–85; M. Pitsch, *Essai de catalogue*, 174–90.
14. L.-S Mercier, *Le Tableau de Paris*, vol. 10, p. 191.

four pairs of breeches! We also know that cotton hose were costly and fragile, which argues in favour of the change . . . but no information! Were they sold? buried with the dead? — unlikely for working garments. Or did they escape the notary because they were unworthy of his attention? Certainly, the trousers of the workman and fairground artistes were destined to triumph over aristocratic breeches, but their early history remains obscure. In any case, men from the popular classes were accepting all sorts of novelties in basics and accessories; almost everyone had stockings (81 per cent), three-quarters of the inventories mention shoes, which no doubt means they had been adopted definitively by everyone, if one assumes a first pair bought earlier. There were collars in two-thirds of the cupboards, cuffs in three-quarters of the drawers. The gap between servants and wage-earners persists but more in quantity than style: the former had two or three pairs of shoes to one for the latter, a dozen muslin stockings to their six or seven. Servants were much better off for linen, only a quarter of them had fewer than a dozen shirts, the average was twenty-five, which allowed plenty of changes; indoor garments — housecoats, dressing gowns, night-caps, turbans, slippers — made private life more comfortable for the affluent. Men's underpants, unknown in 1700, are mentioned about ten times. The popular classes of Paris seemed to aspire to better standard of living, authenticated by more frequent changes of linen and other garments, and to show a new feeling for sartorial taste. It is true that heavy materials still predominated, but cottons were overtaking woollen cloth, flannel and nankeens, especially for jackets and waistcoats; silks and swansdowns were gaining ground. The fabric of men's clothing was becoming more varied and inventories were registering the results of a development in textile manufacture, of the speculations of entrepreneurs, in short, of the forces of production already mobilised for massive consumption.[15]

Garments were a bit lighter, and it was no longer unthinkable to attempt some pleasant, cheerful touches. Dark colours no longer completely dominated the scene, blacks, greys and browns made up two-thirds, but warm, bright colours were making progress, blues, yellows, greens and pinks were becoming rather more common. The third quarter of the century in particular saw a rise in striped and checked patterns, testified by Mercier: 'The zebra stripes of the King's anteroom have become the model for present fashions; materials are all striped; coats and waistcoats are like the beautiful skin of a wild ass. Men, old and young, are striped from head to foot: even stockings are

15. F. Braudel and C.E. Labrousse, *Histoire économique et sociale de la France*, vol. 2 *1660–1789*, pp. 227–250, 514–27, 545–53.

striped . . .'.[16] The word had been given, and the popular classes were taking in this air of fashion. This new masculine consumption proves there was widespread variety, a feeling that it had become necessary to keep up appearances, a sense of visual gaiety, all in all a real revolution. Solid, utilitarian virtues had come to terms with the frivolous; those who lived in the shadow of the rich and powerful showed a consumer capacity directly linked to their imitative faculty, increased by the contacts of their daily relationships.

Women undoubtedly took the lead. Their wardrobe made spectacular progress, and showed enormous variety. The petticoat was still the main item, 95 per cent, but now, in 57 per cent of the wardrobes of women of the wage-earning class, and 63 per cent of those of servants, it was combined with a dress, which had not been mentioned in the earlier inventories. Aprons were now worn by the majority, and corsets by as many as half. Chamber-maids and the more affluent had the full panoply, augmented by jackets, 'caracos' or long, loose jackets, mantlets and pelisses. Fashion decided the variety of combinations, set off the female figure to better advantage, and multiplied the indispensable trimmings. The coif was still worn (51 per cent) but was rivalled by head-dresses and bonnets; fichus and neck-bands tended to supplant the old neckerchief: all these items appear in 96 per cent of the inventories. Decorative cuffs and muffs for winter were becoming common; an increase in the number of gloves (18 per cent) was a sign of affluence (30 per cent among servants). Most wardrobes contained one, or even several pairs of shoes. The *Parisienne* was changing her shoes and providing work for the four thousand masters of the two cooperating guilds of cobblers and shoe-makers. For the women as well as the men of the Parisian popular classes, the shoe was a conquest of the century of Enlightenment.[17]

Like men's clothing, but even more so, the gamut of women's clothing had new resonances, depending less on the solid and utilitarian than on a concern for effect, originality of styles, colours and motifs. Underclothes were neat, shirts and camisoles of fine linen, and drawers were beginning to be worn. This shows a new relationship to the body, restricted to the well-to-do, but soon to be imitated by a growing number; increased stocks of linen, which made more regular changes possible, were aimed more at comfort than a show of luxury. The basic factor was the lightness of the materials, there was less wool and cloth, more cottons and silks. The *femme du peuple* was better dressed, and the servant-woman even more so; she might enjoy the

16. L.-S. Mercier, *Le Tableau de Paris*, vol. 10, p. 191.
17. Ibid., vol. 11, pp. 21–2.

supple range of satins, soft taffetas, gay *toiles de Jouy*, and the Parisianised exoticism of Siamese and Persian cloths and nankeens. The influence of current fashions could be seen in new shades in the colour range: less than a quarter of materials were black, grey or brown; a good quarter were white; rather less than a quarter, red; the rest included blues, yellows, greens, and especially countless cool pastel shades such as russet, canary, turtledove, *gorge de pigeon*, winecolour, puce-brown. The Parisienne now had a quicker eye and more subtle awareness; contrasts were less extreme in the street scene, it was less easy to distinguish social classes, things changed according to the season or the dictates of taste echoed by countless voices, paraded by the elegant, and progressively imitated and reshaped. The evolution of textile motifs is illuminating from this point of view: stripes predominated (20 per cent), but they competed with flowers, sprigs, checks. In this respect there was no difference between the average inventory of the labouring classes and the servants except in abundance and attention to detail; even the gap in their fortunes was closing, but without ever completely disappearing in spite of this levelling of appearances.[18] Take stockings as a test case: every servant owned at least a dozen pairs, they were often white, grey or black, sometimes flesh-coloured, sometimes striped, most of them cotton, but a good third silk; working-class women had a half-dozen pairs, generally white, rarely coloured, usually cotton, occasionally silk. The culture gap was maintained by this possibility of a better choice from a wider range of products, colours and quality. The revolution in women's fashions was the result of a slow circulation of models. Rétif de la Bretonne sang its praises, whilst Mercier was an impassioned observer.

For both of them sartorial novelty was an integral part of the great social shift made possible by the urban machine which was beginning its slow progress, far from the countryside: 'While gold and silver braid appears on the servants' livery, the hempen smock scarcely covers the ploughman and the vine-grower. The labouring class [refer-

18. F. Ardellier, '*Essai d'anthropologie urbaine*', Anne Geneviève Lou, cook, estate of 500 *livres*; 3 dresses and petticoats, 2 camisoles and petticoats, 1 loose jacket and skirt, 1 mantlet, 2 aprons, 11 more skirts of white linen, dimity or cotton, 2 under-petticoats, 6 pairs of dimity pockets, 3 gauze caps, 6 lace caps, 2 stomachers, 8 bonnets, 3 caps, 17 *fichus*, 3 pairs of stockings, 3 pairs of cuffs, 34 linen shirts, 6 muslin camisoles (no mention of shoes), value 317 *livres* (which amounts to 60 per cent of the fortune of this unmarried woman servant).

Jacqueline Maris François, chamber-maid, estate of 15,800 *livres*: 11 dresses and petticoats, 2 dresses and aprons, 3 mantlets, 2 aprons, 15 pairs of pockets, 7 skirts, 12 corsets, 8 with lining, 4 stomachers, 4 Valencienne-style caps, 4 muslin head-dresses, 11 caps, 19 bonnets, 16 lawn and muslin *fichus*, 5 pairs of muslin cuffs, 4 pairs of gloves, 6 pairs of cotton mittens, 1 of velvet, 4 pairs of leather shoes, 1 of cloth, 18 muslin shirts, 10 pairs of linen drawers, 2 camisoles, 3 mob-caps, 12 pairs of stockings, 43 kerchiefs, value 316 *livres* (2 per cent).

ring here to peasants] sees the valets in their braided cloth and cham-ber-maids in silk dresses, even with a few little diamonds. This wretched class is beginning to think of itself as far beneath the servant order . . .'.[19] Mercier, who denounced the growth in servant numbers in the towns, clearly saw their refracting effect: they become adept at copying their master 'after a certain time', for better or for worse. 'Farewell, maidens with massive petticoats, the silent daughters of Europe's poor', one might already say of the *femmes de peuple*, who were watching and imitating them in their own way, 'the *grisette* is happier in her poverty than the daughter of the bourgeois. She starts her career at an age when her charms still dazzle; her poverty gives her complete freedom, and her happiness sometimes comes from having no dowry. . . . A taste for adornment is added to the basic needs of life: variety, as bad a counsellor as poverty, keeps telling her softly to add the resources of her youth and her face to those of her needle.'[20] In the demoralising city where models of taste abounded, working-class girls were carried away by the combined effects of necessity and of the spectacle of unnatural, immoral riches; they took their place in the society of conventions; far from being liberated, they risked being lost. Sébastien Mercier saw the popular classes losing their simple ways, compromis-ing their health and their true nature in the fragile conquest of appear-ances: 'In general the Parisian is obliged to be sober and cannot afford good food, all in order to give his money to the tailor and bonnet-maker . . .'.[21] The consumption of clothing was one of the mechanisms animating the town theatre, dear to the disciple of Rous-seau, where both personalities and social relations were corrupted. The life-style of the idle, dedicated to the game of masks, to ostentatious frivolity, to a non-transparency of being,[22] became the norm for an increasing number, and that is why, in its crucial phase, the Revolution insisted upon a reappraisal of the modes of dress. The modernity sensed by Mercier lay in this downward spread of the habits of court and city — which had been the restricted public for an earlier innova-tion — towards the silent majority; and this change of custom which the Industrial Revolution would accelerate, already represented a confusion of exterior roles, therefore of conditions, a profound shift in perceptions and therefore of language and awareness, precluding the advent of a 'fetishism of merchandise'.

Rétif saw and observed this change as if it were a *fête*. Monsieur Nicolas was not rich, but the day he was received as a journeyman-

---

19. L.-S. Mercier, *Le Tableau de Paris*, vol. VI, pp. 100–11.
20. Ibid., vol. VIII, pp. 117–18.
21. Ibid., vol. VIII, pp. 120–4.
22. J. Starobinski, *Jean-Jacques Rousseau, la transparence et l'obstacle*, Paris, 1957.

printer, his parents gave him his first suit of grey camlet with gold-thread buttons; in the evening after work, when he was preparing to set off on a spree, he washed his face, put on his breeches of black drugget, smoothed his white cotton stockings over his calves, donned his shoes of polished leather with silver buckles and his great, green bergopzom coat, all tasselled and frogged, and finally, with his short sword and powdered hair — he did not wear a wig — he was ready to pass himself off with the tender-hearted *grisettes* and pretty shop girls in the rue Saint-Honoré as some dashing cavalier.[23] In the early 1760s, Rétif had not yet become the 'nocturnal spectator' pacing the town draped in 'an old blue cloak', hidden beneath 'a broad felt hat', who boasted that he had not bought a garment from 1773 to 1796. At that time he knew how to cut a dash and live beyond his means, just as in old age, on the other hand, he loved to appear before the rich badly dressed. The itinerary of his life shows a theatrical sense of dress and how 'taking some slight pains'[24] already meant choosing to appear what one was not. In the eyes of the moral observer, costume played its part in the corrupting effects of the city. This was the real sartorial revolution, born of a modest affluence. 'I happened one day to have on a black lustrine jacket and white silk stockings, and I was on my way to see a young beauty. Well then, on the way, I was surprised to find myself proud and disdainful. I shrank from the touch of the common man . . . .'[25] Clothes borrowed from other classes transmitted prejudices and vices. A poorly-dressed man became an object of suspicion and the black coat of the popular classes a danger signal. For dark shades were still thought suitable for the popular classes, as the inventories prove; black was not reserved for rich *dévots*, spies, and churchmen,[26] as Mercier observed: 'Black clothes are wonderfully adapted to mud, bad weather, thrift and the reluctance to take pains over one's toilette . . . '.[27]

Two strategies were combined in Rétif's response to clothing: social seduction, which might indicate corruption or progress towards equality, and the cleanliness which dictated the real sartorial education. This conversation between two laundry-maids reveals some ways of making life more equal:

> One of these girls said to the other: 'You were swanking on Sunday with your white trimmed dress! My, it did suit you.' — 'I should think so! It

23. Rétif de la Bretonne, *Monsieur Nicolas*, pp. 33–4, 46, 80, 89.
24. Idem, *Les Nuits*, p. 1199, 2549.
25. Ibid., pp. 2519–20.
26. Contrary to the rather hasty affirmation of R. Cobb, *Death in Paris*, p. 25.
27. L.-S. Mercier, *Tableau de Paris*, vol. 1, p. 239.

belongs to a fine lady and was made by an expert, Mistress Raguidon in the rue Guillaume . . . I'd be a fool to buy my own clothes! I wear white every Sunday, something different every time! Ladies like that never dirty anything; I do it for them and cut quite a dash! Stockings, shirt, shift, none of it's mine. . . . What about you, Cataud?' — 'Oh me? don't breathe a word! or I'd tell on you like you'd told on me, and we'd be in the same boat. I lend hankies, shirts, collars, stockings to grenadier Latereur.' — 'And I lend things to Lamerluche, the foot-watch, jackets to little Marion, and shirts to Javotte, and then I hire some out . . .'.[28]

Thus a new elegance was appearing in the ways of the popular classes. *Les Nuits* recounts the fascination with dress on the part of the nocturnal spectator who can no longer tell the 'real sylph' from the 'foolish working girl'. A pretty pearl-grey taffeta dress or a clinging dress of white satin could change the girl who was used to wearing a coarse dress and calico petticoat into a woman of quality.[29] In a host of anecdotes, countless Pygmalions clean, scrub, dress, transform and conquer pretty working girls.[30] Precise description of feminine costume was part of an ethic preoccupied with remaining true to Nature and resolving social contradictions.

It was in support of this lesson that Rétif called for hygiene in dress. On every page the contrast between white dresses and linen and black mud was related to a philosophy of femininity, a morality which exorcised anything dirty, unhealthy, disturbing: 'love of cleanliness' was the key to all virtues; a girl who had the misfortune not to be clean would bring every kind of misfortune upon herself, but the opposite was also true. 'Look at that little Sophie who was taken from poverty and adopted by rich people; they were delighted by the cleanliness of the rags she was wearing, they were torn but clean as a pin'.[31] Without referring to it directly, Rétif was pointing to the great lesson of Good Manners: cleanliness was, above all, suitability — of clothing to the person and to the proprieties of age and station.[32] Neatness of apparel crowned a whole apprenticeship, involving, amongst other things, physical deportment, table manners, learning silence. It was a discipline and the affirmation of victory over the savage instincts and animal nature of *le peuple*.[33] This was demonstrated by the behaviour of poor

28. Rétif de la Bretonne, *Les Nuits*, pp. 182–3.
29. Ibid., pp. 580, 887–92, 1041.
30. Idem, *Les Contemporaines*: more particularly, 'Le Nouveau Pygmalion', pp. 35–41 and 'La jolie fille de boutique', pp. 147–8.
31. Idem, *Les Nuits*, pp. 3135–6, 'La couturière malpropre'; *Les Parisiennes*, pp. 50–1.
32. C. Rimbault, 'Le Corps', pp. 82–4. See, for example, A. de Cortin, *Bouveau traité de civilité*, Paris, 1673; J.-B. de la Salle, *Les Règles de la Bienséance et de la Civilité*, Paris, 1713.
33. Rétif de la Bretonne, *Les Parisiennes*, pp. 45–52.
34. Idem, *Les Nuits*, pp. 372–3.

people amusing themselves, on carnival days, by throwing rubbish and filth over the beautiful white clothes of fine ladies.[34] Rétif's discourse echoed the hygienists, plus his own social symbolism and personal obsession. Dress, like housing, had its part to play in improving the moral standards of the poor. The long lists in the inventories show that they were acquiring the wherewithal of this lesson which they had inherited; the observations of Rétif and Mercier prove that they were rapidly applying it. The popular classes were no longer in rags, they had to be clean, they washed their shirts, and bits and pieces.

'There is no city where people use more linen than in Paris and where laundering is worse. Take the shirt of a poor workman, tutor or clerk which goes through a brushing and beating every fortnight; soon the poor devil's eight or ten shirts are worn out, torn and in holes. . . . So anyone who has only one or two doesn't give them to be beaten by laundry girls; he becomes his own launderer, to preserve his shirt. And if you don't believe it, walk across the Pont-Neuf on a summer Sunday at four in the morning, and there at the riverside on the corner of a boat you'll see several fellows with nothing on under their coats, washing their only shirt or kerchief . . . .[35]

On 4 September 1763, François Fontaine, a fifty-six-year-old manual labourer, was taken by the harbour police before the tribunal of the Hôtel de Ville for indecent exposure; he defended himself by explaining 'that all he did was to take off his shirt to wash it because of the lice . . .'.[36] In the city, such was the fate of a wretch dressed in rough clothes, with a coarse jacket, woollen stockings and thick shoes, wearing an old wig, 'who dressed the day before for the day after, and the day after sometimes for the rest of the week'[37] as Diderot, a keen observer of the ways of the people, remarked. The population of Paris was changing all the time; an unstable society threw together old and new city dwellers with newly arrived peasants; the lucky ones were integrated into the restricted circle of those who had more or less made it; the poor and unfortunate tramped the streets, all participating in a spectacle where sartorial norms were in a state of flux. The Parisian milieu favoured acculturation in all sorts of areas and clothing was certainly not the least important for the labouring classes, for they could, in their way, operate a special method of distribution. Going

35. L.-S. Mercier, *Le Tableau de Paris*, vol. 5, pp. 102–03; also J.-A. Perreau, *Instruction du peuple*, pp. 179–89: 'The lower classes, and the poorest among them [he is speaking of peasants] have no possibility of changing their clothes, but they can keep them neat and clean by washing them, and exposing them sometimes to the air, sometimes to the fire; for most of them are made of woollen fabrics, and wool is very unhealthy if it is not kept clean . . .'.
36. AN. Z^{1}H 620, 4 September 1763.
37. D. Diderot, *Le Neveu de Rameau*, Paris, 1972, ed., pp. 91, 178.

from norms to manners, novelists and *littérateurs* could testify, if not
to everyday ways of dressing, at least to the effect clothes had on other
people. The influence of dress, even of linen, in romantic situations
and anecdotes designed to illustrate the picturesque in popular life,
may reveal a sense of sartorial usage, prove to be a fairly reliable echo
of their perceptible changes, and give some indication of the means by
which the concern for dress was reaching the popular classes.

From this point of view, we should examine that literary tradition
which extends from Marivaux to Rétif in which peasant men and
women, *parvenus ou pervertis*, play an active part in the denunciation
of urban corruption. For all the novelists, the vital factor was the
importance of imitation in the transmission of behaviour patterns and
the acquisition of customs. For young peasants in novels, going to
town meant setting foot 'on the moon', for behaviour, therefore the
rules of the social game, was no longer easy to read; in short, they all
had to be educated.

Take the Parisian journey of Jacob, the *paysan parvenu* invented by
Marivaux.[38] He is not exactly a poor man, but the son of an established
vine-grower, owning land and crops, producing the best local wine, a
champagne which sells well in Paris; he is the cock of the local walk,
and a tenant farmer to his lord. Jacob is single, he goes up to the city
where his brother has preceded him and married a 'comfortably off
tavern keeper'; he does not intend at first to settle in the city, merely to
deliver the annual supply of wine. He stays; 'the first days I had spent
there had stirred my heart, and I suddenly developed a taste for
money . . .'. So he is a voluntary migrant, he has cash and manners, he
is on the make and he will succeed. 'I was eighteen or nineteen; they
said I was a handsome lad, as handsome as a peasant can be whose face
is at the mercy of the sun and work in the fields. But apart from that, I
really was quite good looking . . . .' For him a change of appearance
would open the way to success; in a few days he had to drop his rustic
ways and peasant clothes. The scene of this change? The mansion of a
great lord. The tutors of this transformation? The house servants 'who
fell for him at once', the chamber-maids, blonde Toinette and brunette
Geneviève, a lackey who takes a liking to him, and the mistress herself
who advises and keeps an eye on him. 'That same evening they called
me to be measured by the tailor of the house . . .', 'two days later, they
brought my new clothes and linen and a hat and all the rest of the
outfit.' Curled and powdered, the young rustic is cleaned, whitened,
dressed, civilised; he can make his entrance upon the stage of urban

38. Marivaux, *Romans*, Biblio. de la Pléïade, Paris, 1949, 'Le paysan parvenu',
pp. 568–76.

life. Of course, Jacob speaks of the attractions of the city, the ruses which offer some a chance of success, the necessary cultural and personal trump-cards. What comes across even more strongly is the need for a complete change of manners and the part, both symbolic and real, played in all this by dress. The conquest of Parisian customs starts with a change of costume: for a new décor, a new skin!

Forty years later, Rétif takes up the same theme and the same action. If poor Edmond fails where Jacob made his fortune, it is perhaps because circumstances are more difficult, and certainly because his creator wishes to persuade his readers not to yield to the lure of the city: 'A fortune made in the city by real merit is the big prize in a lottery; a hundred thousand lose for the one man who wins . . .',[39] and to convince them for once and for all of the dangers of urban immorality. But the process remains the same, and it may be that the cultural baggage acquired, ways of hearing, seeing and doing, have been in the long term more important than the temporary deculturisation of countless sons of the soil. Women are no different from men: for Marivaux's Marianne, as for Edmond's sister, entry into Parisian society is effected through sartorial metamorphoses. The heroine of the 1730s will succeed in breaking into society, the other will fail, but at the outset they share identical chances. Let us follow Marianne.[40]

She brings with her a good provincial upbringing: 'I had learnt to make all sorts of little trimmings for women, a skill which was later to prove very useful . . .', a pleasing face, the resources of her wit and the strength of her virtue. Her entrance into city life is brutal, her modest protectress dies at the inn, her belongings are stolen, but she is gradually assimilated, and the start of a new future is marked by the gift of a new outfit. 'I had chosen it; it was impressive but modest, such as would have suited a high-born girl of slender means. After that, M. de Climal mentioned linen, and indeed I needed some . . .'. With this fine linen temptation arrives but 'having thus settled the little question of conscience, my scruples vanished, and the linen and clothes seemed to me a fair prize . . .'.[41] Marianne's dress symbolises more than worldly seduction, it means a rupture in her way of life, joining the social throng, acquiring new sensibilities. All in all, novels of apprenticeship and conquest call upon three main functions which establish a dialogue between reality and fiction: amorous strategy, social masks, and Utopia.

For the first, clothing was essential both for the libertine's seduc-

39. Rétif de la Bretonne, *Le Paysan perverti, ou les dangers de la ville*, La Haye-Paris, 1776, 4 vols., vol. 1, pp. iv–v, 30–60.
40. Marivaux, *La Vie de Marianne*, pp. 94–109.
41. D. Diderot, *Le Neveu*, p. 108.

tions (look at M. de Climal, look at Rameau, the nephew, dreaming up his role as a go-between: 'Couldn't you explain to the daughter of one of our good citizens that she is badly dressed; that pretty ear-rings, a bit of rouge, some lace, a dress *à la polonaise* would suit her to perfection?');[41] for sexual parade, even the most ordinary amorous by-play. In *Monsieur Nicolas* and *Les Nuits*, as well as *Les Contemporaines*, Rétif has drawn up an anthology.[42] Everything is there: the daily appraisal — 'Jeanne still looked like a *grisette*, although she was in evening dress' — remarks on the art of coquetry and the artifices of charm: 'dressed like this, she was appetising . . .'; 'he had Félicité measured for a green taffeta "polonaise", he wanted bunches of ribbons on it and gold tassels on the hips . . .'; observations on the voluptuous efficacy of good dress, and the well-known fetishism of footwear. Secondly, Parisian novels use clothes to mark social distance, but also to blur outlines; as in life, one has the costume of one's state (he was dressed as a clerk, she as a butcher-girl), but at the same time conventions are changing, the *grisette* dresses like a bourgeoise, the journeyman like a master, the valet acquires and transmits the art of appearances, the marquis pursues his adventures in a great-coat of coarse camlet. The attraction of dress inevitably leads to a confusion of ranks. Finally, the life conjured up by novelists confers on romantic clothing its utopian dimension, which may be sexual — Rétif's *Monsieur Nicolas* or *Les Contemporaines*, or the *Fille de trois couleurs*[43] — frequently social. Utopian fiction, which uses reason to judge everything, defines imperatives and habits. But its overall aim is to allot each man his usual costume and keep everything in its place. Nevertheless, the imagination of the novelist can open up new vistas; this is the meaning of the figure of the journeyman Loiseau.[44] This friend of Rétif, a member of the fun-loving typographical quartet of the 1750s, comrades in work and play, whose joys and pains are part of the fascination of *Monsieur Nicolas*, earns enough to dress well, but dresses in ascetic frieze cloth, takes care of his linen and wears his hair

---

42. Rétif de la Bretonne, *Les Nuits*, pp. 580, 590, 645, 781–3 (Putting masculine shoes on a woman, this charming practice no longer exists . . . . When my little Isabelle becomes my wife, she will be dressed in the most feminine way possible from head to toe . . .), 1041, 1113, 1165, 1171, 1179, 1217, 1271, 1431, 1472, 1512, 1595, 1719 (Aglae had a low-cut white dress with a round bonnet in which she looked charming), 1836–8, 1873, 1931 (you have turned up your skirts higher again), 2150, 2171, 2218 (she was adjusting her garter in the alley), 2284–5, 2311–60 (high heels), 2372, 2419 (the bold lackey), 2439, 2425 (the dresses cut), 2788, 2857, 2865, 2960, 3135. In *M. Nicolas*, one might cite pp. 31–3, 75, 143 (Zephire had put on a little linen dress), 144–5 (Loiseau went out with Manon . . .), 159, 227–8, 277, 288, 293, 484–5, 502 (in this voluptuous outfit I took her . . .). In *Les Contemporaines* see 'Les Trois belles charcutières', 'La Petite laitière' and 'La Jolie fille de boutique'.

43. Idem, *Les Contemporaines*, VI.

44. Idem, *M. Nicolas*, vol. 3, pp. 114–89.

cut like a pudding basin; he affects a severe style of dress, he is already
an incorruptible. Loiseau is the incarnation of the educated, thought-
ful, republican popular classes, indifferent to the bewitching magic of
clothes. When the time has come for political hopes to be realised,
Hébert will cry, linking female nature and the evil spell of dress:
'Those bitches of women, with their accursed chiffon have always
screwed up men and their families'.[45]

Thus norms and customs were defined, a repertoire of behaviour
patterns registering the birth of a consumer society based on obsolescence. But obsolescence also presupposes a life-style within the pattern
of daily life from which one can extrapolate three main features:
household management, which considers how and when things are to
be renewed; popular purchasing habits; and finally, a consequence of
the overall trend, the family scene, which we may glimpse from the
garments worn by victims of the tragic accident on 30 May 1770, and
by the bodies which ended up in the Basse Geôle de la Seine between
1796 and 1800.

Family consumption of clothing is not easy to reconstruct for as we
have already seen, the budgets of the popular classes are practically
unknown. Ordinary people kept no accounts or expense books. The
incomes of most urban wage-earners were absorbed by essentials,
bread and lodgings, and it is difficult to measure the influence of the
Parisian economy on the evolution of living standards.[46] We must be
content, as were their contemporaries, with a general estimate. At the
beginning of the eighteenth century Vauban attempted to evaluate
what a weaver and a manual worker would have left after paying for
the 6 lbs of bread needed daily by a family of four. If the family had
about 150 *livres* a year, they would spend more than 60 of these on
food, and more than 40 for a single room in Paris. [47] The remaining 50
livres would have to pay for heating, light and, as Vauban says, 'the
purchase of a few bits of furniture, if only a few earthenware bowls,
clothes and linen . . .'.[48] This reckoning allows the modern commen-
tator to draw a moderately hopeful conclusion: the working-class
family must have had enough to eat, and managed to survive the major
crises, but they were already on the breadline, for fluctuations in prices
and the risk of unemployment could reduce their means to zero: a
single day laid off work, an upsurge on the corn-market, threatened
most members of the popular classes in Paris with a reduction in food

45. Cited by G. Lascault, *Figurées, défigurées*, p. 36.
46. M. Morineau, 'Budgets populaires', pp. 203–15.
47. Ibid., p. 212.
48. Vauban, *La Dîme Royale*, ed. Coornaert, Paris, 1933, cited by M. Morineau, pp.
233–5.

and forced them to resort to charity. Nothing here suggests that on a single wage they could afford anything at all beyond the basic necessities. Only by working overtime and pooling their resources and earnings in a family enterprise could they manage to acquire a little mobile capital; as we have seen, bachelors and couples with few children had a slight advantage. Often, they were the first to keep a wardrobe, occasionally the first to buy something beyond basic necessities, although most would have invested in something other than clothing. In this respect, one can see the advantage enjoyed by servants; their earnings were regular and they could pick up their masters' cast-off clothing, either as a gift or for a modest sum paid to the butlers and top women servants who were in charge of wardrobes.

In the years before the Revolution something changed, and evidence is more precise.[49] Budgets reconstructed with real certainty for the peasant of l'Aunis, the weaver in Picardy and the master silk-worker in Lyon allow us, for lack of a better source, tò make a comparative estimate of the wardrobes of the popular classes in Paris. Around 1765, a bachelor peasant earning 183 *livres* a year would devote 66 per cent to his food, which was improving, 18 per cent to housing — including taxes — leaving 16 per cent for clothing.[50] At Abbéville, a family of four had 370 *livres* a year, of which two-thirds went on food, 20 per cent on the home, leaving 10 per cent for clothes.[51] In a typical Lyon household, around 1785 — and here we are dealing with the upper stratum of the *classes populaire* and the lower middle class — out of more than 2,000 *livres* in the kitty, about 50 per cent was spent on food and less than 15 per cent on renewing their wardrobes; it must be noted that extra expenses were involved in the home and the workshop, as well as various expenses for the children.[52] Nevertheless, the independence of the *maître fabriquant* was precarious, and a rise in prices could bring him down towards the level of his workers.[53] Overall, allowing for the fact that conditions in Paris were more favourable as regards wages, perhaps less favourable as regards prices and consumer habits, we have here the range of possible spending

49. M. Morineau, 'Budgets Populaires' pp. 225–8, 229–30, 454–7.

50. *Memorandum on the Necessity of diminishing the number of holy days*, n.p., 1763. Budget for a single peasant wage-earner (the figures rounded up to the nearest whole number): food, 109 *livres*; house (lodging, heating, lighting and including a tax of 12 *livres*, 40 *livres*; clothing, 27 *livres*.

51. M. Morineau, 'Budgets populaires', p. 230: food, 240 *livres*; house (not including tax), 104 *livres*; clothing, 26 *livres*.

52. Ibid., pp. 471–9: expenses for workshop, 593 *livres*; house, 392 *livres*; food (reckoned for four people, that is the artisan couple and two workmen), 804 *livres*; clothes (for two people), 138 *livres* (7 per cent of the total family receipts, 15 per cent of the family expenses, reckoned for two); 314 *livres* remaining.

53. Ibid., pp. 456–7; M. Garden, *Lyon*.

power: 24 *livres* for the single migrant worker, 138 *livres* for an artisan and his wife, less than 10 *livres* for a textile worker. All things being equal, the popular classes who had jobs might devote between 10 and 15 per cent of their meagre income to dress; a hard-working single boy or girl, as Rétif proved, could afford to dress up, a married man with two wages coming in could provide, more or less, for his own and his wife's clothing, depending on how many children he had to keep. A servant was always privileged, and had a chance to show off, and change his clothes more often. It is interesting to see how often wardrobes were renewed and what items were chosen.

Academicians in La Rochelle calculated that the rural labourer would acquire every two years: four shirts at 48 *sous*, a collar at 1 *livre*, two kerchiefs at 10 *sous* each, two pairs of stockings at 30 *sous*, six pairs of gaiters at 16 *sous*, an ordinary hat at two *livres*, a coarse woollen cap, another *livre*, and for a new linsey-woolsey coat, 22 *livres* — an old one bought at the second-hand shop, 10 *livres*; this leaves clogs, eight pairs of willow wood or six pairs of strong wood, 4 *livres* 4 *sous*, and let us not forget the laundering of shirts at 4 or 5 *livres*. Altogether, including footwear and maintenance, 32 *livres* a year, and we must remember that most of the above could only be replaced slowly: one year for clogs, two for the rest. Most new arrivals settling in Paris at the same time probably had in their luggage if not this minimal wardrobe, at least the consumer habits it implies. Calculations for Lyon enable us to more precise about replacement rhythms and to measure the effect of modest affluence in an urban milieu.

The *canut* would own a more expensive coat changed every eight years for 80 *livres*; for his daily work he wore a *matelotte* jacket and breeches, renewed every three years for 30 *livres*, and a hat likewise, 12 *livres*; he would wear out two shirts a year, 10 *livres*, two pairs of stockings, two kerchiefs, a cap and a hair-net, all coming to 12 *livres* and, finally, two pairs of shoes and one repair bill would cost him 12 *livres* most years; a bit more variety, a warmer coat, clothes for work, shoes instead of clogs, perhaps generally a less rustic quality were the outcome of urban consumer habits and a more secure situation. His wife spent rather more — 80 *livres* a year to his 50 — so the dimorphism of Parisian wardrobes was linked with excess consumption, and no doubt registered the effect of more rapid replacement. In the provinces, the *canut*'s wife would change her dress and skirt (30 *livres*), blouse, mantlet and corsets every three years — like her husband she would go through two chemises a year, also two pairs of stockings, two neckerchiefs, two pairs of pockets, two aprons, two pairs of shoes and one of galoshes, a round cap for work, a night-cap, and another for going out. This gives us a ceiling based on essentials and calculated in a crisis period to justify an increase in costs: 138 *livres* a year when, at the same time, the wardrobe of the average wage-earner in Paris, including linen and reckoned at second-hand prices, was worth 133 *livres*. So the accumulation of clothes, which we have glimpsed for the majority of workers, certainly raises the issue of market possibilities and the system of re-sales which enabled people to achieve higher standards at lower cost. The importance of such possibilities for dress generally is indicated by the wardrobes distributed by the *bureau de ville* in 1751, to mark the birth of the Duc de Bourgogne, to 600 young betrothed couples 'from the artisan classes, or labourers, or others for whom inadequate reserves or return on their work means that they cannot provide for themselves'.[54] Each fiancé received a coat of Elbeuf cloth, a shirt, woollen stockings, a pair of shoes and gloves; the girls received, together with a dowry of 300 *livres*, a dress and its petticoat made from a mixture of silk, linen or cotton, a cap, a neckerchief, a pair of muslin sleeves, a pair of woollen stockings, shoes, gloves and a flowered hat. In the middle of the century marriages in the city kept pace with new consumer patterns, they set a reasonable standard which was within the reach of the majority as they started out in life, and established the threshold of sartorial expectations among the more settled members of the popular classes.[55]

The sales system enabled them to meet new demands. Their clothing was bought from countless tailors, dressmakers, sewing-women, sellers of fashions, cobblers or shoe-makers, who would cut, sew, pin, pink, tack, hem and embroider miles of cloth, cut and tap leathers by the dozen; all these were mobilised firstly to serve the rich and and the affluent, the Parisian, French or European clientèle of fashion. Rue Saint-Honoré, 'the quintessence of urbanity' with its fashion shops, hatters, furriers, jewellers, was the dazzling nocturnal shop-window of this world, with its girls 'decked out like guild chapels'. It was there that Rétif would judge elegant evening costumes and assess 'the new revolution in women's dress which is due to the exquisite taste of an adored queen'.[56] But neither new nor fashionable garments, with rare exceptions (recourse to the local dressmaker or tailor, or sewing within the family) were within the reach of everybody. People generally went for their clothes to second-hand dealers. There, coats and all sorts of garments would pile up at the end of a complex circuit.

54. H. Vanier, *La Vie populaire en France*, Paris, 1965, p. 188.
55. Rétif de la Bretonne, *Les Nuits*, p. 163. The Nocturnal Spectator makes an inventory of the bundles of two lovers, a clerk and an orphan girl: 6 men's shirts, collars, stockings, 1 cotton bonnet, 2 pairs of white drawers in one packet, and in the other 6 women's shirts, stockings, bonnets, round and very clean, a few ribbons, 2 lawn aprons, 2 silk skirts, 2 loose jackets, 2 pairs of pockets . . . .
56. Ibid., pp. 2284–95, 2310–15.

First it was fed by the rich selling to old-clothes dealers and *marchands de mode* — 'instead of giving her old clothes in the usual way to her chambermaid, she would send for a woman who traded in outfits, and sell them almost new . . .'[57] says Rétif in *Les Parisiennes* — but also by a small business set up by their servants, especially personal servants of the great: all sorts of bits and pieces were cleaned, stitched, stripped of ornaments that could be used again; buttons were changed, lace altered, the clothes of the popular classes were repaired from the costume of the affluent. Second-hand dealers also got their stocks from auctions held after inventories, like the women-criers of Vadé or Taconnet[58] ('Lots of linen — it's all 'ere, nearly new, every day I'm 'ere at this end of the Pont-Neuf'). But selling was not exclusively a preserve of the rich or their servants, it was also practised when required by the poor. On a bad day, M. Nicolas sold his shirt to the second-hand women in rue Saint-Victor, to pay his rent. 'The first woman offered me 12 L. for what I was selling, four shirts which were worth at least 48, so I thought I could ask 24; the woman left to be replaced by another who offered me 9 . . .'.[59] People might also be driven to it by coquetry and imitation, like the fashion seamstress 'who loved to be smart, so she made an inventory of all her old things, gave part to Lisette (the apprentice) and sent her to Saint-Esprit to sell the best of it so that she could get herself something new'.[60]

And finally there was theft: a third of the 9,000 offences judged between 1750 and 1790 at the Châtelet were thefts of effects, linen and outer garments,[61] and from 1774 to 1790 the judges, who saw only those who got caught, passed sentence on more than 500 individuals for stealing clothes.[62] The details of these cases reveal a varied collection: 161 thefts of garments, 62 of handkerchiefs, 35 of linen, the rest involving a great range of petty larceny, pieces of cloth and stuffs, skeins of wool, scraps of lace. It was all fair game for these particular delinquents, who tended to be young men (only 25 per cent were women) and generally opportunists; they would snatch a garment lying around at a window, bits of clothing drying on the laundry-women's racks, possessions that had been entrusted to someone. The

57. Idem, *Les Parisiennes*, p. 163.
58. Vadé, *La Pipe cassée*, pp. 30–4; Taconnet, *Parade et Héroïde poissardes*, Paris, 1759, pp. 21–2.
59. Rétif de la Bretonne, *M. Nicolas*, vol. 4, p. 411; *Les Nuits*, p. 1179 ('Your husband is ill, when you have sold all his clothes, where will you turn?').
60. Ibid., pp. 2485–6.
61. A. Farge *Le Vol d'aliment*, p. 114 (310 crimes against persons, 10 per cent; 2,168 thefts, including 87 thefts of food).
62. C. Aubry, *La Jurisprudence criminelle du Châtelet de Paris sous le règne de Louis XVI*, Paris, 1971, pp. 106–10.

marauders rarely operated with the efficiency of those observed by the 'Spectateur Nocturne', in the rue de Grenelle near La Halle, where houses were systematically pillaged, and the rue d'Orléans where prostitutes' dresses and petticoats disappeared through their windows.[63] Dealers of both sexes, although closely watched by the police, contributed to this fruitful trafficking, about a hundred of them were in trouble with the law during the last forty years of the *Ancien Régime*;[64] the majority were occasional delinquents, driven by their failure to integrate themselves into society, or by extreme poverty; a minority were out-and-out rogues and regular criminals, men and women, who used their professional skills to make a living for themselves. Occasionally this little band made good police auxiliaries and efficient informers, because their work placed them at the centre of trading activities which were not always easy to categorise as legal or illegal.

So a lively, colourful milieu, close to the popular classes in its recruitment, way of life and habits, existed to clothe them.[65] It had its hierarchy dictated by the clientèle, the place and the means of selling and acquiring stocks. The women selling fine dresses and old-clothes dealers were the shrewdest, most of whom had open shops with heaps of old clothes, jewellery, fabrics and carpets. The junk sellers of both sexes at Saint-Esprit kept shops full of old clothes and linen; the register of one of them, Anne Jeanne Marière, who bought and sold to the lower strata of *le peuple*, shows all the garments and fabrics recorded in inventories: velvet for dresses, lustrine for coats, fustian for waistcoats, woollen cloth for jackets and breeches, muslin for fichus and mantlets, 'siamoises', Indian calico, cottons, nankeen, pekin for skirts, petticoats and jackets, silk for blouses.[66] Women selling old clothes and hats walked the streets shouting their wares, serving as go-betweens for more affluent shop-keepers.[67] This society had its

63. Rétif de la Bretonne, *Les Nuits*, pp. 645–6, 1059–60.
64. D. Dutruel, *Les Revendeuses à Paris dans la seconde moitié du XVIIIᵉ siècle*, Memoire de maîtrise, Paris 1, 1975, pp. 184–96, 109–209.
65. Ibid., pp. 19–76.
66. AD Seine (Archives de Paris), D 4 B 6, 49, 2957, 4 October 1773.
67. In the *Cris de Paris* and *L'Iconographie parisienne*, the spread of images is:

	No. of images	Cris de Paris (%)	L'Iconog. parisienne (%)
Town (leisure, circulation, culture and unspecified activities)	476	56	—
House (furnishing, construction, Sweeps, water-carriers)	75	11	26
Food	145	23	50
Fashion and clothing	70	10	24

habits, rhythms, manners, and pitches like the pillars of les Halles, Saint-Esprit, the quai de la Ferraille, quai de l'Ecole, under the Pont-Neuf; they tramped the town, cutting, restitching, taking apart and re-making the ordinary garb of the people. In the eyes of observers they were besmirched with all the faults of the popular classes: dirty, disorderly, confused, noisy, marginal and with strong criminal tendencies.[68] The poverty of the popular classes was stamped with this bad reputation, which masks the fact that almost the entire city was making use of old clothes; it is also the mark of Parisian adaptability to market conditions dictated by conspicuous expenditure and redistribution. 'It offers an expedient for countless citizens of slender means who would otherwise be obliged to go without basic necessities' thought the lawyer Des Essarts.[69] Ultimately, it proves that practices of re-routing clothes existed by which the popular classes in Paris used and appropriated other people's things, and by a spontaneous adaptation created their own codes and affirmed their personality, and it is this specific language that we must rediscover in the theatre of the streets.

But, due to the lack of documentation, it is not easy to glimpse a picture of daily life. Instead of paintings and iconography, whose deciphering would require expert examination for anything more than the illustrative use that is normally made of them, we can turn, however, to sources which have their origin in violence and death. Two catalogues may be consulted: the first is the list of the dead and their effects drawn up by the Paris police in the aftermath of the appalling catastrophe of 30 May 1770, which claimed 132 victims;[70] the second, the registers from the morgue which exist for the period 1796–1800 and which include 184 accidental deaths and suicides.[71] But to make the clothes of the dead speak, we must make a few caveats. The accident in the rue Royale left on the cobble stones a majority of women who were not able to escape from the mêlée — 88 as opposed to 44 men — all their garments are described with one exception, the clothes of a day-labourer's wife, which were returned to her husband before being inventoried. The clerks in the Basse Geôle received, and

68. L.-S. Mercier, *Tableau de Paris*, vol. I, pp. 208–10 ('Marchés'); vol. II, pp. 253–5 ('Piliers des halles'); vol. III, pp. 180–1 ('Revendeuses').

69. Des Essarts, *Dictionnaire*, on the second-hand clothes trade. In all, there were probably more than 4,000 salesmen and women working in the second-hand market. The police register Y9508 for 1767–9 — the only one preserved — numbers more than a thousand: 1,129 women, 240 men. Cf. D. Dutruel, 'Les Revendeuses', pp. 37–9.

70. AN. Y 9769 and Y 15707. I am grateful to Arlette Farge for giving me these references and dossier numbers.

71. AD. Seine (Archives de Paris), D 4 VI 7: we have studied only 184 of the police reports contained in this dossier, 404 in all — those for Year IV, Year VIII, and those concerning bodies brought out of the river. For the documentation and a social and cultural approach, see R. Cobb, *Death in Paris*, 1979.

scrupulously described, 142 male victims of suicide or accidental death, 34 of whom had been wearing no clothes, either because they had been bathing naked in the river, or because the clerks were negligent; out of 42 female corpses 11 were 'without any sort of clothing', but it is impossible to know why. In both cases, bureaucratic concern dictates the repetitive and monotonous compilation of lists; the investigators in 1770 were concerned to limit the psychological effect of an accident which quickly assumed symbolic significance,[72] to ensure the gratitude of the bereaved — only six corpses were not identified — and to return to their families the poor legacy they were wearing on their backs; for the *juges de paix* of the Directory and their medical clerks in the 1796–1800 sources, this careful identification was all the more natural since the police force had just gone through the Revolutionary crises and was struggling to stem the rising tide of violence.[73] It was in the interests of the police-controlled society of the eighteenth century to identify corpses that had suffered violent death — accident, crime or suicide — for nothing was more embarrassing than 'corpses in the cupboard' and police cases unsolved. Even as early as this, every detail counted in this department: special marks or a piece of clothing missing, both the presence and the absence of evidence, might enable scrupulous bureaucrats to solve the unique problem posed by the individual strangeness of each corpse that landed by chance on the wet slabs of the Basse Geôle du Châtelet. We must remember that what we are considering — the clothing in particular — was in each case stamped by violence, brutally in 1770, insidiously three decades later. In the rue Royale, men and women lost shoes in the mêlée, and rogues had, in some cases, begun to plunder the corpses. In the morgue, the men and women were all better shod, often in spite of prolonged immersion in the river, since they are recorded as having had not only buckle-shoes but also shoes with laces, and even half-boots. Here the reports indirectly confirm a general trend — few people in Paris went barefoot — and underline a technological micro-revolution — the spread of laces and the eclipse of buckles. The same applies to shirts, although the sources here are not entirely reliable. In 1770 and again in 1796, they were described with great precision (coarse or fine cloth, worn or new, embroidered, stained); why then their repeated absence — and absence of details — in a number of records? *Un peuple* without shirts? But in 1770 they included an architect, a lawyer and a woman dealing in women's clothing. In the year IV, we find that six out of twelve men had no shirts. The

---

72. S. Kaplan, *La Bagarre*, The Hague, 1979.
73. R. Cobb, *Death in Paris*, pp. 32–41 ('Le Juge de paix et l'historien').

following year they were all wearing them. The clerks must have got tired and careless, or inherited corpses undressed after inspection — and the police reports do not contradict the inventories — since Parisians cannot have been walking the streets with nothing on under their jackets or dressed only in breeches. In the same way, hats and head-dresses disappeared, flying off in the mêlée, or swallowed by the current.

Furthermore, the clerks' records give us a social sample that is not fully representative. First in age,[74] and sex — too many women in 1770, too few in 1800, for fewer women committed suicide — not many children or young people, a lot of adults and old men, which biases the conclusions in the same direction as the notarial inventories. Socially the whole of Paris is represented: the elite and the affluent, masters and shopkeepers, but especially the popular classes: 65 per cent in 1770, 60 per cent between 1796 and 1800. In both cases, the image is very close to that projected by the 1749 marriage contracts. So we get a valid picture of the Parisian choice of clothes on a May evening, and for every month in the year towards the end of the century of Enlightenment (See Table 6.3).[75]

The first thing to note is the uniformity of dress, for men and women, through these thirty years. For men, two combinations of garments predominated: breeches, trousers and shirt, or jacket and coat, breeches, trousers, shirt. The coat was often preferred by old

74. Ages calculated in 1770 and 1796–1800 compared with the pyramid of ages in France in 1801, in J. Dupaquier, M. Reinhard and J. Armengaud, *Histoire Générale de la Population Mondiale*, Paris, [n.d.], p. 258

	1770	1796–1800	1801
0– 9 years	7.5	4.5	21.9
10–19 years	17.0	10.0	18.4
20–39 years	24.7	43.5	30.4
40–49 years	13.8	17.0	11.6
50 years and over	39.0	25.0	17.7

75. Cf. A. Daumard and F. Furet, *Structures sociales* (in %):

	1750 (Paris)	1770	1796–1800
I. Merchants, officers	11.0	6.4	11.0
II. Small shopkeepers, artisans	27.0	30.0	28.0
III. Popular classes	62.0	63.6	61.0

Table 6.3. Wardrobes according to police reports (% of total in brackets)

	1770		1796–1800	
Men	Number of cases: 44		Number of cases: 108	
Jackets	34	(80)	41	(37)
Coats	26	(59)	20	(19)
Breeches	37	(84)	63	(59)
Trousers	—	—	44(+4)	(41)
Waistcoats	7	—	81(+11)	(75)
Frock-coats, cloaks	4	—	11	(11)
Shoes	7	—	59(+1)	(52)
Stockings	33	(75)	66	(61)
Shirts	18	(41)	96	(88)
Kerchiefs	23	(51)	12	(11)
Drawers—	—	—	9	(8)
Women	Number of cases: 88		Number of cases: 31	
Dresses	9	(11)	2	(6)
Skirts and/or petti-				
coats	86[a]	(98)	28[b]	(93)
Loose blouse	52	(60)	19	(61)
Jumper	5	(3)	7	(22)
Mantlet	13	(12)	—	—
Cloak	3	—	—	—
Apron	40	(45)	10	(30)
Pockets	23	(26)	17	(55)
Shoes	2	—	12	(31)
Corset	17	(18)	14	(44)
Stockings	57	(65)	24	(77)
Shirts	28	(34)	26	(80)
Kerchiefs	45	(51)	10	(31)

Note: [a] [36 (2) 17 (3)]   [b] [14 (2)]

men, the waistcoat, rare in 1770, had become common before 1800 —
75 per cent of cases. Trousers, unknown in the time of Louis XVI,
clothed the posteriors of four Parisians out of ten under the Directoire.
A job-lot of frock-coats and great-coats protected the shiverers in May
1770, or were found on the backs of the affluent in winter months.
Any sort of seasonal adaptation was a matter of class, piling on
garments was very rare except for waistcoats, a rather dubious way of
combatting the cold. Differences of fortune and condition are immediately striking, a whole world of manners and habits separated
d'Argenton, a *négociant* dressed in a braided overcoat made of Silesian

cloth, breeches and a fine shirt with face inserts,[76] or Pierre Legros, a well-known ladies' hairdresser (Melchior Grimm deplores his disappearance),[77] with his cloth and scarlet jacket, both with gold braid, his black velvet breeches, linen shirt, silk stockings,[78] from poor journeymen like Guillaume Goubert in a coat and jacket of bluish cloth, black serge breeches, cotton stockings, coarse shirt,[79] or Jean Cléry, fished out of the Seine in a red-and-white-striped velvet waistcoat, with two pairs of grey drill trousers, shirt and truss.[80] For all of them, the hygiene of underpants was virtually unknown — none at all in 1770, nine between 1796 and 1800. They acquired essentials, but life remained precarious for many, and the differences between them are explicit in their appearance.

There is no very marked variety in women's outfits. Marie Auroux, wife of a timber-merchant, had dressed in two petticoats, an ordinary household shirt, a gauze tippet and white cotton stockings; she was twenty-four when they picked her up in the rue Royale; Marie Fournier, sixty-year-old wife of a water-carrier, was wearing a shirt, two petticoats (one serge, the other of *calemande*) and an old pair of loose pockets, no stockings.[81] Thirty years later, Marie Gyon, employed in the Poitevin Baths, fell into the Seine at the age of twenty, wearing a poor calico petticoat, a blue-and-white-checked loose blouse,[82] a linen chemise and black woollen stockings. Clothing was fairly uniform for most of them, four-fifths wore petticoats (or skirts, for the distinction between *jupon* and *jupe* is not always clear) loose smock and shirt; a corset indicated the superior ways of servants, girls working in the world of fashion, or the wives of good artisans. There were camisoles, some slightly superior low-cut dresses, a few mantlets, not many cloaks, but they all wore stockings, a good number of checked aprons, and the pairs of pockets essential to good housewives. On the evening of 30 May 1770, only a few servants or seamstresses and a small number of widows or established shopkeepers had dressed up: Anne Josèphe Godeau, aged twenty-four, a chamber-maid in the rue Royale, in her dress of Indian cotton; Marguerite Simonet, aged sixteen, a seamstress, with her white cotton pleated blouse, her little

76. AN. Y 9769.
77. M. Grimm, *Correspondance littéraire*, vol. V, p. 21, 1 July 1770 (Legros had a European reputation as a ladies' hairdresser.)
78. AN. Y 9769.
79. AN. Y 9769.
80. AD. Seine, D 4 V 17, Year VII, 13 Florial (Jean Cléry was aged forty when he was fished out of the river at the Pont de la Révolution, Pont Royal).
81. AN. Y 9769.
82. AD. Seine, D 4 V 17, Year V, 24 Messidor (Marie Gayon was twenty-one. She fell in the river accidentally while stepping from one boat to another).

Table 6.4. Colours of clothing, according to police reports (in %)

	Men		Women	
	1770 100 = 92 mentions	1796–1800 100 = 355 mentions	1770 100 = 120 mentions	1796–1800 100 = 116 mentions
Grey	34.0	27.0	12.6	8.0
Black	22.0	9.0	8.4	7.0
Brown & musk	7.0	7.0	4.2	6.5
White	13.0	20.0	22.6	35.0
Green	5.5	5.0	1.6	2.0
Yellow	6.0	4.0	3.5	4.5
Orange	18.5		29.0	
Olive		15.0	24.3	23.0
Blue	7.0			
Red	5.0	13.0	18.4	14.0
Pink				
Patterned	6.0	74.0	Patterned 50.0	48.0
Striped	2.0	55.0	19.0	26.0
Checked	1.0	4.0	15.0	7.0
Flowered & sprigged	3.0	5.0	13.0	9.0
Spotted	—	10.0	3.0	6.0
Plain	91.0	80.0	Plain 63.0	75.0

bodice of calico, her two printed petticoats and her cloak of calico stuff; Marie Cottier, sixty-two years old and the widow of an inn-keeper, was wearing a dress and petticoats lined with black taffeta shot with gold, a scalloped shirt, white cotton stockings, two under-petticoats of pique and calico, a lace cap and red and green silk garters.[83] Among the *femmes du peuple* who had come to see the fireworks, as among those whom the hazards of their wretched life cast in the river, everything spoke of necessity, with only a few superfluous touches, some silk, small accessories, little luxuries of underclothing. The general picture is in accordance with the average levels found in notarial inventories. Colours and materials give a much clearer indication of changes that occurred during a century (Tables 6.4 and 6.5).

It was a motley crowd that packed into the place Louis XV, the men wearing black jackets, grey coats, brown or dark breeches, the women in white skirts, white and red blouses, blue petticoats, *déshabillés* of blue and white calico; white stripes and checks were most common for

83. AN. Y 9769.

Table 6.5: Fabrics in wardrobes, according to police reports (in %)

	Men		Women	
	1770	1796–1800	1770	1796–1800
	100 = 108 mentions	100 = 359 mentions	100 = 341 mentions	100 = 142 mentions
Wool: ratteen camlet, serge, knitted ⎫	62.0	48.0	14.0	18.0
Wool mixture ⎭				
Cotton: cottonade, Indian calico, cretonne, dimity, silk muslin, nankeen, pekin, cotton velvet	12.0	24.0	54.0	50.0
Silk: satin, damask, taffeta	4.0	6.0	3.5	4.0
Linen: hempen linen, canvas, drill	18.0	20.0	25.0	28.0
Leather	4.0	1.5	—	—
Miscellaneous	—	0.5	3.5	—

aprons. Here and there a patch of dazzling colour, yellow, orange, or a fabric dyed in a cooler shade such as green, or sombre shades of black or brown gave nuance to the colour values. Thirty years later, with the Revolution stabilised, the palette of masculine colours was splashed on ordinary clothes; the variety of fabrics, fantastic colour combinations, subtlety of contrasting shades composed a new visual order; the people were leaving their grey jackets in the cupboard and donning lilac coats, white cotton waistcoats with yellow stripes, bottle-green breeches, cutting a dash in camisole-jackets or pink Revolutionaries' jackets (*carmagnoles*) with dark spots, the acme of smart outfits: Michel Datte, an elderly printer, was an old-fashioned figure in his slate-coloured camlet jacket, and his black satin breeches;[84] Charles d'Aubigny, a twenty-five-year-old tavern boy fished out of the La Grenouillère quay had chosen, on the morning of his disappearance, a Revolutionaires' jacket of striped violet nankeen over trousers of the same fabric, two waistcoats, one red silk, the other dimity piqué, blue stockings and pointed shoes,[85] only one of which remained. Blue and white, red and white, blue and red were the most frequent colour combinations. The women wore scarlet petticoats — indeed, petticoats of every shade — bodices and aprons with a variety of motifs and soft

84. AD. Seine, D 4 V 17, Year VI, 8 Brumaire.
85. AD. Seine, D 4 V 17, Year V, 19 Messidor.

colours; they were less innovative than the men. This shows a double liberation: in relation to the old dimorphism by which eye-appeal was restricted to women, leaving men the majesty and uniformity of dark colours; and in relation to the social system of appearances by which colour was an affirmation of establishment and power paraded in the passing show, and emphasised by superfluous details. With a pronounced simplifications of forms, the refined show of *les grands* has percolated down to *le peuple*, as if in defiance of prevailing difficulties and despair.[86]

Two more factors are revealed by this trend: the culmination of the textile revolution, and the custom among the popular classes of re-routing material possessions. The new consumer goods predominated in the clothing of those who drowned in the year VIII, woollens had lost their overwhelming ascendancy; light fabrics, cheaper calicoes and cottons had taken over. It is not certain that the popular classes were better covered, but it is certain that they were forced to renew their clothes more often, and were thus obliged to enter the consumer market. At the same time, via the second-hand clothes dealers, there was an adaptation of manners hitherto restricted to the refined circles of the aristocracy and fashion. In the greyness of ordinary life, clothing allowed some sensual responses and choices, such as the play of light and colour, and perceptual pleasures — which Rétif shows playing their part in amorous adventures — or like the tactile pleasure of handling fabrics that were not so harsh and coarse, of putting on more supple and lighter clothes, and the capricious amusement of picking out a particular detail, adopting a style. The victims of accident or suicide entered the water in their everyday clothes, moulded to measure by work, habit and bearing, chosen with an empirical utilitarian sense in details — like buttons[87] or second-hand bits of uniform — without much regard for the fashions of the new privileged groups or for patriotic and political bric-à-brac. The people modelled their dress as they constructed their living space.

In the eighteenth century in Paris the popular classes underwent a sartorial revolution, they passed from the days of the durable and the dependable, handed down many times, to those of change and renewal; they displayed a new sensibility. The eye became keener, the passing show more mobile, the notes of a higher world of fashion sometimes made themselves heard. Contrasts between men and women were less marked, though they did not disappear, but a feeling for adornment was acquired by all. Does this assessment seem too

86. R. Cobb, *Death in Paris*, pp. 76–7.
87. Ibid., pp. 78–9.

optimistic because it does not take into account paupers and down-and-outs? Perhaps, but I feel there are two lessons to be drawn from the reading of police reports. First, they speak of the culture of the poor, therefore of a specific activity; reading through their monotonous litany it would be wrong to think of the masses dressed in worn, stained, patched clothes. Of course, the aspect existed: expressions like 'mean', 'old', 'worn', 'torn', 'patched' were used 36 times in 1770, 57 times around 1798; but the clerks were on those occasions checking more than 550, and more than 600 items of clothing. The ragged were a minority. Secondly, it is more important to see how the popular classes came to terms with the material conditions imposed on them than to imagine them miserable and indifferent to appearance. The culture of poverty, as it became established at the beginning of the Revolution, was made up of compromises; it expressed a general trend, it adapted to a certain rhythm of material obsolescence. For the first time in history, a huge consumer system, based on the ephemeral, and allowing for a certain element of excess, was experimenting with popular dress. Social divisions of appearance were established on these new frontiers.

PART III

Popular Culture

CHAPTER 7

Reading Habits

But this rabble never reads, it never will read as long as it is a
rabble. . . .

Rétif de la Bretonne

From the seventeenth century the urban world was a
world of culture and privilege, and in the constellation of French
towns the capital enjoyed an undeniable superiority. Culture in Paris,
fashioned in the shadow of the monarchical state, benefited from a
network of facilities and institutions which enabled it, throughout the
eighteenth century, to maintain its progress and consolidate its advantages as the leading centre of book production, undisputed metropolis
of academic life and its provincial extensions, crossroads of scientific,
philosophic and literary innovation and, at the same time, the centre of
theological thought and university tradition. There is no need to dwell
on such a familiar picture, but it is important to realise that this
acculturising process, directed primarily at the social elites, could not
fail to have its impact upon the popular classes. Paris, no doubt more
than any other city in France, offered cultural opportunities. Because it
produced and circulated books, papers and pictures, because it retained and attracted authors and potential authors, because every kind
of writing could be found there, the capital had built up a specific
culture in which habits and behaviour were modelled on recent knowledge, and where the chance to meet and communicate gave a sense of
hope and the possibility of acquiring a culture of their own to the most
impoverished and illiterate. The newcomer, temporary or permanent
migrant, found in Paris more than just a city atmosphere, such as a
villager might find spending a few hours at his local county town, he
entered upon a life of a quite new and different kind, he could become
a different man. There are two ways of rediscovering how this new
popular-class being was created: by looking at cultural activities and
habits which depended upon familiarity with the printed or written
word; by looking at ways of life and leisure revealing a specific
sociability which observers did not always understand.

Reference to the reading habits of the popular classes in Paris immediately conjures up an image which presents a problem — that of the supposed upsurge in reading which we associate customarily with the Enlightenment as a whole. Let us listen once again to Sébastien Mercier, in his *Tableaux de Paris*, when he is depicting book-sellers and book-lovers:

> People are certainly reading ten times as much in Paris as they did a hundred years ago; if you think of the multitude of small booksellers scattered all around the place, set up in shops at street corners and sometimes in the open air, selling old books or a few new pamphlets that keep on appearing . . . [You see groups of readers] standing as if magnetised around the counter; they are in the way of the shopkeeper, who has removed all the seats in order to force them to stand; but that does not stop them remaining for hours bent over books, busy perusing pamphlets, making advance judgements of their merit and their fate. . . .[1]

A text as remarkable as this in its picturesque precision is of course open to a variety of interpretations. The perceptive observer was originally struck by the progress of the book, but this first impression was reinforced by the idea that there was a widespread public of intelligent, active, avid readers, with a keen appetite for knowledge, quick to judge and even to debate in Paris on the eve of the Revolution: an opinion supported by every genre of writing and apparently based on fact. And finally, Mercier tells of the strategies deployed by shopkeepers to cope with the growth of a clientèle which suggests a spontaneous sociability within the bookshop, an eagerness to devour the books and publications piled on the stands, in the midst of running battles over chairs and hurried debates, in a flash of brief controversy and the excitement provoked by a growing number of readers who were more and more demanding, more and more confident of their ideas and judgements. So Parisians were reading and re-reading, but which Parisians and what books? Access to reading was undoubtedly the result of an accumulation of cultural privileges which a number of recent studies have proved to be both selective and open; it stamped urban social groups in the same way as indications of fortune or badges of prestige. To be able to read was an advantage which was all the more useful since the whole of French society was steeped in oral peasant cultures and because, for a great number of the Parisian popular classes, the first decisive years of seeing and doing had been spent in a rural environment where visual communication and action predominated. This is why it is important to make clear how, in a society

---

1. L.-S. Mercier, *Le Tableau de Paris*, vol. 12, pp. 151–5; cf. *Ami*, vol. 5, pp. 54–6.

dominated by the written word, even a halting ability to read could utterly transform the ordinary perceptions and mentality of the popular classes.

Who could read among the popular classes? As elsewhere, we must use the test of signatures which, required for official documents — marriage contracts, wills, witnessing at law, interrogations, witnessing an inventory after a death — enable us to trace how widely basic writing skills were diffused.[2] In the eighteenth-century city there was a high probability of a correlation between the ability to sign one's name and complete literacy, although it is not entirely proven and a fundamental doubt is thrown upon the interpretation of signature counts, which do not enable us to distinguish between different writing abilities. The ability to read does not call into question a relationship to social and religious norms as much as the mastery of writing, which offered the possibility of escape and liberation from traditional constraints:[3] active and passive literacy cannot be distinguished in the ability to sign one's name. Finally, we must not forget the psychological significance which makes the act of signing so important as a social affirmation of identity.

In the present state of research, we can say that the study of elementary education in eighteenth-century Paris has scarcely begun, and we can work only from fragmentary and heterogeneous data. But two characteristics appear quite clearly: globally, Parisian literacy was long-established; moreover, it progressed in the eighteenth century along lines which, for lack of investigation, are difficult to establish precisely. From the end of the seventeenth century, figures obtained for Paris appear to be far above the national average: 85 per cent of men and 60 per cent of women were capable of signing their wills; on the eve of the Revolution more than 90 per cent of men signed, and the number of women went up to 80 per cent. It may be objected that making a will is socially a very selective act in that it favours the propertied classes and cultured groups; in fact, one Parisian in ten made a will in the reign of Louis XIV, 15 per cent during the reign of Louis XVI. Moreover, results observed in *quartiers* with a strong popular-class base are no different from the general high success rate: around 1700, in the Montmartre *quartier*, where 40 per cent of the

2. For all comparisons and analyses in connection with the problem of signatures, see F. Furet and J. Ozouf, *Lire et écrire*, Paris, 2 vols., 1977, particularly, vol. 1, pp. 16–44, 229–59; J. Quéniard, *Culture et sociétés urbaines dans la France de l'ouest au XVIIIe siècle*, Lille, 1977, 2 vols., vol. 1, pp. 112–241. The average percentage for partners signing their marriage certificate was 28.7 for men and 17.4 for women (1686–90) and 47.4 and 26.8 respectively between 1786 and 1790.

3. R. Chartier, *L'Entrée dans l'écrit*, Critique, 1978, pp. 973–83.

4. P. Chaunu, *Mourir à Paris*, pp. 233–5, 292–5, 394–5, 428–30, 457–61.

testators were from the popular classes, more than 77 per cent of the men and 64 per cent of the women signed their names; in the same period, in the parish of Saint-Nicolas-des-Champs, where a good third of the wills which came before the notaries were from the popular classes, more than 90 per cent of men and 70 per cent of women signed their wills. Between 1750 and 1790, in the parish of Saint-Paul, literacy averaged 87 per cent; in the rue Saint-Honoré — where a third of the sample of testators came from the *petit peuple* — it was 93 per cent. So it seems that those who made wills in Paris were acculturated, although it remains true that the act of making a will undoubtedly ratifies the cultural privileges of the native Parisians and that the unequal social distribution of literacy will not show up very clearly. It is, however, logical to assume that illiteracy at the lower levels of the social ladder resisted the strong acculturation pressures for a long time. Inventories made after death give a better idea of the real social state of popular education.

Around 1700, 85 per cent of men and women servants who survived their partner signed the notary's document, women rather less often than men, responsible servants always more than the rest; around 1789, 98 per cent of the survivors were able to sign. If you include the witnesses present, of an equivalent social standing — servants or members of the lower strata — the proportions drop by 8 and 5 points around the same dates.[5] Undoubtedly, Parisian servants enjoyed a remarkable elementary education very early, and they became more at home with writing as the years went by. This appears first of all in their concern to preserve notarial documents, various certificates and even miscellaneous papers and correspondence. More than half the married servants kept a copy of their marriage contract at home, in a quarter of the inventories a will is mentioned, and two-thirds signed notes acknowledging debts, registers or account books. Some were prompted by a sense of family continuity or legal prudence to build up coherent collections of documents over two generations; Alexis Thorin, chef to the Baron de Breteuil, had four inventories, two wills and two marriage contracts connected with his family. As the century went on, even the poorest servants were keeping twice as many documents as at the beginning. There was every indication of regular familiarity with writing and counting: writing desks, desk-seals, pens, sand horns appear in the more privileged cases, and about a third of servants owned bureaux, *secrétaires*, writing-cases and desks. From the seventeenth century on, to be able to read and get something down in writing was a decisive factor in professional and social integration; for

5. F. Ardellier, 'Essai d'anthropologie urbaine', pp. 106–10.

Audiger in his *Maison réglée*,[6] for the abbé Claude Fleury in his *Devoirs des maîtres et des domestiques*,[7] there could be no doubt that servants (the men at least) had to be able to read, write and count; it was a matter of efficiency and smooth running of the aristocratic household. For women,[8] the question did not even arise, as their chief duty was 'to be good and honest'.[9]

A century later Madame de Genlis, writing the *La Bruyère des domestiques*, and Jean-Charles Bailleul, reflecting upon the *Moyens de former un bon domestique*,[10] were still stressing this advantage. 'This alone often procures a good situation', thinks the first, in her optimistic, liberal way; '. . . but the servant himself sometimes has most cause to fear the basic elements of education: because he knows his letters and numbers, he fancies he is a clever man and above his condition', argues the second, who has clearly perceived the social consequences of education for servants and been disturbed by them. That is why, even if it was necessary to have educated servants in order to be better served, one would always try to keep them in their place, and remind them 'that they are ignorant men'.[11] However, observers were at one in noting that Parisian servants read more than the average, travellers noticed private coachmen reading on their seats and lackeys poring over pamphlets at the back of the carriages;[12] Sébastien Mercier saw everywhere valets who could read and erected this into a positive act of faith in the illuminating virtues of books: 'These days, you see a waiting-maid in her back-room, a lackey in an anteroom reading pamphlets. People can read in almost all classes of society — so much the better. They should read still more. A Nation that can read carries within it a particular and happy strength which can defy or confound despotism . . .'.[13] Monsieur Lebrun, editor of the *Journal de la mode et du goût*, replied to his subscribers who were complaining that they had not received their copies of his periodical: 'This decision — the suspension of deliveries — will be carried out most rigorously, because it is not right, if servants are seizing the books, that we should supply them twice to their masters'.[14] The remark is interesting because it

6. Audiger, *La Maison réglée et l'art de diriger la maison d'un grand Seigneur*, Paris, 1692.
7. C. Fleury, *Devoirs du maître et des domestiques*, Paris, 1688.
8. M. Botlan, 'Domesticité', p. 271.
9. Audiger, *La Maison réglée*, p. 83.
10. Madame de Genlis, *Le 'La Bruyère' des domestiques*, Paris, 1828, 2 vols., vol. 1, pp. 7–8; J.-C. Bailleul, *Moyens de former un bon domestique*, Paris, 1782, pp. 25–30.
11. M. Botlan, 'Domesticité', pp. 272–3.
12. A. Soboul, *La Civilisation de la Révolution française. La crise de l'Ancien Régime*, Paris, 1970, p. 447.
13. L.-S. Mercier, *La Tableau de Paris*, vol. 9, p. 334.
14. C. Rimbault, 'La Presse féminine au XVIIIe siècle', Thesis, 3e cycle, EHESS, 1981, pp. 30–5.

signals a circulation of publications within the house, from the antechamber to the butler's pantry. But these remarks by observers and the
lessons drawn from inventories risk erring on the side of excessive
optimism, and signatures in interrogations of the accused at the
Châtelet give different results.[15] On the one hand, the general average
of signatories, taking men and women together, drops to about 50 per
cent, based on the last twenty years of the *Ancien Régime*; on the
other hand, the sexual dimorphism, not nearly so evident in notarian
documents, reappears here in full force: 62 per cent of men signed their
document, but scarcely 16 per cent of the women. This confirms the
advantage enjoyed by male servants in Paris, but it is not peculiar to
them, for it is found among all the accused questioned by the judges.[16]
By contrast, ordinary female servants in the most precarious situations, whom bad luck and hard times had brought before the tribunal,
were certainly more ignorant than the rest of the accused: only 16 per
cent of them could sign their name, as against 33 per cent of the men.
This shows the result of an advanced regional acculturation in which
women were always the losers;[17] the Parisian servant class, sustained
daily by rural migration, exaggerates the general contrast in town and
country, underlining once again the difference in professional qualifications. All in all, at a comparable level of fortune, the signature was
undoubtedly an attribute of servants integrated by work, marriage and
success, who might acquire an elementary education in the course of
their service, but this seems to have applied exclusively to men;[18]
women almost always remained 'as ignorant as the moment they
arrived in Paris'. Between the sombre, even desperate picture revealed
by the legal interrogations and the, generally speaking, quite dazzling
picture obtained from notarial documents, the ambiguous cultural
position of servants is clearly revealed. The demands of masters might
encourage literacy in aid of better service: this was the case already in

15. M. Botlan, 'Domesticité', pp. 275–8.
16. P. Petrovitch, *Crimes et criminalité*, pp. 248–50; 61 per cent of men signed their
statements, 33 per cent of women, an average of 52 per cent of defendants.
17. J. Dupaquier, *La Population rurale du Bassin Parisien à l'époque de Louis XIV*,
Paris, 1979, pp. 380–6. The average rate of literacy was 38.6 per cent of men, 12.5 per
cent for women between 1671 and 1720; M. Fleury and P. Valmary, 'Les Progrès de
l'instruction élémentaire de Louis XIV à Napoléon III, according to the investigations of
Louis Maggiolo', in *Population*, 1957, pp. 71–92; based on the same grouping as the
Maggiolo data, the results for the demographic catchment area for Paris are 53 per cent
for men, 33 per cent for women; for the *départements* close to the capital they are 63 per
cent and 38 per cent respectively.
18. M. Botlan, 'Domesticité', p. 277. At the age of twenty, 58 per cent of male
servants signed; at thirty, 75 per cent; at forty five, 85 per cent. For women of the same
ages the figures are only 17 per cent, 12 per cent and 42 per cent; the very slight increase
in the higher age groups cannot be regarded as significant, in view of the small number of
cases.

the seventeenth century with senior servants, and essentially men; on the other hand, employers' fears or passivity might curb or inhibit the progress of elementary education: this was the case with non-specialist personnel, especially women. Thus, compared with the lower orders in the countryside, only servants who inherited money were certain to get on, whilst the urban popular classes rose to the top only by their individual aptitudes and determination, and could improve themselves only if they went into the houses of enlightened employers: 'like master, like servant'.

Among Parisian wage-earners the ability to sign one's name was much less apparent than among servants under Louis XIV: 61 per cent of male wage-earners signed the inventory after the death of a spouse, but only 34 per cent of women could do so; under Louis XVI this cultural split was considerably reduced: 66 per cent of men and 62 per cent of wives were capable of signing; this recovery by women was quite spectacular and the lessening of the gap between the sexes suggested by the inventories indicates the multiplication of educational opportunities in the town and in the cultural and demographic zone of the capital. Around 1750, two-thirds of lower-class men signed their names, but scarcely half the women:[19] A decisive change has come about, the explanation of which is complicated by the mixing of social classes and by emigration. In the faubourg Saint-Marcel, a study of 15,000 signatures, 67 per cent of whom were Parisians and more than two-thirds lower-class, confirms this positive conclusion: in 1792, 68 per cent of the inhabitants of the faubourg could read and write.[20] Other *quartiers* present an analogous cultural scene: for example, in the Marais, where 90 per cent of the 3,000 *cartes de sûreté* analysed were signed, and also among families drawn from the popular classes in the rue Saint-Denis where 86 per cent of men and 73 per cent of women signed their marriage contract;[21] in both cases, there was only a very small gap between Parisians and migrants — 8 points for those in the section de la place des Fédérés, 4 for the newly-weds on the north–south axis; however, 84 per cent of *Parisiennes* were literate, and only 62 per cent of women from the provinces. In all cases the data are not affected by age: rates of literacy were very much the same for journeymen and their fiancées of about twenty-five to thirty, as for the forty to forty-five age group in the inventories; as many twenty-year-old *sectionnaires* signed their cards as those aged thirty, and only

19. M. Moulon, *Recherches d'anthropologie urbaines à partie des inventaires après décès a Paris, 1750–1760*, Memoire de maitrise, Paris 7, 1977, pp. 61–5.
20. H. Burstin, 'Faubourg Saint-Marcel', pp. 384–8.
21. H. Davet 'La Rue Saint Denis au XVIIIᵉ siécle', Thesis, 3ᵉ cycle, Paris I, 1976, typescript, pp. 177–80.

around the age of fifty did they appear less educated.[22] In the same
way, differences attributable to levels of wealth are less significant than
those established for other cities and towns, like Lyon, but the results
are not as conclusive as those obtained by a study of marriage contracts. Two frontiers, which sometimes crossed, appear clearly defined: lack of professional qualifications and social failure.

There is an obvious correlation between literacy and occupation. In
the faubourg Saint-Marcel percentages of illiterates were higher in
sectors of work which did not require much specialisation and in
which employers of the increasing mass of workers could draw upon
the endless flood of newcomers — casual and day labourers, porters,
dockers, masons, building workers, carters, coachmen, transport
workers all achieved lower than average scores: 57 per cent illiteracy in
non-specialist jobs, 46 per cent in building, 52 per cent among trans-
porters and carters. On the other hand, the rates of literacy were above
average among the artisans, journeymen and assistants, these having
acquired both professional skills and a level of culture very close to
that of master artisans; the workers in the Gobelins factory, with 87
per cent literacy, looked like scholars in the world of suburban
workers. These figures, which apply only to the male working population, recur in the section des Fédérés; all jobs where contact with
clients and professional requirements demanded book-keeping and a
certain amount of correspondence, therefore a basic command of
writing, were at the top — food, clothing, precision skills, furnishing
and timber trades. All non-specialist jobs and small street-trades could
accommodate a high percentage of illiteracy. The same contrast appears in the signing of inventories: from 1700, three-quarters of
wage-earners in the corporations signed their names, as did half of
their wives; around 1780, the figures were 80 and 65 per cent respectively; half the day-labourers, casual workers and independent wage-
earners signed their inventories in the time of Louis XIV, but less than
a quarter of their wives did so; in the reign of Louis XVI, the figure for
the men had still not reached two-thirds, but the women had caught up
with them. Cultural homogeneity of the sexes was encouraged by the
Parisian ambience, but it would not have occurred if the acculturation
levels at the points of departure had not been well-advanced. In the
popular faubourgs, and in the central *quartiers*, illiterates came from
further afield than literates, and they filled the labouring jobs and
unrewarding occupations; men from Savoy, Limoges, Cantal and the

---

22. F. Rousseau-Vigneron, 'La section de la place de penchant dans la Révolution', in
Contributions à l'Histoire démographique de la Révolution Française, 3rd series, Paris,
1970.

Auvergne were the least educated and the least inclined to settle permanently in the capital. In the Bonne Nouvelle section 500 masons were registered, and three-quarters of them came from Limousin and spoke the patois that Rétif made fun of: 'None of them seemed to me to have the accent of the Parisii, they all spoke strangely, singing, roaring, yelling . . .'; more than half of them were illiterate. These were the *gros ouvriers* that people spoke of with fear.[23]

The criminal records reveal an illiterate wage-earning society and make it possible to estimate the influence of poverty and failure: three-quarters of those accused of stealing food, both men and women, claimed they could 'neither read nor write', and the signatures studied around 1730 prove no great familiarity with writing.[24] Among petty criminals on the riverside 60 per cent of the delinquents were totally uneducated; around 1785 rather less than 40 per cent still claimed to be unable to sign their interrogation. Casual labourers, carters, porters and unskilled workers made up between half and two-thirds of this shifting population whose cultural character changed little during the century, and which included few women (8 per cent around 1730, 7 per cent around 1785). As everywhere, female delinquency was lower, but female illiteracy much higher: four-fifths of female petty delinquents could not sign their names.[25] In the same way, the dossiers on women arrested by the *matéchaussée* in the Ile-de-France — most of whom were provincials looking for work in Paris or the large villages and small towns on the outskirts — show that most were illiterate: only 7 per cent of those arrested could sign their deposition.[26] Material deprivation and intellectual poverty characterised the wandering horde of delinquents who were recruited for the most part among rootless recent migrants, but they were fairly exceptional in a population of men and women who were literate to a very large extent. The *peuple de Paris* could read, write and count, and it is understandable that Rétif should be concerned at the situation for, if the populace was familiar with reading and writing, was there not everything to fear,[27] still more as far as women were concerned. His misogyny breaks out in the *Gymnographes*, where he defines 'the duties of women from every class of citizen'; daughters of the popular classes must busy themselves only with work, 'as writing and even reading could only be prejudicial

23. M. Reinhard, 'La Révolution', pp. 78–9.
24. P. Petrovitch, *Crimes*, 248 (of the women tried at the Châtelet, only 33 per cent signed); A. Farge, *Le Vol d'aliment*, p. 127.
25. G. Picq, M. Pradines and C. Ungerer, 'La Criminalité', p. 115.
26. D. Lefèbvre-Weisz, 'Analyse de la délinquance féminine dans les environs de Paris de 1750 à 1790, d'aprés les archives de la Maréchaussée', Thesis, IIIe cycle, Paris 1, 1979, pp. 104–09.
27. Rétif de la Bretonne, *Les Nuits*, pp. 3355–6.

to them',[28] indicating his concern to defend to the last the traditional roles of women — good daughters, good wives, good mothers — according to which cooks who could not read made the best soup![29]

The diatribes of Rétif contrast with the reality in the capital and surrounding region which were strongly acculturised after a century and a half of literacy dictated by the Counter-Reformation. Between the middle of the seventeenth century and the end of the eighteenth century teaching institutions had multiplied in Paris; four types ensured almost complete schooling for boys and a steady improvement in the situation for girls.[30] Parish and hospital chantries — like Bicêtre where Rétif met his brother who was teaching there, and devoured the thirty or so books collected by the Jansenist Fuzier[31] — were intended for little boys, who sang the offices and received some basic teaching until their voices broke, thus obliging them to leave the choir school. The *petites écoles* which, from 1672, were organised in 170 units in the forty-three parishes, each had a master and mistress who took boys and girls separately, for a school fee; they were supplemented in the eighteenth century by free charity schools founded by the parish organisations and the clergy, such as the one of Saint-Sulpice which attracted the teaching order of the Christian Brothers, or the establishments in the faubourg Saint-Antoine (almost twenty) founded by the Tabourin Brothers.[32] If you add the authorised boarding schools run by laymen, classes opened temporarily or permanently by religious congregations (some male, but mostly female), the educational work for Savoyards and young provincials carried out by the establishment of the abbé de Pontbriand and, for example, hospitals teaching young orphans, by 1789 there were nearly five hundred establishments of elementary education which depended on the Church and which were available more or less free to children from modest homes.[33]

To these must be added the 174 licensed master writers and arithmeticians who, in addition to their expertise in commercial writing and accountancy, also provided well-attended lessons in writing and arithmetic, competing with the aspirations of small schoolmasters. The

28. Idem, *Les gymnographes*, The Hague, 1777, pp. 40–69.

29. S. Maréchal, *Project de loi portant défense d'apprendre à lire aux femmes*, Paris, 1801.

30. R. Chartier, M. M. Compère, D. Julia, *L'Education en France du XVIᵉ au XVIIIᵉ siècle*, Paris, 1976, pp. 45–85.

31. Rétif de la Bretonne, *Monsieur Nicolas*, vol. 1, pp. 185–205.

32. M. Fosseyeux, *Les Écoles de charité à Paris sous l'Ancien Régime et dans la première partie du XIXᵉ siècle*, Paris, 1912, pp. 48–64; A. Gazier, 'Les Écoles de charité du faubourg Saint-Antoine', in *Revue internationale de l'enseignement supérieur*, 1906, pp. 212–40.

33. F. Langlois, 'L'enseignement primaire payant à Paris, 1770–1790', Mémoire de maîtrise, Paris 10, Nanterre, 1975.

mâtre écrivain Paillasson wrote, in the *Encyclopédie*, in praise of the
body to which he belonged, which defended sound principles of
writing and which taught elementary commercial techniques, indispensable both to the economy and to the culture of the capital.[34]
Finally, the precentor of Notre-Dame and the episcopal authorities
had to beware of the competition from clandestine tutors, unofficial
teachers who kept open classes in spite of the interdicts: between 1770
and 1790, 116 of them — 74 women and 42 men — were prosecuted.[35]
Compared with the rural and urban provinces, and in spite of persistent inequalities, for women and for recent arrivals, they were not far
from achieving 100 per cent schooling for the popular classes in Paris.
A town-dweller had an excellent chance of learning to write, to some
degree at least, even if his or her education was directed chiefly towards
the disciplining of children and the making of good Christians.[36]

All the evidence suggests that the above was true. More than half of
the wage-earners' inventories mentioned personal papers — slightly
fewer than among servants, but nevertheless enough to show these
acquired habits were widespread. We must consider here the importance of letter-writing, which was in no sense restricted to the social
elite; it is simply that refined products of the art sent by the ruling
classes have been preserved, but those humble letters, ill-written and
ill-spelt, exchanged by poorer men and women have rarely been found
— or, indeed, sought. Nevertheless, private and confidential correspondence did exist among the popular classes, no doubt encouraged by
the regular functioning of the parcel post and the creation of the *petite
Poste* to deliver mail within Paris. Three situations in particular gave
rise to written messages among the popular classes: love affairs, family
exchanges and business correspondence.

Many indirect references in *Monsieur Nicolas*, *Les Nuits* and *Les
Contemporaines* indicate the frequency of sentimental, even erotic
letters: Madame Knappen's pretty chamber-maid exchanged well-
phrased, quite spicy letters with the journeymen in the workshop
where Rétif was working; Monsieur Nicolas delivered his seductive
messages to the shops in the rue de Grenelle where the dressmakers
read them aloud to each other, making love by letter.[37] In a package
left in the rue Transnonain by a butcher's daughter, the Nocturnal
Spectator discovered the notebooks in which she kept copies of the

34. J. Bonzon, *La Corporation des maîtres écrivains et l'expertise en écritures sous
l'Ancien Régime*, Paris, 1899.
35. F. Langlois, 'L'Enseignement primaire', pp. 70–2.
36. J. Kaplow, *Les Noms des Rois*, pp. 176–7; one can no longer subscribe to the
author's rather hasty judgement that 'educational possibilities were very limited for the
children of the popular classes'.
37 Rétif de la Bretonne, *Monsieur Nicolas*, vol. 3, p. 299; vol. 4, p. 80.

letters 'she wrote to the man she loved, and her lover's replies . . .'.[38]
Agnès Lebègue, Rétif's wife, 'wrote gallantries in the midst of poverty', which meant she spent her days composing an amorous correspondence, the discovery of which suggested to the writer the publication
of *La Femme Infidèle*.[39]
   The epistolary form affected by the novelist no doubt owes less to a
studied romantic effect or the fashion for epistolary novels than to a
need within himself which, in this case, conformed to general social
practices. As with other authors, the letters invented are always
presented as authentic, but in Rétif's novels, particularly, they reflect
an activity dictated by patterns of *sensibilité* which were universal.
With Rétif, fiction vibrates to the rhythms of real life: *Monsieur
Nicolas* shows the importance of letters exchanged between those who
have left and those who have stayed behind.[40] It would be an illusion
to imagine that migration broke all the bonds between migrants and
their families: of course, some would have wanted to sever connections, but for the others there was always some way of writing or
having letters written — public letter-writers were there for that
purpose, and friends — not forgetting the news that could be transmitted *viva voce* and that compatriots would bring with them as they
disembarked from river barge or stage-coach. But for many people,
reading and writing letters, giving and receiving news was nothing
extraordinary. Jacques Ménétra, a journeyman-glazier, during his *tour
de France* kept in touch with his family in this way, sending news from
every town where he stayed any length of time, and receiving affec-
tionate greetings and sometimes a little money from Paris. An elementary education was a considerable advantage in work and for getting a
job; it was by writing that you could find out where the good jobs
were, receive the money needed for the journey by post, and fix
conditions of employment by letter. Ménétra was capable of running
the affairs of widows who employed him, he wrote their letters, and
when a dispute broke out, his abilities singled him out as the man to
bring about a settlement.[41] For his employers and for his friends, part
of the prestige of a Parisian journeyman rested on a small treasury of
education. If the *Paysan Perverti* and the *Paysanne Pervertie* are
epistolary novels, it is because they are dramas of separation high-

   38. Idem, *Les Nuits*, pp. 127, 176, 185, 203, 405, 465, 2226 (the daughter of a
respectable artisan threw herself in the river, and a note was found in her pocket), 2208,
1057; after his death they found this note in the pocket of a servant imprisoned for theft:
'love of Eufrasie caused me to seek to improve my fortunes; for love, shame and jealousy
I am resolved to die . . .'.
   39. Idem, *Monsieur Nicolas*, vol. 3, pp. 470–1.
   40. Ibid., vol. 3, pp. 390–1, 409–10.
   41. BHVP, MS. 676, fos. 30–1, 52, 55, 62.

lighting one fact above all else — the meaning of separation revealed as a result of having experienced the collective impact of Parisian life. The letter in a novel, as in real life, was part of a chain of communication between village and capital, between districts in the town, and between members of the family; it prolonged the conversations it reported, it could be read aloud to an audience; it was an instrument of information and change. One can understand the dismay of moralists when they saw in its widespread popularity an abuse by the people of an edifying education intended originally to control and uplift. There is no doubt that this useful patrimony could be acquired easily in Paris for, apart from educational institutions available free of charge, you could always find some voluntary instructor; an elderly relative, educated friend or amorous acquaintance might serve as a tutor to the children of the popular classes. Thus, for some time, Monsieur Nicolas spent his Sundays after dinner teaching writing and reading to his landlady's young children, Manon and Théodore, and to their friend Colette, a sixteen-year-old laundry-maid.[42] Parisian booksellers quickly realised this was a profitable market. Countless treatises, guides and manuals were published and reprinted to direct the relationships of the untutored and lavish useful advice upon autodidacts of love and epistolary sociability.[43] The vogue for 'secretaries', 'courtiers', 'lovers', 'ladies', 'French soldiers' and 'families' testifies to a diffusion beyond bourgeois and aristocratic circles.[44] The adult member of the popular classes could learn from them 'how to write politely on all sorts of subjects', and find a model for formulas suited to all circumstances of life, which would then blossom in his speech and from his pen like the shrewd commentaries drawn from proverbs or the wisdom of the *Messager Boiteux* or the *Grand compost des bergers*.

However, people could usually read before they could write. It was with pride that the errand boy replied to the question: 'Are you learning to read?' 'Oh yes, Mademoiselle, I can read writing . . .'.[45] He may have learned in Latin — this was recommended around 1700 by the *Philémon-Trotet*, a basic text book for the *petites écoles* — but also in French — the *Pitel-Préfontaine*, another school book used frequently in Parisian lessons, preferred this method, following the example of J.B. de la Salle and the charity schools.[46] This apprentice-

---

42. Rétif de la Bretonne, *Monsieur Nicolas*, vol. 3, pp. 576–7.
43. *Le Livre dans la vie quotidienne*, Paris, 1975, pp. 109–12.
44. The most notable success was Puget de la Serre's book, *La Secrétaire à la mode*, Amsterdam, 1655, known to have gone through about fifty editions; it was part of the *Bibliothèque Bleue de Troyes* as early as 1730.
45. Rétif de la Bretonne, *Les Nuits*, pp. 1561–5.
46. F. Langlois, 'L'Enseignement Primaire', pp. 92–105. These two Parisian manuals went through several editions around 1770–80.

ship in writing skills meant acquiring a careful technique: the cutting of the pen and the command of a physical control which involved the general posture of the body, the positioning of fingers and hand, the coordination of movements.[47] For little urchins it was a physical and moral remedial lesson, which many found difficult;[48] at all events, it crowned elementary schooling in the same way as simple arithmetic, which gave the learners the mechanics of numeracy which were indispensable in adult life.[49] And the fact is that familiarity was as important in all this as was the basic skill. In a population for whom it was not a daily practice, writing occupied a special place, for it was a sort of insurance and reserve strength, and it could be used even if one was not always in a situation requiring its use;[50] in any case, the indicator of the presence of written manuscripts proves that reading among the popular classes had purposes other than access to knowledge and channels other than the possession of books. Obviously, writing lent itself to the accidental and superficial, as much as to essentials. The emancipation of the individual and the constitution of the modern family presuppose the act of preserving written papers and their increasing use. Inventories prove that personal papers and family papers had become progressively necessary and customary. Their disappearance, which was linked with the rapid devaluation of their importance and the poor conditions for preservation in popular-class homes, should not conceal from us the real importance of these archives of daily life. A whole chain of attitudes and practices link together demanding our attention: religious procedures giving rise to certificates of baptism, of death, and of good life and morals; civil and administrative regulations demanding contracts, the division of property, inventories, trusteeships; family connections leading to legal documents, personal letters, and papers of all sorts. A whole system of accepted ways of thinking and acting was fashioned by these customs which brought the individual before the priest, notary, clerks of the Treasury and the tax-farmers, forcing him along a path marked out more and more by the registry office. It was not for nothing that the Comité de Sûreté générale in the Revolution created the *carte d'identité* — an identity card, except for the photo. The *carte civique*, which was copied in a register, made it possible for the authorities to get to know the people better, to control suspects and prevent disorders — a police observer remarked, when the cards were renewed in 1793, that it was important to prevent 'troublemakers and conspirators

47. G. Vigarello, *Le Corps redressé*, Paris, 1978.
48. R. Chartier, M. M. Compère, D. Julia, 'L'Education', pp. 126–35.
49. Ibid., p. 136.
50. Y. Castan, *Honnêteté et relations sociales en Languedoc*, Paris, 1974, pp. 121–6.

infiltrating the workers . . .'.[51] At the end of the eighteenth century in the popular areas of Paris the frontiers between private and public life had already become unclear: people were always having to show their papers.

Literacy enabled people to read and write, opened the door to all sorts of knowledge, but it did not necessarily, in Paris at least, lead to the possession of books. Between 1750 and 1759, out of about four thousand inventories after death, involving all social categories, less than a quarter mention the presence of books.[52] Paris, capital of the book trade, controlling more than half the printed production in France, was a city where people apparently read less than in provincial towns like Rouen or Rennes.[53] These contrasts support the idea that access to the printed word involved a whole range of factors including means, job, social situation and the cultural habits of families, but they also suggest other hypotheses. The first concerns documentary sources: in the capital, replete with culture and won over to books from the middle of the seventeenth century by the efforts of its printers and publishers,[54] the notary's document is not such a clear and faithful measure as in provincial society, where books were still scarce. The second hypothesis involves conditions of daily life in Paris: the population was crowded into confined lodgings which did not encourage the preservation of fragile things, and where perhaps books, rather less rare as consumer-objects than elsewhere, may have been thrown or left lying in corners, in any case hidden from the eye of notarial investigators. In a society which was already partly accustomed to profusion, it may have seemed natural not to count everything, there were sins of omission in the information, in so far as the users were blasé and more insensitive; so books and pamphlets of practical culture or pious texts of no great commercial value may have been left out of the valuation by the very fact that there were so many of them. Accumulation can lead to waste, and consequently a number of light-weight, badly presented, low-cost publications may have disappeared. Finally, a last possibility must be suggested: in Paris books were not the only means of access to the printed word; for men of letters, libraries and private collections played their part; for the masses, one must consider a different visual culture in which the book was only one element among others; for most people, the periodical, broadsheet, occasional political

51. M. Reinhard, *Contributions à l'histoire démographique de la Révolution française*, 2nd series, Paris, 1965, Introduction, pp. 11–15.

52. M. Marion, *Les Bibliothèques privées à Paris au milieu du XVIIIᵉ siècle*, Paris, 1978, pp. 94–8.

53. J. Quéniard, *Culture*, vol. 2, pp. 536–76.

54. H. J. Martin, *Livre, pouvoir, et société à Paris au XVIIᵉ siècle*, Paris–Geneva, 2 vols., 1969.

writings, a picture sometimes with, sometimes without, words, a poster, manuscript or printed song, a placard or even a sign were possible media which sustained the effects of very high literacy. Accumulation, exchanging and waste may explain the small number of book *owners*, a number which may be attributed not to the failure but to the success of urban culture.

Not many books were preserved in the homes of the popular classes: around 1700 they were recorded in 13 per cent of wage-earners' and 30 per cent of servant inventories after death; between 1750 and 1759 it was still 13 per cent out of 800 legacies made by wage-earners, and 20 per cent out of more than 200 servant inventories; around 1780 the percentage was over 35 for the lower classes and close on 40 for servants.[55] So, at first, journeymen, assistants, day-labourers and casual workers read much less than servants and chamber-maids, but the gap was perhaps less pronounced if one allows the probability of books in some homes, as suggested by the listing of book-cases in about ten instances. However, neither wage-earners nor servants in Paris could pass as avid readers, even if they still shared this trait in the middle of the century with other social strata whom one would confidently expect to own books: minor civil servants and clerks (14 per cent), and rentiers (23 per cent). At the end of the century servants, who lost ground around 1750 — a 10-point drop compared with 1700 — made less progress overall than wage-earners. The bookshops were probably winning readers but without the gap shrinking between literacy and reading, which tends to emphasise the importance of cultural heritage and tradition; perhaps the old-established Parisians read more and the more numerous newcomers caught the habit only after one, or even two generations. Ownership and preservation of books were part of a general integration.

Three characteristics mark out *le peuple* from the whole body of readers in Paris: the possession and age of books depended both on levels of wealth and the scale of professional qualifications; the average number of single volumes was low but the total number of books owned rose clearly between 1700 and 1790; and, finally, the apparent content of their meagre libraries remained the same (see Table 7.1).

The uneven distribution of books among servants followed a fairly clear hierarchy: the majority of readers were found among those of above-average means; upper servants who were close to their employers always had more books than others, although these positions — for

55. F. Ardellier, 'Essai d'anthrophologie urbaine', pp. 108–110; (the rate of 55 per cent includes probable cases, attested by the presence of book shelves); M. Botlan, 'Domesticité', pp. 278–9, has found that, out of a total of 196 cases, 33 per cent were certain.

Table 7.1. Distribution of books among the popular classes

	(1) Wage-earners	Servants	(2) Wage-earners	Servants
1700				
Number of book owners	5	10	8	21
Average number of books (in vols.)	2	3	10	12
Number of collections over 10 vols.	1	3	2	10
More than 50 vols.	—	1	—	2
Religious works — wage earners 87% servants 91%				
1780				
Number of book owners	8	22	26	33
Average number of books (in vols.)	6	12	24	28
Number of collections of over 10 vols.	5	14	18	28
More than 50 vols.	—	—	—	4
Religious works — wage-earners 91% servants 97%				

(1) = below-average fortunes   (2) = above-average fortunes

example, coachmen — may have been combined with a certain afflu-ence; finally, with certain exceptions, women read less than men. In 1778, Pierre-Martin Sauvage, valet and upholsterer to the Cardinal de la Roche Aymon, left his heirs an estate of 28,000 *livres*, which was a considerable sum; but in the lumber of his possessions there were only some fifty books on religion and history.[56] Marie-Elisabeth Fronteau, an unmarried chamber-maid, left an estate of 10,000 *livres*, but she had a library of more than two hundred books — an indication of an unusual special interest.[57] Generally speaking, around 1780 one butler out of three was a proven reader, one valet out of five, one chamber-maid out of six, but only one maidservant out of eight and one stableman out of ten; doormen, ushers and concierges came close to the average scores. A comparable hierarchy existed among wage-earners: those with below-average means were always less likely to have books, and if they had any, they had fewer; journeymen in guilds

56. AN. Min. Cent. I, 573, 30 May 1778.
57. AN. Min. Cent. CXI, 373, 6 February 1787, estate evaluated at 9,826 *livres*.

and specialised trades always owned more books than day workers, labourers and small street-traders. At his death, Guillaume Thorel, a journeyman-cartwright and a bachelor, left 3,000 *livres*, and had about twenty volumes; with his calf-bound Bible in quarto, his *Dictionnaire Historique* in octavo, his *Guide des Pécheurs* by Louis de Grenade, the *Vie de Saint Jeanne de Chantal*, and a few more devotional works, this man with no family, living with his master, might pass for a man of culture, with a touch of religiosity, and his little collection was already a library.[58] Around 1780–90, such an example was no longer exceptional among the popular classes: with a hundred volumes, the ribbon-maker Matthieu Ferry might almost be called a collector; Jean-Pierre Dumon, another journeyman-cartwright, kept about fifty volumes on different topics, Charles Durand, cabinet-maker, a good thirty, François Guenet, an ordinary day-labourer, could claim twenty titles.[59] In short, books were gaining ground everywhere among the *petit peuple*, and journeymen or shop assistants read nearly as much as master craftsmen or shopkeepers.

The second peculiar characteristic of the diffusion of books among the popular classes is a greater familiarity with the printed word than elsewhere: there are two indications of this — the presence of single volumes and the size of collections. It was less common to own just one book in Paris than in the provinces; from 1700, where there were books there were several: among wage-earners, only three cases out of thirty involved the ownership of a single book, among servants, less than five out of forty; around 1780, the proportion was still lower. If we remember that the valuers were only interested in works 'meriting description', we see this shows considerable progress. Moreover, the average number of books inventoried doubled in both social groups and the total number of works had multiplied by a factor of five on the eve of the Revolution.[60] So among the popular classes in Paris there was not the drop in reading habits that characterised the towns of western France;[61] The popular classes in Paris were undoubtedly reading more at the end of the eighteenth century. Whereas under Louis XIV only three wage-earners and a dozen servants owned more than ten volumes, in the time of Louis XVI more than twenty journeymen and about forty servants had passed this stage. On the other hand, there was no change above fifty volumes — three cases at the begin-

58. AN. Min. Cent. IV, 356, 17 December 1710.

59. AN. Min. Cent. XXVIII, 523 (1786); XXVIII, 23 June 1783, XXI, R 532, 2 September 1785; XXII, 65, 14 October 1790.

60. F. Ardellier, 'Essai d'anthropologie urbaine', pp. 108–09; and R. Arnette, *Les Classes inférieures*, appendices; wage-earners: around 1700, mentioned 107 times; around 1780, 584; in Botlan, 'Domesticité', 310 mentions in 1700, 2,700 in 1780.

61. J. Quéniard, *Culture*, pp. 770–3.

ning of the century, four at the end — this was no doubt a barrier which was crossed only exceptionally by someone inspired by a passion for piety or erudition, or with an unusual education, and beyond this group we are speaking of a cultured elite. But the dividing line between those who owned more than ten works and the rest is also important, for it coincides fairly closely with the limit of the average fortune and especially that of the ownership of writing-desks and bookshelves, and in more than half the cases for the popular classes and for servants it coincides with the acquisition of pictures, paintings, prints, engravings and the thousand things that create an individual personality — watches, jewellery, devotional objects. Thus among the popular classes there appeared, in their relationship to cultural pursuits, an homogeneous group, whose behaviour patterns raise the question not only of the acquisition of writing skills and a taste for reading, but also of a sense of propriety and comfort, that is, a certain tone half-way between the cultured ruling class and the uneducated populace. In other words, Parisian popular culture was formed from a combination of ordinary practices and habits and texts which had come from elsewhere: it was above all a matter of appropriation. Like writing, reading is an act of mediation susceptible to infinite modulations, and nothing in notarial records tells us how to distinguish between fluent reading which presupposes the regular handling of books, the irregular, infrequent deciphering of print often linked with pictures, or reading aloud, shared among several people, which may have been an act of friendship, even love, or sociability. Autumn and winter evenings spent in company were not limited to the country, or rather, one does not see why new arrivals in the town should have given up one of their former habits. Rétif bears witness. 'We went to a lady friend of this friend, and there we found a group of people playing at being sociable. We sat by a fire, artistically placed . . .'.[62] But the touch of malice emphasises what separated this friendly gathering of people with little financial standing from the manners of the city salons of the ruling elites. However, it is clear that books circulated in Paris, they could be lent, re-sold, given, read privately or in company.

The records of the notaries show that popular culture in Paris was crushed beneath the weight of devotional literature. The predominance of books of piety was total and remained constant from 1700 to 1789; and it was always more evident among women and those who owned few books. The book most often cited was the New Testament of the Bible, followed by a whole procession of pious works designed to improve, edify and instruct the people: *Manuel Chrétien, Journée*

---

62. Rétif de la Bretonne, *Les Nuits*, pp. 2697–8.

Chrétienne, Doctrine Chrétienne, Année Chrétienne, Semaine Sainte, Instruction Chrétienne, Méditations Chrétiennes, Offices, Missel, Vespéral and *Heures.* As well as manuals intended to organise the religious life of the popular classes, there were a great number of lives of the saints, but works of theology or lofty meditation were less common. What we see caught in the notaries' sieve is only a tiny part of this consumption; it gives no idea of the variety of cheap publications for ordinary use, which we must seek elsewhere: in the catalogue of the Libraires Troyens, or the lists of the Bibliothèque Bleue which are known to us.[63] Nevertheless, it does stress two important features of the religious culture of the people of Paris: the way it put a more learned culture into an ordinary, everyday perspective, and its role as a distorting echo of the christianising zeal of the elites.

This vast bulk of religious reading was a wager with time. It was possible only at rare moments, and in general was only conceivable within the family, or at times of personal prayer. This is why the little pious texts postulated a Christian organisation of life, according to formulas very close to those in the almanacs. *Heures, Calendriers, Semaines, Offices, Mois, Missels, Années,* ... *Chrétiens* included extracts from the Bible, summaries of the liturgies, ways of celebrating religious holidays, in short they taught *Pratiques, Exercices, Conduites.* The lives of the people were to be modelled upon the principles of the great reformers of the seventeenth century for a more personal salvation by the daily practice of temporal duties and the teaching of parental example.[64] In the last analysis, the need to live one's life in the 'memory of death' must guide the truly devout.[65] Moreover, this new religious sensibility which triumphed in mass publications had no difficulty in coming to terms with older ways in which faith in divine mercy and the intercession of the saints was fundamental, exemplified in all the works describing the life and death of Christ, lives of the saints, hymns and Christmas cards.[66] The transformation of the single model of the *Art de Mourir* into a multiple model adapted to a great variety of uses for mass production shows a similar adaptation for, as in the *Bible des Noëls* and in the whole range of popular religious books, traditional sensibility and the new attitudes could coexist.[67] This was, no doubt, the result of the acculturising efforts of the

63. A. Morin, *Catalogue descriptif de la bibliothèque Bleue de Troyes*, Paris–Geneva, 1975; H. G. Martin, 'Culture écrite et culture orale, culture savante et culture populaire dans la France d'Ancien Régime', in *Journal des Savants*, 1975, pp. 225–81.
64. Abbé Perreau, *Instruction au peuple*, Paris, 1786, pp. 60–71.
65. D. Roche, 'La Mémoire de la mort', in *Annales*, ESC, 1976, pp. 76–119.
66 J.-L. Marais, 'Littérature et culture populaire aux XVIIe et XVIIIe siècles', in *Annales de Bretagne*, 1980, pp. 65–105.
67. D. Roche, 'La Mémoire' pp. 115–18; J.-L. Marais, 'Littérature', pp. 90–2.

Church, involving all forms of culture — the printed word, writing, pictures, singing and music. The overall aim was the ordinary moral education of the people; it was the permanent association of the good of religion with that of society. Texts which questioned the purpose of educating servants showed a revealing anxiety about the threat to masters from servants who had been over-educated.[68] 'Gentlemen, I do not wish to be murdered in my bed', Voltaire half-joked as he distanced himself from his valets. Similarly, abbé Perreau accepted that the popular classes should be educated, but only within certain limits and in order to maintain the appointed order of things; reading and writing were to enable children of the labouring classes 'to carry out their duties within society'.[69] In other words, clerics, moralists, observers and philosophers were at one in thinking that in the long term Christian and moral readings might lead to a change of behaviour, involving social mobility, and even the functioning of a society affected by dreams of equality. The significant alteration in the format of wills which appeared between 1720 and 1730, that is to say, a whole generation before it occurred in the provinces, signified an abandoning of procedures, if not of convictions; it was not echoed in inventories after death which continued, right up to 1790, to register the apparent triumph of pious texts.[70] This source masks a change which went deeper.

If one accepts the conclusions of P. Chaunu, one can understand how the messages of terrorist preaching, haunted by death and the after-life, together with the message of a moral teaching that was dedicated to a Christian annexation of life concerned to civilise the savage behaviour of the popular classes, could, after two centuries, lose their original force and, paradoxically, encourage the popular de-christianising tendency which was to reach its climax in the spring of 1793.[71] In this sphere, it is less a question of a brutal rupture, than of slow transformations and gradual substitutions in ways of behaving, and of the absorbing of life-styles copied from the upper echelons of society. The education of the popular classes was undermined by the libertinage of the great and the inadequacies of the clergy, thought Rétif, as he estimated fearfully the political effects — observed in the unrest of a people without principles — of the changes that had taken place during the century.[72] But an enormous variety of publications show that we must not identify popular culture simply with the

68. M. Botlan, 'Domesticité', pp. 284–6.
69. Abbé Perreau, *Instruction*, pp. 62–3, 66–7.
70. P. Chaunu, *Mourir à Paris*, pp. 433–65.
71. A. Soboul, *Les Sans-culottes Parisiens en l'an II*, Paris, 1958, pp. 282–99.
72. Rétif de la Bretonne, *Nuits à Paris*, pp. 3233–4.

distribution of devotional literature; the printed word in Paris exerted its influence in other guises as it had done for a very long time.[73]

First, there was all the literature hawked around by pedlars, in which the official and the clandestine were combined, and occasional and permanent themes alternated to familiarise the popular classes with new horizons. The colporteur had been a fact of life in Paris since the sixteenth century, and from Louis XIV to Louis XVI his role had in no way diminished: there were more than 120 authorised colporteurs after 1713, and an increasing number of unofficial pedlars, crying their wares openly or selling secretly low-quality publications and a host of clandestine editions printed in cellars and attics in the city, or imported from abroad. A denizen of the streets and open air, always on the move, quick to appear and disappear, the colporteur haunted every part of the capital city, knew his customers and how to escape the watch, selling all sorts of things as well as books, to boost his business. Mercier observes: 'Police spies wage war on the colporteurs, a race of men who trade in the only good books one can still read in France, which are consequently banned. They are horribly ill-treated; all the police bloodhounds pursue these poor creatures who do not know what they are selling and would hide the Bible under their cloaks if the Lieutenant of Police took it into his head to ban the Bible. They are put in the Bastille for selling silly pamphlets that will be forgotten tomorrow . . .'.[74] The observation is only partly correct: it is true that colporteurs of all kinds made up more than a third of those condemned to the Bastille between 1715 and 1789 for publishing offences, but they sold all sorts of things, not only clandestine books. Readers among the popular classes could get supplies more easily and cheaply from them than from publishers' bookshops, and in an emergency they knew how to defend the pedlar against the police.[75]

On top of his basket or his tray this peripatetic salesman placed the little booklets covered with *papier bleu* which had early attracted a market among literate Parisians. Booksellers in Paris were selling them from the second half of the seventeenth century; the Oudots of Troyes had set up shop in Paris about 1665. Throughout the eighteenth century journeymen and servants could choose from the traditional titles of *la bibliothèque populaire* and find religious consolation — 43 per cent of the Oudot catalogue in 1789 — recipes for a better life, or the shallow messages of utilitarian pedagogy which drew their strength

73. R. Chartier, 'La Ville acculturante', in *Histoire de la France urbaine XVIe – XVIIe siècles*, Paris, 1981.

74. L.-S. Mercier, *Le Tableau de Paris*, vol. 1, pp. 188–9.

75. J.-P. Belin, *Le Commerce des livres prohibés à Paris de 1750 à 1789*, Paris, 1913, pp. 80–6.

as much from common sense as from illusions of magic — *Abécédaires, Comptes, Faits, Médecines des pauvres, Miroirs d'astrologie, Almanachs* and *Calendriers*. They might also resort to the imaginary and escapism — novels, tales, serious stories or farces.[76]

Mercier praised the almanac which went from hand to hand in different guises — *Messager Boiteaux, Etiennes Mignonnes, Almanach chantant*.[77] More research is needed into the history of this popular laughter fed by a great number of cheap booklets ranging through all the registers of parody (*le Testament de Michel Morin*), comic rhetoric (*Les Adieux de Tabarin*), fantastic compilations of words, proverbs and objects, initiation into slang or the scatalogical humour of the art of farting![78] Booklets in the Troyes lists depicting Paris and its inhabitants were not negligible, *Cris de Paris, Tracas de Paris, La ville de Paris en vers burlesques, Les Filoutiers du Pont-Neuf, Le Déjeuner de la Rapée* (which passed from the fishwives' repertoire to the Bibliothèque Bleu), *Le Pain de Gonnesse* — all these titles offered the poor a familiar, burlesque vision of their ordinary lives.

In addition to this basic repertoire, there were occasional pamphlets, newspapers and political writings which had an enormous circulation. From the birth of printing to the growth of the great popular press of the nineteenth century, the first had been a vehicle for primitive information which threw together the evocation of the marvellous in all its forms, the fascination of the monstrous and criminal, and escape into the world of supernatural catastrophes or dreams of miracles. A whole cultural form oscillated between the familiar realism of death sentences shouted in the streets before every execution, and an imaginary world which was not without echoes in the Paris of mysteries and sects, hysteria and miracles, riots against such unnatural happenings as the kidnapping of children and girls to satisfy the whims of the great.[79] The popular classes discovered in all this a dynamic of the supernatural which all the preaching of Catholic reformers never managed to eradicate. Newspapers were less accessible because of the subscription charge, but they could be read in the butler's pantry, at the cabaret, even in a small tavern or smoking-saloon kept by a man with some

76. H.-G. Martin, 'Culture écrite et culture orale, culture savante et culture populaire dans la France d'Ancien Régime', pp. 246–7. Religion in *Catalogue Morin*, 28 per cent, in Oudot's inventory of 1789, 43 per cent; fiction (novels, short stories, theatre songs) 41 and 28 per cent; utilitarian literature (informative and educative), 30 per cent and 27 per cent.
77. L.-S. Mercier, *Le Tableau de Paris*, vol. 12, pp. 297–9.
78. J.-L. Marais, 'Littérature', pp. 93–5.
79. R. Kreiser, *Miracles, Convulsions, and Ecclesiastical Politics in Early-eighteenth-century Paris*, Princeton, 1978, pp. 140–80; *Chroniques de la Régence, journal de l'avocat Barbier*, Paris, 1885, 8 vols., vol. 1, pp. 136–7.

pretentions to culture.[80] News of the world, discussions of the future of certain individuals, information about daily bread and work, the *affiches* and *avis divers* were consulted by all and thus reached the popular classes. Luxury products reserved for the affluent, newspapers in fact reached a wider audience, for they went from hand to hand in the entourage of subscribers, their titles were bawled out in the streets and they were placarded on walls; their contents were discussed everywhere. In 1789, freedom of the press favoured the immediate development of a journalism which, without being exactly popular, did not escape the attention of the popular classes.[81] At that time, political writings with a massive circulation again achieved a publicity they had not known since the time of the Fronde and the Mazarinades. The extraordinary impact of the lampoons and brochures on sale after the convocation of the States-General cannot be explained without assuming a familiarity with the habit of reading that had been sustained for more than a century by the clandestine presses. Before 1750, this familiarity was passed down by the reading of Jansenist propaganda deeply rooted in the popular-class parishes in the centre and in the faubourgs. There was a whole production ranging from pious manuals to illustrated prayers, from journals to a brochure relating the miracles of Deacon Pâris, which the spies of the *lieutenant général* had some difficulty in tracking down, for it circulated from the top to the bottom of the social scale. 'Monsieur, is it true that we won't go to confession any more when the constitution is passed?' a lackey asked one evening as he was preparing his master, Lawyer Barbier for bed, to which the latter replied: 'That shows the impertinence of the common people'.[82] Around 1750 and after 1770, inferior books from Jansenist presses were interspersed with pamphlets, lampoons of a satirical and defamatory, sometimes pornographic kind, which, as a result of their low cost, reached a very wide audience, and by their scabrous nature, a type of mind susceptible to scandal. A popular public was awakening, thirsting for news, hungry for discussion, easily roused to enthusiasm and, in some cases, to action.

In this panorama of culture the song played an important part. It took up and completed several of the functions associated traditionally with the writings hawked by colporteurs; as a hymn, it was a means of Christian persuasion and a considerable part of basic religious culture

---

80. Rétif de la Bretonne, *Les Nuits*, p. 1685; ibid., p. 2055 — 'A publication happened to come into my hands'.
81. R. Darnton, *The Business of Enlightenment, a Publishing History of the* Encyclopédie, *1775–1800*, Harvard, 1979, pp. 481–90, and 541–2; L.-S. Mercier, *Le Tableau de Paris*, vol. 10, pp. 295–8.
82. *Chroniques de la Régence*, vol. 2, p. 29 (January 1728).

was acquired by singing; as a lament, it could accompany a fantastic or realistic evocation of the contemporary scene, and play its own part in the concert of official political propaganda (around 1780 Parisian recruiting officers tended to enrol young men to the sound of *Adélaïde et Fine lame*, a song in praise of the American War of Independence). Songs familiar in ruling-class circles were whistled and commented on by people in the street; finally, songs were also a means of escape and relaxation, a way of evoking daily life, accompanying work, creating a rhythm for housework. People sang in attic rooms, workshops and streets, at crossroads and on bridges. The seller of songs was a stock figure of the street scene; Moreau le Jeune has left an excellent portrayal of one: on his platform, violin resting on his shoulder, he is holding out in his right hand the song-sheet for sale, and in a wallet hanging from his belt he keeps the copies intended for customers; behind him a picture tells the story he is relating, and a group of elegant idlers and working-class people are gathering round.[83] These travelling *chansonniers* would set up their pictures and offer their little books of songs at all the strategic points of the world frequented by the popular classes: the boulevards, the Pont-Neuf, the squares:

> Some sing sad Holy Canticles, others naughty songs, often only forty steps away from each other. . . . The merry song woos the audience away from the seller of the scapulary; he is left standing all alone on his stool pointing his stick in vain at the horns of the tempter Satan, enemy of the human race. Everyone forgets the salvation he is promising to run after the song of damnation. The reprobates' singer celebrates wine, good food, love and the charms of Margot, and alas, the twopenny piece that was hovering between the hymn and the vaudeville song drops into the wallet of the worldly minstrel.[84]

In a lively vein, Sébastien Mercier illustrates here a characteristic trait of the culture of the popular classes and we should complete his picture by recalling how the song lent itself to cultural interference, to imitation by the popular classes of those learned themes which they might distort and adapt; 'It goes from one singer to another, growing as it goes', Boileau had already explained. All this afforded the popular classes a sphere of freedom they could enjoy at their leisure.[85]

---

83. M. Pitsch, *Essai de catalogue sur l'iconographie*, p. 145; other examples on pp. 14 ('perched on chairs we sang the Bourbonnaise'); 96 (*Les Chansons du boulevard de Barbarie*, by Berthaud); 111 (*L'Orgue de Barbarie*, by Bouchardon); 87 (*Fanchon la Vielleuse*, by Fragonard); 113 (*La Place Maubert et la place des Halles*, by Jeaurat); 121 (*Le Marchand de chanson de juillet*); 141 (*L'Erection de la statue de Louis XV*) by de Machy.

84. L.-S. Mercier, *La Tableau de Paris*, vol. 1, pp. 285–7.

85. H. Davenson, *Le livres des chansons*, Neuchâtel, 1946, pp. 81–8.

This leaves the pictorial image, representing the last of the ways in which the written or printed word could affect the popular classes. Almost always accompanied by a text, by hymns, laments, legends, information about the people and places represented, it played a triple role in popular culture: it was an efficient medium of Christian moralising, an instrument of political propaganda, and finally a form of entertainment presenting moralities, games and jokes. Pictures originally came before books, but in Paris during the century of the Enlightenment they followed close behind, permeable, like books, to every kind of influence. The inventories confirm that they were to be found everywhere: among 56 per cent of wage-earners, around 1700, and 61 per cent around 1780; among servants during the same periods, 56 per cent and 40 per cent, the latter figure representing a drop which indicates either saturation or a transfer of attention to other things. The *variety* of forms is of prime importance — paintings, engravings, prints; secondly, the predominance of religious pictures (50 per cent among servants, 65 per cent among wage-earners); and, finally, their increasing diversity on the eve of the Revolution: as well as pious pictures, there were landscapes, townscapes, portraits, even mythological or political scenes. All in all, it was a familiar medium of popular culture that had a wide circulation in the capital (Table 7.2).

Songs, the books of the colporteur and popular pictures formed a unity which was practically indissociable in their modes of production and diffusion. The printed word reached the popular classes, shaped their awareness within a Christian moralising tradition, but it also helped them to take stock of their individual personalities — the more affluent of the popular classes generally managed to acquire all these badges of culture, together with the host of things that establish a personality and encourage the development of the individual, such as the possession of watches for men: around 1700, 13 per cent of servant and 5 per cent of wage-earner inventories record a watch; by 1790, the figures have risen to 70 per cent and 32 per cent. This shows a fundamental conquest in which servants were in the vanguard: with a watch, one entered another world of time, a more rational and mechanical way of reading the passing of time, and a different way of creating and shaping it. The triumph of the watch-making industry in Paris, imported, like many mass-produced clandestine books, from Switzerland, moved the Parisian popular classes into the age of time as a marketable value, the new time of the world of Kant; while a few people — curious, rich, or neo-amateurs — reached the shores of fantasy and escapism by acquiring strange non-essentials, so that geographical maps, dictionaries, scientific instruments, musical scores and a few musical instruments turned up here and there as if they had

Table 7.2. Distribution of pictures among the popular classes

	(1) Wage-earners	Servants	(2) Wage-earners	Servants
1700				
Owners of paintings/ prints (%)	28	36	17	20
Average number of pictures owned	7.9		8.6	
Total number of pictures in the category	341		484	
1780				
Owners of paintings/ prints (%)	43	20	18	19
Average number of pictures owned	6.4		22.0	
Total number of pictures in the category	392		863	

(1) = below average fortunes   (2) = above-average fortunes.

lost their way. Were they individual gestures of a strong personality, or the collective apprenticeship of a mutation based upon the habits of the ruling classes? It is very difficult to say, in so far as these manifestations almost always coincided with high levels of wealth and the occupations with the highest qualifications. In any case, for a minority it meant, alongside the acquisition of a culture based on knowledge, the acquisition of a culture based on life-styles, a new art of self-presentation in which the influence of intermediaries reigned supreme, but to which most of the popular classes could not aspire. When Rétif recalls the readings he shared with companions in furnished rooms or with his pretty sweethearts, he gives an idea of the possibilities open to people who worked in the book trade. They could read *Thérèse Philosophe* or *Le Portier du Chartreux* quite cheaply, though they cost more than 24 *livres* when sold 'under the counter' around 1780; this helps us to understand how, here and there, the popular classes might have undergone a transformation.[86] Servants were daily agents of this transformation, but so were the travelling singers or clandestine pedlars of pictures and lampoons. As a clerk in the administration wrote to

86. Rétif de la Bretonne, *Monsieur Nicolas*, vol. III, pp. 189, 199, 399.
87. P. Manuel, *La Police de Paris dévoilée*, Paris, Year II, 2 vols., vol. 1, pp. 66–7.

the Lieutenant of Police in 1788: 'It is clear that the songs offered in the streets to amuse the populace are giving them notions of liberty; the vilest *canaille* regard themselves as the Third Estate, and no longer respect their betters. It would be most useful to impose strict censorship upon all those vendors on the Pont-Neuf in order to stifle this spirit of independence . . .'.[87]

The Parisian popular classes were changing, and no doubt reading played its part in this change. However, more than the content of what they read (which could be alienating or liberating), it was its very diffusion which, as it accelerated, fermented the change. First, because buying books or pamphlets, even if it is nothing very unusual, involved a financial act; secondly, because reading demanded a physical effort which marked a victory over the poor conditions of lodging, lighting and over-crowding, as well as over the difficulty of deciphering the badly-printed characters; finally, it was a break with oral habits and the usual leisure practices. This concentrated effort by the reader facilitated the development of the literature of colportage, explained the appearance and disappearance of various titles, encouraged a broadening of themes, revealed a strategy of appropriating different sorts of knowledge, and thus, by active adaptation, opened the way to other reading.[88] Popular culture, in Paris as elsewhere, had its roots in an old *sensibilité*, but it is inconceivable that it could remain impervious to the variety of the cultural show which surrounded it on all sides. By their disdain or their repeated attempts to exercise control, the social elites, clerks and administrators, proved they had not managed to impose uniformity upon the cultural confusion of the masses. The debate did not involve only books and reading. Urban reading practices, especially those of the popular classes, must be set in a wider perspective involving all the processes of urban acculturation in which the same permament debate between control and savagery was pursued. The inventory can only be prospective; if it reveals areas hitherto neglected, it proves above all that reading is a spontaneous act, and as such an agent of urban legibility expressed through channels not directly connected with the spread of the printed word, like signs, posters and street names.

For the literate in Enlightenment Paris the act of reading was an immediate, rapid response, for it was also linked with the first active attempts to provoke and stimulate the public, through which countless messages were passed and behaviour patterns diffused. First of all there was the sign-board, a good indicator of ordinary modes of perception because it was so long-established and subjected to so many police

88. J.-L. Marais, 'Littérature', pp. 103–05.

Table 7.3. Imagery of sign-boards in Paris (%)

	Taverns in 1789	Hôtel-Dieu and its houses (16th/ 17th centuries)	Houses in the Cité and Louvre areas (15th/16th centuries)
Topography	5.0	4.0	1.0
Objects	19.5	22.0	41.5
Animals	12.0	20.0	18.0
Plants	2.5	3.0	3.0
Mythology	3.5	6.0	4.0
Hagiography	19.0	27.0	26.5
Trade	14.0	3.0	5.0
History, politics	19.5	10.0	0.5
Miscellaneous	5.0	2.0	0.5
(Total number of cases)	(212)	(298)	(266)

interventions. A familiar part of the environment, it was first a land-mark for getting about the streets, for it identified houses before places of business; signs gave character to an address that possessed, as yet, no real individuality, and took the eye with its picturesque composition and the meaning conveyed by its inscriptions. It derived from a way of reading space based on a physical response to detail, and an unconscious, almost random apprehension of some flora or some shape that was significant to the purchaser, stroller or lover seeking a shop, some touch of local colour or the house of his sweetheart. So it was part of a rhetoric of information, playing a role similar to that of the modern poster, but with time on its side, for, without being entirely permanent, a sign was durable and could be moved with the business or shop. So it was an inducement to buy and to consume, mixing various cultural elements with those based upon demand and those arising from early forms of advertising to the world, objects and people which symbolised a particular manufacture or sale: a hat for the hatter, shaving bowl for the barber, grapes for the wine merchant, or the more complex symbol of the patron saint of a corporation — Saint Eloi for goldsmiths and Saint Nicholas for grocers (Table 7.3). There was an element of chance here, as Sébastien Mercier showed, for the image could leave the house and the area and be used again elsewhere, thanks to the hardware merchants on the quai de la Mégisserie.[90]

89. E. Fournier, *Histoire des ensignes de Paris*, Paris, 1884; J. Grand Carteret, *L'Enseigne*, Paris, 1902; M. Charpe, *Les enseignes de cabaret et de marchands de vin à Paris au XVIIIe siecle*, Mémoire de maîtrise, Paris 1, 1979.
90. L.-S. Mercier, *Le Tableau de Paris*, vol. 1, p. 118.

Thus the code of perception required continual spontaneous adaptation because people had to find their way through it all. The artisans who invented and created the signs also had their say. Their choices refer, if not to a popular culture, then at least by their collective dimension, to everyday usage. Professionals gathered together in St Luke's Academy — the corporation of ironworkers and blacksmiths, painters, sculptors, carvers in wood and stone and metal-workers — all shaped with their hands images drawn from familiar models, from memories and from personal or professional learning. There was nothing passive or static about this work, for anything might provoke a new sensual response or interpretation. The cultural memory of the artisan ranged over motifs which had to evoke a response in the memory of clients, and drew from an arsenal of common themes — natural, religious, political, even linguistic. It also had to play with forms and formulae, combine images and inscriptions in an art form that was both realistic and fantastic. To the elite, the sign was a mutilator of language and colour, but to the popular classes it was a spectacle and a simple stimulant with an inexhaustible potential for dreams and creativity. It was always susceptible to more than one reading: a buyer of curios was not a stone-throwing urchin, and a journeyman in search of an atelier or shop was not the commissioner enforcing law and order. So the message varied according to the role of the reader. It is impossible to imagine passivity of eye, mind or imagination in front of an image; the sign could instruct, seduce, hold or mobilise the gaze and the intellect of the people, as a more extended study of the motifs would show. Religious imagery predominated in the designation of houses. Images of favourite trades, emblematic objects, animals and plants, mythology and history, even an overflowing of spontaneous humour, which included irreverent puns: *à l'Episcié, au Gracieux, au Puits sans Vin*, not forgetting, out of the list of inn signs condemned by the thunder of the *dévots, le Juste prix, le Cygne* [sign] *de la Croix, le Teste Dieu, le Saint Jean-Baptiste*.[92] Captions and images fascinated the elite: 'The sign-board offered an image of a race of giants to the most stunted people in Europe: a sword-guard six feet high, a boot as big as a hogshead, a spur as broad as a carriage wheel, and a glove which could have housed a three-year-old child in every finger'.[93] Sébastien Mercier is evoking the fascinating

91. M. Coyecque, *L'Hôtel-Dieu de Paris au Moyen Age*, Paris, 2 vols., 1891, vol. 1, pp. 201ff.; A. Berty,/ 'Les Enseignes des maisons de l'Ile de la Cité', in *Revue Archeologique*, 1860, pp. 75–113.
92. M. M. de la Mure, 'Le Cabaret parisien à la veille de la Révolution', Thesis, Ecole des Chartes, Paris, 1979.
93. L.-S. Mercier, *Le Tableau de Paris*, vol. 1, pp. 204–5.

spectacle of the Paris street, the variety of hundreds of pictures enlivened by their polychromatic boldness, which first evoked a familiar world, but then a world of dreams and exile, the exotic and fantastic (lions are red and horses green) and won the laughter and connivance of the public.[94] Signs were soon brought under control. The Enlightenment police proscribed them, in order to avoid accidents when they fell down in a high wind, and because they jutted out into the street, restricting the movement of carts and causing endless bother to the people in the houses on each side.[95] A decision of the 1660 council scrapped the protective coverings, and in 1669 signs were reduced to one standard size and their height fixed at 15 feet, but this did nothing to prevent the disorder. In 1761 Sartines outlawed them, and according to Sébastien Mercier Paris was 'a town shorn of its signs'. This was the beginning of a decisive change and the metamorphosis of the sign: from now on it was only used to indicate a place of business, and it did not overhang the public way but stretched across and above the entrance and the bays of the shop, so that it became both a fresco and a painting, and the traditional way of reading them tended to disappear. But at the same time, at the end of several centuries of skirmishing between the Church authorities and the painters of popular images, enlightened men began to reflect upon the pedagogic value of the painted signs.[96] Abbé Teisserenc felt they offered the possibility of an officially organised model for popular instruction. If their height, size and projection could be standardized, they would help to create a unified urban decor, encourage trade, and fill the state coffers by a small charge levied on every new sign. Above all, with their combination of image and text they would serve to educate everyone. For this purpose, their subject should be chosen from every kind of literature, and for each craft and commerce a theme, subject matter and combination of forms and colour established. Thus the popular classes as a whole could learn historic facts, chivalric orders, weights and measures, monies, and the tools and work of the different trades. The street would become a school; shopping would become an apprenticeship in elementary practical culture, and walking would enable people to check their knowledge, and enjoy making discoveries. Teisserenc even considered using the supports for street lighting so that messages could be understood and interest aroused at any time of day. The smashing of the general rules controlling the highways, despite the change of regime, meant that the abbé Teisserenc's Utopian scheme for adver-

94. J. Adhémar, *La Peinture d'enseigne au temps de Balzac*, Archives de l'Art Français, 1978, pp. 307–12.
95. Des Essarts, *Dictionnaire*, vol. IV, p. 524.
96. Abbé Teisserenc, *Géographie parisienne*, Paris, 2 vols., 1762.

tising and educating at the same time could never be realised. His ideas
arrived either too early or too late, for painted signs had for several
centuries created a pedagogy of information and enabled the poor to
read and dream.

The poster is better known. It too usually combined words with an
iconography whose apparent naïveté has held the interest of specialists
in popular art forms. Nevertheless some historical comment must be
made on a medium which became familiar to the popular classes in
Paris so early, was destined to be short-lived, and was from the first
available free of charge.[97] It demanded special presentation in which
clarity, layout, choice of type, the distribution of black and white, the
importance of margins and the part played by illustrations were all
decisive elements in affording instant, lively reading not only for the
individual but also for the group, as any painting which highlights the
activity of the bill-stickers or a crowd gathered round the placard
shows.[98] The white of the paper and the black of the print stood out
against the grey wall, the spectator's attention was captured by the
voice of the man deciphering and transmitting the purport of a message
which was almost always announced to the sound of trumpet and
drum before being stuck on the walls. Posters were essentially the
work of royalty, parliament, the municipality and the Church, they
transmitted authoritative communications, edicts and ordinances,
municipal and police regulations, prohibitions and programmes, notices of executions, quotas of the shares of the Compagnie des Indes
and winning lottery numbers. In this way, everything concerning the
ordinary life of the people was placarded, *requêtes de la ville* — similar
to our local notices or authorisations and building permits — sum-
mons to assemblies and to join the militia, market price lists, and news
of military victories. News, broadsheets, spectacles and theatres, invi-
tations to a festivity — such as jousting on the river or fireworks — all
served as a manifestation of power but at the same time made possible
a change of attitude towards the city, a change of habit and custom,
and a general familiarity with written information. People soon acquired a taste for information, however light-weight, and the 'oblique
gaze of the people' learned to adopt these peaceful paths and pick up
various coded messages stamped on the memory while strolling in
quest of adventure or by listening attentively to a host of expert
autodidacts, skilled in discussing the rights of King or city, the weight

97. F. Emel, *L'Affiche*, Tours, 1971.
98. Le Colleur d'affiches par Bouchardon; J.-B. Raguenet, *Le Cabaret de l'image
Notre-Dame*; G. Canella, *Les Halles en 1828*.

of a sack of beans or the price of a cord of wood, the entertainment value of some show at the theatre or the disappearance of a famous actor. The poster was a book for all to read, which changed every morning when the forty official bill-stickers arrived with paste and brush to decorate the city anew. Sacred and profane, politics and leisure took turns to clothe the naked walls.[99] Thousands of eyes contemplated the posters, and thousands of individual wills saw a common thread running through them; notices of funerals and weddings punctuated the destinies of all.

Posters even provided an opportunity for leisurely dreaming, whether on 'an invitation to the public to win a fortune', inviting people to try their luck in the bureaux of the Royal Lottery,[100] or the posters of charlatans guaranteeing a cure for all ills, or better still, those advertising enrolment in the army, relaying the recruiting officers' skill through the printed word.[101] One example among thousands:

Noyon, 1766. A Notice to the Flower of Youth, the *Artillerie de France*, *Corps Royal* and *Regiment de Fère* are advised that this is the Picardy Regiment. Our men Dance three times a week, play *aux battoirs* and spend the rest of their time at Skittles and Prisoner's Base, as well as at the Practice of Arms. Pleasure rules, all the soldiers are well-paid and well-rewarded for a place as artillery guard or officer of fortune at a salary of 60 *livres* . . . .

The imagination could soar at will around a text with such a variety of appeal for the popular class, repeated references to authority that gave a pleasant ring of power to the reading, provincial solidarity, the charm of a life of pleasure and play, together with security in old age. How many young men were fascinated by all the pictures suggested by this sort of reading? No doubt, many more than there were readers of Monsieur Guibert or the chevalier d'Arc. The poster made its points effectively and was in a sense less deceptive than books. Situated somewhere between the oral and the written, it illuminated a sphere where the common sensations were by definition acculturising and might even offer the chance of freedom.

The Parisian popular classes manipulated the seditious placard in their own way.[102] It was an old custom born with the printing industry itself and brought up to date by religious disputes and political discord. It was the nightmare of the Parisian *commissaires* who set

99. L.-S. Mercier, *Le Tableau de Paris*, vol. 4, pp. 45–7; ibid., vol. 6, pp. 73–9; ibid., vol. 12, pp. 10–12.
100. Advertisement for the bureau of Citoyenne Thevenet, 121 rue Créqui, 1793.
101. An old-time recruiting poster, *Le Magasin Pittoresque*, 1833, p. 390; ibid., 1862, p. 131.
102. P. Datz, *Histoire de la publicité*, Paris, 1894, pp. 85–105, for legislation.

spies and informers to watch the walls. All to no avail — as soon as the political temperature began to rise, posters would sprout on walls like mushrooms after a downpour. Hordes of lampoonists would set the clandestine presses creaking, colporteurs relayed them in the streets, the popular classes bought, looked, passed comments. Before the Revolutionary explosion, two high points increased the flow of an otherwise regular movement recorded in police reports and gossip columns: between 1725 and 1730, at the time of the Jensenist troubles, 'a simple poster struck the first blow', says Barbier,[103] and started the 'war of the placards'; and also from 1768 to 1775 at the time of the grave political and economic crisis that shook the capital and kingdom.[104] From November 1763, Sartines recommended his myrmidons to keep watch at suitable street corners and to search the *quartiers* for authors of subversive texts; but the latter came out in undiminished abundance, demanding cheap grain and the dismissal of ministers. They expressed the 'opinions of the poor', was how the *commissaires* described these increasingly bloodthirsty appeals, which were 'badly written and badly spelt'. Posters therefore relayed rumours, they were a direct medium of political thought, the only one that enabled the popular classes to express their opinion of political life. Putting up posters was certainly a dangerous practice whose impact was less significant in periods of calm.

Sébastien Mercier leaves an ambiguous record of posters: on the one hand, he shows the clandestine bill-stickers at work, eluding police vigilance; on the other, he thinks the placards no longer meant much to the people who were 'absorbed by their pressing needs', 'having lost track of public events and any desire to laugh'. This emphasises the continued practice of bill-sticking, and its potential for swift mobilisation — proved again in 1789. It also confuses times when the popular classes laughed at political posters emanating from the upper echelons of society, such as the famous placard directed at the Minister d'Argenson during the Regency: 'Lost, one black dog with a red collar and flat ears . . .', and times when they posted the placards themselves. Such a capacity represented a cultural act.

Other opportunities for reading were introduced when the city was made legible in a new way. The numbering of houses, which was inaugurated at Caen about 1770, became part of Parisian mores about

103. *Chroniques de la Régence*, vol. 1, pp. 42, 59, 111, 134, 187, 403; ibid., vol. 2, pp. 22, 54, 56, 75, 83, 93, 110, 168, 169, 246: the most famous of the placards dated 3 February 1732, 'by order of the King, God is forbidden to perform miracles in this place . . .'.
104. S. Kaplan, *Bread, Politics and Political Economy in the Reign of Louis XV*, The Hague, 1976, 2 vols., vol. 1, pp. 319–23.

1780: 'Arriving at the Nouvelle Halle, I went and sat opposite number 14 . . .', writes Rétif.[105] It was an important innovation for it imposed on everyone a new way of looking at things: mental arithmetic and rational organisation replaced kinesthetic sensation and familiar perception. Dwellings which before were difficult to differentiate when described in picturesque terms, took on a more concrete reality, and this helped to speed up the traffic of people and things, now less likely to get lost. The reading of a house number became part of modern awareness in the same way as other procedures of measurement, and it partly dispelled the darkness covering and perhaps protecting an essential area of daily life. An air of equality was implied by the numbering of the *portes cochères*, rejected by the great lords, but it was accompanied by increased surveillance and the threat of fiscal pressure which inspired the popular classes to protest against the work. So it was carried out at night to avoid trouble. The Constituent Assembly and the sections would accustom the poor to a more rational approach to the deciphering of space without yet establishing the present system of street numbering imposed by Préfet Frochot in 1805. In this area the popular classes moved within a quarter of a century into a different world, and the enterprise was completed by naming the streets.[106]

The standardized establishment and posting of street names had a similar effect, although it involved different motivation. The important date here is 1728 when, on the orders of *Lieutenant de Police* Hérault, they began to put up on the street corners in Paris 'two pieces of tin with the street name in big black letters . . .'. Of course, the novelty was not the street name, which had been known since time immemorial, but the attempt to generalise a daily information procedure by a simple and inexpensive process. The name of each street became more legible, and it was easier to designate the new roads and therefore to play with the toponymy of the highways. People's perambulations took on a new character and were made easier. It is difficult for us to understand how these new practices altered the way in which the popular classes saw the town, but the planners meditated upon these changes and showed what was at stake.

Abbé Teisserenc felt it served the interests of a well-policed state, concerned to facilitate the relationships essential to modern life and communication between the inhabitants of the city or between them and the world outside.[107] Why not use familiar itineraries and casual

---

105. Rétif de la Bretonne, *Les Nuits*, p. 2984.
106. J.-C. Perrot, 'Domesticité', vol. 2, pp. 664–7; J. Pronteau, *Les Numérotages des rues de Paris*, Paris, 1966.
107. Des Essarts, *Dictionnaire*, vol. 3, pp. 519–20; Piganiol de la Force, *Description de la ville de Paris*, Paris, 1765, vol. 1, p. 32.

strolls to teach Parisians geography! The 865 streets of the capital lent themselves to this operation, it was just a matter of changing the names, which was easy 'since street names were arbitrary signs', and reorganising Parisian toponymy according to the map of the kingdom. The streets would be called after French towns lying in their direction; to complete this educational procedure for Parisians, the signs would also have indicated the *quartier* which would take the name of a province, and the distance from the capital to the town mentioned. Thus, the rue Montmartre would become the rue de Rouen and the sign would state: VIth district, Normandy, Rouen 28 leagues. The rue Saint-Martin would be called rue de Lille, rue Saint-Denis would be called Amiens, the rue du Bac, Bordeaux, and the rue de Faubourg-Saint-Marcel, Marseilles. The gates of the capital would henceforth take the name of the foreign countries to which they opened the way: Germany for the barrière de Montreuil, and Canada for the sortie du Roule. There was no obstacle that could not be overcome in order to make the city clear-cut and uniform, and to facilitate the control of the popular classes.[108]

Parisians were spared this plan of abbé Teisserenc; it aimed to remodel the past too fast and too completely, but parts of it could be implemented. At any rate, it had its antecedents in the names of provinces given by the site-developers to some streets in the new *quartiers*. Between 1820 and 1830, the 'quartier de l'Europe' grouped the names of the European capitals in its street network. The century of the Enlightenment tended to make the street a theatre, a school and a pantheon. During the Revolution abbé Teisserenc's lesson did not seem incongruous. In 1793, Citizen Chamouleau proposed to the Convention that the names of the virtues should be applied to the different communes, so that: 'At all times the people will have the name of a virtue on their lips and soon morality in their hearts'. At the *Comité d'Instruction publique*, abbé Gregoire reopened the dossier and wanted to combine political lessons with moral pedagogy. 'Is it not natural that one should go from the Place de la Révolution to the rue de la Constitution which would lead to the way of happiness . . .?'[109] A celebration of great men could thus punctuate the leisure moments of the popular classes. The nineteenth century would continue to write this chapter, and the Parisian authorities would accustom strolling citizens of whatever class to changing labels. Prudery would modify the familiar organisation of the collective world; in

108. Abbé Teisserenc, *Géographie parisienne*, pp. iii, iv, ix–x.
109. J.-C. Perrot, p. 665; P. Grunebaum-Ballin, *Le Système de dénomination topo-graphies pour les rues . . .*, *La vie urbaine*, 1959, pp. 251–63.

the old *quartiers*, brothel-ridden streets of ill-fame would change their names; in 1809 rue Tire-Boudin in the heart of the old district of Les Halles became the rue Marie-Stuart; the rue Trousse-Nonain, or 'Tumble Nun', already disguised as Tasse-Nonain, became rue Beaubourg; rue de la Pute-y-Muse or 'Idling Tart' escaped a change of title for it was concealed under the vague label of *petit-muse*; and in the same way the scatological collection of rues Merdeuses, Merdelet, Chieurs and Chiards would disappear, as the rue du Petit et du Gros-Cul, du Gratte-Cul and du Poil-au-Con had already gone. Republican, imperial and royal morality carried on successfully the indexing begun by the Catholic reformers, and the people were obliged to change their ways.

Growing literacy, increased reading, pictures and songs all meant that in Paris the man in the street more or less had to read. But in the acculturising city the sphere of utilitarian and practical reading is something that scarcely appears in inventories, although it is in this, and in ordinary daily perceptions that we must seek the origins of the major change in the behaviour of the popular classes. Over and above mere ownership of the printed and written word, a host of incitements were at work changing their way of life.

CHAPTER 8

Life-Styles

Popular culture in Paris was made up of a multitude of acts unified by certain behaviour patterns and a characteristic socialisation. It would be impossible to give an overall description here, but we can sketch a study of some relationships which are significant for what they tell us about the influence of urban sociability and ways of using space, and because they reveal the ordinary ways in which the popular classes lived their lives and experienced their city. The historical problem which must be solved involves the intrinsic meaning of the working-class way of life. For the moral observers it was *per se* deculturising. For Sébastian Mercier, 'a poor man cannot be happy in Paris', solitude was his lot; the young Rétif knew this even before he trod the pavements of Paris — 'nobody knows anyone else'. Using criminal records, historians have uncovered the aura of misery, neglect and violence which was the usual fate of those who transgressed the norms, but which was also to some extent the general lot. Now the writings of moralists and economists speak the same language as police records, as we have already pointed out, a language of suspicion and incomprehension; they can give only an indirect account of what was a confused awareness of a collective destiny: the culture of the poor. We have to come to terms with this. Among other possible approaches, there are two ways of reconstructing these life-styles: first, to extrapolate a paradigm of relationships from their ways of organising life within their day-to-day surroundings; secondly, to take the tavern as a focal point from which to study the range of attitudes which characterised the condition of the popular classes in their daily work and leisure, in their habits of ordinary sociability and in their misdemeanours.

Let us start with the figures. If we take inventories after death and identification of bodies in the morgue in 1770 and around 1796, what can we learn about loneliness? Wage-earners and servants did not die in isolation, but within a certain support system and without having broken completely with their provincial origins (Table 8.1).

234

Table 8.1. Social support system

	1695–1715		1775–90	
	Wage-earners	Servants	Wage-earners	Servants
Proxy	20	18	45	42
No known relatives	35	36	15	21
Family represented by relatives	45	46	40	37

For each period this represents a total of several hundred people, a sufficient number to indicate the existence of three main networks of relationships. First, the family — those who travelled to the spot, those who got someone to represent them, and those who were already on the spot; grandparents were very rare, sons- and daughters-in-law not common, but uncles and aunts played a vital role as they were often guardians to their nephews and nieces, and at each period made up between a third and a quarter of the relatives present; brothers and sisters, brothers- and sisters-in-law and cousins made up the rest, that is, the majority. Second in this group of witnesses came people from the deceased's place of work: either other servants or connections from the workshops and shops. Masters or employers rarely appeared except, perhaps, in the case of bachelor journeymen with no family and old widowed servants who were more or less isolated. Finally, there were neighbours, but these made up less than a tenth, which should not surprise us, since for 'inventory' read 'patrimony'.

The sociology of these gatherings is an interesting indication of permanence and stability, and even of some social mobility. Among wage-earners, three-quarters of the relatives occupied a position similar to the deceased, a casual labourer was a son, and often also a brother of a casual labourer, a day-labourer had a day-labourer for an uncle. A quarter of the witnesses occupied superior positions, a proportion which did not change much from the time of Louis XIV to that of Louis XVI; a journeyman might have a relative who was a master-craftsman, or a day-labourer might be connected with a trade apprentice, or have a cousin or nephew who was a clerk. Finally, for those who had arrived quite recently from the provinces, a small number of jobs and social situations from the rural world were recorded, in rare cases an established *laboureur*, more frequently a relative who was a vine-grower, a gardener or a farm labourer. We should not be surprised that this moment of family dislocation reveals the wage-earner society as stable and little changed through one or two

Table 8.2. Social mobility in 1749 (%)

	Fathers						
	Domestic servants	Day-labourers	Crafts- or tradesmen	Peasant labourer	Others	Small Shopkeepers	Upper-class
Sons							
Dom. servants (287)[1]	5.0	3.0	15.0	33.0	12.0	10.0	22.0
Day-labourers (47)	2.0	21.0	9.0	38.0	13.0	9.0	8.0
Craftsmen tradesmen	4.0	3.0	31.0	11.0	6.0	29.0	16.0
	Husband						
Wife							
Domestic (301)	27.0	3.0	22.0	8.0	6.0	19.0	15.0
Day-worker (66)	12.0	30.0	20.0	8.0	8.0	13.0	9.0
Tradeswoman (558)	10.0	6.0	28.0	3.0	2.0	38.0	13.0

[1] Number in sample

direct or collateral generations. This confirms the analysis[1] of marital relationships based on certificates in Paris for 1749: a third of the journeymen and guild workers were doing the same job as their fathers; another third were sons of artisans and shopkeepers, which indicated their expectations rather than a social decline; 16 per cent came from higher social milieux and the rest from the lower wage-earning levels. Casual workers and labourers were less fortunate because their fathers were usually from the country or casual labourers themselves. The principle of endogamy verified by a comparison of the social situations of wives and their husbands confirms this general stability and the unequal chances of labourers as against journeymen or artisans, since two-thirds of the latter made a match in the guild fraternity, but only one-third of the former. In choosing a wife they did not break through the customary barriers, and the wage-earners' *carte du tendre* encroached very little on the territory of their social superiors — only 10 per cent of cases. From wedding to funeral, family life proceeded within horizons which changed rarely, where situations identical in their geographic and sociological origins were consolidated, and where immobility was the rule and change the exception (Table 8.2).

1. A. Daumard and F. Furet, *Structures familiales*, pp. 65–78.

The social profile of relatives and witnesses at inventories of servants is a much more open one. From 1700, more than a third were master craftsmen and shop-keepers (37 per cent), a good number were Paris bourgeois (19 per cent), there were servants (15 per cent) but few from the lower ranks of wage-earners or country folk (12 per cent). In more than a tenth of the cases the upper classes were represented as close or distant relatives. Relationships between servants and the middle classes in the capital confirm the possibility of integration; masterships and investment income were their common horizon. There was little change around 1780, but the number of peasant relatives increased, especially of journeymen and day-labourers — one lackey might have a casual labourer for a brother, another a labourer uncle (24 per cent). This may mean that there was an increase in the global number of servants recently arrived from the country, and a slowing down of the chances of breaking into polite urban society. The 1749 marriage certificates confirm the first two features, for 45 per cent were sons of peasants and 10 per cent sons of artisans and shopkeepers; they add a third factor — 25 per cent of the servants came from the *bonne bourgeoisie*, either to perform superior functions or because there had been a decline in their circumstances.

They chose their wives mostly from the servant classes, then from among wage-earners, and, lastly, from the world of the shop and the workshop. A chamber-maid would marry a valet who was the son of a servant, the lackey a waiting-maid who was the daughter of a servant, a good workman or a small artisan. Matches with a superior social rank were rare. Servants stabilised, rather than improved, their position by marriage.

The files at the mortuary offer conclusive proof that the Parisian popular classes were never entirely alone (Table 8.3).[2] Suicides and the victims of accidents had lived within a double support system: the wider family network, and the network of daily relationships. Family respondents represented a clear majority after the 1770 accident, when only a quarter of the victims were not claimed. First, husband and wives came to identify their partners, then fathers and mothers, while children, brothers and sisters made up a third. In short, it was mostly close relations who were affected by the fatal crowd disaster. Employers and friends did not have time to act. On the other hand, these represented a clear majority of witnesses at the Basse Geôle. Of course, there were still relatives — 35 per cent of the respondents, especially husbands, wives, sons, daughters, sons- and daughters-in-law. But a crowd of neighbours, friends, workmates from a building site, com-

2. AN. Y 15 707 and H 1873.

Table 8.3. Social response to accidents according to mortuary reports, 1770 and 1796–1800

	Men				Women				Total
	(1)	(2)	(3)	(4)	(1)	(2)	(3)	(4)	
1770									
Husband and wives	1	—	10	14	—	1	1	5	32
Parents and grandparents	1	—	3	9	—	1	2	6	22
Sons and daughters	1	—	2	7	2	1	3	2	18
Brothers and sisters	—	—	3	10	—	—	2	5	20
Uncles, aunts and cousins	—	—	1	4	—	—	—	—	5
Employers	—	—	—	4	—	—	—	1	5
Friends and workmates	—	—	1	2	—	1	2	4	10
Total number of respondents									112
Not known: 33 out of 132									
1796–1800									
Husbands and wives	2	2	7	17	—	—	5	6	39
Parents and grandparents	2	1	4	19	4	1	1	5	37
Sons and daughters	—	2	4	10	—	—	—	1	17
Brothers, sisters and in-laws	1	2	9	24	2	—	2	3	43
Uncles, aunts and cousins	1	2	2	11	—	1	—	7	24
Employers	—	2	13	16	—	—	—	3	34
Friends and workmates	12	28	27	135	10	11	12	28	263
Total number of respondents									457
Not known: 22 out of 184 cases									

(1) Interminate categories   (2) Superior categories   (3) Workmen and shop-keepers   (4) Members of *le peuple*

panions from a workshop, pals from the regiment turned out to perform an act of recognition which was often an acknowledgement of a more brotherly and lasting bond, a last gesture of curiosity, or a fleeting goodbye. Jean-Pierre Leroy fell from the Pont de l'Unité opposite the

Tuileries and drowned on 10th Messidor, year VI; on the 11th his father-in-law, the glazier Rondu, his brothers-in-law, Delaistre, a painter, Thérault, a small publican, and Jean-Pierre Leroux, a confectioner, turned up; they all lived in the same *quartier*, in streets close to the victim's home. On 19th Messidor in the year VI, Nicholas Grépart, a Savoyard from Comblat, was drowned; three days later his father and brother, both casual labourers, came to identify the body; like the victim they all lived in rue de la Chaussée d'Antin. Thus to their last moment the victims were integrated in a support system, all had connections in the city where a multiplicity of human relations were possible.[3]

All these networks were related to space. The hearth and home were the focal point for family loyalties. Perhaps it has been too quickly assumed that popular-class families did not exist until they became aware of family feeling worked out by the elite as early as the late seventeenth century, and diffused through schools which disciplined children outside the home.[4] At the lower end of society, the history of the family is supposed to coincide with the history of living standards.[5] But this is to forget that the majority of the lower-income groups had shaped· their own behaviour patterns and awareness through several centuries of urban life. Not only did the *famille populaire* exist but perhaps it had always existed, carrying within it a mode of relationships all of its own. It will be objected that there could be no family life because people had to live in unbearable confusion and because there were no children. But this was not so. We have seen that continual overcrowding was indeed the lot of the popular classes, which suggests they had their own proxemics and created their own characteristic social, family and perceptual relationships. The families of the popular classes adjusted to the lack of space and made the best of it, couples adapted to the impossibility of privacy, parents and children accepted an environment of smells and sexual sights that had already long been unacceptable to the affluent. The working-class home accepted smells — of bodies, dirty water, cooking, the morning *café au lait* which had become a commonplace for the Parisian popular classes from the eighteenth century. They also accepted the noise, the shouting, scolding, snoring, farting and belching that so shocked the authors of the *Civilités puériles et honnêtes*: Sébastien Mercier was right — the common people were always raising their voices when the bourgeois and aristocracy lowered theirs. But crowding was not loose-living and

3. R. Cobb, *Death in Paris*, pp. 57–69.
4. P. Ariès, *L'Enfant et la vie familiale*, Paris, 1960, pp. 451–9.
5. J.-L. Flandrin, *Familles, parenté, maison, sexualité dans l'ancienne société*, Paris, 1976, pp. 94–100.

did not rule out a certain style, perhaps a different mode of happiness, simple but already subtle, unruly but at the same time balanced.[6]

It is said there were no children among the popular classes. Children were abandoned or put out to nurse, they ran away from home, were collected into schools or spent their free hours in the streets, only coming home to sleep. Let us be clear about two things: at least in Paris, abandoning children was not peculiar to the poor; paying for wet-nurses was not confined to the popular classes, and did not rule out the return of survivors to their parents' home. The number of foundlings in Paris rose during the eighteenth century: about 1,000 were abandoned around 1700, more than 5,000 by 1790, but 40 per cent of these children came from the provinces. The rest came from all sectors; first there were the illegitimate, 70 per cent, but also the 30 per cent legitimate; so far as the children of the *classes populaires* are concerned, we have, for 1778, the following results based on 1,199 cases (percentage in brackets):

Journeymen, casual labourers, wage-earners, small trades	348	(29)
Servants	85	(7)
Master craftsmen, shopkeepers	294	(24)
Bourgeois — rentiers — higher categories	472	(40)

The abandoning of their children by the popular classes, common in the parishes of the faubourg Saint-Antoine or the Centre, was, in fact, less frequent overall than among shopkeepers and master craftsmen (one quarter), and the upper classes. Poverty was to blame, especially in critical times, provoking this irrevocable act; but so was a certain life-style practised by the affluent, those who were climbing the social ladder, the petty bourgeois, and it did not necessarily exclude a wish to take the child back when the difficult spell was over. Many children were born of debauchery, but they came from all classes, and if they came from *le peuple* it was because the *corruption des moeurs* (as Rousseau would say) operated essentially at the expense of lower-class girls. This is not simply an invention of history. 'A surfeit of progeny' was a fact of life as much for the rich as the poor, if not more so.[7]

6. Ibid., pp. 99–100; R. Hoggart, *La Culture*, pp. 63–5.
7. C. Delasselle, 'Les Enfants abandonnés à Paris', in *Annales*, ESC, 1975, pp. 187–218.

Which leaves the foster children, two-thirds of whom were destined, through inadequate care and the practise of wet-nursing, to certain death. But there again, these fundamental choices were not confined to the popular classes.[8] First, because the monthly payments to the nurse ruled out the poorest wage-earners; in 1792 there were no children of casual labourers among the 644 children put out to nurse in the villages of the southern periphery (percentage in brackets):

Journeymen	155	(24)
Servants	41	(6)
Master craftsmen, shopkeepers	283	(44)
Bourgeois — higher categories	165	(26)

On the contrary, less than a third of the parents were Parisian wage-earners, but this may be an under-estimate because one must bear in mind the prices, which were more or less expensive according to the distance.

Neither abandoning babies nor putting them out to nurse was typical of the family behaviour of the popular classes. One is not sure that the parents resigned themselves to these dramatic separations, or that the wife of a worker was unmoved by this choice dictated by necessity. It was essential that women should go out to work to help to support the family, but abandoned children were not always forgotten.[9] Urban life imposed its law, and imitation of the intermediate social levels imposed models, such as the Malthusian or libertine ways of the rich, or the ways of running their businesses and their lives adopted by the *moyenne bourgeoisie*. A minimum of wealth was required to avoid total alienation and the dislocation of the family; sometimes it was achieved, won, lost, and won again, and we have noted how important children were in the precarious consolidation of patrimonies. Thus a whole strategy was organised around couples whose isolation was only relative. The extended family no longer lived together at one hearth, but they were still united by daily or weekly contacts, sometimes sharing the same jobs, meeting at the same festivities, ceremonies, funerals, weddings, arrivals and departures. And everywhere there were children.

---

8. P. Galliano, 'La Mortalité infantile dans la banlieue sud de Paris (1774–1794), in *Annales de démographie historique*, 1966, pp. 138–78; J. Kaplow, *Les Noms des Rois*, pp. 115–17.

9. A. Farge, *Vivre dans la rue*, pp. 64–8, particularly the text cited on p. 68, Y12719.

In the day, of course, the children of *le peuple* filled the schools and jostled on the streets and the quais; the *commissaires de police* were wary of such tricks as splashing passers-by, tying pans to the tails of cats and dogs, bombarding each other with rotten fruit, clods of earth and stones. On July afternoons they sunbathed on the sand by the river — in which some were drowned.[10] Others started work very early, with father or uncle or a nearby master-craftsman to whom their family apprenticed them.[11] They learned manual skills and were conditioned to life by strokes of the cane and by crude wit. But as Mercier says:

> Children in Paris are charming until the age of seven or eight. As they are brought up in the midst of a crowd they very early acquire an ease of manner. They certainly don't look stupid; they are quite familiar with the ways of the world and the city's problems: a confident look says they were born in the capital and are already at home in all its bustle. . . .[12]

This capacity of Parisian children to adapt was a general feature of the popular classes: it was a positive effect of overcrowding, which made them learn young. Those who had paid employment could have their children at home with them — the nurslings that had survived, children who had not run away and who had escaped the appalling fact of infant mortality. With their parents they shared joy and pain; they accompanied them on a day out — there were twenty-one of them below the age of fifteen among the hundred victims of the *Bagatte*; they learned their roles, authority for the boys, docility for the girls, a sense of work, and that *frondeur* attitude typical of the popular classes. By the firelight they could dream of independence, of leisure and comfort, and could learn their letters and numbers, turning the pages of the *Catéchisme* and the *Almanach*, the *Clef des songes* and the *Miroir des femmes*. It was there too that the important moment of the meal gathered everyone around the family table.

The ritualistic character of the meal (at which the family roles were played consistently, and basic wisdom transmitted — 'don't put your finger in your nose', 'chew your food slowly', 'he who steals an egg will steal an ox') was stressed by the painters, who depicted the ritual of grace before meat.[14] A picture by Lebrun, which was popularised in prints, shows a collective attitude. The family is consciously present

10. A.D. Seine (Paris) D4, U, 7; see also AM, Z'H 656.
11. BHVP, MS. 678, fos. 4–20.
12. A. Farge, *Vivre dans la rue*, pp. 128–30; G. Picq, M. Pradines and C. Ungerer, 'La Criminalité', pp. 138–9.
13. L.-S. Mercier, *Le Tableau de Paris*, vol. 12, pp. 131–7.
14. P. Ariés, *L'Enfant*, pp. 403–7; J.-L. Flandrin, *Familles*, pp. 102–04.

and, no doubt, conscious of its collectivity, which is not linked directly and uniquely with the possession of a house and bourgeois privacy, but is built into their rituals: for example, of eating. Meals would bring everyone home, but the food was not always warmed or prepared there at the hearth, it was bought from food-sellers and sellers of left-overs.[15] These *marchands des viandes* — there were perhaps 6,000 of them all over Paris, both men and women — 'sell retail what they have bought retail', vegetables, eggs, fish or meat but also cheese, salt and fruit. In particular many of them filled the empty bellies of the popular classes with left-overs from high-society meals. This provided even the most impoverished among them with a pittance which must not be thought of solely in terms of the 'hideous scraps' and the 'public bowl' described by Sébastien Mercier.[16] Left-overs were a second-hand business, the servants saw to that, and there was a whole hierarchy of dishes readily available; anyone who had an easy-going butler as a neighbour could come to an agreement with him to enjoy some of these crumbs from the rich man's table. For most of the popular classes, excluding servants, it was a basic necessity, a means of varying a diet based on household bread, for the mixture of meats and vegetables, 'the treats', of these food retailers cost only 17 *sous*, while a pound of tripe cost 9 *sous*. Were the popular classes well fed? The moral observers were convinced that the food-sellers were poisoning the poor, indicating their obsession with decay and poison as part of their denunciation of urban corruption. However, it it reasonable to assume that eating standards improved during the eighteenth century. The Lieutenant of Police, Lenoir, recalls the fact in his memoirs, and such calculations of Parisian food rations as it is possible to make are perhaps not far out, if we allow for differential consumption and this phenomenon of redistribution by the food-sellers.[17]

It is difficult to determine what happened to the 350,000 sheep, 120,000 calves, 80,000 cattle and 40,000 pigs that reached the market of Les Halles every year, according to Lavoisier's figures: the stomachs of the rich could not have coped with it all. It is clear that the popular classes did eat when times were normal — albeit less than 2,000 calories a day, which was not exactly gluttony — but even in the eyes

15. D. Dutruel, 'Les Revendeuses', pp. 28–33, 49–53.

16. L.-S. Mercier, *Le Tableau de Paris*, vol. 8, pp. 74–5 ('Marmite perpétuelle'), 218–23 ('Mets hideux'); ibid., vol. 3, pp. 201–05.

17. M. Benoiston de Chateauneuf, *Recherches sur la consommation de la ville de Paris, en 1817*, Paris, 1821; R. Philippe, 'Une opération pilote, l'étude du ravitaillement de Paris au temps de Lavoisier', in *Annales*, ESC, 1961, pp. 564–8; J. Kaplow, *Les Noms des Rois*, pp. 127–36. Kaplow makes some useful criticisms of Philippe, but on second-hand food sales reflects the viewpoint of the contemporary bourgeoisie and high society: 'the fried *pâtons* were like machine oil'. Why machine? Doesn't Kaplow enjoy eating fried sausages in the open air?

of Mercier and Rétif, 'the servants look stout and fat'. Crisis times were another matter, and when the market price of wheat rose, this meant a crisis for the stomachs of *le peuple*. If things were going well, a little party might bring the family together, either at home — sending to the cook-shop for the food — or at the tavern. The first glass of wine was raised in honour of the grandfather.[18] The interest of these practices for us is to show how everyday life bred a particular ingenuity; the women had to use their wit and versatility to keep things going. The families of the popular classes created their own habits of eating and drinking which had no connection with those of the rich: fill your stomach with the well-seasoned produce of the cook-shops and food-sellers, enjoy a good snack now and then, even if it is not prime quality; reasons both real and symbolic made the family meal an act with a character of its own.[19] Family feeling came across in these habits which were linked with outward sociability and which achieved a balance between the demands of privacy and collectivity.

Around the home, local solidarities wove another thread in the daily life of the popular classes. When Mercier mentioned neighbours he claimed they did not know each other,[20] but the *Tableaux de Paris* is full of significant anecdotes which prove that everybody knew everybody, in the house, in the street, in the *quartier*. The wretched, cramped buildings imposed this public life-style, and family quarrels or the quirks of particular individuals could not escape their neighbours on either side, above or below. Relationships grew out of daily familiarity, a regular greeting, a few words, borrowing matches — 'au clair de la lune . . . je n'ai plus de feu' — salt and pepper, or a pan or a soup tureen. Quarrels might cause these encounters to degenerate into a feminine brawl about a door left too wide open or too tightly closed, a lost well-rope, a bucket of rubbish that overbalanced and hit its mark. Tenants cohabited and, to escape the stress inherent in any overcrowded collective living, they had to adapt generally to the material conditions, and to space that was permeable and open.[21] Private and public mingled closely in the itinerary of the house with its strategic points: meeting places for the inhabitants where discussions and conflicts might arise, always observed and supervised. 'Passing a house whose passage was open, I heard piercing shrieks. I climbed the stairs, a madman ran down, I dashed into a lavatory . . . the whole house was awake now and people were talking to me from the

18. Rétif de la Bretonne, *Les Nuits*, pp. 1615–16.
19. R. Hoggart, *La Culture*, pp. 70–5.
20. L.-S. Mercier, *Tableau de Paris* vol. 1, pp. 60–1.
21. A. Farge, *Vivre dans la rue*, pp. 32–6.

windows. . . .'[22] First there was the passage, defended by its secrecy. Every passage door had its lock, every tenant had his keys, and if he forgot them he was forced to wander round all night, for the proprietor or main tenant locked up around 11 o'clock.[23] Gallants and marauders would emerge to disturb the neighbours; people would pass through to get to the stairs, the yard and the other buildings.[24] They would meet, greet each other and 'the trouble was that people left their water there as they went by, and coming home one would meet a man pissing, quite unconcerned, at the foot of the stairs'.[25] In the slightly superior houses the master of the passage was the door-keeper, sometimes an artisan, a cobbler, tailor or public scribe; 'he works at his sedentary task and has only to pull a string. In big houses, the door-keeper has nothing to do; he drinks and warms himself idly all day in his lodge'.[26] Parisian porters were informers and observers jealously guarding their prerogatives, they ruled the world of tenants with benevolence or tyranny and knew everything, nothing escaped their influence.[27] Regular life was organised around the stairs and punctuated by the landings. Every storey was a separate world with its own social colouration and style. In the house in the rue Galande where Rétif took lodgings, the second floor was occupied by Sophie Grandjean, the beautiful pastry cook who had just married a 'nobleman from Picardy'; the third by a pretty butcher-woman; on the fourth lived Bonne Sellier and her seven lodgers — she had been chamber-maid to the Princesse d'Epinay, had some *savoir-vivre* and was then married to a drunken journeyman-printer; on the fifth floor a governess, Zoé Delaporte, lived in front, and a hatter and his daughter at the back.[28] This microcosm had its habits, people met on the landings, an open door or an incident would bring out all the inhabitants in a spontaneous gathering: 'I saw this young person surrounded by her fat neighbour, his wife, Thérèse, and her two friends . . . they did not attempt to conceal their joy'.[29] A thief would be pursued, or a lover hidden in the lavatory; neighbours drawn by the noise would glue their eyes to bedroom doors, the ensuing din would bring the whole neighbourhood to the windows; the stairs were for chit-chat and gossip, a vast sounding-box, a place for adventures. Everyone was on

22. Rétif de la Bretonne, *Les nuits*, pp. 101–02.
23. Ibid., pp. 176, 431, 1711–12, 2023.
24. Ibid., pp. 117, 263, 493.
25. S. Mercier, *Le Tableau de Paris*, vol. 4, pp. 90–1.
26. Ibid., vol. 5, pp. 27–8.
27. Rétif de la Bretonne, *Les Nuits*, pp. 37, 1055, 1539, 3228 ('I heard from the doorman . . .').
28. Idem, *Monsieur Nicolas*, vol. 1, pp. 53–4.
29. Idem, *Les Nuits*, pp. 1446–9.

the watch there, for the lower classes had their fears and phobias and their interests to protect, and thieves, informers, gallants, pimps or jokers might have the whole house up in arms. Once the alarm had been sounded, people would be waiting for the intruders at the foot of the stairs, armed with broom handles and meat skewers and hoping the *commissaire de police* would come. Family reunions, the loves of the young and the not-so-young — everything occurred with a spontaneous candour and in a brotherly spirit that did not always exclude violence. The sociability of the building played its part in unforgettable quarrels between couples, rows with the landlord, arguments among tenants in which the women were particularly involved, for it was they who watched over the family territory and guarded its boundaries against the neighbours, defending their reputation as a good housekeeper, or their honour as a wife. The day-to-day existence of the people was made up of this capacity for solidarity, this aptitude for brutality, even fury.[30] These collective responses were acquired early, and could be seen in the actions of young journeymen who united to achieve a better standard of living. Like good fortune, poverty was shared. Monsieur Nicolas made up a trio with Boudard and Chambon, a printer and a clock-maker; they shared expenses, the stew simmered on the hearth, they ate meat every day and managed to live on 3 *livres* a week. Marriage was to be a disaster for Rétif, as Agnès Lebègue, who had known better things, blushed for their wretched ways: she could not bear eating what the poor ate, patching clothes, making a penny go a long way! The result was misery for the couple.[31] Rétif's promotion to foreman at Quillan's on 18 *livres* a week improved their standing, Agnès Lebègue took in sewing, 'we both worked. . .'. The household prospered.[32]

There was no division between house and street, into which the whole neighbourhood overflowed from nearby houses, workshops, shops and taverns. Around every inhabitant a *quartier* took on its shape, made up of daily contacts and changing reputations. Individuals worked round the corner from where they lived, sometimes in the very house they lived in, and if they moved house they never went far. Jacques Ménétra was born in the house in the rue du Cloître-Saint-Germain-l'Auxerrois where his father kept a shop, and his whole childhood was spent between the rue de la Grande-Truanderie near Les Halles, l'Eglise Saint-Germain, the parish of Saint-Eustache, the

30. A. Farge, A. Zysberg, 'Les théâtres de la violence à Paris au XVIIIe siècle', in *Annales*, ESC, 1970, pp. 984–1015.

31. Rétif de la Bretonne, *Monsieur Nicolas*, vol. 3, pp. 16–18, 462–3, 560–1.

32. G. Chaussinand-Nogaret, *La Vie quotidienne des Français sous Louis XV*, Paris, 1979, pp. 69–75.

Seine quaysides and the Pont-Neuf. It was in the house of his father and grandmother, the little parish school room, open shops in the streets and boats on the river that, with kids of his own age, he learned the facts and the pleasures of *l'existence populaire*. At twenty he had hardly ever crossed the Seine, and it was easier for him to set out on his *tour de France* than to go to the faubourg Saint-Marceau. Once established as a journeyman, he felt positively exiled in the rue du Petit-Lion-Saint-Sauveur near the rue Saint-Denis, which was less than five hundred yards away.[33] Going through this busy little world thousands of times, one would become known, classmates sided with each other in their quarrels, fathers acted as referees, and uncles came to the rescue.[34] Barbers knew every beard and each wig and they could inform the observers, 'they know all the local anecdotes'. The barber's shop was a news office, and in the evenings and on Saturdays and Sunday mornings men would wait their turn, talking about politics and the problems of the day. Every day the barbers watched the comings and goings, discovered who was friendly with whom, and picked out new faces.[35] If you didn't belong to the neighbourhood, 'people give you a very hard look'.[36] Solicitude and distrust were two major components of popular culture in Paris. They were instructive among all those who had a job and a home but they also affected newcomers, who then developed their own solidarity. Everyone feared vagrants, wanderers and strangers, who were suspect more for their rootlessness than their manners. Extreme poverty provoked tolerance, even solidarity when the people rioted to save the downtrodden from arrest[37] and attacked the *archers* and the guard. It was not the poor they suspected, but the other, the stranger, and foreign frontiers were the nearby boundaries of the *quartier*, parish and neighbourhood. Part of the morality of the *peuple révolutionnaire* had its roots in this mentality.[38]

Any enquiry into popular culture has, very soon, to confront the tavern.[39] There are several reasons for this: it was the privileged spot

---

33. BHVP, MS. 678.

34. Rétif de la Bretonne, *Monsieur Nicolas*, vol. 3, pp. 207–08, 463–4. We know that Rétif was fond of the left bank. He settled first in the rue des Poulies, in the Louvre district, then crossed the Seine to the rue Saint-Julien-le-Pauvre, then rue Galande, then cours d'Albret near the place Maubert; two short stays on the right bank, in furnished rooms in the rue Sainte-Anne and in the rue Quinquampoix left unpleasant memories; he then wandered between the rue de l'Université and the old college of Presle, where he settled in a fifth floor attic room, in the *quartier* place Maubert, BHVP, MS. 678.

35. Idem, *Les Nuits*, pp. 466–7, 673, 1700, 1954–9.

36. Ibid., pp. 1088, 1135.

37. A. Farge and A. Zysberg, '*Les Théâtres*', p. 1006; A. Farge, *Le Mendiant un marginal*, pp. 312–28.

38. R. Cobb, *Death in Paris*, pp. 57–69 (esp. 64–9, 'Protestation populaire'), 111–13.

39. J. Kaplow, *Les Noms des Rois*, pp. 35–139; A. Farge, *Le Vol d'aliments*, pp.

for the kind of massive consumption that developed in the city, thus it
was a meeting place, where eating and drinking were an excuse for
day-to-day conviviality; then it enables us to see how the practices of
everyday sociability, as well as wrong-doing, were organised: violence,
delinquency, rebellions and revolts all emanated from the tavern;
finally, taverns were particularly closely watched by the police which,
apart from producing abundant archives, led to arguments about the
importance of law-breaking and freedom of speech. Here again, we
must be wary of the police commissioners' reports, as they rarely had a
good word to say about the guilty — those who flouted opening and
closing hours, committed fraud and indulged in all kinds of petty
crimes; as for the observers, they were divided between fascination
with the canaille — 'to see Paris without seeing la Courtille . . . is like
seeing Rome without seeing the Pope' — and disgust and fear: 'The
countless multitude of taverns are the cause of drunkenness, theft,
debauchery, idleness, a passion for gambling, quarrels, unhappy marriages and the ruin of poor families . . .' vituperated the virtuous Des
Essarts,[40] and Sébastien Mercier went further, saying: 'In these smoky
dens you will find nothing but idle workmen'.[41] Taverns have been too
readily linked with illicit life, whereas they were a perfectly ordinary
part of daily living, providing thousands of hungry and thirsty Parisians with food and drink. So far as these establishments were concerned, the municipal authorities were caught between two fires: they
had to control a shifting, turbulent area, a task made all the more
difficult because the tavern was an integral part of daily life and of the
popular tradition of physical excess:[42] at the same time, they did not
want their regulations, constraints and surveillance to dry up the
revenues, essential to the city and to the state, that poured in from
duties collected by customs officials on drinks coming into Paris. The
police had to regulate and intervene to prevent excesses, but they had
also to know when to turn a blind eye or even to protect the tavern.
This last was a difficult task at a time when the Church and its
preachers, as well as philosophers and economists, were demanding
increased vigilance in this area because it was thought to have adversely
affected the working lives of the population. These groups were united
in opposition to popular 'idleness', and for two centuries Catholic
bishops had consistently denounced debauchery, dance and profanity,

182–3; idem, *Vivre dans la rue* pp. 72–7; idem and A. Sysberg, 'Les Théâtres', pp.
1006–7; (esp.) J. Nicolas, 'Le Tavernier, le Juge et le Curé', in *L'Histoire*, 1980, no. 25,
pp. 20–8.
    40. Des Essarts, *Dictionnaire*, vol. 1, pp. 412–15, 482–4.
    41. L.-S. Mercier, *Le Tableau de Paris*, vol. 2, pp. 12, 81–4; ibid., vol. 10, pp. 207–08.
    42. J. Nicolas, 'Le Tavernier', pp. 20–1.

as well as the irreverence which contrasted the tavern with the tabernacle; surveillance of taverns was part of the repression of furtive leisure. For economic moralists this necessity was linked with the incitement to work and the criticism of unemployment. In their view, workers were too inclined to idleness; the number of official holidays hampered the growth of production, and the tavern and its debauchery curbed the zeal to work. All the detractors of the customs of the popular classes were at one on this point: it was essential to outlaw occasions when working energies might be wasted, and to extol the workshop over the tavern.

In Paris the matter was complicated by the confusion about these establishments and their function, and by the geography of public houses. Popular consumption involved several aspects of the commercial and corporative system whose roles were complementary, but none the less competitive where they overlapped. In order to drink wine, the popular classes had to go to the tavern where the wine merchants retailed drinks and usually, provided meals; the latter theoretically came from the nearby *traiteur-rôtisseur*, a guild, well-established since 1695, which was not allowed to serve drink unless the member was a *traiteur-aubergiste*. To obtain beer, cider, fortified drinks, sweet liqueurs, lemonade, ice cream, coffee or drinking chocolate, the regulations stated that the customer must go to the *limonadier* who, as well as providing the above-mentioned refreshment, could keep a shop and sell vinegar, or open a counter and café, or even install a smoking-room, billiards or tennis court. In fact, although they were subjected to daily surveillance by the *maître-jurés*, the frontiers between the guilds were perpetually being eroded; people ate and drank anywhere, it was a matter of convenience. In their ordinances the police tended to lump all the sellers of drink together — they would restrict *all* wine-merchants, tavern-keepers, *limonadiers*, sellers of brandy, of wine and so on . . . .[43] Customers went from one establishment to another for a glass or *rince-cochon*, a quick snack or a more copious meal, and the vigilance of the guilds abated. The wine-merchant Maillard, who kept a tavern at la Maison Blanche, poured coffee and liqueurs for his customers, while the inn-keeper Cartellier, a wine-seller on the Champs-Elysees, spoke of his coffee 'au Grand Turc'.[44] Cartouche escaped from the Châtelet through a fruiterer's cellar, but unfortunately four soldiers of the guard were in the shop

---

43. For example, the police ordinance of 12 February 1734 and the sentence passed on 30 June 1789.
44. M.-H. de la Mure, 'Le Cabaret parisien au XVIIIe siècle', Thesis, L'Ecole Nationale des Chartes, Paris, 1979, typescript, pp. 13–14 (Y 11824 and ZIG 212).

drinking brandy.[45] Masters of the guilds of *rôtisseurs* and tavern-keepers watched over their members' rights but allowed double membership, even association within the same family, neighbourhood or house. Finally, in this survey of Parisian libations, we must not forget the grocers who sold rum, doormen at great town-houses who might occasionally retail the proprietor's wine, and the ushers who had a monopoly in royal or privileged houses. So there was no shortage of opportunities to wet your whistle! In all, it has been calculated that in 1790 there were 4,300 involved in the lucrative sale of wine, rather fewer than the 1780 total of 2,000 wine-merchant–tavern-keepers plus 2,800 *limonadiers*, calculated from the guild lists; if we take the figure for inn-keepers this was about 700 for 800,000 inhabitants — one establishment per 1,143 people. Overall, this meant one for less than 200 inhabitants; by comparison Lyon, a particularly bibulous town, offered its population only one wine shop per 700 inhabitants,[46] an indication of the importance of the trade in Paris.

There were taverns all over the city, but we have to distinguish between the centre and the periphery. In the heart of the city the Poor Tax returns reveal the density of the population in the parishes near the river, Saint-Eustache, Saint-Gervais, Saint-Paul, Saint-Jean-en-Grève, Saint-Germain-L'Auxerrois, Saint-André-des-Arts, Saint-Nicolas and Saint-Médard, and on the great axes of the rue Saint-Denis, rue Saint-Martin, rue Saint-Antoine, rue de Seine and the rue Saint-Jacques. On the left bank, the *faubourgs populaires* had high densities of taverns, but in the aristocratic *quartiers* to the west and east they were proportionately thin on the ground. The situation was linked directly to economic activity, the River Seine, the ports, the market of Les Halles, *quartiers* with a dense artisan, commercial and popular population; in 1792 there were 500 wine shops in the faubourg Saint-Antoine and nearly 800 in the faubourg Saint-Marcel — that is, one per eighty inhabitants! This shows also the influence of traffic and of movement, for the great arteries of Paris were lined with countless taverns and *estaminets*. So it is not surprising to find this is also the topography of criminality and violence.[47] In the centre of Paris, the tavern was a place of freedom, as well as of eating and drinking.

Once past the *barrières*, the trade changed in character and was dictated by the shifting of the fiscal limits, therefore by urban growth; beyond this perimeter there were mostly *guinguettes*, or small suburban pleasure gardens, which had their origins in the seventeenth

45. *Chroniques de la Régence*, vol. 1, p. 167.
46. G. Durand, *Vin, vignes, vignerons en Beaujolais du XVIe au XVIIe siècle*, Lyon, 1979, pp. 32–8, 89–90.
47. A. Farge and A. Zysberg, 'Les théâtres', pp. 990–3.

century. The wine was cheaper there and the popular classes adopted them to pass their leisure time on Sundays, Mondays and official holidays, that is to say, about a hundred days a year. *Guinguettes* flourished throughout the eighteenth century and proved a blessing to little villages threatened by the town, villages such as Gentilly, Montrouge, Ivry, Vaugirard and le Groscaillou on the left bank; Charonne, Belleville, Ménilmontant (where Rétif, Boudard and Loiseau went on the spree) and the suburbs of la Courtille au Temple, la Nouvelle-France (between the faubourg Saint-Denis and Montmartre), les Porcherons and la Petite-Pologne — of eighty-three houses in the rue des Martyrs at les Porcherons in 1780, twenty-five were taverns! The vicissitudes of the fiscal war which tended to include the *guinguettes* within the tax perimeter are well-known.[48] The annexation by the tax-farmers of an enlarged taxable area in which a large-scale trade in wines and spirits had been developed provoked a revolt among the tavern-keepers in defence of their interests and the rights of the popular classes, those great consumers of cheap wine. Fraud and guerilla warfare between tax officers and smugglers were commonplace in the last fifty years of the *Ancien Régime*, and turned into open war and rebellion with the building of the tax-farmers' wall; between 1785 and 1789 about fifty cases were judged at the Election and the *cour des Aides*; the movement culminated in the pillage and burning of the customs posts in July 1789.[49] The consumer rebellion found an outlet in political protests, and popular hostility to the tax system was crystallised in insults to the administering clerks and assaults on buildings. Wine merchants and caterers were willing intermediaries, and a whole population joined with them in the name of freedom to defend deeply-rooted habits.

Thus, in old Paris and on the outskirts there was an entire hierarchy of establishments differentiated by their clientèle and the variety and quality of the services offered. In Mercier and Rétif we can follow this confused itinerary, which was all a matter of nuance, even of the moment, leading from the café frequented by smart, respectable people, but also by 'the idle and indigent', 'artisans and tradespeople', to the shady tavern in the suburbs, via the ordinary *estaminet* and the *guinguette* where the popular classes and men of the world rubbed shoulders.[50] In working hours during the week idlers and wasters, the

48. R. Dion, *La Vigne et le vin en France des origines à nos jours*, Paris, 1959, pp. 519–25.
49. P. Krumnow, *Les Rébellions populaires contre les employées de la ferme générale à Paris de 1775 à 1789*, Memoire de maîtrise, Paris 7, 1976, pp. 10–20.
50. L.-S. Mercier, *Le Tableau de Paris*, vol. 2 pp. 12ff. (*tabagies*), 81–4 (*jours fériés*); ibid., vol. 8, pp. 142ff. (*cabarets*); ibid., vol. 10, pp. 207–09 (*le lundi*); Rétif de la Bretonne, *Les nuits*, pp. 1582–3, 1685–6, 1823–84 (billiards), 1801–1907 (cafés), 1907–13 (*Cabaret de la rue de l'Abre-Sec*), 1987–9 (*La Mère Thorel*).

unemployed and journeymen on the spree were everywhere, but in the evening and at dinner time, on Sundays and on holidays, there was an enormous crowd and the temperature would rise.

The physical setting of these establishments lent itself to this sort of occasion, and is worthy of our attention.[51] The Parisian tavern was usually situated between the street and the yard, which often allowed a number of easy entrances: at Bonneau's in the rue Girard-Beauquet there was an exit into the rue du Petit-Musc, while the yard served both as a store and as an extra room, and could easily be turned into a summer garden with trellissed vines, tables in the shade and a game of boules. In the suburbs it was the courtyard which gave the *guinguette* its air of a great country inn. Depending on the size of the business, the clientèle, and the acumen and wealth of the owner, the wine-shop might take over the upper storeys, usually the mezzanine and first floors. As everywhere, space was limited, a fact which distinguishes the tavern from the café, where there was plenty of room, and from the establishments on the outskirts of the city which could be extended more easily. It was a world well-defended by doors which were glazed only at the top, with a solid grille like the windows; police regulations stipulated the grille, but reports on break-ins, which give useful information on such details, prove that it was not always effective. Interior arrangements were dictated by the dual function of the establishment, as the wine-merchant sold drinks either to take away or to be consumed on the spot.

The shop, with its wooden counter covered with lead, stone or tin, its cupboards and chests to store utensils for wine and all kinds of domestic linen catered for neighbours as well as for thirsty passers-by. Its size and luxury would vary according to the custom, but in most cases the equipment was scanty and simple; half-litre mugs, flasks, small carafes, glasses, dishes and plates, barrels, brass or stoneware pitchers, washing-up bowls and furniture, worth 1,000 to 1,500 *livres* in the rue Mouffetard, and 2,000 *livres* in the rue Saint-Honoré. Customers sat round a few wooden tables, on stools or benches; two to four tables was the average for about fifteen drinkers but some drinking-rooms could accommodate thirty to fifty people crowded on to cane chairs or at trestle tables of rustic pine. In his leafy tavern Mercier counted sixty places argued over by second-hand clothes dealers and tramps; in the rue de l'Arbre-Sec Rétif described a room crammed with a noisy throng, and prints have popularised Ramponeau's famous *Tambour Royal* at la Courtille:[52] shop and counters, a vast fireplace, shelves laden with pots, customers with their jugs ('come and buy new

51. M.-H. de la Mure, 'Le Cabaret', pp. 103–21.
52. M. Pitsch, *La Vie populaire à Paris*, plates 18, 22, 52, 72–4, 88, 475.

wine from the famous Ramponeau at 4 *sous'*), the jostling crowd, serving-men and women, ice-cream sellers and oyster-women. It was a scene of disorder and congestion which was unbearable for Mercier; for Rétif, it was all physical contact, elbowing, a hurly-burly encouraging every sort of relaxation after the fatigue of work. The eyes and ears of the bourgeoisie were astonished by this upheaval, and the sense of personal space could find no satisfaction in this hubbub. Anyone who wanted peace in a tavern either had to find it in himself, as Rétif managed to do, must quit the premises for some superior establishment, or else hire a side-room suitable for a little supper, furtive meetings or amorous romps. Monsieur Nicolas knew how to hide in the *guinguettes* of the Bois or Gros Caillou with his friend Boudard, when he was sought by the informers for his clandestine printing.[53] The Parisian tavern-keeper would knock up nooks and crannies out of the available space, offering his customers a choice between unruly, boisterous company and brief privacy; people might meet anywhere and on different levels; private and public lives would overlap. The tavern had no connection with the neo-classical pleasure gardens and Vauxhalls dreamed up by Ledoux and Lequeux.[54] It took shape spontaneously, combining old-fashioned vertical construction with a more modern horizontality in a way which encouraged congestion.

The café, given that it was more elegant and attracted a superior clientèle, belonged to a different order of things. The Nocturnal Spectator conveys this impression, for the lovely hostesses attracted him as did the chance of hearing an interesting argument; he would go in to write a letter, read the advertisements, and scour the public papers. His chosen cafés were in the rue de la Montagne Sainte-Geneviève, on the boulevards, at Manoury's in the place de l'Ecole, where he watched the draughts players, at Procope's, kept in 1785 by the *limonadier* Dubuisson, at the Régence, where he might see Jean-Jacques Rousseau who went to play chess there with the glazier Ménétra,[56] or at the café Aubry in the rue Saint-Jacques, where the game was dominoes.[57] His itinerary was initially a literary game, and he piles on the contrasts and picturesque viewpoints, but beyond this we see the peaceful sociability of polite discussion and physical comfort. Binet engraved this familiar décor for Rétif — tiled floor, Louis XVI panelling on the walls, the scene brightly lit by *girandole* chand-

53. Rétif de la Bretonne, *Monsieur Nicolas*, vol. 3, pp. 84–5, 101–02, 114; ibid., vol. 4, pp. 23–4, 26, 45, 500.
54. BN, prints, 78 C 85837–840, 65 C 24868.
55. AN, Y 11518, 3 May 1789; J.-C. Perrot, *Genèse d'une ville moderne*, vol. 2, pp. 686–7.
56. BHVP, MS. 678, fos. 249–51.
57. Rétif de la Bretonne, *Les Nuits*, pp. 2163–4.

eliers, the habitués at the orderly little tables, newspapers, and the central stove which attracted attention and determined the grouping of the customers. The Parisian café offered its clients an orderly, civilised and transparent space which favoured a sociability quite different from that found in the dockside tavern, smoking-saloon or billiard saloons. Montesquieu in 1720, Diderot in 1750, Rétif and Mercier around 1780, all perceived that these establishments fulfilled different roles. It was not so much a question of the sociology of the clientèle, which simply underlined the diversity of social contacts and the mingling of age groups and ranks, but rather of very delicate nuances in life-styles.[58] One important fact should certainly be noted: police reports and literary sources agree that women went to taverns. In reports on police raids, it is not only *femmes du monde* and prostitutes who are mentioned, but also reputable housewives, the wives of shopkeepers and artisans, and apprentices and working-girls, who went alone or in groups, with husbands, workmates or lovers; some, unashamedly, took their children. They can all be seen in the print of the Tambour Royal. We meet them in Mercier, who darkens the picture and increases the picturesque values in a confused throng of female thieves and old-clothes dealers, loud-mouthed fishwives and vegetable-peelers, all drinking and arguing with thirsty males. As for the Nocturnal Spectator — this is his *voyeur* side — he insists on the licit and illicit amorous play when Virgine sells her maidenhead and Agathe defends her virtue. In *les Parisiennes*, only women in the last three categories frequent taverns: the daughters of artisans, the daughters of workmen, and the shameless women of the people — *les Pouliches* — who go there alone or *en famille*, which bourgeois women would never dare to do.

This, then was the development: ordinary festivities were organised around two poles, 'the ignoble tavern', as Michelet called it, and the café — the former for the popular classes, the latter for the bourgeoisie. In the one, pushing and shoving was the rule, gestures were provocative and voices loud, the characteristics of an old style of urban life were taken to extremes, everything moved, circulated as if driven by a need for social intercourse and human proximity. A social order was created which was partly outside the norms; a well-cut coat would transform the journeyman, a neat white dress make a superior person out of a curvaceous *grisette*, deceiving the dandy who sauntered in. The tavern allowed for the mask adventure, the darkness lent itself to every encounter, it tolerated the social mix which work and the *atelier*

58. In about 100 police summonses for 1789, 463 people were involved: shops and merchandise, artisans — 135; journeymen, wage-earners, servants — 317; soldiers, police, various — 261; bourgeois and the upper classes — 8.

almost always proscribed. Close contacts animated the crowded scene: like the habitat of the *classes populaires*, it was a hot-house. The café with its decorum, its mirrors, organisation, comparative silence encouraging intellectuality, its spaciousness preserving distance, belonged to a different, a tepid world.

If Parisian taverns represent one of the modes of expression of popular culture, it is because it was there that the people schemed against official controls, and imposed their own rules and mores, starting with time schedules outside the code of Church and the economy. Throughout the century the *police des moeurs* had multiplied their regulations, insisting upon 8 p.m. closing in the reign of Louis XIV, 9 p.m. in the reign of Louis XV and 10 p.m. in the reign of Louis XVI. In 1784, according to police reports, it was fixed at 10 p.m. in the winter, and 11 p.m. in the summer.[59] But the multiplication of announcements and infringements proved how impossible it was to enforce these regulations. There was no end to the drinking houses open until long after midnight, and noted by the nightly patrols of police and the watch. The proprietor would not dream of opposing the wishes of his customers. Charles Tarlé, a taverner in the rue Pagevin, was an early-to-bed chap, at 11 p.m. he had shut up shop:

> almost immediately his nephew came knocking at the door saying that the citizens who had supped with him were asking for two bottles of wine; he refused, saying that it was too late, whereupon they told the defendant's nephew they wanted it and there was no justice around to impose a fine, and they were doing the policing. The defendant refused again, but his wife persuaded him to let them have it, saying: 'my dear, they are decent people who don't get drunk . . .'.[60]

Consumers imposed their laws, and used taverns and smoking-saloons as and when they liked. The police chased them and the publicans opened in the grey dawn at 4 a.m. or 5 a.m., and closed when they could. Night life and the Sunday holiday were only a small part of ordinary day-to-day business which obeyed its own laws.

The attested flouting of regulations concerning closing times during divine service on Sundays and holidays confirms this plasticity. Police indulgence easily adjusted to repetitions amounting to common practice; the number of fines imposed at the police courts for infringements against closing times dropped between 1700 and 1789. The offensive of the *dévots* and ecclesiastical vigilance lost the battle in Paris before it did in the provinces. One might even wonder how the legislation could

59. M.H. de la Mure, 'Le Cabaret', pp. 123–5.
60. AN, Y 152 17, 31 July, 1789.

be applied in a city where the multiplicity of parish churches and convent or private chapels would seem to require continuous closing of the taverns on the Lord's Day.[61] Police pursuit was half-hearted, preachers thundered, moralists scolded, the people drank and the force of consumer habits imposed illegal habits of dissipation. It became a necessity of life, 'the poor of this City, who have a right to relaxation like the rich, can only find it now in taverns', the administrators would sigh during the Revolution. Popular sociability ruled the day and displayed before the eyes of respectable people the scandal of irreverence, waste and every sort of excess in which 'the underground world of dispute rose to the surface'.

This is how the tavern had appeared to the Parisian authorities as early as the fourteenth century, when magistrates and priests were perturbed to see it become the haunt of beggars and vagabonds.[62] Since then, and especially in the eighteenth century, the growth of trade and population, and the improvement of the police system highlighted the criminal aspect of the institution, indeed its influence in generating crime: spies and informers were paid to unearth its secrets. In the seething popular underworld three main features appear: the first was directly linked with the frontier-role in the life of the city of a whole diurnal and nocturnal world poised between the legal and illegal; the second arose when innocent pleasures and ordinary meetings turned sour through drunkenness and violence; and the third was linked with various forms of protest, from meetings of journeymen-associations to the plotting of revolution.

The tavern was the theatre for a whole range of activities, all both more or less legal and more or less illegal: trafficking, theft and prostitution were the aspects highlighted by police raids. In the half-light thieves would plan the next job or get rid of their booty, and the publican, often a receiver and as often a spy, would circulate stolen objects, remnants of cloth, gold snuff-boxes, and cutlery. The tavern world where discreet or naïve habitués rubbed shoulders with cunning or clumsy crooks, was primarily a vast redistribution centre, the flea-market of the day. Everyone was aware of it, including the victims of the rogues, who would go there to negotiate with the men who robbed them. It was all carried on in an atmosphere of familiarity to the sound of mugs drained in the pipe-smoke, rogues and honest men knew each other; 'that kind of man knows neither pretence nor perfidy', thought Mercier of 'l'habit noir', who ran a profitable line in trafficking. Taverns, especially on the *barrières*, were warehouses for

---

61. M. Ferté, *La Vie religieuse dans le diocèse de Paris au XVIIe siècle*, Paris, 1962.
62. B. Geremek, *Les Marginaux parisiens au XVIe et XVe siècles*, Paris, 1976, pp. 309–11.

illicit goods, stolen or smuggled, lead stolen from roofs, clandestine books of pornography or philosophy; they also harboured the exile who did not want to leave the city, the thief on the run or the girl betrayed.

Idleness, drunkenness and evil associates haunted the minds of police, moralists and fathers of families, including the wig-maker who locked his son up, because 'far from devoting himself to work he goes to taverns every day and mixes with bad company which can only lead him into vice . . .'.[63] Master-craftsmen would see their journeymen drinking away their wages in taverns, while deceived husbands would go there in search of their wives. The tavern meant the ruin of business, artisans and families, for it destroyed good management and unity. In the taverns servants on the spree, runaway children, bad workmen and bad parents proved that the line between enjoying oneself and loose-living was a very fine one, and that the popular classes were losing their sense of morality in the absence of official control. Weekly drunkenness, when the people drank for a whole week, and daily drunkenness were more an irritation to the police than an excuse for a systematic intervention, for the drunks were too numerous and even included members of the watch. Social vigilance was not yet fully mobilised against drinkers, but bacchic excesses might lead to prison for those who lost control, swore at the watch or pissed on the police.

There was not a night-watch that did not round up its contingent of tarts in the taverns. Parisian street-walkers went there leisurely prospecting for fops — Mercier thought that there were over fourteen thousand of them — the police accepted the situation and the informer often doubled up as pimp; the wine merchant made his profit out of the oldest profession in the world. Prostitutes would accost the customers — navvies looking for supper, soldiers of the guard, tailors' assistants, horse-dealers. They would get them to buy a bottle, or a glass of brandy, and take the gullible off into furnished lodgings or neighbouring rooms. There again the publican would make his profit — 'these wretched creatures are charged twice as much as respectable women' — but the situation was not to everyone's taste and sometimes proprietors, tenants and neighbours would tackle the publicans and the girls, while respectable women trembled for their husbands. Fights and quarrels might break out and all — prostitutes, pimps, deceived fops, crafty servants, abandoned wives and rich men who had been robbed — might end up in front of the *commissaire*.

For itinerants and the drop-outs reduced to any expedient, the tavern offered endless resources; the latter were easily caught stealing

63. AN. Y 11031, 9 June 1787.

cutlery; but the former were more cunning, real rogues, often organised in gangs, who went for the watches and snuff-boxes of affluent
customers, and were rarely caught.[64] The craft of the sneak-thief
demanded skill, nimbleness, speed, a respectable appearance, a quick
eye and mind, in short, an apprenticeship in a technique which would
enable them to spot a fat wallet, to organise a break-in by night and
remove the cash-desk and silver from the tavern, and to spirit away
anything that was lying around. It was a specialist, not an amateur
business, as Rétif observed; they were at home in the tavern crowd like
a fish in water.

When these many encounters turned nasty, violence would break
out. The most innocent fights arose from excitement among good
companions at the end of a meal. Anything might give rise to an
argument, the quality of the wine, the price of the bottle, a stare, a
too-hasty word. The women might demand that their honour be
defended and voices would rise. Soldiers on the spree, tipsy workmen
and heavy-handed tavern-keepers were the usual protagonists in these
chance brawls, which expressed not so much social animosity as a
brutal explosion of violence between people from the same background, companions at work and play. Soldiers from different regiments would fight, and journeymen from different trades —
quarrelsome, rowdy carpenters against pliable, prudent wig-makers,
water-carriers against street-porters or dockers. Most ended up before
the police, who only became really nasty if blood flowed, the patrol
was attacked, or the plaintiffs who had been robbed were knocked
about too much. Knife-thrusts often remained anonymous.

The tavern owed much of its bad reputation to these brawls, which
were, in fact, an integral part of a pattern of regular and characteristic
relationship in the life of the *classes populaires*. They emphasised the
permanence of violence and the prestige attached to strength. People
who knew each other well or total strangers might resort to such
brawls because the wine and the atmosphere had relaxed the usual
constraints and closed their ears to reason. Fighting among the popular
classes was less a deliberate act of transgression than a manifestation of
a code of behaviour which was essentially physical, so the tavern was
at such moments the theatre for a ritual. 'If the fumes of adulterated
wine lead to a row, oaths and fists are brought out simultaneously, the
guard come running, and without them this dancing mob might have
killed each other to the sound of the violin. The populace are used to

64. P. Peveri, *Vol à la Tire er répression dans le Paris de l'époque des Lumières
(1750–1775)*, Mémoire de maîtrise, Paris 8, pp. 40–2, 89–106.
65. M.-M. de Caylus, *Histoire de Monsieur Guillaume Cocher*, Paris, 1970, pp.
13–17.

the guard, and rely on them to contain them and to end the frequent arguments that break out in taverns. . . .'

As Sébastien Mercier clearly saw, words came before blows, oaths and threats before fisticuffs. An insult would provoke the offended adversary to action, stung by a slur upon his or her good name, offended by the sexual (slut, bugger), moral (rogue, thief, nark) or status (old dog) connotative. Above all, the attack was verbal: 'You bloody swine. I'll kill you for that', 'I'm going to break you in half', 'Do you want my sword up you', 'I'll blow your brains out'! The intervention of the owner and onlookers would take things a stage further. The publican would defend the honour of his establishment, his clients would weigh in with something and friends would have to take sides. Monsieur Guillaume, a coachman, has left us a vivid account of a brawl in a *guinguette*. Mademoiselle Godiche and Mademoiselle Babet, dressmaker and hairdresser respectively, started things off with comments about each other's clothes and appearances, an exchange of insults and slaps led to blows and hairdos were ruined; the men joined in, tailor against servant, soldier against cabby, 'you can't stand by and see decent citizens insulted'. Weapons were rare — only a few knives, one pistol, and a handful of swords in a hundred brawls. Blows, improvised weapons, and wrestling, which tore collars and sent wigs flying, usually came before thumping and tripping, but unfair blows 'outraged the onlookers' who disapproved of treacherous attacks. Out of a hundred fights, there were only ten serious wounds and one serious eye wound, but torn hair or lost garments were not thought worthy of comment. It is easy to understand the terror felt by respectable people at these regular weekly fights, in which the noise, shouting and broken furniture were part of a cultural performance. The element of display, provocative sexual abuse and exaggerated gestures made these brawls a charivari in popular *mores*, belonging to the sphere of gaming, fêtes and physical exchanges. In the landscape of the popular classes, a rough-and-tumble or a hail of blows were like marking the end, almost deliberately, of a fine summer evening or autumn Sunday.[66] The police certainly feared such fights less than secret plotting and insurrection in the smokey refuge of taverns.

Cabals to protect wages, unlawful assemblies, passions and protests fermented in the cabarets of the Centre and the pleasure gardens of the faubourgs. Workers' meetings were forbidden, as was the selling of books and pamphlets, but meetings were held and books circulated.[67]

66. Rétif de la Bretonne, *Les Nuits*, pp. 1908–10.
67. G. Martin, *Les Associations ouvrières au XVIIIe siècle*, Paris, 1900, pp. 75–6, 92–124.

The incessant vigilance of the *lieutenants de police* and surveillance by informers achieved nothing. While masonic meetings were tolerated by the police and held in well-known taverns, meetings of journeymen remained forbidden and were closely watched. But affiliated branches of the *devoirs*, or secret societies of workers, braved the prohibitions, meeting in the lesser taverns and inns where they found a friendly welcome, some assistance and a little money, information about places where they might find work, or about work generally, all lavishly offered by *mères* and *roulers*, who acted as agents for the hire of workers. Guild ceremonies were held in taverns — initiations, affiliations, elections and celebrations for arrivals and departures. There was food and drink in abundance, and all the authorities agreed that taverns were an all-too-frequent source of infringements against the privations of Lent and against the 'regulations concerning morality'. In the pre-Revolutionary years there was a spate of police injunctions to prevent seditious meetings. In 1776 the strike of the journeymen-binders was activated by Lidy, who kept a tavern in the rue du Mont-Saint-Hilaire, and 'who gave dangerous counsel to the workmen', as well as accommodation and meals on credit; in the *guerre de barrières* Caille, a tavern-keeper in la Nouvelle France, mobilised men against customs agents and the guard.[68] In 1789, newspapers, pamphlets and lampoons were passed around in taverns in spite of the prohibitions; helplessly, police observers disguised as cook-boys or wig-makers watched it happen. In creating a different culture, tavern society came all the more readily to adopt a challenging or questioning stance, since the line between legal and illegal remained so vague. This difference, which was fundamental to the lower-class way of life, made it seem strange and dangerous to some, but the very stuff of life to others, for it was *le peuple* who fixed the rules and wrote the scenario.

The tavern was the theatre for many aspects of ordinary life: a great variety of activities took place there quite legally. It was a familiar extension of family and working life centred around eating and drinking, and the place where most people spent their leisure hours. Taverns played a regular part in professional activity. Workers sought refuge there, for tavern-keepers with rooms to let specialised in particular trades: S. Kaplan has picked out the taverns of the journeymen-bakers all over Paris, and in *Monsieur Nicolas* Rétif gave the addresses of some good lodgings for printers; they would gather in the public room and share the hearth. They came to discuss work; Ménétra received a commission there, Hanriot, a journeyman-printer, had an appointment with an individual introduced to him in the shady offices of the

68. P. Krumnov, 'Les Rébellions', pp. 12–29.

rue Saint-Jacques, such and such a confidential agent would recruit servants and grooms for an aristocrat, another would entice workers away to the provinces or even to the colonies, recruiting sergeants would pick out the innocents and trick them with wine or girls into enrolling in the King's armies. The tavern became an employment agency, a mart for situations vacant, a door to adventure.

Taverns served as a base for all trades. Second-hand dealers went looking for customers and the *fripiers* offered old clothes for sale, individuals such as Tiéchar who sold his old clothes at Coppin's wine-shop in the rue de la Mortellerie, while women selling kerchiefs harangued the customers at the Tambour Royal. In rainy spells or sudden squalls the tavern provided shelter for a while, and a good-natured owner, perhaps a compatriot, might look after the meagre stocks of a man selling old hats or prints. Coachmen would go in to drink a half-litre and play cards with bourgeois lackeys. Waggoners, carters, carriers had their own stages along the arteries of the Centre and towards the *barrières*. They would arrange deliveries, and there was a lively traffic in goods, bales of cloth and chests of pottery in which the publican was at one and the same time client, warehouseman and middle-man. Pierre Ormancey in the rue Montorgueil would collect the takings for the fishmongers from Dieppe; neighbouring artisans entrusted him with messages and commissions. The tavern was a crossroads between the stable world of the capital city and the shifting world of people on the move. Every sort of transaction and business was carried on there; in the good places Rétif could always find pen and ink which had already served creditors to draw up their notes, sweethearts to write love letters, the persecuted to make a petition, and provincials to scribble a line to their families. Everything passed from hand to hand in the tavern — papers, cash, business letters, negotiable effects, contracts. The swarming world of small or big business glittered in countless temples of Mercury.

Family sleeping and eating arrangements among the popular classes depended on the taverns. People could be found eating and drinking there at every hour of the day and night from sunrise to closing time. In the crisp early morning workers would be ordering a glass of white wine, around ten o'clock artisans, shop-keepers, journeymen and assistants would be emptying a few bottles, strollers would pause to enjoy a few oysters opened by the oyster-seller on the doorstep, and the local women would share a bowl of soup and glass of wine. Peak hours were dinner-time, between 11 a.m. and 2 p.m., and supper, between 5 p.m. and 9 p.m., when a wave of local regulars would join the customers who were passing through. Rétif might be watching quietly outside Thorel's in the rue des Mauvais-Garçons, where

Mother Thorel in little over an hour would feed about 120 guests — all chewing vigorously around tables which seated twenty or thirty people, jostled by the hostess and her girls; they were allowed a quarter of an hour to eat. Rétif would note the workmen, tailors' assistants, carpenters, saddlers, locksmiths. He went in to try the food for 'it is not enough to look, you have to eat . . . '. Besides, he was used to it: when he lived in the cour d'Albret, he would go down for his meals at the tavern on the corner. His description of Madame Thorel's establishment contrasted with his usual diatribes, and suggested a less sordid scene. The atmosphere was cheerful, the hostess a good natured fat woman, the son cooked at the fire, while the two well-built daughters served at the tables and put any lads with wandering hands in their place. Young workman and scruffy old bachelors came there to eat — for 6–10 *sous* according to the quantity — and for company. This was fairly typical. In a cook-house in the Port Saint-Paul, a young Burgundian ate a copious supper (cost, 4 *sous*): 'For this great city of Paris is so admirably organised that it provides something for every pocket; they served him quite a good piece of roast meat and a salad, and he had a choice of a different course, his glass was rinsed clean and they put a jug with nearly three litres of water on the table, after asking if he wanted wine, and cut him a great hunk of bread (all that) with no inconvenience other than having ill-dressed neighbours at his table . . . '.[69]

Tavern-going was part of the daily rhythm of the life of the popular classes: work interrupted for a few minutes (too many of the petty delinquents on the quaysides hung around drinking); a little stroll before getting back into harness at the task or tool left at the work-site. Workers did not yet have to clock-on very strictly and time was fairly cheap, for there was plenty of labour available and it was interchangeable. If the journeyman was irreplaceable, the master could wait; he might even go and have a glass with him; Ménétra did much as he liked with all his bosses, and a journeyman-carpenter, his wife and father-in-law spent four hours in a tavern in Fontarabie; François Pinget, an official measurer of grain, who was a bit tipsy himself, complained that the casual labourers too often downed tools to go for a drink. When work was over, they would drift quite naturally back to the tavern. The break became an institution and the propensity for drinking was a way of recuperating from the fatigues of the day.

For they really lifted their elbows: over the whole population, including women, babies and children, a half-litre per head was drunk every day. The police noted an increase in consumption in taverns: a

69. Rétif de la Bretonne, *Les Contemporaines*, vol. 2, pp. 47–8.

journeyman settled in at Graillot's in the rue de Cléry downed his litre and a half, three drinkers ordered 2 litres between them, five others shared 15 *pintes*, that is about 14 litres, in three hours. These drinkers were often reported drunk in the police statements which pinned down the unlucky ones who could not hold their liquor, exceeded their capacity, or got into trouble. It represented an appreciable calorific intake in the ordinary diet. Some men with heavy labouring jobs — carters, dockers, water-carriers — got their second wind from brandy. Then eating helped to prevent them getting drunk. Monsieur Nicolas preferred the hearty tavern meals to the poor fare provided by Agnès Lebègue. Eating out was always a treat, and family life-styles allowed for it somehow.

Police reports and Rétif's observations provide us with a picture of basic eating habits, together with a range of additional dishes. Wine and bread were the staples; a good salad, beans, a slice of meat, a portion of tripe or a piece of cheese added variety and interest to meals that were more or less filling. Two characteristics should be stressed: the fact that the system was extremely adaptable, and the apparent contradiction between pre-Revolutionary poverty and the pressures of the popular classes at the taverns. The important thing was that they ordered on the spot or outside, they brought home food bought more or less at their door, if necessary they added to it, there were no hard and fast menus. The adaptability of people's eating habits was part of the general social pattern, 'you can live at all prices'. The variety of consumption was endless, one journeyman would pay a *livre* for a good meal, while somebody out of work would make do with 5 *sous'* worth of bread and cheese, Mother Thorel and the tavern-keeper César sold filling soups for 10 *sous*. Theoretically, the wage-earner or labourer who had lost his job as a victim of a period of crisis could not afford it; in fact, we have seen that conditions of work allowed for an extra effort, people in work were rarely managing on a single salary, women and children would pick up odd jobs very early. Finally, the culture of the poor indicated a certain solidarity, and tavern-going was part of a system of give-and-take between the fortunate and unfortunate. On the fringes of poverty there could be an economic system of giving that can never appear in historical statistics, and it was encouraged by the tavern with its spontaneous conviviality and adaptable consumer habits. Poor and less poor would take their turn to share-out. Between basic necessities and the prodigality of special festivities every nuance was possible, and this is what the moralists reproached the people with: 'The populace live only in the present, if they can earn enough for their needs in three days, then they only work three days and get drunk on the fourth. But when they lack basic necessities, they are wretched, they borrow, don't pay, and ruin the baker, shoe-maker and wine-merchant, everything goes to pieces'.[70]

Living from day to day was part of popular culture, within a way of life adapted to the conditions of work in pre-industrial Paris, a vast, uncontrollable work-site. It was part of that working-class insubordination which went right through the century and found echoes in Delamare, Barbier, Mercier and Rétif. It was based on a desire for freedom with regard to work, wages and employment, which meant it was permanently at odds with the imperatives of the economy and guild policies. It presupposed, not so much the disintegration of some idyllic social relationship between masters and journeymen, but the perennial confrontation of different cultures. It drew its strength from improvisation, collective solidarities within the family, from the neighbourhood and district, and found expression in the system of debts, an attempt to multiply jobs, the black economy, and pilfering from employers. All the thieves on the quaysides were taken in for petty offences, stealing logs, a measure of grain, a bale of hay, bucket of coal, pitcher of wine, they were circumstantial acts, quite unpremeditated, usually carried out by one man — in fact, a sort of instant recouping from the gigantic mass of bric-à-brac lying around the ports, a multifarious, day-to-day fraudulence that eluded even the police, who saw only the surface of it. The people could survive, even the poorest wretches, because there was still the possibility of an economy of expediency based on countless little procedures which were contrary to order and morality, whose reverse side was inevitably the spontaneous hedonism of the *fête*.

And we are back to the tavern, the place for mass eating and drinking on Sundays and holidays, and for parties improvised by well-to-do journeymen. The popular classes moved *en masse* from the town to la Courtille, from the Cité to la Glacière, from the Louvre to Chaillot or le Gros Caillou. To have a little meal in a private room with a pretty girl, eat a calf's head at la Rapée or fish stew at Port Saint-Bernard, indulge in a little spread for four at the Bois or Ménilmontant, was nothing out of the ordinary for Monsieur Nicolas. Weddings and family celebrations were opportunities not to be neglected, and the popular classes would club together for an entertainment: Rétif was invited to the marriage of a waterman and a pretty girl from the suburbs; at 6 in the evening the guests who had been drinking and dancing threw themselves upon the food — fried fish with matelote sauce, fricassée — they rose from the table still singing at about 10

70. Idem, *Les Nuits*, p. 1860; Anon., *Les Porcherons*, Paris–Stenay, 1773; E. Fournier and F. Michel, *Histoire des hôteliers, cabarets, hôtels garnis*, Paris, 1851, pp. 365–9.

p.m., after the dessert. The cost of the food had been shared between them. We are into the world of popular gaiety and to finish we must identify its components: conviviality, a sense of appearances, *joie de vivre*, and gaming.

Amusement was not a solitary business, the popular classes came together in merry companies of friends and neighbours, in age groups and in families. The anonymous poem below, written in 1773 by an unknown *poissard* describes these bacchic assemblies with sympathy and understanding:

> From every *quartier* of the city,
> on Sundays and holy-days, there a procession
> of decent folk from every trade,
> cobblers, tailors, wig-makers,
> fish-wives and patching women,
> vegetable-peelers and laundry-maids,
> serving-girls, lackeys and scrubbers,
> dandies from the harbour or porters,
> and here and there soldiers
> and their fishwives
> who, with no fear of the devil,
> turn their backs on the sermons
> and gallop off to the pleasure-gardens
> where the cheap wine is drunk. . . .

The Sunday spree would bring everyone out, but no fine day would go by without some effort at adornment, and the festive proceedings began with a change of appearance, staring with the men.

> The free and easy air of these pilgrims,
> their chat and everything about them
> show that here as elsewhere
> they all mean to look like somebody
> — while stockings, fine shoes, white-powdered hair
> adorn these merry hearts who are going off,
> delighted with themselves, to say their sweet nothings;
> they wear *jabots* and cuffs,
> trim white shirts,
> little hats with great bands,
> kerchiefs in waves around their necks,
> red plush breeches,
> cane in hand or tucked under the arm,
> linen or cotton jacket
> with mother-of-pearl buttons;
> head forward, elbows back,
> wearing their gloves summer or winter,
> and their hair drawn back in a net, a plait or a great knot. . . .

Female elegance matched that of the gallants:

Short shift and long sleeves,
a few trinkets in their ears
doing wonders for their finery,
a muslin apron
across which a key-chain hangs from belt to pocket,
and above in the middle of the bib
they put the bouquet
which is the seal of their lover.
Red or brown, their short skirts
are just right for springing about in the gavotte. . .
patterned stockings of thread or cotton
drawn tight to the leg. . .
fine shoes of grey or blue
with flame-coloured heels. . . .

The elegance displayed at la Courtille was part and parcel of the general sartorial revolution and the urge to break with everyday clothing. Then a great feasting would begin and people would drink and gorge themselves, but the cult of the good life was unimaginable without dancing, noise, shouting, violins and hurdy-gurdies.

To cut a dash, laugh, shake a leg,
and then end many a gamble
with many and many a slap,
which afterwards gave each the pleasure
of making it up:
this is where hearty pleasure
never had time to languish. . . .

These were the permanent pleasures of the people, making up for the lenten fare of the week, swigging from the jug, murmuring sweet nothings, bawling, dancing the jig, gavotte, minuet, quadrille and, if only for a moment, affirming their freedom of body and mind. Hope is a physical thing, and in the liberation of the *fête* the reality of the life of the popular classes briefly centred upon excess and the wasting of time and money. It was their turn!

And lastly there was gaming, which went on everywhere, on Sundays and holidays, a striking symbol of disorder.[71] There were all sorts of games: billiards, which in the week brought together pimps, ser-

---

71. On prohibitions, Le Poix de Freminville, *Jeux*: on police sentence of 18 February 1718, J. Huizinga, *Homo Ludens*, Paris 1951; idem, *Le jeu au XVIIIe siècle*, Aix, 1971; L. Dubois-Dillange, *La Police et les tripots à la fin de l'Ancien Régime*, Archives Historiques et littéraires, II, Paris, 1891.

vants and idlers, and which cost twice as much in winter; draughts and chess, which were played especially in cafés; piquet, triumph, dominoes and countless games of chance, regularly condemned and forbidden by royal ordinances and decrees of the *Parlement*; dice; drawing cards like basset, lansquenet and faro; lotto, hoc, English Chance, roulette and raffles, the three-card trick and official or clandestine lotteries. In Paris the people gambled like the great, even if the stakes were lower. Tavern-keepers encouraged this passion in spite of police sentences, of closures and of being fined. If one player was arrested, one gambling den closed, one wine merchant punished, immediately ten new players, ten gambling houses and ten wine merchants would spring up in their place. The police were compromised, but the moralists hated gambling: 'I hate gamblers and drunkards' said Rétif, in a significant association of ideas, during a sombre itinerary which depicted bourgeois billiards, and tramps playing at Ricci's at the quai de la Ferraille, punters, journeymen robbed of their wages, and housewives who had staked their all on the wrong number in the royal lottery. Tavern dissipation came to its height in gambling and brought quadruple disorder for the man enslaved to his passion, for his family ruined by Chance, for the private economy of money squandered, for the state threatened by unlawful assemblies, and by the passions aroused at gaming assemblies. If the King tolerated lotteries, it was because it was a means of boosting the revenue, and the greatest theologians had recognised their legitimacy; they were no more and no less than a form of borrowing justified by their charitable purpose and they showed the intervention of Providence to be beneficial if it allowed public lotteries and condemned private gambling, although the latter continued to enjoy popular favour.

Popular gambling, like that of the aristocracy, derived from the need for sociability, but above all it was part of an economy of expediency which characterised the life of the labouring classes. By the intervention of chance, gambling was a means of reversing roles and confirming the general belief in the redistribution of fortunes by Fortune. The nuance infused by the people into the social universality of gambling stemmed from a magical concept of chance, the intervention in individual destinies of propitious or unpropitious factors, providence or the devil. So, unlike aristocratic gaming, the repression of popular gambling owed less to religious morality than to an urge to impose order upon social conduct. What the clergy, magistrates and police were attempting to control was a frontier of superstitions. It is true that belief in magic was not confined to the popular classes — Casanova, for example, was given to reading books of magic and conjuring the planetary hours — but in the taverns and streets of Paris when punters,

Conclusion

CHAPTER 9

The Police and the People

Commissaire de police: the laws have entrusted to him the happiness
of the people of an immense city. This thought must uplift his soul.
Des Essarts

To respectable people the culture of the poor was
strange and primitive, a business of living from day to day without
being able to plan, all confusion and disorder. Reading the reformers
and moralists, one can see what was at stake when they spoke of
'policing the people'. It meant, first and foremost, knowing, being
informed, in order to inform the King and the ministers about everything that was going on. That is why order in the city depended on the
progress of police institutions and the development of surveillance.
Since the Frondes and the curbing of the last great popular revolts, the
monarchy knew that, in order to govern the bubbling cauldron that
the capital would become, Parisian society had to be the subject of a
searching curiosity which left nothing hidden from the eyes of those in
authority; everybody's actions had to be known, each individual had
to be identifiable. The plan was to be applied to all, as in all Utopias.
But beneath this fiction, administrative activity was lost in the obscur-
ity of individual passions, allowing the storm of collective disorder to
gather. Every sphere, religious, cultural, social and economic, and
every social level, was affected by this necessity. The popular classes
did not escape. If they were not the only target of the new policing,
they were certainly in the front line of the police assault. Around 1750,
François Jacques Guillauté (or Guilloté), an officer of the *maréchaussée*
of the Ile de France, said in answer to the question: 'What is a city
police?' 'It is the surveillance of an infinite mass of small objects', and
this is how he proposed, in a memorandum highly coloured by a
policeman's imagination, to shape the destiny of the popular classes.[1]
To subjugate the people, one must divide and command; to prevent

1. J.-F. Guillauté, *Mémoire sur la réformation de la police de France, MDCCXLIX*,
Paris, 1974.

crime, the magistrate's eye must be everywhere. This could be achieved by a systematic division of the city into twenty *quartiers* of twenty sections, of twenty houses numbered street by street, each storey given a number, every lodging a letter; *commissaires*, inspectors, managing agents, upon whom the system of surveillance depended, would provide the overall control. Every inhabitant, furnished with a certificate, would be known to the fiscal and highways departments, to the police and to the census officials: a central bank equipped with revolving filing cabinets (designed and coloured by Gabriel de Saint-Aubin with some graceful rococo touches) would bring it all together, and twelve clerks could obtain at a glance any information required for action. Everything was to be regulated, known, counted, arrivals and departures, good citizens and bad, 'there would be no safety for them except in the forests or outside the kingdom . . .', 'any workers plotting the destruction of a manufactory would lay down their lives there . . .'. We can see that Jacques François Guillauté's reform had a lot going for it; even if it was not applied, it showed what was involved: immobilising the popular classes in time and space.

To achieve this, the police held three trump cards: control of work, surveillance of morals, security of food supplies. In order to control the popular classes it was necessary to keep the workers in a subordinate position, which, as S. Kaplan and M. Botlan have demonstrated, could be achieved by a general application of the servant–master relationship; increasingly, servants became wage-earners, while at the same time the workers were being assimilated into the ancillary world, and the principle of domestic authority prevailed even beyond the Revolution.[2] That is why the popular classes were not allowed to refuse work: religion, economics, morals were all opposed to their subversive demand for the right to be idle and for freedom of action. The good worker, the good servant did not object, went to Mass, did not plot; work was a civilising force and its own reward. To realise this ideal, policing facilitated the control of corporate bodies and the surveillance of independent tradesmen. This was essential and Turgot's reforms of 1776 set things moving: spying on the *devoirs*, intervention against strikes, the *voies de la rigueur* enabled them to control popular protests concerning jobs, wages, and the freedom of work. The use of the *certificat* — without which you could not be taken on by another employer — and the *livret* — introduced for certain corporate bodies around 1775 — were the extreme expression of social control. In the decade before 1789, these tensions were apparent to all observers; for Mercier and Rétif insubordination had reached a peak, but the police

2. S. Kaplan, 'Réflexions' pp. 17–77; M. Botlan, 'Domesticité', pp. 21–41.

had things under control. Paris was a safe city:

> It would be impossible for a riot to degenerate into sedition . . . the city has generally been peaceful since the days of the Fronde. . . . But once let the Parisian popular classes off the leash, if they did not feel that the constabulary, on foot or horse, the *commissaire* and the officer of the watch were on their trail, there would be no holding them back; released from their accustomed control, the populace would give way to violence which would be all the more cruel because they themselves would not know where to stop.

Mercier here reveals a certain clairvoyance, which was partly vindicated by the events of the summer of 1789, but as far as controlling the popular classes was concerned, the Le Chapelier law maintained the essential principle of intervention, individual freedom did not extend to any sort of cabal, working-class agitation became a criminal act, even a political plot, and it remained a crime against the ruling classes.

Morals were the second object of police regulations and of class tensions.[3] The safety of the city lay behind the pursuit of marginal elements — delinquents, criminals, beggars, prostitutes — but also it prompted all the measures aimed at policing the population, leading men away from the brutality and violence attributed to the savages of the faubourgs and still-rustic provincials. It also lay behind everything concerned with the surveillance of social exchanges, writings, books, exchange of letters, discussion groups, none of which could be tolerated because they were moving away from the Enlightenment and might provide the fuse for violent confrontation. Thus, every aspect of daily life was taken in charge through the combined efforts of the police authorities. Certainly it would be wrong to imagine their instructions and activities as a perfectly tuned machine functioning without any problems or setbacks, for the city was there with its shadows and its own territory offering many resources, and the police had their own weaknesses, they could sometimes be bribed — especially by keepers of gaming dens and the *belles abbesses* of the convents of prostitutes — the *commissaires* were only human and the *lieutenants généraux* open to persuasion. But the system maintained its impulse and direction, the great encircling action worked, beggars and prostitutes were put in poor-houses and, even if there were a few riots against the poor-house warders, even if forced labour in prisons was only partly affected, the efforts either to exclude or to integrate continued throughout the century. The system must not be seen as an abstract power extending its network over the wretched women,

3. A. Farge, *Vivre dans la rue*, pp. 163–243.

vagabonds and rogues, but as the corporate action of many forces which were busy shaping, redressing, civilising, the acts of men who were known, seen in the street, the tavern, their office, or at the guard house. The history of the *commissaires* and of the *lapins ferrés*, as the people called the guard, remains to be written, but there is no doubt that to know it would help us to understand the ambiguity which characterised the relations of the workers and the poor with the police, a combination of familiar complicity, enforced tolerance and interference borne with difficulty.[4] Spies and informers who were known by their dress, their walk, even by the way they knocked, like the tax-clerks, were detested by the ordinary people: 'I felt really humiliated to have been taken for a spy . . .', writes Rétif at the end of one of his many misadventures. On the other hand, the popular classes were quite ready to call the *commissaires* and the watch and the guard to capture a crook or a thief. Solidarity and antagonism came to terms somehow or other. The same crowd that was attemping to lynch a thief *à la lanterne* before the eyes of the German, Reichardt,[5] might defend beggars against the *archers*, drunks against the guard, and prostitutes against the officers of the watch. Admiration for Cartouche did not prevent people from clinging to their scanty possessions, pitying the victims, wanting to carry out their own rough justice and showing hostility towards delinquents who did not spare even the most impoverished. In short, this modern system of surveillance and punishment had its limits as well as its support. In a capital city where streets were cleaner and safer, drains less stinking, and violence better controlled, the popular classes were no longer quite themselves, but they were still at home, and might find opportunities to escape this attempt to suppress their individuality. In the long term, modes of conduct were being established, savagery was being tamed, education and culture were making new people, the *police des moeurs* were nibbling away at misconduct in an atmosphere of calm and constraint.

The important thing was that the Parisian popular classes did not revolt; they became excited, they grumbled, their temperatures soared, but they did not explode, as long as 'plenty of provisions arrived'.[6] This was one aspect of the police vocation, like the art of governing men, one way in which the royal State after the reign of Louis XIV was able to safeguard itself against popular protest. In a world where the fear of bread shortages was confirmed by economic crises when nobody could control the forces of nature, the tyranny of grain

---

4. M. Foucault, *Surveiller et punir*, Paris, 1974, pp. 66–7; J. Kaplow, *Les Noms des Rois*, pp. 230–7.
5. J. Reichart, *Un Prussien en France*, Paris, 1892, pp. 307–08.
6. S. Kaplan, *Bread, politics* . . ., vol. 1, pp. 52–91; ibid., vol. 2, pp. 555–639, 677–702.

governed the general fatalism and necessitated a constant policy of intervention in the cereal market — cereals still represented 80 per cent of the diet of the masses. At the beginning of the eighteenth century, a *commissaire de police* in Paris, Nicolas Delamare, formulated principles to ensure the maintenance of social order: the king, father and provider of all, was responsible for the fate of his subjects, and it should be possible to mobilise all the organs of royal administration to carry out this policy. The Parisian popular classes, by their number and their habits, played a special role in the whole system, for the authorities dreaded explosions in Paris more than anywhere else. The black year of 1709 was there to justify this attention. The control of grain had two consequences for the labouring classes: first, its absolute necessity justified the intervention of the State in the name of the general good and, secondly, it explains their inveterate hostility towards powerful merchants. The attitude of the consumers was conditioned by this principle, permanent need created dependence and the magic belief that in times of crisis this control would and could deal with monopolies and the mysterious plot to starve the crowd. From the cold days of the winter of 1709 to the hot days of the summer and autumn of 1789, this same mentality governed popular protest. The police and the people were linked by a tradition which held that the problem of grain was a matter of politics, not economics. To say that the popular classes had no political awareness would be to forget this, or to reduce it to a primitive awareness of survival; but the policing of grain was a policy which had become almost a mystique. This is why at the time of the reforms of 1763–4 and 1774–5, the popular will torpedoed the modernisation of the economy — the harvest of liberalism for people starving to death — long live the imposition of price controls! Theory must not triumph over centuries of practice, the king could not want his people starved in the name of private interests. The capital refused to play the liberals' game of *laissez-faire* and *laissez-passer*, because its traditional authorities, the *prévôt des marchands*, the *lieutenant de police, procureur général du Parlement*, the local *commissaires de police* knew what would happen. The recourse to grain paid for by the royal treasury, price controls, propaganda — at the darkest hours they displayed on the quais sacks of good wheat intended to reassure people — none of these measures prevented rises in price, therefore increasing pauperisation, but they did succeed in assuring food supplies: nobody actually died of hunger. The rights of consumers, the old community ideal, had to prevail over the rights of producers. Richard Cobb has noted this profound and lasting coincidence of the interests of the people and the police at the height of the Revolution. To have bread in the house was 'the simplest and most definitive statement of the economic policy so dear to the *sans-culotte* . . . '.[7] For the popular classes, the king was perhaps doomed when threats of the rumoured 'famine pact', to starve the poor and enrich the profiteers, circled through the network of popular information, pamphlets, placards, songs. The politicisation of the Revolutionary masses in Paris was implicit in this economic protest movement as was their indifference and fatalism. The history of popular politics is still not closed and to understand it, it would be useful to know the pattern of existence in which they were woven.

Servants, who were distrusted in the Revolution, played an important part in the society of the France of the *Ancien Régime*. The servant class embraced many nuances and extremes of success and failure, well-paid or insecure situations. From one extreme to the other, participation in the sophisticated life-style of the ruling classes varied, and everywhere women were underprivileged compared with men. Nevertheless, because of their number, they performed one precise function. In aristocratic society a vast hierarchy of often useless servants was part of the ostentatious expense of the privileged. In the antechamber, their idleness echoed that of their master's, and their physical and sartorial appearance reflected the might of the men they served. Their very celibacy made a reserve of energy.[8] This model of behaviour developed in the shadow of the courts was diffused throughout the kingdom by the aristocracies of service and justice. And indeed, servants formed a screen between the classes, and assumed a vital role in the sphere of public display where everything was designated by theatricalised attributes.[9] The servant was part of the décor, even if he also performed most of the unpleasant tasks which the technological state made necessary or social rank forbade. In the process, he partly adopted the values and behaviour of the class on whom he depended, and appropriated them in a play of loyalties. When the rich, and not-so-rich, bourgeoisie copied this aristocratic pomp, they echoed it without attracting the same consensus which supported a different kind of ostentatious life. Which explains why observers would denounce the insolence of servants towards their new masters.[10]

It seems that, in order to compensate for this loss of identity, servants played another role. Between the rulers and the popular classes, they displayed the virtues of outward show. The variety and

7. R. Cobb, *La protestation populaire*, p. 235.
8. T. Veblen, *Théorie de la classe de loisirs*, Paris, 1970, pp. 41–6.
9. J. Habermas, *L'Espace publique*, pp. 17–27.
10. Abbé H. Gregoire, *De la domesticité chez les peuples anciens et modernes*, Paris, 1814, p. 144.

number of these outward appearances was abundant evidence of the superiority of *savoir-vivre* over *savoir-faire*. So, by appropriating the marks of good taste and the ways of the privileged, servants played a part in a decisive change of behaviour. Through them, various attitudes filtered from the world of the ruling élite to become part of the patrimony of the masses.

This appropriation first affected the richer wage-earners, but it offered everyone a model of new hope, and the aspiration to satisfy new needs which were partly an artificial creation. The fact that anyone who had been given his chance could enter into a new consumer system in which abundance and all it stood for triumphed over scarcity had as powerful an effect as any to be observed in the ideological sphere. But at the same time it promoted the organisation of space and objects, a sense of comfort leading to better standards, and the affirmation of the group and the individual through the presentation of appearances and objects.

By the end of the *Ancien Régime*, the popular classes were being mobilised. Since 1700 they had seen their living conditions both deteriorate and improve; the common fate was made up of fortune and misfortune, success and failure. Many intermediaries — servants, rich wage-earners, cultured journeymen — had taken part in the appropriation of ruling-class values and manners. The consumption of clothes and all kinds of other improvements had changed the usual order of things and made basic dependencies seem harder to bear. At the same time, there was a more refined awareness, and growing cultural demands which had to come to terms with old ways of living and consuming. *Le peuple de Paris* were never as happy or unhappy as people imagine, their primitive happiness was constantly threatened, and their lives remained a territory where the strange and the familiar walked hand in hand.

---

11. J. Proust, 'Les Maîtres', pp. 162–3.